HOMES with CHARACTER

Fifth Edition

Hazel Thompson Craig

Bennett & McKnight *a division of* **Glencoe Publishing Company**

Send all inquires to:
Glencoe Publishing Company
17337 Ventura Boulevard
Encino, California 91316

Printed in the United States of America

ISBN 0–02–668040–8 (Text)
ISBN 0–02–668060–2 (Teacher's Resource Guide)

1 2 3 4 5 6 7 8 9 10   90 89 88 87 86

TABLE OF CONTENTS

Chapter 1

Shelter: A Universal Need

Since the beginning of time, people have required shelter in order to survive. Shelters served as protection from the weather and wild animals. They were places where people could carry on everyday activities free from danger. Slowly, shelters evolved into homes and reflected the living styles of their inhabitants.

Look closely at these steep canyon walls where long ago, Indians built high cliff dwellings. The overhanging walls of the canyon provided excellent protection from other tribes. The largest cliff house contains more than 200 rooms, much like a modern apartment building. Some sections are two, three, or four stories high. The structure also has many underground rooms which may have been used for meetings and special ceremonies. About 400 people may have lived here at one time. It is believed that most of these homes were built over 900 years ago in an area in southwestern Colorado that is now called Mesa Verde.

Throughout history, home designs have served as symbols for people's ideas, beliefs, and ways of living. Each culture has contributed to our heritage different styles of architecture, decoration, and home furnishings. Today, these designs are reflected in the homes and living styles of the 20th century.

PREVIEWING YOUR LEARNING

After you have read this chapter, you will be able to:
• Explain why shelter is a basic need, shared by people of all times and places.

• Describe how housing choices are influenced by people's social, psychological, and spiritual needs as well as by their physical needs.

• Explain how different societies and civilizations have made contributions to home design, furnishings, and decoration.

• Give examples of architecture of the past that have contributed designs and ideas to today's homes.

TERMS TO KNOW

archeologist—a specialist who studies the remains of past human life and activities

architecture—the art of designing and building structures; a style of building

civilization—a cultural development that has a high level of technology and order

classical—having to do with ancient Greece or Rome; traditional

community—a group of people with common interests living in a particular area

culture—the collection of ideas, skills, values, and customs of a group or society

environment—the physical, social, and cultural conditions that influence the life of an individual or community

prehistoric—existing in the period before written history

primitive—very simple

society—a community, nation, or broad group of people having common traditions, interests, activities, and institutions

technology—the methods used to produce objects that are needed by a society

EARTH-SHELTERED HOUSES

FEATURE

Caves provided natural shelters from harsh weather and hungry animals for prehistoric man. Today's builders are rediscovering Mother Earth's natural protective qualities in what they consider a "new" idea—the underground construction of earth-sheltered houses.

Using the earth's natural insulating qualities is not a new concept at all. In 200 A.D., the ancient Romans who settled in Tunisia built their homes underground. They found that the milder, more constant temperatures below the surface of the earth provided wonderful protection from the North African heat. The Berbers, who inhabited the same region 1400 years later, carved their dwellings right out of the ground, rather than backfilling earth around a structure as the Romans did. Today, in some rural provinces of China, more than 10 million people have made homes beneath the same fields that provide their food.

With new construction technology and materials, such as high-performance concrete, treated wood, and waterproofing systems, earth-sheltered homes can be built in a wide range of ground and climate conditions. The recent development of pre-insulated panel walls have made the construction costs of underground houses comparable to those of conventional, aboveground structures. Underground homes are easier and cheaper to heat or cool than aboveground homes. The earth covering also provides protection from violent weather and fire, as well as soundproof shelter from noisy highways, airports, and industrial areas. And the earth-sheltered home-owner can enjoy the luxury of blasting a stereo to the maximum without disturbing the neighbors!

PRIMITIVE KINDS OF SHELTER

Shelter—together with food, water, and clothing—is a basic requirement for human survival. People in primitive societies have always depended on shelters that existed naturally or were easily made from the materials at hand. In more advanced civilizations, people have learned to change materials into new forms and to change their surroundings in order to improve their living conditions. Although most people today live in the more complex kinds of shelter we take for granted, primitive kinds of shelter are still used all over the world. Both simple and highly developed kinds of housing meet the human needs for shelter and living space.

Many factors influenced the kinds of shelters people developed in prehistoric times. These factors included climate, the shape of the land, and the natural resources at hand for building. The location of shelters was influenced by nearness to water and food. Because the earliest humans lived by hunting, their shelters were usually temporary. No matter how crude, these shelters were of vital importance to people's survival.

Caves

To the earliest humans, who lived in a world filled with danger, caves and overhanging rocks provided natural shelter. The use of fire for warmth and light helped to make caves more livable. There, the hearth became the center of family life. Caves also became a place for performing religious rites. Primitive art found in caves is thought to have been drawn by hunters to gain magical powers over wild game.

Within recorded time, caves have played some part in historical events. In recent years, a number of scrolls from Old Testament times have been found in caves near the Dead Sea. A hillside cavern, used as a stable, was the birthplace of Jesus in Bethlehem. Also in the Near East, a cave protected the Prophet Mohammed during his flight from Mecca to Medina.

Caves, which are cool in summer and warm in winter, offer many advantages as a modern form of shelter. Whole communities live in caves in some parts of the

Prehistoric hunters made these paintings on the walls of a cave in France about 17,000 years ago.

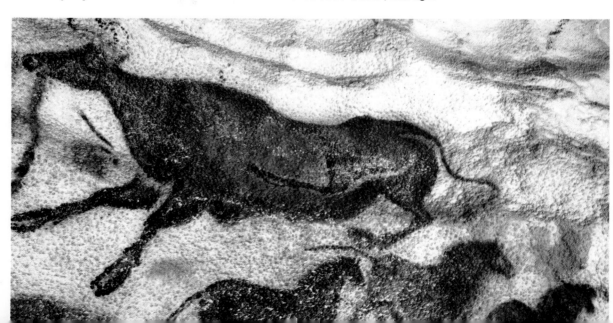

world. Near Granada, Spain, a large community of gypsies lives in caves. Rock in this area is so porous that a series of rooms with dome-shaped ceilings can be hollowed out for a home. Such homes may have electric lights and even plumbing, with fresh water piped in from natural springs.

Throughout history, people have sought shelter in caves in time of war or natural disaster. Today, caves would be the safest shelters in case of an atomic attack. Among the largest caves in the United States are the Carlsbad Caverns in New Mexico, Mammoth Cave in Kentucky, and the Luray Caverns in Virginia.

Tents

Tents of various kinds have been in use since prehistoric times. The simplest type of tent is the pole tent. The wigwams and tepees of many North American Indians are typical forms of the pole tent. Even with limited technology, the Indians succeeded in developing a number of intricate tent structures. The shape of these structures varied from the simple pole tent, beehive tent, and rounded hogan to gabled structures such as the Iroquois longhouse. The type of materials used by a particular tribe depended on the resources at hand. The Eastern Woodland Indians used tree bark to cover a framework of poles. The seed-gathering Indians of California and the Great Basin used grass mats over poles, and the buffalo-hunting Indians of the Great Plains used buffalo hides.

Tents still provide a home for many wandering herdsmen. In Mongolia, nomadic people have for centuries lived in dome-shaped tents called *yurts*. The beehive-like frame of the tent is made of strips of wood crisscrossed like latticework. The sides are covered with large sections of heavy felt or skins laced together with strips of hide. Canvas is often used over the felt to make the yurt almost waterproof. The entire structure can be taken apart and moved, as the herdsmen travel from one pasture to another.

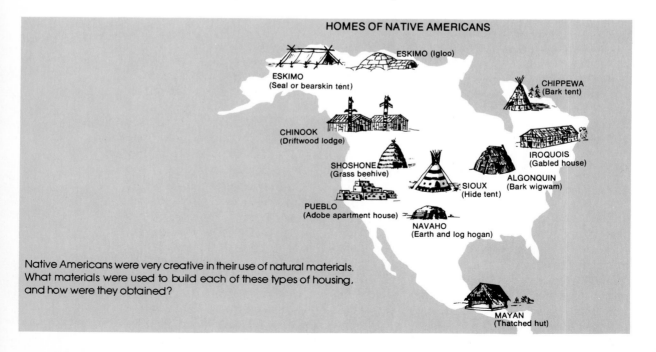

HOMES OF NATIVE AMERICANS

ESKIMO (Igloo)

ESKIMO
(Seal or bearskin tent)

CHIPPEWA
(Bark tent)

CHINOOK
(Driftwood lodge)

IROQUOIS
(Gabled house)

SHOSHONE
(Grass beehive)

SIOUX
(Hide tent)

ALGONQUIN
(Bark wigwam)

PUEBLO
(Adobe apartment house)

NAVAHO
(Earth and log hogan)

MAYAN
(Thatched hut)

Native Americans were very creative in their use of natural materials. What materials were used to build each of these types of housing, and how were they obtained?

Modern tents used by campers are similar in design to early tents used by North American Indians and nomadic people.

The Bedouins, Arab nomads of the desert regions of North Africa and the Near East, also live in tents. Tents are well suited to their way of life, as they herd their sheep and goats across the desert in search of water and new pastures. Camels are used by these nomads to carry tents and supplies from place to place.

Tents are often used today by campers as temporary shelters. Sizes range from one-person tents that weigh less than three pounds to large family tents that sleep six or more people. For those inside of them, tents provide shelter from rain and snow as well as some protection from the cold.

Tree Houses and Houses on Stilts

People in primitive societies discovered that high places as well as caves provided safety. They built grass-covered structures on the branches of tall trees as a refuge from wild animals. Ladders made of vines provided access and could be pulled up at night or in time of danger. Some people in tropical regions of South America, Africa, and Asia still live in tree dwellings.

Structures built on poles over water were another primitive type of shelter. The remains of prehistoric lake dwellings have been found in several areas of Switzerland. These buildings were made of wood and had thatched gable roofs. They were built on platforms which were set on heavy logs that had been driven into the lake and held in place by large rocks. The platforms also had a sheltered area for tame animals and walkways with fenced edges. A number of platforms and their houses made up a community where people could move about without descending to the ground.

People in more advanced societies also built their communities in places that offered protection. Ancient cities in many parts of the world were built on high ground, often with walls around them. Many medieval castles were built on high hills to provide a view of the surrounding countryside. Castles on flat land often had moats, which were deep trenches filled with water, around them for protection. The great Aztec city of Tenochtitlán was built on islands with bridges leading to it.

Houses like these are well suited to the tropical climate of the Fiji Islands in the Pacific.

The Zulu of South Africa live in houses made of wood and woven grass.

Grass Huts

In a hot, humid climate such as that of the islands of the Pacific and areas of Africa, tall grasses or reeds are plentiful. The people of Hawaii, Tahiti, and Samoa have used these materials to build cone-shaped or beehive-shaped huts. The roofs of these structures are slanted in order to shed heavy rains. In Samoa, many houses are round, with cone-shaped roofs supported by poles. These houses have no walls, but grass mats held by ropes can be let down like blinds for protection from the weather.

People in many areas of Africa also live in grass huts. The huts are usually round with dome-shaped roofs. The structures have a framework of bamboo and reed. Grasses are carefully assembled and tied in place over the entire framework. In some areas, the sides are covered with clay.

Igloos or Snow Houses

People who live in severe climates often have special problems in obtaining shelter.

The Eskimos of Alaska and northern Canada do not have at hand common building materials like wood. They have defied their harsh environment by using the only available resource—snow—for building houses called *igloos.* Igloos are dome-shaped structures made by fitting together blocks of compacted snow. As the inside surface melts, a coating of ice is formed. The snow outside provides enough insulation to keep the igloos comfortable in sub-freezing weather. An opening at the top permits air to flow through and smoke from the fire to escape.

Mud Huts and Mud-Brick Houses

Mud is a building material that is available almost everywhere. Very early in human existence, people learned to make shelters by spreading mud over a framework of branches. Baked by the sun, these crude huts provided protection in desert areas. In time, people discovered they could mix straw with clay and mold the mixture into small rectangular forms, or bricks. This was a major technological achievement. Houses made of these bricks are particularly well suited to warm, dry climates.

Dwellings in the ancient civilizations along the Nile, Tigris and Euphrates, and Indus rivers were made of mud bricks dried in the sun. Indians of the American Southwest used the same type of brick, called *adobe,* to make structures several stories high. In some tribes, many families built their homes together in a group called a *pueblo* by the Spanish. In the pueblo, the roofs of the lower stories formed porches for the floors above. As protection from attack, the first story originally had no windows or doors. People entered through a hole in the roof. Access to the roofs was provided by ladders, which could be raised in time of danger. Pueblos had rooms for social and religious uses, as well as for family living.

This pueblo, located at Taos, NM, has been the home of the Pueblo Indians since prehistoric times.

ARCHITECTURE IN ANCIENT CIVILIZATIONS

In the transition from primitive to civilized societies, two changes were particularly important: namely, the taming of animals and the raising of crops. As prehistoric people gained a dependable food supply, they began to live in permanent homes. A number of homes located together made up a community.

Living in a community had many advantages. One of these was safety. Early towns often had walls to provide protection in time of danger. Because farming and herding provided food throughout the year, people could carry on activities, such as crafts, that were not essential to survival. Over a long period of time, people began to work at specialized tasks, such as farming and bricklaying.

With survival no longer a problem, the population of permanent communities increased rapidly. This increase led to a more highly organized society within the community and to the development of more complex religious and political thought. Economic life was also affected. As more raw materials, food, and goods than a community needed were actually produced, people began to trade with other communities. Slowly, communities grew into cities and became centers of civilization.

The oldest known city is Jericho, which was located in the Near East close to the present city of Jerusalem. Jericho developed in a desert oasis near a huge natural spring. Prehistoric cave people from the nearby hills visited the spring. By about 8,000 B.C., the oasis had a permanent community of people who built round houses of sun-dried brick.

Mesopotamian Architecture

Over the next 5,000 years, as Jericho and other scattered communities declined, new cities grew up in Mesopotamia, the area between the Tigris and Euphrates rivers. These cities became the earliest centers of civilization. The first civilization that arose there was the Sumerian. The people of Sumer, a name meaning "land between the rivers," brought together the knowledge and skills of many communities. Advances in weaving, pottery making, metal working, and decorative arts improved the Sumerian people's way of life and expanded their concept of the world. The Sumerians also contributed to civilization two important inventions, the wheel and a written language.

Because stone and wood were scarce in the river valleys of Mesopotamia, the Sumerians built their houses of mud or clay mixed with reeds. Later, they used bricks, a more durable building material. Wealthy Sumerian families lived in two-story houses with many rooms. The middle class of professionals, craftsmen, and government workers lived in one-story homes, usually built around a central courtyard. Homes of the unskilled laborers were often built in rows. These houses usually had flat roofs and only one door.

The houses shown in this model of Ur, a Mesopotamian city of 4,000 years ago, are made of sun-dried brick. In what ways are these buildings and the pueblo shown on page 7 similar?

Among even the earliest cities, religion was an important part of life for both the individual and the community. Awed by the mysteries of life—birth and death, feast and famine, drought and flood, daylight and darkness—people attributed these events to unseen spirits or gods. One aspect of Sumerian civilization was a highly developed religion, which was interwoven with the social and economic life of the community. Records concerning population and trade were kept in the temples. Both written language and a system of mathematical symbols were developed to aid in keeping these records.

The religious life of the Sumerians was centered around temples and was directed by priests. The temples built by the Sumerians as places of worship were rectangular in shape and built in levels, one above the other. These step pyramids, or *ziggurats,* rose to great heights so that the priests could be closer to the gods. The palaces of the kings were also built in levels and had beautiful courtyards and terraced gardens. The temples and palaces represented the great technical knowledge and architectural skill of the Sumerians and their civilization.

Egyptian Architecture

While the Sumerian cities were thriving, another civilization was developing along the Nile River in Egypt. Over many centuries, the Egyptian civilization produced some of the greatest architectural works of the ancient world. The cliffs at the edge of the Nile Valley provided various types of stone—limestone, sandstone, alabaster, and granite—from which the Egyptians built long-lasting monuments.

The great works of architecture in ancient Egypt were expressions of religious beliefs. The earliest of these great structures were the Pyramids, built before 2,000 B.C. The Pyramids were royal

The Great Pyramid of Cheops near Cairo, Egypt, covers about 13 acres (5 hectares) at the base and is more than 450 feet (137 m) high. It was built about 2500 B.C.

tombs, designed to provide a safe resting place for the god-kings. Within a pyramid were rooms completely furnished so that the kings would want for nothing in the afterlife. For four thousand years, the Pyramids have remained a marvel of engineering knowledge and construction.

In later centuries, Egyptian rulers built their tombs in the towering rock cliffs along the upper Nile. The tombs were built on the west shore of the Nile so that the spirits of the dead could pass into the afterlife with the setting sun. Near Thebes, now called Luxor, the ancient Egyptians built the huge stone temples of Karnak and Luxor. The temples were on the east shore of the Nile. This site was the social, economic, governmental, and religious center of the surrounding communities.

The earliest homes in Egypt, like those in Mesopotamia, were built of mud, and later of sun-dried bricks, with earthen floors. These simple structures continued to serve as the homes of poorer Egyptians. As nobles gained power and wealth, they began to build villas with beautiful courtyards and gardens. The growing civilization and wealth in Egypt led to interest in and support for many forms of art. Because of its uniqueness and beauty, ancient Egyptian art is still an important influence on decoration and design.

Crete: The Minoan Style

The early history of Crete, an island in the Mediterranean Sea, is less well known than that of Mesopotamia or Egypt. Ruins of cities and palaces indicate that an ancient civilization existed in Crete between 2,000 and 1,200 B.C. What became of it remains a mystery.

In the late 1800's, archaeologists began to solve some of the mystery. At Knossos on the north coast of Crete, they uncovered a huge palace, the home of King Minos. At other sites, they found large villas with beautiful art objects, metalwork, and a written language that has still not been translated. Each discovery added new knowledge about the people of ancient Crete and their civilization, which became known as *Minoan.*

The statues in this courtyard of the Temple of Luxor in Egypt are of the pharoah Ramses II. What are some characteristics of Egyptian architecture?

The Minoan civilization was unique in a number of ways. Because the island of Crete is mountainous, the people of Crete could not depend on agriculture for a living as the Egyptians and Sumerians had. Instead, they turned to the sea. As they learned to build seagoing ships, they began to trade with the cities of Egypt and the Near East. They exchanged their beautiful art objects of bronze and gold, fine glazed china, and delicate jewelry set with gems for the food and resources needed at home. In time, Minoan trade reached to all parts of the Mediterranean world. Safe on their island, the people of ancient Crete developed a high level of civilization.

Perhaps the greatest achievement of the Minoan civilization was its architecture. When the palace at Knossos was finally uncovered, it revealed a maze of rooms set around a great central courtyard. The rooms included a throne room, treasury suite, courtrooms, weaving quarters, bedrooms, kitchens, and bathrooms with toilets and two sets of drains. Many of the walls were decorated with frescoes, or paintings done on wet plaster. Minoan homes were simpler, being made of either brick or wood.

Religion had little influence upon Minoan art and sculpture. Their arts were created mainly for decoration. The artists chose their themes from the world around them—plants and animals, sea creatures, and court scenes which showed people dancing, playing musical instruments, and grappling with bulls. Many art objects have been found in palaces and in private homes. The museum in the town of Heraklion has on display urns, figurines, statues, musical instruments, coins, and even bathtubs, along with many other items which were in everyday use almost four thousand years ago.

Archaeologists have known for a long time that the Minoan civilization ended

The huge Palace of Minos at Knossos, Crete, was built before 1600 B.C. The paintings are frescoes, done on wet plaster.

suddenly, but they were puzzled about the cause. Some scientists now believe that the sudden collapse of the Minoan civilization was due to a terrific volcanic eruption on a nearby island. The earthquakes, tidal waves, and fire that followed the eruption may have ruined the cities and structures of Crete, including the palace of Minos. At about the same time, Greek invaders may have conquered the island. With the destruction of the Minoan cities, the center of civilization shifted to mainland Greece.

ARCHITECTURE IN THE CLASSICAL AGE

The civilizations and highly organized societies that grew up in Greece and Rome produced much great architecture. In their great public structures—temples, civic buildings, and stadiums—the Greeks and

Romans introduced new principles of design. These principles and the classical styles based on them were to influence all later architecture.

Greek Architecture

Greece, in early and classical times, was divided into a number of city-states. Although traditional gods were worshiped throughout the city-states, certain places were considered sacred to particular gods. The city-state of Athens was sacred to Athena, goddess of wisdom. On a high hill, called the Acropolis, in the center of their city, the Athenians built a temple to the goddess Athena. This temple, the Parthenon, was both a religious shrine and a symbol of the Athenian state.

The Parthenon is made of marble, one of the most durable building materials. This temple combines massive size with delicate design and perfectly balanced proportions. The colonnade, the sloping roof, and the

triangular pediment became characteristics of classical Greek architecture. For more than 2,000 years, Greek architecture has been revived and adapted in new ways.

Roman Architecture

Roman architecture, which developed later than that of Greece, borrowed many ideas from Greek design. The Romans also contributed a number of original features, including the dome, the arch, and the vault. For building materials the Romans used not only marble but also brick, limestone, cement, and terra-cotta. These materials provided more flexibility in the design and decoration of buildings.

Many of the large structures built by the Romans had a religious purpose. The Pantheon, built to honor all Roman gods, combines a Greek-style colonnade and pediment with a Roman-style dome. Other structures, such as the huge basilicas, were government buildings used for courts of law, official records, and public meetings. Many of these were located near the Forum, or civic center. In addition to civic and religious structures, the Romans built

The Parthenon, one of the world's greatest works of architecture, was built before 400 B.C. It was 237 feet (72 m) long, 110 feet (34 m) wide, and 60 feet (18 m) high. The columns were 34 feet (10.4 m) high. The temple was partly destroyed several centuries ago by an explosion of gunpowder. The drawings show typical designs used in Greek architecture.

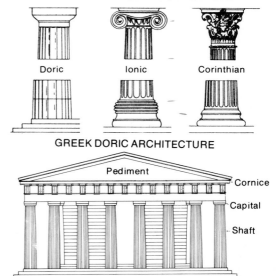

DETAILS OF GREEK ARCHITECTURE

Doric   Ionic   Corinthian

GREEK DORIC ARCHITECTURE

Pediment
Cornice
Capital
Shaft

The Colosseum, with its round arches, is a classic example of Roman design. What modern structures resemble it? The dome, another characteristic feature of Roman architecture, was often used in temples, such as the Pantheon.

great engineering works such as aqueducts, bridges, and sewers.

Home architecture, at least for wealthy families, improved greatly during Greek and Roman times. Many of these families had town houses as well as villas in the country. Their houses had a central court, called an *atrium*, around which the rooms were grouped. Many of these homes had baths with running water, sewer systems, and heat which circulated through tiles in the walls. The Romans were the first to use glass instead of oiled paper in their windows. Oil lamps provided light at night.

In the city of Rome, many homes were built in rows, much as town houses are today. Shops occupied the front or first floor of many buildings. Some people lived in apartment buildings which had as many as six stories. A stairway in a central court led to each story. Poorer families lived in mud or brick huts similar to those in Sumer and Egypt.

ARCHITECTURE OF THE MIDDLE AGES

By the fourth century A.D., the power of the Roman Empire, which had controlled the whole Mediterranean area for hundreds of years, began to decline. One reason for this was the invasion by tribes less civilized than the Romans. Another reason was lack of leadership which Roman rulers had once provided. The thousand years between the defeat of Rome in 476 and the Renaissance in the late 1400's is called the Middle Ages or medieval era. During this time, separate civilizations developed in the eastern and western areas of the Mediterranean world.

Byzantine Architecture

One of the last great Roman rulers, Constantine I, realized that the far-flung Roman Empire was breaking up. He decided to move the capital of the Empire from Rome to Byzantium. This city, renamed Constantinople and now called Istanbul, is located on the Bosporus, a narrow waterway between the Black Sea and the Mediterranean Sea.

Constantinople became not only the political capital but also the religious capital of the eastern Mediterranean. It became the center of the Eastern Orthodox Church, while Rome remained the center of the Roman Catholic Church in the western Mediterranean. The influence of the Orthodox Church spread through eastern and southeastern Europe.

Byzantium, which had been an ancient trading city, was also a crossroad for ideas. A new style of architecture developed there, which combined elements of classical Greek and Roman architecture with the ornateness of Asian design. This style became known as *Byzantine*. Byzantine art was closely related to the Eastern Orthodox religion. Churches built in the Byzantine style were often domed structures,

This mosaic, characteristic of Byzantine art, is in a church in Ravenna, Italy.

having interiors decorated with mosaics or paintings and elaborate carvings.

As the Roman Empire declined in the western Mediterranean, the Byzantine Empire grew rich and powerful in the eastern Mediterranean. With the spread of the Eastern Orthodox religion, Byzantine art became an important influence on architecture and design in eastern and southern Europe, particularly in Russia and the Balkan region.

The capture of Constantinople by the Turks in 1453 brought an end to the Byzantine Empire. The Turks, an Asian people who had been converted to the Moslem religion, brought with them elements of both Asian and Moslem design. These included the use of mosaics, tapestries, glazed tile floors, and oriental rugs for interior decoration. The exterior of windows and doorways included inlays, carved stone grillwork, and elaborate surface decorations. Villas were built with beautiful gardens and enclosed courtyards with fountains.

Some elements of Moslem design had been brought to Spain earlier by the Moors, who were also Moslem. During the 700's, they had spread across North Africa and invaded Spain. The Moors, who ruled part of Spain until the late 1400's, had an important influence on architecture and the decorative arts in Spain. Later, designs from Moorish art were brought to America by the Spanish.

Medieval European Architecture

After the decline of Roman rule, a new political, economic, and social system called feudalism developed in western Europe. Feudalism was a system of owning and using land and was based on social classes.

The Turks added towers of Moslem design to the Byzantine church Saint Sophia in Constantinople.

The Alhambra was a Moorish fortress in Granada, Spain. What examples of Moslem design can you identify?

In theory, land belonged to the king. He in turn could grant the use of it to nobles who would fight for him. The land held by each noble was actually worked by peasants who made their living from the land and gave yearly payments to the nobles.

Because the nobles had to protect their lands against enemies or invaders, they lived in fortified castles. Castles were often built on hilltops, where they could easily be defended. Castles in level country were usually surrounded by a moat with a drawbridge. Below or near the castle were the homes of the servants and peasants. These homes, with one or two rooms, were made of timber, brick or adobe, or stone and had thatched roofs.

Castles had huge ornamented fireplaces and were often furnished with massive carved furniture and beautiful wall tapestries. Although they were imposing structures, castles were not designed for comfort; many were dark and cold, as well as foul-smelling from smoke and refuse. Nevertheless, they did provide protection. In time of danger, many people took refuge within the castle walls.

During the Middle Ages, the Church helped to preserve culture and a sense of unity in western Europe. In every country, monasteries were built where monks carried on religious and educational work. Some monasteries were designed in a style known as *Romanesque*. These buildings had low arches and thick walls, with few windows.

Later in the Middle Ages, a new kind of architecture, called *Gothic*, appeared. This architecture, which was religious in inspiration, reached its finest form in the great Gothic cathedrals. Usually a cathedral was built as the church of a bishop or archbishop. Most cathedrals were located in the towns and cities that arose in the later medieval era with the growth of trade and commerce. The first cathedrals were built in France. Later, the style spread to other countries.

Bodiam Castle in Sussex, England, is a typical medieval castle. What protection does the castle have?

Gothic architecture emphasized height and a sense of lightness. The use of pointed arches, often set on pillars, made it possible to build structures of great height. The high, thin walls of the cathedrals were supported from outside by braces called flying buttresses. Large windows made of stained glass added a jewel-like beauty to the interior. The Gothic cathedrals expressed in artistic form the spiritual aspirations of medieval people. They reached upward from a difficult life on earth to a better world beyond.

The Gothic style of architecture was adapted for a number of different uses. The central square of most medieval towns was surrounded by guild halls and a town hall, often of Gothic design. Houses were in rows, with the upper stories extending out beyond the lower stories. This design was later used in colonial homes in America.

Chartres Cathedral, the half-timbered house, and the Norman farmhouse show different aspects of Gothic design. What special features does each have?

RENAISSANCE ARCHITECTURE: THE CLASSICAL RENEWAL

During the 1400's, a new era known as the Renaissance began to emerge in western Europe. The Renaissance was marked by new scientific and geographic knowledge, by the recovery of classical learning, and by remarkable achievements in architecture and the arts.

The Renaissance Style

The early Renaissance began in the cities of Italy—first in Venice and Florence, later in Rome and other cities. In the late Middle Ages, the cities of Italy had begun to trade with the Moslem cities of the Near East. The Moslem culture was advanced in sci-

The Villa Rotonda at Vicenza, Italy, was designed by Palladio. What features of classical design does it have?

entific knowledge and had also retained some of the classical learning that had disappeared in western Europe. Trade brought not only goods but also knowledge back to the cities of Italy. This cultural exchange contributed to the Renaissance.

As families in the Italian cities gained wealth through trade, they became patrons of the arts. They sought architects to build beautiful palaces, often in the classical styles of Greece and Rome. In addition, they encouraged painters and sculptors to produce great works of art. The classical revival was also expressed in the religious architecture of the Renaissance, together with masterpieces of religious sculpture and painting.

One of the leading Renaissance architects was Andrea Palladio, who adapted the heavy classical forms to a lighter and more refined style. Palladio also wrote books about architecture, both the classical style and that of the Renaissance. These works and Palladian designs influenced the architecture of later centuries in both Europe and America.

Late-Renaissance European Styles

Renaissance architecture, like the Renaissance itself, spread from Italy to the countries of northern and western Europe. There, it was adopted by the rulers of the growing nations and used in the design of royal palaces and government buildings. Members of the nobility built beautiful houses in this style both in the city and country.

In some areas of western Europe, the decline of feudalism meant greater freedom and better living conditions for the common people. The peasants who owned their own land sought to improve their living conditions. In the cities, the rising middle class also had money to spend for better housing and a pleasant home environment. However, the serfs who worked on the land and the poorer workers in the cities continued to live in poverty.

The Palace of Versailles in France is of baroque design.

The Queen's House at Greenwich, England, is of English Renaissance design.

Late-Renaissance Styles in England

The Renaissance style of architecture spread from the continent to England, where it was used in churches, palaces, and mansions on country estates. Two outstanding architects of the late Renaissance age in England were Inigo Jones and Sir Christopher Wren. Besides designing many structures, Wren took part in rebuilding London after the Great Fire of 1666.

Just as the 1600's marked an important era in English architecture, the 1700's were noted for the design of interiors and furnishings, particularly furniture. The growing wealth from overseas trade, as in the Italian cities earlier, encouraged interest in the arts. Again, trade brought not only wealth but also new ideas and designs. Thomas Chippendale, a cabinetmaker, used designs that were influenced by Chinese art. Sheraton, Hepplewhite, and the Adam brothers used classical decorations to create furniture with an elegant, formal style. By combining furniture, interior decoration, and structure in a total design, the Adam brothers introduced a new era in architecture. The styles of 18th-century England set a standard of tradition and taste that has remained an important influence on interior design and decoration.

C A R E E R

ARCHEOLOGIST

P R O F I L E

Archeologists study objects and architectural structures of earlier cultures, especially those of prehistoric and ancient cultures. Fossils, relics, artifacts, and monuments provide valuable information about different civilizations. These items may be recovered from excavation sites in all parts of the world.

By studying data collected from these sites, archeologists reconstruct what life was like in these earlier cultures. They attempt to identify the specific age of each object and try to interpret how it may have been produced and used by the people in the particular society. These findings help us to understand better how a culture may have developed from the simple to the more advanced levels, or, in other cases, why it disappeared.

If you are interested in becoming an archeologist, you should have a strong interest in history and in the study of civilizations and their people. You also need good organizational skills, inventiveness, analytical ability, and an understanding of statistical and mathematical analyses.

To become an archeologist, you must obtain a master's degree in a social science area, plus training in the field. You also must be willing to travel to excavation sites and, at times, live in primitive settings.

REVIEWING CHAPTER 1

SUMMARY

People have always needed shelter in order to survive. In prehistoric times, people used caves, or created tents, tree houses, or mud huts from available materials. As people began to live in permanent communities, they built structures of brick and stone.

All civilizations have developed great public structures as well as homes. The Sumerians and Egyptians built pyramids and temples. The Greeks and Romans introduced new principles of design in their temples and public buildings that greatly influenced later architecture. During the Middle Ages, new styles, such as Byzantine and Gothic, developed. The Renaissance revived the classical styles and introduced new furniture and interior designs.

Rulers and people of wealth have always built homes of great luxury, such as villas, castles, and palaces. Homes of average people have always been simpler, but often the designs have been adapted from the more elaborate styles.

FACTS TO KNOW

1. Explain why shelter is considered a universal human need.
2. Name three types of prehistoric housing. What are several advantages and some limitations of each kind?
3. Describe the changes in people's ways of living as they settled in permanent communities.
4. Name three ancient civilizations and a contribution each civilization made to architecture.
5. Describe the influence climate and availability of resources had on the architecture of one early civilization.
6. Name five design features introduced by the Greeks and Romans. How did these designs influence later architecture?
7. Describe the design of a Gothic cathedral and explain several reasons for the design.
8. Explain the meaning of the term *Renaissance*. How did Renaissance architecture reflect this meaning?

IDEAS TO THINK ABOUT

1. Compare primitive kinds of shelter with the housing we have today. In what ways are they alike? In what ways are they different?
2. What conclusions can you draw about the people of ancient civilizations from their architecture? Give examples to illustrate your answer.
3. How do the climate, land surface, and available resources influence the kinds of housing used in your community?

ACTIVITIES TO DO

1. Choose one type of prehistoric housing to study in depth. Prepare a report describing how it was made, what group of people used this type of housing, where and when it was used, and what customs or traditions were related to its use (if any). Make a drawing or model showing the housing.

Chapter
2

America's Housing Heritage

Throughout America there are many different styles of architecture. If you travel down the streets of a city, suburb, or small town, you will probably see a variety of housing styles. On some streets, all the homes may be similar in style, whether they are individual houses or apartment buildings. On other streets, the styles may differ from house to house dramatically—from Cape Cod to Southern colonial, from Mediterranean to modern. Where did these designs originate? How did they evolve into the styles of homes that people live in today?

To better understand the wide variety of housing styles, you have to look back into history. The early colonists built homes similar to those they had left behind in Europe. Thus, different styles developed in different sections of the country, depending on where the colonists came from.

Over the years, architects have designed homes that contain many of the features and details that appeared in earlier homes. These include different styles of roofs, windows and shutters, porches and verandas, columns, fireplaces, balconies, and doors. So, whether you live in a city, suburb, small town, or rural area, many of the homes in your community probably have their roots in our early history.

20

PREVIEWING YOUR LEARNING

After you have read this chapter, you will be able to:

• Explain why the design and structure of homes in various parts of the country differ.

• Identify typical English, Dutch, German, Swedish, Spanish, and French contributions to American architecture.

• Recognize examples of American styles, such as Federal, Greek Revival, and Victorian.

• Describe the effect of the growth of cities on housing and living conditions.

TERMS TO KNOW

clapboard—a thin board usually thicker along one edge, overlapped to cover outer walls

dormer—a window that projects from a sloping roof

eclectic—selecting what seems best from various styles

gable—the triangular piece of wall between the sloping sides of a roof

gambrel—a roof with a lower steeper slope and upper flatter one on each of its two sides

mansard—a roof with two slopes on all four sides, the lower slope being very steep

shingles—small thin pieces of building material laid in overlapping rows to cover a roof or the sides of a building

stucco—a plaster that forms a hard covering and is used for walls

tenement—a dwelling occupied by several families

terra-cotta—a brownish orange clay used for vases, roofing, and building decorations

veranda—a large porch along one or more sides of a house

FAMOUS HOMES IN FICTION

Since our nation was founded by men and women who were seeking a better place to live, it naturally followed that "home" became an important theme for American novelists. Several authors felt that the American home was not just a mere dwelling, but that it represented our heritage and lifestyle.

In *Uncle Tom's Cabin,* Harriet Beecher Stowe's novel, the lowly shack of a Southern slave was a place filled with warmth, compassion, and humanity. In contrast is the mansion Tara from Margaret Mitchell's *Gone with the Wind.* With its majestic columns and fluttering white curtains, it was more than just a home to Scarlet O'Hara—it represented the wealthy and elegant lifestyle of the Southern plantation which she was determined to protect.

For Nathaniel Hawthorne, *The House of Seven Gables* in Salem, Massachusetts symbolized "ill-gotten" wealth that brought misfortune as it passed from one generation to the next. In Edgar Allen Poe's *The Fall of the House of Usher,* the gloomy, antiquated mansion seemed to predict and symbolize the approaching death of its owners.

In *The Little House on the Prairie,* Laura Ingalls Wilder depicts the purposeful lifestyle of the American frontier people. Home was a simple log cabin with an attic for food storage, a small bedroom for sleeping, and a single big room for cooking, eating, and living. It was hard work just to survive in the wilderness, and one's home provided primarily shelter from harsh weather and wild animals.

Thus, through literature, we gain keener insights into what the homes of our American ancestors meant to them.

THE COLONIAL ERA: EUROPEAN INFLUENCES

The founding of English, French, and Spanish colonies in America during the early 1600's became the basis for three distinct architectural traditions in our nation. English colonists settled at Jamestown in 1607; the French established Quebec in Canada in 1608; and the Spanish founded Santa Fe in 1610. In each place, the settlers used familiar styles of building, adapting them to the new surroundings. These styles had an important influence on the types of architecture that have developed in our nation.

English Influences

The influence of English architecture on colonial housing was greatest along the Atlantic coast, particularly in the New England and Southern Colonies. The first distinct forms of colonial architecture developed in New England. The early settlers there used house forms they were familiar with in the old country. Because wood was plentiful, it became the most common building material.

The early village restored at Plymouth shows how English settlers lived during the colonial era. The homes that have been restored there are far more comfortable than the crude dugouts or bark-covered structures the Pilgrims first lived in. After the first sawmill was built in 1640, clapboards of smooth lumber were used to cover the original walls of split logs and caulking. The earlier thatched roofs were replaced with shingles. Window openings were small and covered with oiled paper to keep out the cold.

Early colonial styles A number of different colonial styles developed in New England during the 17th century. All of these homes were rectangular in form. The roofs were variations of the steep slanted roof or the gable roof. Each style had its

Early colonial homes built in New England during the 17th century have strongly influenced housing designs in our nation.

ROOF STYLES

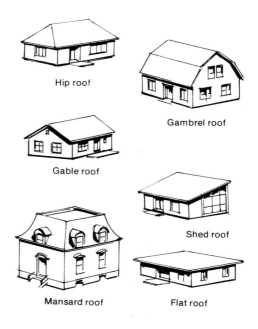

Hip roof

Gambrel roof

Gable roof

Shed roof

Mansard roof

Flat roof

Garrison colonial

Cape Cod: the Captain Gray House, Orleans, MA

Saltbox

own unique characteristics. Adaptations of all these colonial styles are used today.

New England, or Northern, colonial was one of the earliest styles built in America. It was characterized by a rectangular form, gable roof, plain clapboard exterior, and small windows. Sometimes, several more gables were added as the size or wealth of the family increased. Houses of this kind, called multi-gable, resembled the stone farmhouses traditionally built in the Cotswold Hills in England.

The saltbox, named for its resemblance to the box colonists kept salt in, evolved

from the early Northern colonial style. It provided more space on the first floor by adding a lean-to at the back and extending the gable roof over it. The entrance and walls, with clapboard or shingle sides, were severely plain.

Another early house design was the garrison colonial, in which the upper story extended beyond the lower story. This style was called garrison colonial because the overhang construction was first used in forts and blockhouses. The main entrance was either centered or at one side. Originally, the chimneys at one or both ends of the house were loosely attached, for quick removal in case of fire. The best-known example of the garrison colonial style today is the home of Paul Revere. The oldest wooden house in Boston, it was built about 1676. Revere bought it in 1770.

The Cape Cod style originated late in the 17th century. Among its features were a central chimney, a broad gabled roof, and sides covered with rough shingles that were allowed to weather in the ocean air. Even when there was a second floor, the first floor usually had one or two bedrooms.

The style of early Southern colonial houses was less varied than that of New

Early Southern colonial: a 17th-century house at Williamsburg, VA

England. Most houses of that era were made of wood, with one-and-a-half stories, dormer windows, and a chimney at each end. A central passageway provided the air circulation needed during the hot summers of the South.

Georgian design During the 18th century, the early colonial forms of architecture gave way to more imposing styles. These designs were based on the Georgian architecture being developed in England. Most of the Georgian houses in the colonies were built by Northern merchants and Southern plantation owners. The Georgian style, made possible by the growing wealth of these colonists, provided a new level of comfort and elegance for colonial homes.

The Georgian house was far more spacious than the early colonial home. It was built in a large rectangle, with a hip roof, and had a high chimney on each side. The windows were large and often had shutters. Steps led to a paneled front door, which sometimes had columns set on each side. A center hall with rooms on both sides gave the interior a balanced, formal effect.

In New England, Georgian homes were usually made of wood. The center of the roof was often flattened and enclosed with

Georgian colonial: the Wythe House, Williamsburg, VA

railings to form a "captain's walk" or "widow's walk." There, a wife might watch for her husband's ship to return. In the South, the Georgian style was also known as Southern colonial. Most of these houses were built of brick. Many of the great houses of this style were built on plantations, often on a hill overlooking a river. Some of the finest examples of Georgian architecture are found at Williamsburg, the colonial capital of Virginia. Because the Carolina and Georgia colonies were settled mainly during the Georgian era, the design of many houses there was also strongly influenced by that style.

Another version of the Southern colonial style appeared in South Carolina. In Charleston, planters from the West Indies introduced a tall, narrow town house with floor-to-ceiling windows and multi-story porches. These houses were made of brick

and stucco and were often ornamented with beautiful wrought-iron work. This type of house was particularly suitable for the hot climate of lowland South Carolina.

Throughout the South, plantations usually had many separate buildings behind the main house. These buildings were used for the kitchen, workshops, storage of food and supplies, and homes of the slaves who worked on the plantation.

Dutch, Swedish, and German Influences

The architectural traditions of the Middle Colonies differed from those of the mainly English settlements in New England and the South. Two of these colonies were originally not English: New Amsterdam was founded by the Dutch; and Delaware, by the Swedish. The Middle Colonies also became the home of many German settlers, as well as colonists from England, Ireland, and Scotland.

Dutch colonial designs In 1609, two years after Jamestown was founded, Henry Hudson sailed into the harbor now

Southern colonial: the Cornwallis House, Charleston, SC, and Mt. Vernon, the Virginia home of George Washington

Dutch colonial: the Schenk-Crooke House, Brooklyn, NY

called New York and up the river which was later named for him. The Dutch built prosperous trading settlements at New Amsterdam and Albany. Then in 1655, the Dutch captured the Swedish colony located on the Delaware River. Within half a century, the Dutch settlements were taken over by the English and became the colonies of New York, New Jersey, and Delaware.

The Dutch left a rich heritage to the architecture of American homes. The first Dutch houses were made of wood; later, stone and brick were used, with clapboards for the exterior. The first Dutch homes had steep gable roofs with a slight, concave curve. Later, the gambrel, or broken-gable, roof became the standard style.

Because the climate in New York was less severe than in New England, the Dutch often built front porches on their homes, with benches on each side. These porches were covered by an extension of the roof. Cozy and known as stoops, they were a symbol of friendliness. Another feature of Dutch homes was the double door. The lower half of the door could be closed to keep farmyard animals out of the house, while the upper half could be left open for fresh air. Inside the house, the Dutch emphasized kitchen planning. Plenty of cupboard space was provided for food and utensils. The spaciousness and good design of Dutch colonial houses have helped to keep that style popular.

Swedish design The Swedish colony on the Delaware River, founded in 1638, had a brief history, but its architectural influence was long-lasting. The settlers there introduced the log cabin, a traditional Swedish design. This type of house was also used by early German settlers in Pennsylvania. The log cabin was a practical structure, because the materials used in its construction—logs and clay—were plentiful in America. Logs were hewn, grooved at the corners, and fitted together to form a tight, solid structure. The log cabin, which became the traditional home of pioneers on the frontier, is famous in American folklore. Such cabins are still used for vacation homes and, occasionally, for homes in remote areas.

The log cabin, brought to Delaware by Swedish colonists, was widely used by the colonists. The logs could be fitted firmly together without nails, which were taxed in the colonies. The log cabin was also used by pioneers on the frontier.

German design The colony of Pennsylvania, like the Dutch colonies, was settled by people from many different places. Settlers from Germany were among the most numerous. These people were prosperous farmers, who built large rectangular houses of native stone. Often, they also built large stone or wooden barns. The English Quakers in Pennsylvania used stone to build meetinghouses, or churches, as well as homes.

Spanish Influences

The influence of Spanish architecture in America has been greatest in Florida and the Southwest. The earliest permanent European settlement in our country was built in St. Augustine, Florida, in 1565. A structure believed to be our country's oldest colonial home is located there.

A different type of Spanish architecture developed in the Southwest. This style was a blend of the Pueblo Indian adobe structure and the Moorish style of Spanish architecture. The main features of this new style were the use of the round arch for windows and doorways; rounded terracotta tiles for roofs; balconies and porticoes (long covered walkways); and ceramic tile for interior decoration.

Spanish architectural influences spread through the Southwest, from San Antonio to San Francisco. The earliest structures, such as those at Santa Fe, showed a strong Pueblo Indian influence. Later structures, such as the 18th-century Spanish missions near San Antonio and Tucson, showed a stronger Spanish influence.

In California, the Spanish built a series of missions along the 600-mile road called El Camino Real. These missions, built with the help of Indian workers, were made of adobe and sometimes stone. The thick walls of these structures were effective in

German colonists in Pennsylvania built spacious and comfortable houses of stone, such as the Troxell-Steckel House at Egypt, PA.

keeping out the heat, and the courtyards were suitable for outdoor living and working. The red-tile roofs, arched doorways, courtyards, and porticoes reflected the influence of traditional Spanish and Moorish designs. These features were later adapted in a style known as Spanish Mission, which became popular in Florida and the Southwest.

During the 1800's, under Mexican rule, another design, the Monterey style, appeared in California. It was named for Monterey, the Mexican capital of California. Made with the traditional thick adobe walls and a tile roof, this type of structure usually had wooden door and window frames, a hip roof, and a veranda which encircled the building. New England traders at Monterey extended the roof at the back of the house in a version known as the Monterey saltbox. The Monterey style has been adapted for modern use.

Three examples of Spanish architecture in the Southwest are (below) the Governor's Palace at Santa Fe, NM, built in 1610; the San Fernando Mission near Los Angeles, CA, built in the late 1700's; and the Monterey, CA, Customs House, part of which was built in 1814.

French Influences

French styles of architecture came to America by way of the French settlements in Canada and the Mississippi Valley. The typical colonial farmhouse in late 17th-century Quebec was built of fieldstone, with a steep-pitched roof extending over a porch. French settlers in the English colonies built homes similar to those of Quebec. These houses, usually of stone, had high-pitched roofs and small windows. This style, known as Norman, has been adapted for

Houses in the French Quarter of New Orleans, LA, were often built close to the street, with balconies extending over the sidewalk. Balconies with iron railings—a West Indian style—were also used in Charleston, SC.

present-day use. A later French contribution was the mansard roof, named for the French architect Jules Mansart. This type of roof is found on some houses, condominiums, and small commercial buildings today.

The French colonial style became most fully developed in the lower Mississippi Valley. New Orleans, founded in 1718, became the capital of the Louisiana colony and a center of French influence. In the original design for the city, streets were laid out in squares. This area, known as the Vieux Carré or Old Square, later became the French Quarter. Here, houses were built close to the street, with upper-story balconies that extended over the sidewalk. These features, combined with the same West Indian influences as in Charleston, were later developed into the Creole style. The name *Creole* was given to the American-born descendants of the French and Spanish colonists. Houses built in the Creole style had a hip roof, like Georgian houses; floor-length windows with shutters, like Southern colonial houses; and balconies with wrought-iron railings, like French colonial houses.

THE EARLY NATIONAL ERA: GROWTH OF AN AMERICAN STYLE

Independence from England was important, not only to our nation's government but in every aspect of American life. Architecture was no exception. The years after the War for Independence saw an upsurge of building. Homes were needed for the rapidly growing population. Public buildings were needed for the new national government and the state governments. To meet these needs, American architects sought new styles and forms to express the feeling of a national identity.

The Federal Style

The first truly American style, known as Federal, developed at about the time of the American Revolution. It combined the symmetrical Georgian form with the fine details used by the Adam brothers, English architects and cabinetmakers. The Federal style reached its height in New England. There, merchants who were gaining wealth from the new overseas trade built homes that combined traditional forms with new features. Samuel McIntyre built a number of stately houses in the Federal style in Salem, Massachusetts. In Boston, Charles Bulfinch designed the State House, which is the Massachusetts capitol, and a number of private homes. The Federal style also appeared in coastal cities of the Middle and Southern colonies.

The Classical Revival

During the early 1800's, a new style of architecture began to develop in America. It was based on the classical styles of Rome and Greece. Thomas Jefferson was largely responsible for bringing the ancient classical styles to America. Jefferson was familiar with the writings of the Renaissance architect Andrea Palladio. While in France, he had also seen a number of ancient Roman structures.

As the author of the Declaration of Independence, Jefferson saw the need for architecture to represent the spirit of the new nation. He found the style he wanted in the classical styles of the Roman republic and Athenian democracy. Jefferson added elements of classical design to his home, Monticello, near Charlottesville, Virginia. He

The Federal style, shown in this Salem, MA, house built by Samuel McIntyre, was influenced by classical design.

What classical Greek and Roman designs did Thomas Jefferson use in his home, Monticello, near Charlottesville, VA?

developed the style further in his plan for the University of Virginia. Later, features of classical design were used for the Capitol in Washington and for many state capitols.

The interest in classical design soon led to a new style in American architecture known as Greek Revival. This style, which represented American taste between 1820 and 1840, spread from the Atlantic coast to the Midwest and South. Based on Greek temple design, the Greek Revival style was used in both homes and public buildings. Many old Georgian homes were updated with Greek columns and porticoes.

Certain features of Greek Revival design were used in a special way in many of the plantation homes of the Gulf Coast and the lower Mississippi Valley. There, cotton growing produced new wealth, and some of this wealth was expressed in elaborate architecture and furnishings. Spanish and French verandas and balconies with wrought-iron grillwork were combined with 18th-century Georgian styles and 19th-century Greek Revival features. Along the Mississippi, the main floor of the house was often one level above the ground for protection from floods. Changed economic conditions after the Civil War ended the building of elaborate plantation houses. A number of these houses are preserved in Mississippi and Louisiana as relics of an earlier era.

THE VICTORIAN AGE: A MIX OF STYLES

The era named for Victoria, Queen of England from 1837 until 1901, was a time of experiment in architecture. It produced a variety of styles. Some of these were highly decorative; others had a quaint charm; and many were simply a hodgepodge of design. Although modern architects have ridiculed the Victorian style, many examples of it remain. The white frame houses of the Victorian era are seen most often in the small towns and older suburbs built during the 19th century.

The Victorian age marked the end of traditional designs and building methods. As handbooks of building styles became available, local builders adapted these styles in a wide variety of forms. Architects, too, sought new styles. Some of them adapted traditional forms; others turned to faraway places for the ornate, the exotic, or the extreme in architecture and design.

The Gothic Revival

One of the styles revived during the Victorian era was the Gothic, which became translated into an American form. With the invention of the scroll saw, carpenters used wood to imitate Spanish wrought-iron grillwork. The term Carpenter Gothic is associated with this style. Because of its popularity, often for modest homes, the Carpenter Gothic style spread throughout the country. A later and more elaborate form was called Queen Anne Gothic. Houses in this design were made of wood, brick, or stucco. They featured gable roofs, turrets and towers, and wide porches.

Shadows-on-the-Teche, finished in 1834, in New Iberia, LA, combines Southern colonial, Northern colonial, Greek Revival, and Spanish elements in a uniquely American design.

The style of this house is Carpenter Gothic. Why might it also be called a "wedding cake house"?

Eclectic Design

One of the architects who encouraged the Gothic revival was Andrew Jackson Downing. His house designs were based on those of English manor houses and French, Italian, and Spanish villas. Often these designs were combined in a mixed style called *eclectic*. In addition to European styles, Asian influences were sometimes added.

As the new designs became more extreme, a number of architects began to criticize them. Charles Lock Eastlake, an English architect and journalist, was among the strongest critics. He opposed the imitation of ornate European styles and the combining of earlier styles in a hodgepodge of design. Eastlake introduced a simpler version of the Queen Anne Gothic. His book *Hints on Household Taste* had a definite influence on American taste in house styles and furnishings.

The Truman family home in Independence, MO, is typical of the white frame Victorian houses found in cities and towns across America. Houses of this style were built in the late 1800's.

THE GROWTH OF CITIES:
A NEW AGE

The 19th century was a time of rapid growth for American cities. Colonial cities had developed as centers of trade and commerce. In the century following the War for Independence, the rise of industry hastened the growth of cities all over the country.

The Industrial Revolution had begun earlier in England, with the use of steam for power and the use of machines for producing goods. As a result of these changes, it became efficient to produce goods in factories. After the United States had gained its independence from England, Americans had to produce their own goods. Within a short time, the building of factories began, in order to meet the needs of the growing nation. Among the earliest were textile factories, which were located near rivers for power. New towns and cities grew up around the factories as people moved there to find work. Lowell, Massachusetts, grew up around textile factories; Pittsburgh, Pennsylvania, had steel mills and also became a center of transportation.

Urban Housing Problems

No matter where they were located, expanding cities presented housing problems. Immigration and the movement of people from farms and towns to the cities contributed to urban crowding. In older cities, the increase in population led to the growth of slums. Large numbers of people crowded into structures where only a few had lived previously. New buildings called tenements, often six stories high, were hastily built to absorb the huge numbers of people who needed a place to live. Such buildings had poor water and sewage facilities; in addition, many were fire hazards.

The Queen Anne Gothic style appeared in the later Victorian era.

The Chaney House in Redlands, CA, is eclectic in style. It combines gable and mansard roofs, an Oriental tower, and Chinese fret railing. What features in these two houses are similar?

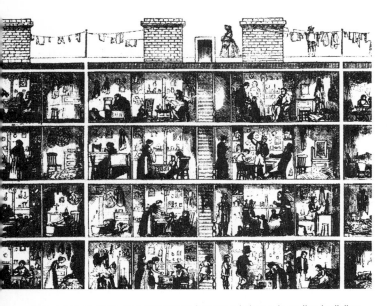

The name *tenement* also applied to the three-story, multi-family houses that were built in new communities at the edge of older cities. In some communities, companies built small houses for their workers.

The crowded urban slums, tenements, company houses, and homes of the poor contrasted sharply with the palatial homes of the "captains of industry." To this group, who had made fortunes in banking, steel, railroads, and other enterprises, homes became symbols of status. Thorstein Veblen, a social historian of the times, described the pretentious homes of the newly wealthy as examples of "conspicuous consumption." Although few families acquired such wealth, their lifestyle influenced American tastes and values.

This cross-section of a New York tenement shows how the building was constructed to contain as many rooms and people as possible.

People in Pittsburgh, P.A., who worked in the steel mills often lived in houses built by the company and rented to workers. These houses were located near the mills.

The Beginning of Modern Architecture

The Industrial Revolution, which had contributed to the problem of urban crowding, also contributed, in time, to the solution of urban housing problems. Inventions such as the elevator helped to make even taller buildings possible. Changes in the design of these structures resulted from the use of new materials, such as glass and steel. The new many-storied structures increased the efficiency of land use in crowded urban areas.

New kinds of transportation, such as the streetcar and subway, made it possible for people to live farther from their work. "Streetcar suburbs" grew up around many crowded industrial centers. Some of the new suburbs had row houses; others had single-family or multi-family dwellings.

The city of Chicago became the scene of many dramatic changes in urban design. Much of that city was destroyed in the great fire of 1871, as London had been destroyed three centuries earlier. As in London, a new generation of architects contributed to the rebuilding of the city. In

The Carson Pirie Scott and Company store was one of the first modern buildings in Chicago, IL. It included many new design features. How are windows like these used today?

Biltmore, the Vanderbilt home near Asheville, NC, is a blend of Gothic and Renaissance architecture.

place of traditional styles and materials, they designed new types of buildings, made possible by modern materials and technology. Most of these buildings in Chicago were designed for commercial use. They met the needs of large-scale businesses, such as department stores and insurance companies. Many of these designs were later used in urban apartment buildings and adapted for single-family homes.

The modern style of architecture that developed in Chicago was based on a new idea—that the design for a structure depended on the building's use, or function. Because decoration was not considered functional, most of the buildings were severely plain. Instead of ornamentation, the building materials themselves provided design interest through the form of the metal framework and the new types of windows.

Modern architecture was in part a reaction to the ornate Victorian styles. It also represented a continuing search for a truly American style, separate from the European influences of the past. The modern style expressed the spirit of the age—a focus on technology, the rise of commerce and industry, and the growth of cities throughout the country. The designs introduced in Chicago became an inspiration to other cities and later to the designers of the 20th century.

c URBAN PLANNER

C
A
R
E
E Urban planners develop comprehensive plans for the use of land and physical facilities
R of cities and metropolitan areas. They compile and analyze data on economic, social, and physical factors that affect land use. As a result, urban planners help guide
P community development and renewal.
R   Urban planners often hold conferences with local authorities, civic leaders, social
O scientists, and land planning and development specialists. They make recommenda-
F tions for what land and physical facilities are needed for residential, commercial,
I industrial, and community uses. Urban planners may also recommend governmental
L measures that will affect land use, public utilities, community facilities, and housing, as
E well as transportation.

Usually employed at various levels of our government, urban planners may also work for private consulting firms. They may have such titles as Chief Planner or Director of Planning if they head a department or unit of a public or private organization.

If you are interested in becoming an urban planner, you need to have the ability to plan, initiate, and direct developmental programs. You should enjoy interpreting data and statistics in order to prepare graphic and narrative reports. Also, you must be able to relate well to people, motivate and direct employees, and maintain good employer-employee and customer relationships.

To become an urban planner, you will need at least an associate's degree in business management.

REVIEWING CHAPTER 2

SUMMARY

The colonists brought to America many different styles and traditions of housing. The English colonists had simple, rectangular homes with small windows and steeply slanted roofs. Later, during the 18th century, more elaborate homes were built in the Georgian and Southern colonial styles, which also were derived from England. Spanish architecture, featuring tile roofs and courtyards, influenced styles in Florida and the Southwest. French settlers introduced the Norman style country house and balconied city houses in New Orleans. The Dutch, Swedish, and German colonists also influenced architecture.

After the American Revolution, new styles of architecture were created that were uniquely American. These included the Federal, Greek Revival, and Victorian styles.

The growth of cities during the 19th century brought urban housing problems. However, the beginning of modern architecture helped improve urban life and inspired designers of the 20th century.

FACTS TO KNOW

1. Describe the contributions two different groups of colonists made to American architecture.

2. Give three examples of how American colonial architecture was affected by climate, land surface, and available resources.

3. Describe the changes in home design in the English colonies from the 1600's to the 1700's. What are two reasons for these changes?

4. Explain why the Greek Revival style was often used for public buildings, such as state capitols.

5. Identify three different styles of Victorian architecture and explain how each one developed.

6. Explain the meaning of the term *eclectic* and give an example of eclectic design.

7. Analyze the effect of the rapid growth of cities and population on housing and living conditions during the late 1800's.

8. Identify two changes in technology that made new designs for building possible in the late 1800's. What new types of buildings were developed?

IDEAS TO THINK ABOUT

1. Why does our country have such a varied architectural heritage from its colonial era? Give examples to support your answer.

2. What traditions and aspects of American life are represented by the log cabin, the Southern colonial mansion, and the white frame Victorian home?

3. How did changes in technology help meet urban housing problems in the late 1800's? How could urban housing problems of today be solved by technology?

ACTIVITIES TO DO

1. Research a building in your community that represents the traditional architecture of your region. Describe the building or make sketches of it to show how its design is characteristic of that architectural style.

2. As a group project, study the history of your community and the architecture used at different stages of its growth. Models or photographs might be used to represent buildings from each stage.

Chapter 3

The 20th Century: New Housing Concepts

During the 20th century, many trends have influenced housing and living conditions.

One major trend during the 20th century has been the constant growth of the population. This has created a tremendous need for new housing. In less than 100 years, the population of the United States has more than tripled: from 76 million in 1900 to over 237 million in 1985. It is estimated that our population will be 267 million by the year 2000.

The population has also changed geographically. During some decades, a great number of people moved from rural to urban areas. In other decades, the shift was from the cities to the suburbs. Today, many cities are showing new growth and development as people move back into urban areas or rebuild old neighborhoods.

What will be the needs of families in future decades? We do not have a crystal ball to answer these questions about the future. However, it is almost certain that the future will bring new changes in housing so as to meet the needs of people better. What are your predictions for future trends? How do you think people will be living in the year 2010?

PREVIEWING YOUR LEARNING

After you have read this chapter, you will be able to:

• Trace the major trends in American home design during the 20th century.

• Describe the changing patterns of urban and suburban development and their effect upon housing.

• Explain the role of government in relation to housing and land use.

• Analyze the effect changing lifestyles will have on housing needs in the years ahead.

TERMS TO KNOW

---

bungalow—a style of house having one or one-and-a-half stories, overhanging roof, and a covered porch

cluster zoning—houses grouped together in clusters with undeveloped land between clusters

duplex—a house or apartment built for two families

foreclosure—a legal proceeding resulting in owners losing their home because mortgage payments have not been made regularly

modular—a standardized unit that fits with others to become a finished product

mortgage—a long-term loan used to finance the purchase of a home

prefabricated—items built in standardized sections at a factory and assembled during construction

solar heating—heating provided by energy from the sun

subsidy—a grant or contribution of money

tract development—a housing development of homes all with the same design

urban renewal—renovation of urban housing

PLANNED COMMUNITIES

**F
E
A
T
U
R
E**

With the population increasing and limited land available for housing, it is understandable why the new planned communities make sense. Reston, Virginia, and Columbia, Maryland, are two examples of planned communities, both located outside of Washington, D.C. These communities—complete with their own schools, shops, business, and recreational areas—are so self-contained that residents virtually do not need to leave their neighborhood. Reston also provides a variety in the type of housing offered: single-family, town house, or apartment. Columbia has a system of minibuses connecting its various areas, so residents do not need to drive.

Projects are also underway to redevelop certain deteriorated areas of large cities into self-sufficient units. Each new unit would have its own apartment complexes, stores, office buildings, shopping malls, and schools. This "city-within-a-city" approach provides residents with the conveniences of a new planned community while still being part of an established urban city.

Because our precious land resources must be shared between housing and food production, future cities may be built on the sea. Huge megastructures may be constructed either to float on the surface in deep water or remain fixed in shallow water. Then, as science writer Isaac Asimov says, it will be possible to catch dinner in your front yard!

THE EARLY 20TH CENTURY

Changes in housing and home design take place more gradually than in other areas of living. There are two reasons for this: homes last a long time, and they represent the largest investment of a lifetime for most people. During the 20th century, a greater variety in designs of houses and types of housing were to become available. Styles of architecture, too, were to become more universal, due in part to improved communication and to the greater movement of population.

During the early 1900's, home styles were still changing slowly. Often, these styles were typical of a certain region. In older areas of the nation, many lovely homes from the colonial era and the 19th century remained. In rural areas and small towns, families lived in single-family houses or duplexes. In large cities, row houses were common. In the fastest-growing cities and industrial centers, many people did not own homes, but lived in tenements or company-owned houses.

New Designs for Homes

The dream of owning a home became a reality for many Americans during the early 1900's. Rising incomes made it possible for more and more people to buy homes. Because they wanted a place to live, rather than style or status, people looked for simple homes that they could afford. A leader in meeting the need for small but livable homes was Edward Bok, editor of the *Ladies Home Journal.*

The small house Edward Bok was concerned with many social causes and in particular with the lack of suitable housing for rural and urban families. Through the columns of his magazine, he was able to spread new ideas concerning homes and home furnishings to a great number of people. One of his contributions was to include in each issue of the *Journal* a section with building plans for small homes. Many families bought the plans and contracted with local carpenters to have homes built.

The small size of the new houses was made possible by several changes in traditional design. The formal parlor and family sitting room were combined to become the living room. Fewer bedrooms were needed because of the smaller size of families. Kitchens, too, became smaller. The use of bathrooms and central heating, however, contributed to both convenience and comfort, in spite of the reduction in the overall size of the house.

The bungalow One new style of house that became popular during the early 1900's was the bungalow. The word *bungalow* comes from *Bengal,* a state in India, where it was used to describe a low cottage with a veranda or small porch. The bungalow design was introduced in California in the 1890's; later, it spread throughout the country. The basic bungalow was an almost square building with one or one-and-a-half stories, an overhanging roof, and a wide covered porch. Building materials ranged from wood and brick to stucco, depending on the area of the country. Some

The bungalow became a popular style in the new suburbs of the 1920's.

California bungalows were built around a patio, in a Spanish style; others were constructed in a post-and-beam style, like a Japanese house. The bungalow was widely used in growing metropolitan areas, such as Los Angeles. Elsewhere, it was often used in "streetcar suburbs," at the edge of large cities.

The prairie house At the same time that the bungalow was being developed in California, a new design, the prairie house, appeared in the Middle West. Frank Lloyd Wright, who created this design, had been an apprentice in a Chicago architectural firm. He realized that the new ideas being used for modern business structures could also be used in the design of homes.

The first houses designed by Wright were in a modern style very different from the traditional. The design gained public attention when the *Ladies Home Journal* in 1901 published Wright's model of a "home in a prairie town." For the next ten years, Wright continued to develop the design of what became known as the prairie house. In place of ornate detail, Wright used uncluttered shapes—rectangular, square, and angular. He used natural materials such as wood and stone, and subdued colors that blended with them. Wright was also interested in the relation between buildings and their settings. He believed that houses should fit naturally into their environment, rather than contrasting with it, and that there should be easy access between indoors and outdoors. The strong horizontal lines of the prairie house blended with the open landscapes of the Middle West.

The modern house The prairie house was only the first stage of Wright's work as an architect. Most Americans were not ready to accept Wright's designs. However, his ideas were accepted in Europe, where they contributed to the International style. After 1935, Wright began a new stage of home design, using geometric forms. This style was in some ways like the International style, which spread to the United States in the 1930's and 1940's.

The Robie House in Chicago, IL, was designed by Frank Lloyd Wright in the prairie house style. Wright believed that a house should provide a sense of shelter, with the hearth the center of the home.

"Fallingwater," the Kaufman house in Bear Run, PA, is an example of Wright's later style. The use of cantilevered extensions was a new feature in architectural design.

The Farnsworth House at Plano, IL, was designed by Ludwig Miës van der Rohe in the International style.

Revival of Traditional Designs

The prosperity of the 1920's brought a new interest in large and imposing homes. As people became more affluent, they turned to styles of the past. Homes of this era represented the revival of traditional English, French, and Early American designs, including the Spanish Mission style in Florida and California.

The prosperity of the 1920's also led to a new awareness of living conditions within the home. Concern for home decoration had been promoted by the first popular book on decorating, *The House of Good Taste*. The author, Elsie de Wolfe, sought to establish certain standards of taste and style in home furnishings and interior decoration. Advertising, too, made people more aware of the desirability for comfort, convenience, and beauty within the home.

Another effect of advertising was to increase the demand for labor-saving equipment. Such equipment—including electric irons, washing machines, and refrigerators—helped make the management of a home easier and less time-consuming.

The automobile, perhaps more than anything else, influenced lifestyles after World War I. Until Ford mass-produced the Model-T in 1915 to sell for $295, only wealthy families could afford to own an automobile. During the 1920's, automobile ownership became common, and people began to spend more time away from home. The automobile contributed to the rise of suburbs and to highway expansion.

Housing During the Great Depression and World War II

The building boom of the 1920's ended with the stock market crash in late 1929, marking the start of the Great Depression. The building of new homes stopped, since people could no longer afford to buy them. As people lost their savings or became unemployed, many families were in danger of losing their homes through foreclosure. People with large homes often converted them into duplexes or apartment units to rent. Second and third floors were often reached by means of added outside stairways or fire escapes in order to save inside space. In the small units within a house, kitchens became kitchenettes and dining rooms became dinettes. The one-room "efficiency" apartment became popular.

During the Depression, many large homes were converted into duplexes or apartment units.

However, many people could not afford even these small makeshift apartments. When they lost their homes, they sought shelter in abandoned warehouses or in shacks made from wood crates, sheets of metal, or canvas that they had salvaged from trash heaps.

During the early years of the Great Depression leaders in government recognized that home building and home ownership were important not only to people but to the economy. In 1934, Congress established the Federal Housing Administration (FHA), which insured loans for home construction and repair. Congress also created the Federal Savings and Loan Insurance Foundation to protect savings in home-financing institutions. The first community planned for low-income families was established at Greenbelt, Maryland, in 1936. It was intended to serve as a model for other communities.

One important step taken by the federal government during the Depression was to provide federal funds for public housing projects. The first of these represented emergency housing; later ones were established by the United States Housing Authority, created by Congress in 1937. These projects were to provide housing for low-income families.

Except for public projects, the housing industry declined between the years 1930 and 1945. The construction of private housing, such as single-family and multi-unit homes, almost ceased during the Depression. During World War II, there was almost no home building because labor and materials were needed for the defense effort. Only emergency housing or housing at military bases could be built. Even remodeling and repair were stricly limited. The result was a growing shortage of housing throughout the nation.

The Greenbelt, MD, development near Washington was the first government-sponsored planned community.

The Pruitt-Igoe Project in St. Louis, MO, was built during the Depression to provide housing for low-income families. It has since been torn down.

THE MID-CENTURY AND AFTER: HOUSING, 1945-PRESENT

The end of World War II marked the start of a new era in American housing. After the war, the return of servicemen and the start of new families led to an increasing demand for housing. After almost twenty years of inactivity, the housing industry suddenly could not keep up with the demand for homes. The purchase of homes was aided by federal loans available through the existing Federal Housing Administration (FHA) or the new VA (Veterans Administration).

Postwar Suburban Growth

The sudden increase in the number of new families after World War II led to the building of new communities. Because land was readily available, and at low prices, the suburbs spread and grew rapidly around most cities.

Suburban homes were usually built on large lots. Many were built in a new design called a "ranch house," a spreading, one-story structure with either a hip or gable roof. Other popular designs were the split-level house, the traditional two-story house, and the split-entry house.

In suburban homes, social life moved to the backyard or patio. Many ranch houses had a family room, recreation room, and a terrace or patio. The openness of the floor plan and the easy access to outdoors contributed to a more casual lifestyle, with an emphasis on outdoor living.

As the suburban population increased, businesses, too, began to move to the suburbs. Shopping malls and industrial parks grew up near suburban population centers and major highways. They contributed to the clutter of landscapes already crowded with businesses and homes. This condition, spread out around major cities, became known as suburban sprawl.

After World War II, suburban areas grew rapidly as new families sought housing. The one-story ranch became a very popular design.

CONTEMPORARY STYLES OF HOUSES

Split-Level House
Living area: 1472 sq. ft.

Lower Level

Upper Level

Two-Story House
Living area: 1010 sq. ft.

Lower Level

Upper Level

Split-Entry House
Living area: 1140 sq. ft.

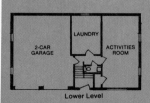

Lower Level

Upper Level

Ranch-Style House
Living area: 1200 sq. ft.

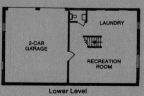

Lower Level

Upper Level

New Types of Development

New approaches to building and large-scale development were needed to relieve the postwar shortage. One solution was to develop a whole area, or tract, at one time. Building all the homes in one area at a time had the advantages of both speed and efficiency in construction. The "development" approach, based on assembly-line methods, also had certain disadvantages. The houses were often small and poorly constructed. The sameness in design was monotonous, and some people feared that they would lose their sense of individual identity from living in such homes. Still, the low price of tract houses appealed to many families and made home ownership possible for more people.

Another approach to the large-scale construction of homes was the use of prefabricated building materials. One of the first builders to use this method successfully was William Levitt. He built a development community, Levittown, on 5,000 acres of Long Island farmland. The 17,447 small homes in the community were almost identical in floor plan and exterior finish. The materials for the houses were prefabricated, or made ready for quick assembling, in factories. Kitchens and bathrooms; walls with doors and windows; roofs, floors, and closets; heating and wiring units—all were shipped as units to the building site. There, they were set up easily and quickly on concrete slabs.

The system developed by Levitt was highly efficient. It provided for streets, water, sewers, electricity, and landscaping, in addition to the sites and completed buildings. The community provided recreational areas, schools, business areas, churches, a town hall, and a hospital. The concept of a planned community was so successful that Levitt built other developments. By 1948, he was putting up 150 houses a week. Other builders have since developed similar planned communities in many parts of the country. Such communities have proved popular; they have also helped to meet the nation's housing needs.

Levittown, NY, went from bare pastures to a completed development in four years.

SITE: 30 Acres

Conventional 54-lot subdivision

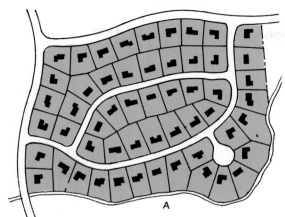

A

Cluster development encourages both efficient land use and conservation. Plan A shows how a 30-acre site would be developed as a standard subdivision. In that type of development, the entire site is split up into single house lots. The landscape becomes monotonous, with little privacy. The road area is extensive, and the dispersed utilities are high in cost.

Plans B and C show alternate uses of the same site based on cluster design. In both plans, individual lot size is reduced in favor of common open-space areas. Because building areas are concentrated, less land is required for roads, and utilities are centralized. Provision for privacy, pedestrian traffic, conservation, and shared use encourages both maximum benefit and efficient land use.

Cluster development: 54 lots

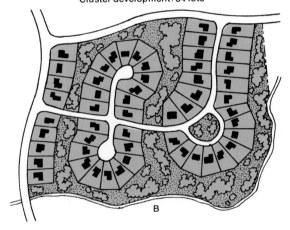

B

Cluster development: 112 townhouses

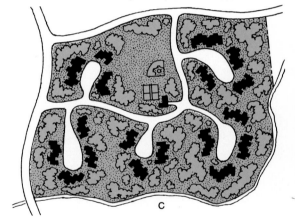

C

The concepts of open-space planning and cluster zoning developed during the 1960's, in order to make better use of the declining supply of land. In cluster zoning, houses are grouped together in clusters, with the space between clusters left undeveloped. Although the density of the housing is high, there is also a great deal of open space for everyone to enjoy.

In open-space development, there is a mixture of housing types, including high- and low-rise apartments, town houses, duplexes, triplexes, and "fourplexes," as well as single-family homes.

The Role of Government in Housing

Housing legislation and regulation have taken place on the local, state, and federal levels. As early as 1656, New York City had regulations prohibiting straw or reed roofs and wooden chimneys. Local communities made the rules for housing construction and placement. Today, local communities still have the power to control the type, size, height, use, and location of buildings through zoning codes. They also regulate construction methods and materials. Building codes set standards for such technical details as wiring and plumbing. Different communities have different zoning and building regulations. How well the regulations are enforced also varies among communities.

Urban renewal has encouraged the renovation and rehabilitation of houses in inner-city areas.

Urban renewal Slums started in America in the early 1800's when large numbers of immigrants moved to our cities. They crowded into already inadequate apartments in areas where family, friends, or other immigrants from their country had settled. To accommodate them, apartments were broken up into one- or two-room units, many with no windows or water. Private houses became rooming houses, often crowding large families into one room. These houses soon became run-down from overuse and poor maintenance. As buildings became slums, they affected neighboring houses and thus slums spread.

The 1937 Housing Act created the Federal Public Housing Program and required communities to eliminate one slum dwelling for each public housing unit built. However, public housing projects were not successful in eliminating slums. Overcrowding, crime, and urban decay continued to spread across cities, creating worsening living conditions. At this time the word *slum* began to be used to refer also to rural or suburban housing that did not provide the basic conveniences and space.

The Federal Housing Act of 1949 marked the start of a new effort to aid urban renewal. It required an approved, workable plan for the redevelopment or renewal of urban target areas by the community. The plan was required to include not only new construction but also renovation and rehabilitation of old housing in the area. Communities were required to consider the design and development of whole areas rather than just buildings or blocks. Loans and grants were made available so that private builders could buy the cleared land and build the planned housing. Under urban redevelopment, communities were required for the first time to establish minimum standards of sanitation, health, and safety for housing.

However, redevelopment also may cause problems. As old buildings are torn down, new homes must be found for the occupants. People who must move to new locations often feel cut off from their friends and familiar surroundings.

Low-income private housing The Depression of the 1930's resulted in very high unemployment. Renters were not able to pay their landlords. Many landlords and homeowners had their properties foreclosed by the banks. Construction of new houses and the upkeep of existing houses were at a standstill. The federal government realized that helping to get new construction started would provide jobs as well as improve housing.

In 1934, the FHA was formed to help families purchase homes. At that time, banks were very reluctant to give out mortgage loans since they had just had so many defaults. The FHA guaranteed the loans by insuring the mortgages that were funded. Because the mortgages were insured, interest rates could be lower. Other ways the FHA helped low-income home buyers were by providing long-term loans, permitting very low down payments, and inspecting the property for condition and quality. Interest rates combined with low down payments meant that more families could afford to buy houses.

After World War II, Congress passed the GI Bill of Rights. Under this act, the Veterans Administration guaranteed loans to veterans to purchase, build, or improve homes. Loans of 100 percent of the purchase price for up to 30 years were available. This enabled large numbers of returning servicemen to become homeowners.

Urban renewal has encouraged the rebuilding of houses in inner-city areas. Often, such structures are sound and well built but need repairs and modernizing. What changes have already been made in these houses? What signs of disrepair can you find?

Some urban families have bought houses for very little money through special home-steading programs. They must renovate the house within a specified amount of time.

Current actions in housing In 1973, after a scandal arose over misuse of funds, all federal money was cut off to builders. The control was switched back to the local level. The 1974 Housing and Community Development Act called for block grants to the states to be used to provide low- and middle-income housing in target areas.

Today, urban renewal funds are essentially no longer available. New public housing is confined almost entirely to housing for the elderly. Some rent subsidies are still available, but in many areas they are not large enough to provide decent housing. The federal emphasis is back to relying on private development and construction. State housing programs are attempting to fill the gap by providing funds for some local housing programs.

Cities are trying to upgrade their housing by buying or condemning properties and reselling the land or the houses to individuals at a very low price. The one condition is that they must renovate or rebuild the property. Urban homesteading programs permit low-income families to buy a house owned by the city for as little as $1.00. However, they must renovate the house and live in it when it is finished.

Other methods used to help lower income families find adequate housing have been the use of rent subsidies, mortgage subsidies, and rent supplements. In 1965, all of the federal housing programs were consolidated under one cabinet level department called Housing and Urban Development (HUD). The new programs included in this act were a rent supplement program that paid a portion of the rent of qualified low-income families and a new subsidy program under which public housing authorities could lease privately owned units for low-income families.

THE FUTURE OF HOUSING

Experience shows that predicting the future of housing involves many uncertainties. The postwar planners of the 1940's and 1950's did not anticipate such changes as the major drop in the birthrate, the energy crisis, or the emphasis on conservation. Nor did they anticipate the need for urban renewal or for the regulation of land use. Although it is difficult to make predictions about housing in the final years of this century, certain trends can be identified.

Trends in Housing Needs

Population changes will continue to affect the housing market. Families are smaller and there are more single-family households. Couples are marrying later, having children later, and having fewer children. These families can use smaller homes, but they want most of the conveniences of a larger home.

There will be an increasing number of elderly single people and couples for whom independent housing will be needed. While community housing for the aged and retirement villages are two possibilities, many elderly would prefer to stay in their own familiar homes. For some families, space must be provided for elderly parents who move in with their adult children. More and more families are having three generations living together, as older children continue to live at home and grandparents move in too.

Housing for the elderly will become increasingly important as more of our population lives into their 70s, 80s, and 90s.

Changes in Housing Construction

Housing construction methods have been slow to change over the years. Because the industry is so fragmented and most builders construct fewer than ten houses a year, traditional methods are most often used.

Nine out of ten single-family houses in the United States are built of wood. Platform frame construction is the most common method for one-story houses. A subfloor, extending to the outer edge of the exterior wall, is put down over the foundation. The exterior and interior walls are then nailed to the subfloor. In this method, the wall framing can actually be put together lying flat on the subfloor. After the wall is finished, it is tilted up into position and nailed to the subfloor. When sections of a house are put together at the foundation site and then lifted into place it is called site fabrication. Even with the use of site fabrication, the construction of a house is a lengthy business.

Although contractors who build only a few houses a year can use traditional methods, builders of development housing need faster construction methods. The most common methods now used are prefabrication and modular construction. Prefabricated housing is produced in a factory where wall and floor sections are built on an assembly line. Then the sections are loaded into a truck and lifted into place on the foundation at the site. Costs can be influenced by the distance between the factory and the site. The wall sections can be complete with the wiring and plumbing lines installed, but usually not the interior finish. Kitchens and bathroom units can be shipped complete.

In modular construction, whole room areas are completed at the factory. The walls and ceilings are finished; the windows, doors, and bathroom and kitchen equipment are installed. These modules are shipped to the site, placed on the foundation, and joined together. Other modules may be placed on top of the first ones. Motels are often comprised of separate modules built for each room and bath, delivered completely decorated and furnished. Module sizes are limited by the width of the trucks that carry them and the width of the roads travelled.

Mobile homes are also available as module units that can be placed on footings and joined together. Two, three, and four units can be joined. Porches or patios are often added. Most mobile homes are never moved from their sites. Modular construction makes it possible for a family to get a home quickly and relatively inexpensively.

New construction methods, such as prefabrication and modular construction, enable homes to be built faster and at lower cost.

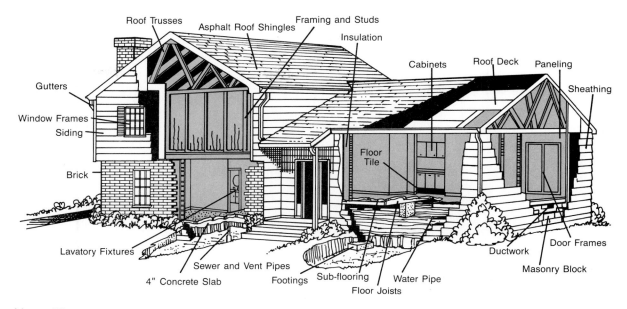

Roof Trusses
Asphalt Roof Shingles
Framing and Studs
Insulation
Cabinets
Roof Deck
Paneling
Sheathing
Gutters
Window Frames
Siding
Brick
Floor Tile
Lavatory Fixtures
Sewer and Vent Pipes
4" Concrete Slab
Footings
Sub-flooring
Water Pipe
Floor Joists
Ductwork
Door Frames
Masonry Block

Many different materials are used in the construction of a house. Prefinished components, such as prehung doors, help builders construct a house more quickly.

Construction Materials

The traditional construction materials are still used today: wood, concrete, bricks, stone, steel, and aluminum. The emphasis is on constructing houses more quickly by doing as much work as possible before the materials even get to the site. Thus, builders can buy doors prehung, windows preframed, floors prefinished, and fireplaces prefabricated. The faster builders can close in the house, the sooner the crew can work indoors. Large plywood sheets, 4 feet wide by 8 feet long (1.2 m by 2.4 m), can be used to cover the exterior walls and roof very quickly.

Concrete is a mixture of cement, sand, gravel, and water. Poured concrete is used for basement floors and walls. Concrete blocks and cinder blocks are inexpensive substitutes for stone. Houses made of concrete blocks are often covered with stucco. Precast concrete modules can be used for houses, hotels, and office buildings. Some experimental houses have been made of concrete sprayed over a form.

Steel is used in single-family houses primarily to provide support in walls over wide openings such as sliding glass doors or window walls. Steel beams support the upper floors over these openings. Steel is also used in the framework of multi-unit structures.

Aluminum is a lightweight metal used for gutters and downspouts, window frames, and heat ducts. Aluminum foil is used as a vapor barrier on batts of insulation. Textured aluminum, made to look like wood, is used for the siding and shutters of houses. People like aluminum siding because it needs no painting and is very durable.

Molded plastics, laminated plastics, fiberglass, and molded plywood can replace more traditional materials. Plastic pipe is lighter and less expensive than copper or brass. Molded plastic walls are used in bathrooms instead of ceramic tile. Some shower stalls and bathtub units have plastic walls on three sides. Plastic foam is

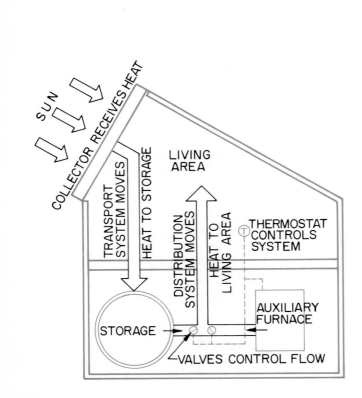

A solar heating system can be active or passive. Active solar systems have large glass panels on the roof which absorb heat from the sun. Hot liquid behind these collectors is then circulated through the house. Passive solar systems depend on southern exposure windows which let in the sun's rays.

used as insulation. Plastic can also be molded and colored to imitate wood, stone, metal, ceramics, and glass.

There are many new types of glass on the market: tinted glass, heat-absorbing glass, heat-reflecting glass, and double-glazed insulating glass. These are used for windows, doors, and skylights.

The development of new construction materials and new ways to use them is helping to cut housing costs. However, the use of new building materials is limited by each community's building codes. For example, plastic pipe is not accepted in some communities for plumbing use.

New Designs for Homes

Solar homes The oil shortage of the 1970's caused the building industry to design energy-efficient houses. These houses contain such features as heavy insulation, double- and triple-glazed windows, and the use of the sun for both active and passive solar heat.

In climates where the sun shines most of the year, solar heating systems can be used. These systems are of two types: active and passive. Active solar heating systems consist of large glass solar collecting panels on the roofs which absorb heat from the sun. Liquid, running through coils behind these glass collectors, absorbs the heat and takes it to a storage tank of water, bricks, or crushed rocks. The storage tank is heavily insulated to keep the liquid hot. When heat is needed in the house, a pump circulates the hot liquid to radiators in the house. Active solar systems are expensive to build because they are custom-designed and custom-fabricated. They also need a second separate heating system to help warm the house in winter or during periods of cloudiness and rain. Efficient heat pumps, which act like a refrigerator in reverse, take heat out of the ground even

in the coldest weather. These heat pumps are run by electricity and are used in conjunction with solar heating systems.

Passive solar systems make use of the location of the glass areas in the house as well as wind breaks and plantings to control the temperature. Passive solar systems require all large glass areas in the house to face south, kitchen windows to face east, and few or no windows on the north. Vertical plantings are needed to shield western windows from the summer sun. In order to work satisfactorily, the southern exposure windows must have a four-foot (1.2 m) roof overhang. The angle of the sun's rays during the winter allows them to enter the windows facing south under the overhang. In summer, the orbit of the sun is higher in the sky and the overhang blocks the sun's rays from entering the window.

Earth shelter homes Another type of construction designed to reduce fuel costs is one in which the exterior walls are built up with earth so that the house is partially underground. Ground temperatures remain fairly constant regardless of air temperatures. Such buildings are therefore less expensive to heat or to cool. Few houses have been constructed in this way, but a number of office buildings and churches have recently used this plan. When parts of their exterior walls are underground, a building seems more integrated into its site.

Other Housing Trends

Because of the high cost of land, new houses are apt to be attached like town houses or built in clusters of three or more houses. The trend is toward smaller-sized houses due to high building costs. However, within these homes, bigger and more luxurious kitchens and bathrooms are being shown. Built-in refrigerators, microwave ovens, and eating areas in the kitchen are desirable features. A new bathroom may contain a whirlpool bath, hot tub, or sauna.

High land costs in the suburbs and long hours spent communting to and from a city have made urban properties more attractive to many people. In some run-down areas of cities, old neighborhoods are being renewed. Old brownstones and small houses are being renovated and sold to middle- and upper-income families. This migration of middle-class people into deteriorating or recently renewed city areas is called "gentrification."

Other housing trends include an increase in special communities that appeal to special groups of people. Retirement communities, singles communities, and recreational communities which feature golf, tennis, boating, or skiing, attract people with similar interests. Others purchase second homes or vacation homes because they are a way of investing money and securing tax savings, as well as being a place to vacation.

Today, a very important factor in the selection of a place to live is security. For more information about present and future trends in housing, see Chapter 23.

C A R E E R

BUILDING CONSTRUCTION INSPECTOR

P R O F I L E

Building construction inspectors oversee and inspect the construction of buildings to make sure that it conforms to the blueprints, the drawings of the architect's plans. They must be sure that the contractor complies with all regulations governing construction. Inspections are made of the materials used in reinforced concrete, masonry, structural steel, and of the electrical, plumbing, heating, and ventilation systems. These materials and systems must conform to specifications. Building construction inspectors also measure distances to verify dimensions and examine the workmanship on such finished products as cabinets, molding, painting, tile, and flooring.

If you are interested in a career as a building construction inspector, you need mathematical skill plus the ability to understand, learn, and apply concepts and procedures. You must be able and willing to accept decision-making responsibility.

You can enter this field by getting vocational or technical training and with experience in the lower level positions of the construction field.

REVIEWING CHAPTER 3

SUMMARY

Housing concepts have changed greatly during the 20th century. They have been influenced by a rising standard of living, changes in population, and new trends in housing design, construction, and materials.

Progress in housing was stopped by the Depression and World War II. The sudden demand for more homes after the war led to a crisis in housing. Suburban and tract developments helped to meet the need for new housing. However, during this time many inner-city areas declined. Government programs have helped aid urban renewal and provide low-income housing.

Changes in housing needs and in people's lifestyles have brought new trends in housing. New methods of construction and types of building materials are helping to cut housing costs. Solar homes and earth shelter homes are two new housing designs that may become more common.

FACTS TO KNOW

1. In what ways did the bungalow and the prairie house differ from house styles of the 19th century?
2. Explain how the Great Depression and World War II affected housing.
3. What factors contributed to the growth of suburbs after World War II?
4. What are the advantages and disadvantages of the "development" approach to building houses?
5. Describe *cluster zoning*. Why is cluster zoning used for communities?
6. Explain how the FHA and the GI Bill of Rights helped people to purchase homes.
7. Describe *prefabrication* and *modular construction*. How do they differ?
8. What is the difference between active and passive solar heating systems?

IDEAS TO THINK ABOUT

1. What factors in the 20th century have enabled more people to become homeowners? What factors may have prevented people from purchasing homes?
2. How can urban renewal better improve housing conditions for low-income families?
3. How have lifestyles changed in the last ten years? How have these changes affected housing needs and trends?

ACTIVITIES TO DO

1. Cut out photographs or illustrations of different styles of architecture from magazines. Label each type of architecture and explain their different characteristics.
2. Prepare a report on the work and contributions of one 20th-century architect. Suggestions include: Alvar Aalto, Marcel Breuer, Walter Gropius, Philip Johnson, Richard Neutra, I. M. Pei, Paul Rudolph, and Frank Lloyd Wright.

YOU CAN DO IT!

New Looks for Rooms

How can you create a new look for a room? Start with the walls—they are usually the largest solid area in a room and are the background for the furnishings. Add architectural interest with moldings or wallpaper borders. Dramatize the room with bold graphics or mirrors. Panel walls for an informal, casual feeling. Stencil a pattern for an authentic country mood. Or, by covering a wall with cork, make a giant-sized bulletin board and decorate it. Each of these do-it-yourself projects can be completed in a weekend.

Add moulding for a traditional effect.

Stencil a design around windows and doors, or across the walls for a country look.

Add a wallpaper border to accent the design features of a room.

Use large mirrors to create an illusion of space and to open up a small room.

Wallpaper one wall of a living room, dining room, or bedroom to create a focal point.

Chapter
4

Influences Upon Housing Decisions

Where will you live? This question may be one that you will have to answer several times during your lifetime. Choosing a place to live is one of the most important decisions a person has to make. Where you live becomes your home—a place that provides shelter as well as space for activities. It can become the center for your family life, social life, time alone, or all of these.

The factors influencing your choice of a home can be many and varied. Do you want to live in a city, a suburb, or in a rural area? Should you live close to work, to your relatives, to your friends, or to recreational activities? Do you prefer an apartment, a house, or a mobile home? How much space do you need? Do you want to rent or buy? What type of community would you like to belong to? How much money do you have available for housing?

Some of these factors are very personal; they reflect your own unique values and lifestyles. Other factors are related to the housing market—the supply of housing that is available within a given area. In this unit, you will discover many guidelines that will help you to make housing decisions. Selecting a home can be a very exciting opportunity. However, only you can decide which choice will meet your needs best and bring the most enjoyment to you and everyone who lives there.

PREVIEWING YOUR LEARNING

After you have read this chapter, you will be able to:
- Explain how people's needs, goals, and values influence their housing decisions.

- Identify different functions that a home can provide.

- Compare the housing needs of people who are at different stages of the life cycle.

- Discuss why financial resources are an important consideration when choosing a home.

TERMS TO KNOW

economics—production, distribution, and consumption of goods and services.

equity—the amount a property is worth beyond what is owed on it

goal—an objective or end for which you are aiming

inflation—a sharp increase in prices

life cycle—the stages of life that the average person or family goes through

lifestyle—way of living

priority—something that ranks highest in order of importance

resource—a source of wealth, supply, information, or skill

standard of living—the measure of how well a home and lifestyle meet people's basic needs

values—a person's ideals, beliefs, and attitudes

BOAT LIVING—YES, IT'S A HOME!

F E A T U R E

Would you be interested in a non-conventional type of home? Would you like to escape the noise, air pollution, and overcrowding that exists around you? Then boat living may be an exciting alternative for you. Many people who have always loved the water find that modern houseboats have all the comforts and conveniences of land housing. Houseboats are like house trailers: they give mobility to people who like being on the go and seeing new places. For the more settled "aboarders," a permanent mooring in a modern marina is like being on vacation all the time.

The first boat dwellers were probably those who used boats for fishing or hauling. In Hong Kong today, large numbers of people live on junks, sampans, and houseboats. In Paris, there are about 200 inhabited boats and floating houses along the Seine River. Amsterdam has over 3,000 houseboats on its waterways.

Here in the United States, the 1950's brought a "boating boom." The development of fiberglass for boat construction made mass production and maintenance easier. As a result, modern boats are filled with many comforts and conveniences, and people are more easily drawn to living on them. However, if you're thinking of buying a houseboat, it is best to rent first before making an expensive investment. You want to be sure houseboating is for you.

DEFINING GOALS

The primary purpose of a home is to provide shelter from both the weather and the impersonal outer world. Your home also serves as the place where you meet your basic needs: sleeping, eating, and taking care of yourself. In selecting housing, you are choosing a place for living not only according to your needs but also according to your activities and values.

Beyond these basic goals, a home represents space of your own, over which you have control. There, you can choose to be alone or together with others. Your home also represents your lifestyle, or way of living. By reflecting your personality, it becomes an extension of yourself.

Just as people in a home influence its environment, the environment of the home affects the outlook and the behavior of the people within it. A home meets the responsibility of providing space for physical needs, such as safety, cleanliness, and health. A home should also fulfill the psychological needs for respect, self-esteem, independence, and creativity. In addition, requirements for privacy, communication, and realizing one's potential should be met. An environment that is supportive physically, psychologically, and socially can provide the sense of security and well-being that change a house into a home.

A home must meet the basic physical needs of a family. It should also help meet the psychological, social, and emotional needs of individual family members.

IDENTIFYING NEEDS

In identifying housing needs, it is important to distinguish between needs and wants. Few people can afford everything they want. Economists recognize that people are always seeking to balance their unlimited wants with their limited resources. Advertising seeks to influence this balance by creating wants and changing wants to needs. Only you can determine your own needs and priorities, on the basis of what you can afford.

Primary Needs

The living space and facilities within the home must meet the basic needs of the people who live there. The space must provide for the functions of living: eating, sleeping, cleanliness and grooming, dressing, working, playing, being alone, socializing, and enjoying leisure time and recreation. The physical environment must support acceptable standards of safety, health, cleanliness, and nonpollution. It must provide protection and security from intruders.

Small apartments are the first housing choice of many young people.

MINIMUM SPACE FOR LIVING

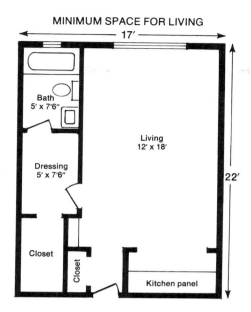

An efficiency apartment provides enough living space for one person.

The space and facilities of the home should enhance its livability. Its conveniences, how efficiently it is organized, and how easily it can be maintained all play an important part in the smooth functioning of a home. They contribute not only to the easy management of the household but also to pleasant living there. These characteristics help the home to fulfill its functions as a headquarters for personal and family life and as a base for dealing with the outer world. The measure of how well a home meets these basic needs is called one's standard of living.

Secondary Needs

The physical environment of the home relates not only to the standard of living but also to the social interaction and emotional well-being of the people who live in a home. A positive environment for living depends on many factors. Among the contributing physical factors are space for individual pursuits as well as family activities; a

provision for privacy as well as togetherness; and room and facilities for recreation and entertainment. Psychologically, one's home should provide a sense of identity and belonging; a feeling of self-esteem; a sense of pleasure and beauty in the surroundings; and a sense of creativity and inspiration. These factors, which contribute to a person's or a family's emotional fulfillment, are related to the quality of life within the home.

Personal values about privacy and sociability influence the need for space and the way in which it is used. Lack of space for individual and family activities can be limiting. Space that is poorly arranged or poorly organized can be socially and emotionally confining. By contrast, good planning and effective use of even limited space can enhance the livability of a home.

Besides being a place for sociability and recreation, the home has increasingly become a personal refuge from a crowded

In this one-room apartment, the couch converts to a bed for efficient use of space.

Privacy can be created for family members in a number of ways. Here a corner of a room is used as a home office. Note the storage space at the end of the desk.

and impersonal world. The necessity for privacy is the result of many factors—crowded urban living, an existence among strangers, distance from one's own family, and occupations involving machines, such as computers or assembly lines, rather than people. These conditions have made it more important than ever for the home to reinforce one's sense of personal identity and belonging.

Through careful planning, it is possible to create home surroundings that reinforce the sense of self. Surroundings that provide emotional support to the individual or family by their very nature enhance the livability within the home. They result in increased aesthetic enjoyment, intellectual stimulation, and interaction among people within the home environment. Some people want their home to create an impression of comfort and relaxation. Others prefer an environment of streamlined convenience. By being aware and planning carefully, you can use space to create the atmosphere and effect that suit you best.

Cost is always a factor in planning the home environment. Beyond cost alone are other factors—imagination, ingenuity, and willingness to do things yourself—which change an empty space with walls, floors, ceilings, and windows into a home. Adapting this life space to support the individual's or family's lifestyle can help to improve the quality of life for everyone within the home.

Changing Needs
A person's housing needs are closely related to one's stage of life. During childhood and adolescence, the young person usually lives within the family home. At some time, often in the late teens, the individual leaves the family home and establishes a separate household. That separateness will continue for most of the remainder of one's life cycle.

The first "home away from home" is likely to be a simple one. It may be a room in a home or dormitory, or it may be a small apartment, sometimes shared with friends. This first home, whether it belongs to a single person or a young couple, is likely to be simple and inexpensively furnished. As the individual or couple gains greater economic security, a move to a larger place is often made. This move may be related to a job promotion, marriage, or the birth of a child. It may also occur when a couple without children needs more space for a changing lifestyle. Families on limited incomes may have less choice about moving as space needs increase, and may have to adjust to the existing quarters.

As personal interests and social activities become more established, people tend to settle in a permanent location. This is likely to be a time of greater social and commu-

nity involvement. More space may be needed in the home to provide privacy, and allow for personal interests, entertaining, and other pursuits. To gain more space, people sometimes decide to buy a home. Some families may decide to settle in the suburbs. The decisions made at this time, however, are often reevaluated as families reach the "empty-nest" stage. Of course, this stage, which is one of great adjustment for parents, does not affect people without children.

A major change in the life cycle comes with retirement. Today, longer life expectancy has lengthened the post-retirement stage for both women and men. At the start of this stage, many people continue to live in their present homes, particularly if their health is good and they are involved in local social and community activities. Sooner or later, a move will probably be made to a smaller home or to a unit in a

DIFFERENT STAGES OF THE LIFE CYCLE

Housing needs may vary at different stages of the life cycle.

housing complex for adults or an apartment building. Changes in priorities during this stage of the life cycle include emphasis on economy, medical care, comfort, interests, and personal relationships.

For senior citizens, further changes in housing may be necessary. Elderly people may have physical impairments and may have given up driving. Outliving one's spouse, brothers and sisters, and friends creates new needs in living arrangements. An older person who is in good health, with sufficient income and varied interests, may not want to move. On the other hand, this may be an opportune time to move to a home where living is simpler. A move to a retirement home or housing for the elderly may be desirable at this stage of life.

RECOGNIZING VALUES

Being aware of one's own values and preferences is an important step in thinking about housing. Each of us has certain ideas and convictions about ourselves and how we want to live. In making decisions about a home, we are applying those ideas to our surroundings and lifestyle. Through conscious choice, we are expressing ourselves and establishing a way of living that in turn has an effect upon us. For that reason, we need to be aware of the choices and decisions we make in choosing a place to live.

Kinds of Values

Values are the ideals, beliefs, and attitudes that are a part of each person. These

EXAMPLES OF ALTERNATIVE VALUES (based on preference, not income)			
CATEGORY	ALTERNATIVES		
Standard of living:	simple/moderate	OR	highest possible
Income management:	balance of saving/ spending	OR	saving not a concern
Spending for housing:	affordable	OR	highest possible
Home ownership as investment:	important	OR	not significant
Purchases for home:	cash/partial credit	OR	all purchases on credit
Household conveniences:	adequate	OR	latest available
Lifestyle:	casual/informal	OR	formal
Interaction focus:	privacy	OR	sociability
Focus of space use:	isolation	OR	togetherness/shared use
Arrangement of space:	convenience/ informality	OR	formality
Use of home:	center for living	OR	minimum use
Setting:	comfort/ convenience	OR	formality
Design:	simple/attractive	OR	distinctive
Character:	spontaneous/personal	OR	fixed/impersonal
Use of color:	personal appeal	OR	interior design
Style:	traditional	OR	eclectic/contemporary

values also characterize each person's behavior. Some values are related to physical needs, such as survival and safety. These are universal among people. Moral values, such as loyalty, honesty, and respect for the rights of others, are usually shared by members of a family, community, culture group, or society.

Material values are associated with possessions that are useful or have worth. Social values refer to interactive behavior, or how a person acts toward other people or groups of people. Aesthetic values, which are related to personal taste and perception, include a sense of beauty, proportion, and style. Material, social, and aesthetic values are directly related to housing and home furnishing. Moral values are important to interpersonal relationships within the home.

Influences upon Values

Many influences affect the values that we acquire. Among these influences are family and friends, culture and tradition, and social and economic changes. These influences tend to affect our values over long periods of time—usually, for most of our lives.

The family, home, and environment we grow up in greatly affect our own values and outlook. Often, we take these values for granted until they come in conflict with someone else's. For example, two people may marry and suddenly realize that their values are in conflict. One partner may have come from a family where order, quiet, and privacy were important. The other partner may have grown up in a family where the lifestyle was more casual, there were always many people around, and possessions were freely shared. In making decisions about their home, this couple will have to resolve some of their differences in values.

Friends and associates often have a strong influence on a person's values.

A home reflects the values of the people who live there. What values do you think are expressed in each of these rooms? Find several other pictures in the text that show different kinds of personal values.

Young people like to identify with people whom they admire. Often, they depend on the opinions of friends concerning clothes, social activities, or the choice of an occupation. While it is important to consider the advice of friends, it is also essential to be aware of your own values and preferences. In a decision about housing, you are the one who will be living in the home that you have chosen.

Most people like to display treasured possessions and items of personal interest in their homes. Such objects add a special character as well as decoration to a home.

Cultural values are the result of long experience and tradition. For that reason, they usually change slowly and are difficult to influence. However, in times of rapid social and economic change—such as the present century—cultural values change very rapidly. Today, the standard cultural values are often replaced by those of subcultures within the whole society. Changes in cultural values have an influence on housing. Many low-income, urban housing developments have not met the needs of residents for informal living space. For example, families accustomed to gathering in the kitchen during meal preparation do not like the new, efficient compact kitchens, because no space for socializing is included.

Changes in Values

The values that people have may change with the times. Social and economic changes often have a direct effect on people's values. In the past century, the shift from a rural to an urban society has changed both family life and housing needs. The sudden growth in population after World War II created a huge demand for single-family homes. In recent years, a declining birthrate and new lifestyles have created a need for smaller homes and greater mobility. A trend toward simpler and more casual living reflects the growing concern for personal, rather than material, values.

For most of the 20th century, a rising standard of living influenced people to seek better housing. In the past twenty years, however, affluence—which valued high consumption—has given way to more modest living—which values the conservation of energy and other resources. During this period of time, social concern has grown, and an adequate standard of living for everyone has become a national goal. This concern has helped to improve the design and quality of some low-cost housing. Social concern has also led to the concept of "open housing," with all members of a community having access to housing without discrimination.

ANALYZING RESOURCES

For most people, cost is the major influence in decisions on housing. The price must be low enough to be within the means of a person or a family. If the cost of housing is relatively high, other things must be adjusted to meet that outlay. In terms of investment, status, or convenience, the sacrifice may be worth it. However, many people choose to spend less than they can afford on housing in order to have more money to spend on recreation, travel, or furnishings.

Buying a home can be a method of forced savings for some people. They may buy a home with less space and fewer conveniences than they would actually like, in order to build up the amount of ownership, sometimes called equity. That equity may later be used as a down payment on a home that more nearly meets their needs.

Skill in managing financial matters is another factor to consider in weighing the cost of housing. The person who can work out a budget for spending and hold to it may be able to afford higher-cost housing than the person who spends less carefully. Because housing is such a basic commitment, knowledge of your priorities and alternatives is important before you make a final decision.

Income

The amount of money to be spent on housing depends on the resources available. For most individuals and families, earned income is the major resource. Income generally includes salary or wages received over a period of time—weekly, monthly, quarterly, semiannually, or annually. In addition to regular salary or wages, people may receive income from property rental, royalties, bonuses, or commissions, and from interest or dividends on investments. Once in a while, a person may receive unexpected income from an inheritance, gift, or part-time work. Most individuals and families plan their spending on the basis of regular income from salary or wages on either a weekly or a monthly basis. Workers whose income is seasonal and self-employed persons whose incomes vary from year to year should budget on a monthly or annual basis but may find that difficult to do.

Traditional patterns of income and employment have been affected by changing lifestyles. At one time, the family was the basic economic unit; today, the growing number of single people means that one income may be supporting only one person rather than several or many. Traditionally, the husband or father was the chief provider; today, more than half of our nation's women are employed outside the home. This percentage keeps rising as the cost of living rises due to inflation.

Having two incomes in a family increases the amount of income available to spend on housing. Today, many families can afford to buy a home only because there are two incomes to support it. However, a second income—like a first income—is not all gain. Some of it will be used to cover work-related costs, such as clothes and transportation, or perhaps child-care expenses, in addition to higher income taxes.

Good money management, while it cannot add to income, can increase the amount of money available for spending. Doing one's own maintenance and repairs or making and renovating furnishings can save money. Good management also influences the general use of income. Two families which have the same number of

It is important that all members of the family practice good money management. Preparing a budget helps many families balance their expenses with their income.

children and which live in similar houses and receive similar incomes will not spend money in the same way. One family may be continually borrowing; the other may be regularly saving. The difference in what they will eventually be able to buy lies in their management of money.

Expenses

Expenses as well as income affect the amount of money a person or a family can spend on housing. The range of expenses an income must cover heavily influences the amount that can be spent for any one item, as well as the extras that can be bought. In any individual or family budget, the cost of housing is a major item. Food for a family is usually the only budget item that could cost as much as, or more than, housing.

Expenses related to housing are of two main kinds—fixed and flexible. Many of the expenses to be covered by income are fixed; that is, they must be paid regularly, and the amount is fairly constant. Certain other types of expenses are flexible; that is, they vary in amount and do not occur regularly. The total of expenses, both fixed and flexible, determines how much income is left over for savings or discretionary spending.

Usually, it is wise to keep a balance between fixed and flexible expenses. Having high fixed expenses may not leave enough money on hand for day-to-day living expenses. However, reducing fixed expenses may result in an undesirably lower standard of living.

Fixed expenses must be met regularly and on time. Prompt payment establishes a good credit rating for you. In terms of housing, it protects your rights, interests, and—if you own your home—your investment. If fixed expenses are not met on time, there may be high interest or penalty charges. If bills for home insurance are not paid on time, the insurance may lapse. In that case, fire or flood could mean a total loss of one's home and personal property.

Because flexible expenses vary from month to month, it may be best to plan for the major ones on an annual basis. Some flexible expenses, such as those for clothing or home furnishings, can usually be postponed. Other types of flexible expenses—such as repairs to plumbing, heating, and cooling systems—cannot be postponed. Health costs are another flexible expense that it is difficult or impossible to reduce or postpone, since earning a living depends, in part, on your health. Some expenses can be reduced by doing repairs yourself or buying less expensive items. Spending for entertainment and recreation can usually be reduced or postponed.

Fixed and flexible expenses change as lifestyles change and as households expand and contract. Good money management adjusts spending according to these changes. Knowing exactly where your money is going and then limiting "impulse buying" can give you better control of your

FIXED AND FLEXIBLE EXPENSES	
Fixed Expenses	**Flexible Expenses**
Mortgage payments or rent	Food at home and away
Installment payments	from home
Interest on borrowed money	Clothing and maintenance
Utilities: gas, oil, electricity,	Doctor, dentist, clinic, etc.
telephone, water,	Recreation and
trash/garbage	entertainment
Transportation: car, bus,	Personal care
train	Personal advancement
Church and charities	School or work expenses
Organization dues	Replacement of home
Social Security and	furnishings
retirement payments	Hobbies
Life insurance	Gifts on special occasions
Health and accident	Home repairs
insurance	
Home insurance	
Personal liability insurance	
Taxes: property, and other	
taxes not taken out at	
source	

Some expenses must be met regularly; others occur only occasionally. What items can you add to each category?

income and greater ability to deal with major expenses such as housing.

At times, a person's financial resources may be affected by the economy as well as by income and expenses. The Great Depression of the 1930's caused hardships and suffering for all Americans. In recent years, inflation—with prices and costs rising faster than personal income—has created problems. During a time of inflation, it is difficult to limit spending in order to meet the rising cost of fixed expenses such as food and housing. Some of the greatest increases have been in health costs, housing expenses and taxes—all unavoidable expenditures.

Personal and Community Resources

People who are willing to invest their own time, energy, and talent on their homes can save money and at the same time increase the livability of their homes. Today,

Do-it-yourself projects can save you money and create a more enjoyable living space.

since the cost of labor has risen, many people do their own home repair and maintenance. New products and inventions, such as self-polishing floor wax, water-base paint, self-adhesive floor tiles, and precut and prefinished wall panels, have encouraged this trend.

People who are skilled in sewing or carpentry can make things for the home that would be extremely expensive to buy ready-made or ready-built. Doing things yourself takes time and energy, but it can also add greatly to the livability, convenience, and value of the home. Painting, wallpapering, and laying floor tiles all add beauty and value to the home at a relatively low cost. They also may give a great

deal of personal satisfaction and enjoyment, and the money saved can be spent for other things.

Community resources, too, can aid in the care and upkeep of the home. Some of these resources, such as libraries and vocational classes, are educational. Others, such as lumberyards, supply stores, and craft shops, provide raw materials. Rental agencies provide specialized equipment for short-term use. Stores, display homes, and craft exhibits can provide ideas that you can use or adapt in your own home. All of these resources can help you to accomplish projects that would otherwise cost a great deal or be impossible to undertake yourself.

WEIGHING ALTERNATIVES

Until now, you have been considering housing from your own perspective, in terms of goals, needs, values, and resources. In all of these areas, you yourself make the decisions. Once you begin to apply your ideas to the housing market, the situation becomes more complex: the precise solution you are seeking may not exist. In that case, you must choose from among the alternatives that are available in the market.

Informing yourself about the alternatives that exist in the housing market is an important part of the decision-making process. Although the total range of alternatives is almost unlimited, there are certain key aspects of the housing market to consider. Among these aspects are the types of

---

THE DECISION-MAKING PROCESS

All good decision making follows the six basic steps. See how they can be applied to housing decisions.

Step 1: Set a Goal
What is your housing goal? Maybe it is to redecorate your room at home. Or perhaps your goal is to live in an apartment after graduation.

Step 2: Review Your Needs, Wants, Values, and Resources
What is important to you? Try to identify specific needs that you have regarding space, privacy, and other factors. For example, think about how you want to spend the time you are at home. What type of living style do you prefer? How much time, money, and skill is available to you?

Step 3: Identify All the Alternatives
How can you reach your goal? Usually there are several choices that you can make. Would rearranging the furniture give your room a new look and make better use of the space? Or do you need some new furniture? Does the room need to be painted? Or would some new accessories create the look you want? What other alternatives do you have?

Step 4: Evaluate Each Alternative
Consider the facts about each alternative that you have identified. What are the pros and cons of each choice? Can you paint your room yourself? Can you find inexpensive furniture at a garage or tag sale, a secondhand store, or in a relative's attic. Evaluate how your resources can be best used.

Step 5: Select the Best Alternative
Based on your evaluation, you must now select which alternative will help you best reach your goal. Then you must follow through on your decision so that you will reach your goal. For example, if you decide to paint your room yourself, the sooner you start, the sooner you will be able to enjoy your new surroundings.

Step 6: Evaluate the Result
After you have made your decision, it is important to evaluate the result. Are you pleased with your decision? In the long run, did you make the right choice? For example, even though it took you an entire week to paint your room and rearrange the furniture, you may conclude you are pleased with the new look; it was a good decision and it was worth the effort.

Each time that you go through the decision-making process, you will improve your skills and be better prepared to make future decisions.

housing available; the advantages of renting or buying; different types of ownership; and methods of financing home ownership. Also important are your requirements for total space and layout, kitchen work space and storage areas, and utilities. On each of these matters, you are applying your own needs and preferences to what the housing market offers. You alone can decide what kind of housing to choose; whether to rent or to buy; and what space, storage, and utilities you need.

Out of the interaction between your wants and the alternatives on the market will come a decision. In making this decision you are acting as a consumer—going into the market and selecting a product. If you understand your own requirements well and have studied the alternatives carefully, your eventual decision should be a sound and satisfying one. The reward will be a home that not only meets your needs but also contributes to and enriches your way of life.

CAREER PROFILE

ARCHITECT

Architects plan and design all types of buildings, from houses and apartment buildings to schools, factories, and shopping malls. They also may work with clients on remodeling homes or renovating office buildings. When working with clients, they must first determine the size and space requirements of the project. Then sketches or perhaps a three-dimensional model of the project must be prepared. Architects write the specifications and prepare the scale drawings that the contractors and workers follow during the actual construction of the building. They may also confer with other experts about site selection, land usage, and financial planning.

If you are interested in becoming an architect, you should have an interest in structural detail and an interest in people. You need spatial ability in order to visualize and draw three-dimensional objects on a two-dimensional surface. Anyone interested in this field must have an understanding of form and design and be able to express creative ideas. Also, good eye–hand coordination is important for drawing blueprints, diagrams, and charts.

To become an architect, you need five years of college leading to a bachelor of arts degree. You must study architectural and engineering principles, design, use of building materials, urban planning, graphics, and the history of architecture. You must also pass a two-day exam in order to receive your license. Architects are employed by architectural firms, land development contractors, and real estate companies. More opportunities for employment exist in large metropolitan areas. Some architects are self-employed and work for others on a contractual basis.

REVIEWING CHAPTER 4

SUMMARY

Housing decisions are easier to make once you have defined your goals, identified your needs, and set your priorities. Your decisions will also be influenced by your values and your available resources.

The primary purpose of a home is to provide shelter; but it also provides a sense of security and well-being and represents your lifestyle. Housing needs may vary at different stages of the life cycle. For most people, cost is the major factor affecting housing decisions. People who can invest their own time, energy, and talent in their homes can save money and enhance the livability of their homes.

Finally, you have to weigh the alternatives that are available in the housing market. Only then can you decide what choice will best meet your needs and enable you to gain the most satisfaction and enjoyment from your housing.

FACTS TO KNOW

1. Identify as many purposes as possible that a home serves.

2. Explain what is meant by the terms *primary needs* and *secondary needs,* and give several examples of each.

3. Identify a number of changes in housing needs caused by changes in the life cycle. Which of these changes apply to individuals who are single? to families? to both? What are some special housing needs?

4. Explain how values can influence housing decisions.

5. Which items in a budget are considered *fixed expenses* and which are *flexible expenses?*

6. List four ways a single person or family can reduce the cost of housing and home maintenance.

7. Identify and explain the steps in any decision-making process.

8. List at least four alternatives that a person should consider when making a decision about housing.

IDEAS TO THINK ABOUT

1. According to your present plans, what is your goal for a first home away from your present home? How did you come to set this goal?

2. What values and special preferences of yours will affect your eventual choice of a home? What characteristics do you value most in a home?

3. In what ways have you adapted your present living space to reflect your interests and personality? How would you expect to do this in your first home?

ACTIVITIES TO DO

1. Using photographs from magazines and newspapers, create a poster display that shows housing alternatives for people who are at different stages of the life cycle.

2. Apply the steps in the decision-making process to some choice related to housing. What factors can you identify at each step? What is your eventual decision? Evaluate the process used in making the decision.

Chapter 5

Evaluating Housing Choices

Very few people can live in their "dream home." Most of us have to compromise and choose from several less desirable alternatives. Compromises involve a lot of evaluation and decision making. When evaluating housing choices, money usually becomes a major factor; it determines how much you can spend to rent or purchase a home. Then, depending on what you can afford and what the market has to offer, you will probably have to make compromises on what you would like.

You always have to consider your own lifestyle and family structure when evaluating housing choices. During people's lifetimes, different types of housing may be best at different times. For some people, their first home of their own is an apartment. Then they may move into a two-family or single-family house, and then they may move back into an apartment. Other people may prefer living in one type of housing throughout their lives.

Once you have gathered information about the housing market in which you are interested, you are ready to evaluate the choices that it offers. But you will need to answer some questions before you can make up your mind. What type of housing seems most suitable for your needs? How long a commitment are you prepared to make to this choice of a home? In terms of income and other resources, what kind of housing can you afford?

PREVIEWING YOUR LEARNING

After you have read this chapter, you will be able to:

- Identify the major types of housing and their characteristics.

- Evaluate a location and neighborhood in which you would like to live.

- Discuss the advantages and disadvantages of renting a home and of buying one.

- Plan the arrangements for moving and recognize potential problems.

TERMS TO KNOW

exposure—the position of a home in relation to the sun and wind

insulation—the material used in structures to prevent the passage of heat or sound

lease—the right to use real estate or other property for a certain length of time, usually by paying rent for it

security deposit—an amount paid by a tenant to a landlord to pay for any future damages caused by the tenant

sublet—a lease by a tenant to another person but with the original tenant still held responsible for the original lease

tenant—a person paying rent for the use of a dwelling

utilities—the services of water, gas, and electricity

veneer—a thin layer of material used as an attractive finish for a surface

THE TWO-FAMILY HOUSE

F E A T U R E

For people who like the privacy of a single-family home but cannot afford the down payment, mortgage, and maintenance bills that go along with it, a two-family house may be the answer. It is a way to enjoy single-family home living with the easy upkeep of an apartment. The two-family house looks like a single home but is divided into two living areas, each with its own entrance. The owner may live in one part and rent the other or may choose to live elsewhere and rent both units. The backyard is shared, and utilities are either metered separately or included in the rental price.

For those who can afford and want to own a home, the two-family house can be a smart investment. As with any home ownership, there are tax and equity benefits. The income gained from the rented portion of the home can partially or totally offset the monthly mortgage payments.

However, the two-family homeowner must handle tenant problems and make necessary household repairs. Renters do not always take care of property as well as owners, and expensive damage may occur. Some of the repair expenses can be offset by requiring a security deposit upon rental. But the key to successful two-family home ownership is choosing a dependable family to share your home. To protect your investment and to insure compatibility, it is vital to interview prospective tenants and check their credit and rental references.

TYPES OF HOUSING

The kinds of housing available have increased greatly since World War II. Until that time, housing consisted mainly of apartments, row houses, tenements, duplexes, and single-family homes. Since the 1940's, housing has grown to include high-rise and garden apartments, multiplexes, town houses, and mobile homes. Having so many types of housing to choose from makes a choice more difficult. At the same time, having many options is an advantage, because you are more likely to find a home well suited to your needs.

Housing is usually divided into two categories: one is based on the number of dwelling units; the other on whether structures are adjoining or freestanding. Apartment houses usually contain a large number of units and are often multi-storied. Town houses and row houses are built with adjoining units. A single-family home represents one dwelling unit and is freestanding, often with some land around it.

In different types of housing, the amount of space and the facilities available vary a great deal. Apartments usually offer the least space and the most limited facilities. Town houses, which often have more than one story, usually provide more living space and better facilities, such as several bathrooms and a larger kitchen area. Single-family houses, in most cases, provide the greatest amount of space and the best facilities. As a general rule, the more space provided and the better the facilities, the more a home will cost.

Apartments: Low-Rise, Garden, and High-Rise

Apartments have been a familiar type of housing in urban areas for most of this century. The demand for them increased sharply during the 1960's, to meet the need for smaller housing units and to provide for a variety of lifestyles. Apart-ments in older, remodeled houses and in compact, new, two-story buildings are usually available at reasonable rates. Garden apartments are particularly well suited for warm climates. They usually consist of two- or three-story buildings with landscaped surroundings. Four rectangular buildings often surround a landscaped court with a fountain or swimming pool in the center. Some of these apartments are entered from balconies reached by open stairways; others have semi-enclosed stairways at intervals between the units. The more expensive apartments may have small individual balconies.

High-rise apartments are found in both cities and suburbs, and in both independently owned and government-subsidized developments. They may be rented, or they may be owned as you will learn in Chapter 6. Some people like the nearness to city attractions that a centrally located high-rise apartment provides. Frequently,

Charles River Park, an apartment complex near downtown Boston, includes this high-rise building.

lower floors contain banks, shops, restaurants, and other conveniences not found in low-rise apartments. The high-rise also provides a kind of privacy which some people want. Other people might consider living high in the sky a disadvantage. They could be troubled by a fear of height or wind-related problems. For them, such impersonal surroundings would result in a feeling of undesirable isolation.

Town Houses

Town houses are built in rows, with common walls. All units provide front and back exposure, except that the end units have three exposures and are therefore more expensive. Town houses in the low-to-moderate price range have almost identical exteriors and floor plans. In the moderate-to-high price range, the front walls may be staggered, and the units may be individualized by differently styled entrances and varied exterior finishes. In the more expensive range, a town house may have its own walk, garage, and private patio or courtyard.

Town houses may be found in either suburbs or cities. In the past ten years, many suburban town houses have been built as alternatives to single-family homes. In cities all over the country, many old row houses are being converted into handsome town houses. These are often well-constructed homes that need new heating or cooling systems, new plumbing and wiring, and some restyling and repair. Town houses offer more space and privacy than most apartments, and they require less upkeep than single-family homes. These homes may be available for either rent or purchase.

Duplexes

The duplex has been popular in small towns since the early part of the century. A duplex is a single building planned to house two families. The two housing units are separated by a common wall. Sometimes the units are one-story high, sometimes they are two. As land has become more scarce, the duplex has become a good housing alternative, providing a

High-rise apartment buildings are more common in urban areas where the population is dense.

Town houses and row houses are attached dwellings that share a common wall with the houses on each side.

home that resembles a single-family home without taking up as much land. Like town houses, a duplex may be rented or purchased.

Single-Family Houses

Owning a home has been a traditional dream of Americans. Whether it is a young couple's first home or a purchase made possible by long-term savings, a home of one's own offers a unique sense of satisfaction. The most desired type of housing in the United States is the freestanding, single-family house set on its own lot or acreage.

A single-family house may be custom built, or it may be a development house, a mobile home, or a prefabricated house. It may be old or new, modern or traditional. However, each single-family house belongs to just one family. Today, single-family houses are 50 percent larger than they were in 1950 and contain more luxuries, such as built-in appliances, air-conditioning, and additional bathrooms.

Unfortunately, the high costs of land, labor, and mortgage interests have put single-family home ownership out of the reach of many young families today, even those with two incomes. People looking for a modestly priced single-family house are more likely to find one in a small town or in a tract or builder development. Some single-family houses are available to rent or to rent with an option to buy. However, these rents are usually very high.

Older houses Existing homes have always made up a large part of the housing market. Some may be relatively new; others may have been built long ago. Today, as prices for new homes are rising very rapidly, more people than ever are buying older homes.

Many buyers of older houses plan to live in them as they are. Other buyers may plan to remodel, making the home more com-

Many of today's single-family homes are mass-produced and assembled at the site.

fortable and convenient as income permits. If they can do part or all of the work themselves, they can add to the resale value of the house. Because remodeling involves technical matters, such as wiring and plumbing, the advice of a builder or architect should be obtained.

City governments have recognized the need to restore rundown urban housing as one part of urban renewal. One interesting program used in many parts of the country is urban homesteading. Under this program, some rundown, inner-city housing is set aside for reconstruction. This housing consists of homes that have been abandoned or left empty after repossession by HUD or the city. The houses are sold for a very low fee to buyers who agree to renovate them within 6 to 18 months. The buyers must also live in them at least three to five years after possession.

Custom-built houses The most expensive kind of home to acquire is a house built according to an architect's design, according to the buyer's specifications. Custom-built houses may be designed in traditional or contemporary styles or in combinations of styles. Usually, such houses are built on large lots—a fact which adds to the original high cost.

Factory-built houses There are two major types of factory-built houses: sectional or panel fabrication, and modular units. Prefabrication of sections or panels takes place on an assembly line. As each panel moves down the line, the frame, outer siding, insulation, electrical wiring, plumbing, windows, doors, and interior walls are installed. Construction time is shortened, and much of the work can be done with unskilled labor. Since the construction takes place indoors, the weather never interferes. Also, since the same plans can be used for many houses, materials can be ordered in large quantities and material waste is limited. Because of these factors, prefabricated housing can be produced at lower costs than conventional housing.

This factory built house was shipped to the site in sections, set on the foundation, and bolted together in only a few days. Landscaping, done later, adds to the overall appearance.

Most mobile homes are permanently parked, often in mobile-home communities. Mobile homes offer the advantages of low cost and little maintenance.

Wood construction is most common for sectionals, but steel, aluminum, and sometimes concrete may also be used. The panels are covered, loaded into trucks or trains, and transported to the construction site. There, the panels are bolted to one another and to the foundation.

Modular units are totally complete units of one or more rooms that are built in a factory. The units are complete with windows, doors, ceilings, floors, electrical and plumbing lines, and all exterior and interior finishes. They may come with carpeting and furnishings. At the site, the modules are placed on the foundation and bolted together. They can be stacked into units of several stories or placed side by side. Housing modules are usually made of wood, steel and wood combined, or concrete. The exteriors may be finished with wood, stucco, or brick. Modular houses usually include a utilities core which contains a complete bath and kitchen. This core may also include the furnace, air conditioner, and laundry facilities.

Sometimes, conventionally built homes include certain parts that are fabricated in factories, such as windows and their frames, doors and their frames, roof trusses, and stairs. For those people with time and talent and, perhaps limited money, factory pre-cut houses are available. Pre-cut houses are delivered disassembled, with all the lumber cut and numbered and an instruction guide. The owner must put the pieces together at the site.

Mobile homes Mobile homes became an increasingly popular form of housing in the decades following World War II. While they are called mobile, most of these homes are erected on a permanent site and are never moved.

Mobile homes are transportable structures up to 14 feet (4.3 m) in width and up to 64 feet (18.9 m) in length. They are a form of factory-built housing. A double-width mobile home consists of two units set side by side. Some double units have over 2,000 square feet of living space. Screened porches, decks, and carports may be attached to the homes at their site.

The design of mobile homes has been greatly improved in recent years. They may be divided into several rooms, have one or more bathrooms, and have modern built-in appliances. The interiors are made of standard dry wall and the outside covering is usually aluminum. Their fire resistance and method of soundproofing have been improved. Construction has been upgraded to meet the HUD standards set in 1976. Mobile homes are usually purchased completely equipped and furnished.

Most mobile homes are financed like automobiles. The loan usually spans seven to ten years, much shorter than that of a conventional home. Because a mobile home is low in cost, the size of the loan is much lower than that of a traditional house. FHA and VA mortgage loans are available if a house is permanently attached to a solid foundation, and if it meets the Mobile Home Construction and Safety Standards.

Mobile home parks charge a fee for the rent of the land, utilities, and parking, but mobile homeowners do not pay property taxes. For this reason, some communities exclude them, and others zone them in outlying areas of town. Some communities have building codes that do not permit mobile homes to be used.

Mobile homes appeal to small families and young couples because of their initial low cost and low monthly finance charges. It is one way for a family to own a single-family home.

This double-width mobile home features a living room, dining area, modern kitchen, master bedroom, two additional bedrooms, and two bathrooms.

Alternative single-family houses

Some people seek nontraditional ways and places to make their homes. Some alternative homes are made by converting buildings which originally had different purposes, to housing. For example, people have made their homes from converted barns, lighthouses, churches, one-room schoolhouses, and windmills. Other alternative houses are architectural experi-ments, designed using new forms, new techniques, or new materials. The geodesic dome, designed by Buckminster Fuller, has been copied in many areas. Houses on stilts or on pedestals have also been built, as well as houses that revolve to follow the sunlight. However zoning laws in some communities do not permit these structures. Financing may also be a problem.

Some people, such as retired people or vacationers, may have permanent homes but want to spend some time in other areas. Motor homes and other recreational

Barns, churches, schoolhouses, windmills, and lighthouses have all been converted into homes that offer alternatives to traditional designs.

vehicles, like campers, make it possible for people to travel inexpensively, using their own self-contained housing. A few people use boats for recreational living or travel; other people live in houseboats that are permanently anchored.

Evaluating the Construction of Single-Family Houses

The shape of the house to be built depends in part on the size and shape of the lot. For a rectangular house, a lot that is 50 feet by 100 feet (15.24 m × 30.48 m) is good, a lot that is 60 feet by 125 feet (18.29 m × 38.10 m) is better, and a lot that is 75 feet by 100 feet (22.86 m × 30.48 m) is excellent. Note how much less lot space a two-story house occupies than a ranch house. Odd-shaped lots limit the design of the house, especially if building codes specify that a house must be set back 25 feet (7.62 m) from the street.

The contour of the land and the makeup of the soil also influence the design of the house and the cost of its construction. The cost of excavating for a foundation or basement will increase greatly if there is rock below the surface. Removing soil and rock or filling swampy land can also be costly. Land that is sloping is particularly suitable for split-level and split-entry houses. In such locations, the basement walls serve to retain the soil of the slope. By contrast, ranch houses require level ground if they are to be built on a concrete slab foundation. The type of foundation to be used is basic to the whole construction of any house. Most two-story houses have a partial or full basement, with small windows above ground. Many ranch-type homes are built on concrete slab foundations. Ranch and two-story houses may be built over a crawl space. In this type of foundation, the floor is built high enough above the ground for a person to crawl in and work on heating and plumbing systems.

For the structural framework, there are several major types to choose from. These

HOUSE STYLE AND LOT SIZE

Two-Story House

Lot coverage: 725 sq.ft.
Living area: 1200 sq. ft.

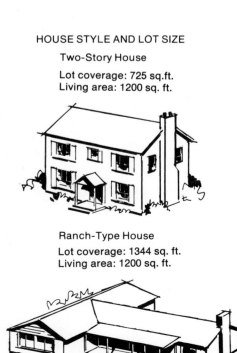

Ranch-Type House

Lot coverage: 1344 sq. ft.
Living area: 1200 sq. ft.

HOUSE STYLE AND LAND SURFACE

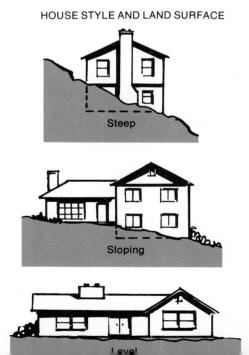

Steep

Sloping

Level

TYPES OF SIDING FOR EXTERIOR WALLS

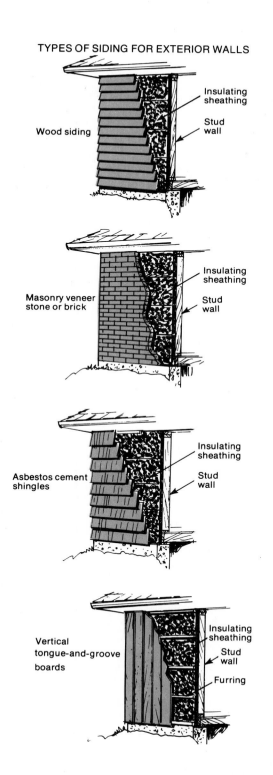

Wood siding

Insulating sheathing

Stud wall

Masonry veneer stone or brick

Insulating sheathing

Stud wall

Asbestos cement shingles

Insulating sheathing

Stud wall

Vertical tongue-and-groove boards

Insulating sheathing

Stud wall

Furring

include the conventional or "balloon" frame, post-and-beam construction, and concrete-block construction. The frame for most houses is made of wood. Steel and reinforced concrete may be used in large structures.

For the exterior walls of the house, a number of popular finishes are available. These include wood siding (both clapboards and vertical tongue-and-groove boards), masonry veneer (brick or stone), asbestos shingles, aluminum siding, and concrete blocks with a painted or stucco finish. Types of interior finishes include wallboard, Sheetrock, ceramic tile, and wood paneling. Wallboard with a thin coat of plaster is the most common and least expensive finish. If a basement is to be used for living space, it is important to make the walls moistureproof. This can be done by installing a framework of two-by-fours to hold insulation with a moisture barrier. The framework is then covered with wallboard or paneling.

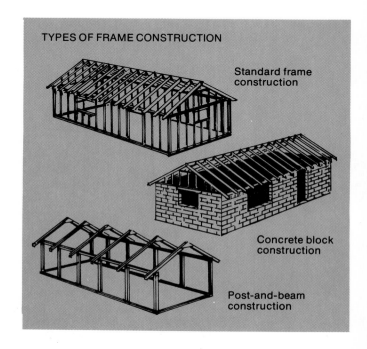

TYPES OF FRAME CONSTRUCTION

Standard frame construction

Concrete block construction

Post-and-beam construction

The design and material of the roof are very important to the appearance and soundness of the total structure. Materials for roofs include asphalt shingles, cedar shingles and shakes, chips and gravel, asbestos tile, slate shingles, and concrete tiles (flat or rounded). For flat roofs, the least expensive type is a built-up roof using layers of tar, chips, and gravel. Wood, asbestos, and asphalt shingles are often used on sloping roofs in temperate or cold climates. In the South, white or light-colored concrete tiles are frequently used on sloping roofs.

MAIN FACTORS IN HOUSE CONSTRUCTION

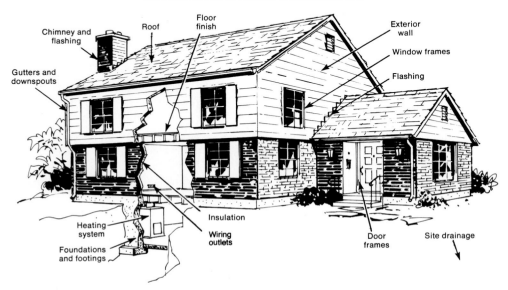

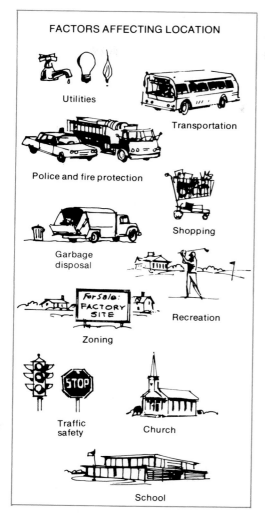

FACTORS AFFECTING LOCATION

Utilities

Transportation

Police and fire protection

Shopping

Garbage disposal

Recreation

Zoning

Traffic safety

Church

School

Each of these factors affect the choice of a neighborhood or community. Different people would prioritize them in different orders. For some families, transportation might be very important. For other families, schools would head their list of priorities.

THE SETTING: LOCATION AND NEIGHBORHOOD

A house does not exist in isolation; it is always a part of some community. A high-rise apartment provides its own self-contained community. However, most types of housing are part of a neighborhood, which in turn is part of a larger community. In choosing a home, you are choosing both your immediate surroundings and your wider environment. There are a number of things to be considered in making this decision.

Location

Convenience is an important factor in location. Nearness to work, schools, churches, stores and shops, and medical facilities affects the time, cost, and effort involved in daily travel. Many people depend upon public transportation for commuting to and from work. Other people want to be able to walk to schools, stores, and parks. However, some people may want to live in a community with specific characteristics that may not exist near their work. People who decide to rent or buy a home far from their work are accepting the inconvenience and cost of twice-a-day commuting.

To families with children of school age, location near schools and public transportation may be an important consideration. Even where school buses provide transportation to and from school, students still need transportation to libraries, after-school activities, and the homes of friends. Nearness to playgrounds and other recreational facilities may also be important.

The location of a home within its environment is important. This is called its exposure and includes its position in terms of both sun and wind. If people are to enjoy a terrace, balcony, or patio, a western exposure is not desirable because of the glare of the afternoon sun. A living area with a

FACTORS AFFECTING ORIENTATION

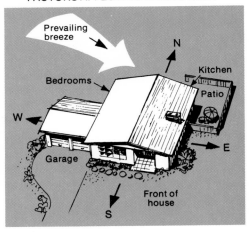

What difference do sun and prevailing breeze make to the location of a house?

northern or windy exposure can be very uncomfortable during the winter months, as well as being very costly to heat. A southern, southeastern, or southwestern exposure is considered preferable for year-round living in areas with both warm and cold seasons. However, in areas where the climate is always warm or hot, these exposures may result in intolerable heat in the summer, particularly if sunlight falls directly on large areas of glass or pavement. If such situations do exist, it is essential to use roofs, plantings, or other shelters to provide shade.

Neighborhood
The neighborhood setting of a house, town house, or apartment affects its value and desirability. If you are buying a home in an established neighborhood, you will want to take a close look at other existing homes. Note whether other houses in the neighborhood are in good condition, with the lawns and yards well kept. If a number of houses in the area are for sale, you should find out the reason.

If you are seriously considering a particular home, plan to visit the neighborhood in both daylight and darkness. Talk with a few of the residents, if possible. Make sure that the streets, as well as all parking areas and entrances to apartment buildings, are well lighted. In multi-unit housing, try to choose an apartment close to a fire exit.

Noise level is becoming an increasingly important consideration in the choice of housing. You cannot control noises outside the home, but you can select a location where noise is less of a problem. Apartments are less noisy if they are not adjacent to or opposite elevators. Parking areas, swimming pools, and tennis courts create noise in any housing development. Single people and older couples may prefer to live where there is minimal noise from children's playing. Families with young children often look for homes on dead-end or quiet streets, where children can play safely. Traffic is an important factor in noise level. Intersections of streets, where vehicles stop and start, can be very noisy. Homes in a development, located some distance from highways and sheltered by a buffer zone of plantings and trees, a wall, or other homes, are less affected by noise and are often more private. A single-family house usually has greater resale value if it is located away from any sources of noise.

Community Services
Good access to community services adds to the livability and value of a home. Typical services to consider are police and fire protection, shopping facilities, hospitals and clinics, places of worship, libraries, recreational centers, and public transportation. For example, if a home is located at a great distance from a fire station, homeowners usually pay a higher rate for insurance. If recreational and medical centers are important to a family and are far away, transportation may become a problem. Find out all you can about the services that you need and want, as well as provision for trash removal, water and sewage, and street cleaning in the area.

HOUSING DECISIONS: TO RENT OR TO BUY

Once you have studied the housing market and know what type of housing you want, you face the decision of how to obtain it. Renting and buying both offer particular advantages and limitations. As part of your decision making, you will want to weigh considerations against your own needs and financial means.

For some people, renting a home offers the most advantages.

Advantages in Renting a Home

For some people, renting is necessary because they cannot afford to buy a home. Others rent because they prefer to. Renting provides flexibility in housing for young people just starting to work, for people who may have to move frequently in their work, for anyone not wanting to establish a permanent home, and for people who do not want the care and responsibility of ownership.

The major advantage of renting is that one monthly payment provides housing, and often some utilities, without further charges for upkeep and repairs. Although a tenant may have to sign a lease for a stated period of time, written permission may sometimes be obtained to sublet or to give 60 days' notice in case of job relocation. Apartments for rent may offer special features, such as recreational facilities or security systems. Many rental apartments have a favorable location in cities near places of employment and cultural opportunities.

Guidelines for Renting a Home

In considering a place to rent, you should obtain information on a number of specific topics. This information should include both your own responsibilities and those of the owner, as well as the facilities and services you are entitled to.

Tenant obligations Before renting a home, you should know just what obligations you are taking on. Before signing a lease, make sure you understand its terms. Make a duplicate copy of the lease and underscore any terms you do not understand. Discuss these with the agent renting the apartment. Be aware that if you sign a lease for a year and decide to move at the end of eight months, you may be responsible for paying a full year's rent before you can move. Make sure the lease has a 60-day vacancy or transfer clause—that is, the tenant or the owner reserves the right to break the contract with a 60-day notice. This clause protects both parties. If the apartment is subsequently rented, you will usually receive a refund for each month's rent collected from another tenant.

Find out what day the rent is due and to whom it is to be paid. Most leases carry a penalty clause requiring the tenant to pay an additional fee if the rent is not paid by a certain date. Be sure to find out whether there is such a penalty and, if there is one, how much it is.

In order to protect equipment, carpeting, walls, and so forth, many owners require a

When looking at a place to rent, be sure to check the exterior of the building and possible parking areas.

security deposit. When the tenant moves, the cost of repairing any damage is deducted from that deposit and the remainder refunded. Make sure you receive the interest due you on your deposit.

Find out exactly which costs are covered by the rent and which you are responsible for separately. Among the charges to consider are those for water, heat, gas, and electricity. If you are paying for these directly, try to get an estimate of their approximate monthly cost.

If you own a car, you may have to provide for parking. Zoning laws in most communities require sufficient parking facilities for residents and guests in multi-unit dwellings. Make sure that your assigned space is near your unit and is well lighted. High-rise apartment buildings often provide underground parking. Find out whether there is an added cost for a parking space there and, if so, what that cost is.

Services, facilities, and restrictions
In addition to your own obligations as tenant, you should know what special services and facilities you are entitled to. Find out who is responsible for managing the building and how this person can be reached in an emergency. Routine janitorial services, such as cleaning halls, stairways, and sidewalks, should be provided. In most new apartment buildings, there is a schedule for painting walls, replacing equipment such as washers and dryers, and doing routine maintenance. In older buildings, the tenant may be expected to take care of decorating and to provide a refrigerator. Get this information in writing.

In checking the facilities, find out whether there are individual mailboxes and whether coin-operated washers and dryers are available. If no provision is made for laundry, find out where the nearest coin-operated Laundromat is located. Ask where trash and garbage are to be deposited and how they are disposed of.

RENTAL CHECKLIST

- [ ] What is the rent per month?
- [ ] Is a security deposit required? If so, how much is it? Will interest be paid on the deposit?
- [ ] Which utility costs are included in the rent? Which costs must you pay?
- [ ] Are there costs for extra services such as parking, pool, or TV antenna?
- [ ] Can the rent be increased before the end of the lease?
- [ ] Can you sublet?
- [ ] Is the apartment well maintained? Is it clean? Is the paint peeling? Is the plaster cracked? Are the floors in good condition?
- [ ] Will the apartment be repainted by the landlord? If not, can you redecorate at your own expense?
- [ ] Does the plumbing work properly? Is there adequate hot water?
- [ ] Do the heating and air conditioning systems work properly? Can you control the temperature?
- [ ] Are the kitchen cabinets and appliances in good condition?
- [ ] Do the range, refrigerator, and dishwasher, if provided, work properly?
- [ ] Are the bathroom fixtures and tiles in good condition?
- [ ] Is the electrical system adequate and safe? Do all the switches and outlets work?
- [ ] Are any windows broken? Do they open and close easily? Are locks provided? Are the windows drafty? Are screens provided?
- [ ] Is ventilation adequate? Is there an exhaust fan in the kitchen?
- [ ] Does the door lock securely? Is there a double lock, a security chain, or a peephole?
- [ ] Is the floor plan convenient? Is there adequate space for your furniture?
- [ ] Is there enough storage space? Is extra storage space available in the building?
- [ ] How soundproof is the building? Are the neighbors quiet?
- [ ] Are laundry facilities available? Are they clean and well maintained?
- [ ] How is trash disposed?
- [ ] Are there any signs of insects, rats, or mice?
- [ ] Are the hallways and lobby clean and well lighted? Is an elevator provided? Does it work properly?
- [ ] Is there a fire alarm? Are smoke detectors installed? Are fire exits provided?
- [ ] Is the outside of the building and grounds well maintained?
- [ ] Is there adequate parking space?
- [ ] Does a manager or superintendent live in the building? If not, whom do you contact for maintenance?

Since some multi-unit housing provides space for storage, find out whether such space is available to you.

Provisions for safety are also important. Safety features include such items as stair railings and lights in halls, on stairways, and at front and rear entrances. If there are elevators, there should be alternate exits. Find out where the fire exits are. Smoke detectors or sprinkler systems are additional safety features to consider. If you are to be billed separately for utilities, find out where the fuse box or circuit breaker is located. Along with services and facilities, tenants may have to observe certain restrictions. Learn what they are. Most apartment buildings have restrictions or regulations concerning pets. In adult communities, there may be regulations about children. Other possible restrictions to inquire about are those concerning alterations and decorating within your own apartment. It is not advisable in any case to install such major things as air-conditioning units or to paint walls without written permission. If possible, get a list of all the restrictions that might possibly affect your apartment.

Advantages in Buying a Home

Owning one's own home can provide a sense of personal satisfaction and belonging. The accepted idea that "one's home is one's castle" recognizes the homeowner's right to privacy and control. At the same time, ownership provides a sense of belonging to a neighborhood or a community. Having a permanent residence also indicates that one is settled and can make long-range plans.

Perhaps the greatest benefits of home ownership are financial. If the home is well cared for and located in a good area, its value often increases at a rate faster than that of inflation. Home ownership offers income tax deductions, since both property taxes and interest on the mortgage are deductible. In renting, these hidden costs are covered by the rent payment and are tax-deductible only by the owner.

While monthly mortgage payments may be high, a part of them represents forced savings. The share of ownership, or equity, in a house increases with each mortgage payment. The equity also becomes worth more as the value of the property increases due to inflation. Homeowners can borrow

Most apartment leases have special provisions relating to painting, redecorating, and remodeling.

Owning a house has many personal and financial benefits. However it also requires maintenance and repairs.

against this equity, if necessary. If the house is sold, the owner's share of the money from it can be used as a down payment for another home. If the owner keeps the home, the property will eventually be fully paid for. Although no more mortgage payments will be due, there will always be a yearly property tax bill.

Owning your home has additional benefits in terms of control and planning. Homeowners are free to remodel and redecorate as they please. They are not subject to many of the regulations for multi-unit housing. Ownership also assures continued possession. If units for rent are converted to units for sale, such as condominiums, the tenant will have to buy one of the units or move elsewhere.

Owning one's home may create problems, however, as well as resulting in benefits. If a home must be sold in a hurry, the asking price may have to be lower than it actually should be. Closing costs for the purchase or sale of a home can be high. Sometimes the monthly mortgage payments are so high that money is not available for maintenance and repairs. In addition to these financial burdens, the care of the home and its surroundings may prove to be more than the owner has time and energy for, and yet the property must somehow be cared for, in order to protect the investment.

Guidelines for Buying a Home

In addition to house-hunting and making arrangements for purchase, buying a home usually involves a long-term commitment. For this reason, making and carrying out the decision usually involves more time and thought than a decision to rent does. Buying a home involves many of the same guidelines that renting does, but it has some additional ones, too.

Housing costs in relation to income

Buying a home involves a much greater financial commitment than renting does, in terms of both the down payment and the long-term obligation. The total monthly cost for mortgage payment, taxes, and insurance is often higher than a month's rent. The cost of utilities (heating, cooking, water, and electricity), repairs, and maintenance are all an owner's responsibility. In the case of an apartment unit that is owned, there is a monthly fee for use of common facilities, in addition to the regular costs of ownership. A person buying a home should realize that in addition to the fixed expenses of the mortgage, taxes, and utilities, there may also be installment payments for furnishings and appliances.

When a buyer applies for a mortgage, the lending agency investigates the applicant's credit rating, financial history, and employment record. Also considered are the number of existing monthly installment payments the applicant has—on a car, appliances, home furnishings, or other items—and how large these payments are. These factors affect the decision of the lending agency concerning the buyer's application.

The buyer must also assess his own financial ability and readiness to undertake ownership. The traditional guideline for buying a home is to pay no more for a home than two to two-and-a-half times your annual income after deductions. Also, you should pay no more for the monthly

Can You Afford to Own a Home?
Owning a home involves many expenditures besides the monthly mortgage payments. Some of these costs must be paid monthly, others seasonally or only occasionally.
- mortgage payment, including interest
- property taxes
- water
- electricity
- gas or oil
- telephone
- insurance
- maintenance and upkeep
- furniture
- decorating
- special assessments
- repairs
- improvements or remodeling

mortgage payment than 20 to 25 percent of your monthly take-home pay. For an accurate projection of expenses for maintenance, add one percent to your monthly mortgage figure for a new home, and two percent for an older home. Your total monthly outlay, including mortgage, maintenance, taxes, and insurance, should not exceed 25 to 30 percent of your income.

Zoning and building regulations Regulations on land use and building construction are especially important to home buyers. Zoning ordinances define the purpose of structures that can be built in certain areas. Locations termed residential are limited to single-family homes and other types of living units. These areas usually do not permit overnight parking of trucks and campers. Areas zoned for industrial or commercial use are for business and industrial buildings. Find out how strict the zoning board is about enforcing restrictions and granting variances in your area. Builders may request a variance to build homes on undersized lots, or to build closer to the street than the zoning law specifies. They may petition to set up portable outbuildings or to add an apartment, office, or beauty shop to an existing home. These exceptions to the standards set by zoning ordinances sometimes lower the value of homes in a neighborhood.

Try to learn about any changes planned for the neighborhood or surrounding area you are looking at. Changes concerning public utilities, such as pipes for water and sewage and lines for electricity and gas, may mean added assessments for property owners in the future.

Property taxes Taxes are a major yearly cost to the homeowner. They increase not only with inflation but also in relation to property values. Find out what the assessed valuation is for the property you are considering and what the current tax rate is. With that information, you can estimate the amount of taxes at present. By getting the same information for the past several years, you can judge how rapidly the taxes have been rising.

Since costs and services differ from one community and part of the country to another, find out what services your taxes pay for. They usually include street construction and maintenance, schools, and fire and police protection. In some areas outside city limits, there may be charges for street cleaning, snow removal, and garbage and trash collection.

Changing conditions may affect the rate of taxation. An unfinished home in a new development may have a low tax assessment. When the development is completed, taxes may rise considerably because the property is then taxed as a finished dwelling. The tax rate may also be raised to finance the building of schools, hospitals, public facilities, parks, and recreational areas. The more you know about plans for such development, the better you can evaluate the tax costs which you as a homeowner will have to meet.

MOVING

Whether you decide to rent a home or buy one, you have to move into it. If your first home is to be a room or small apartment, you may start with very few possessions and accumulate more as you live there. In that case, your first real experience with moving may not come until you choose a larger apartment or a house.

If you have only a small amount of furniture, you may enlist the help of your friends and move everything in a station wagon or rented truck or trailer. Before you undertake such a move, consider your decision carefully. There is always the possibility of personal injury and damage to furniture. If you use nonprofessional help, you may not be able to collect any kind of insurance, in case of accident to anyone or anything.

You can save money by packing some or all of your items yourself.

Moving companies will pack and transport your belongings to your new home for a fee.

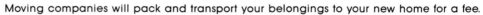

Preparing to Move

As soon as you have made a decision about your housing situation, you should begin to prepare for moving. There are a number of steps you can take well in advance, to avoid the last-minute rush.

—Make plans to end your present lease or sell your home as soon as you have decided to move.

— If you are planning to hire movers, contact several reliable firms and compare costs. When satisfied with one offer, sign the contract with that mover for a specific moving date.

— Before you move, arrange with utility companies to have water, gas, electricity, and telephone service terminated in your present home. If you are moving within the community, arrange to have these services begin at your new address as soon as possible after you move.

— Notify the following about your change of address: the post office; insurance companies; businesses such as banks and stores; subscription departments of magazines; and friends and relatives. You may request special change-of-address forms from moving firms or your local post office.

— Notify all delivery services, such as newspaper, laundry, and milk, to discontinue or transfer service.

— If you are moving out of the area, write letters of resignation to local organizations. If you belong to a religious institution, notify it of your change of address.

— Assemble valuable papers, such as legal documents; insurance papers; canceled checks for the past five years (these are good receipts if a question should arise about unpaid bills); mortgage-payment receipts and any other papers relative to the purchase of a house; birth certificates, health records, and children's school records. Carry these papers with you.

— For future convenience, take along a copy of your present telephone directory.

— Decide which of your possessions you can move by yourself. If you are moving within a community, you will probably want to transfer your own clothes and some personal possessions, and possibly other items. This will save both money and packing time.

Dealing with Movers

Surveys indicate that the most common complaints against moving companies are failure to arrive on the promised day for either pickup or delivery; underestimating costs for packing and shipping; loss of or damage to possessions; reluctance or delay in paying for damage to goods.

If you have contracted with movers, take the following precautions to avoid problems, cut expenses, and aid in the moving process.

— Make sure to have in writing the method of payment and the charges agreed upon, including optional services and liability coverage in case of damage. Also, the contract with your mover should include the dates of both pickup and delivery. It may be difficult to obtain firm dates on small loads, especially if you are moving to a small community, because small loads are stored until there is enough for a truckload going in the same direction.

— Find out how you can cut costs by doing some or all of the packing yourself. Books and clothing are easy to pack. However, china and crystal are more difficult to pack. If you pack these items yourself and breakage occurs, you are not likely to be reimbursed.

— Take a complete inventory of all possessions. Label all boxes and barrels.

— Tag all items according to where they are to be placed in your new home.

— Arrive at your destination before the moving van arrives. Have a money order, a traveler's check, a cashier's check, or cash ready for the driver. As a rule, personal checks are not acceptable.

— Direct the placement of furniture as it is brought into the house. Placement has been included in the moving company's cost estimate.

— Note any damage to furniture or furnishings. Secure estimates as soon as possible for replacement or repairs. Within several days, write a letter to the central office of the moving company and state the damage done and the estimated costs for replacement or repairs. Keep a duplicate of your letter. If your letter is not answered within thirty days, have the secretary of the Better Business Bureau in the area write to the moving company.

CAREER PROFILE

APARTMENT MANAGER

Managers of apartment buildings or housing developments are responsible for the daily running of the building. They routinely inspect the physical condition of the building and its grounds. If necessary, they arrange for repairs or redecorating by staff members or by independent contractors. Apartment managers coordinate the activities of all the employees who help maintain the building, such as those who keep the public areas clean, attractive and safe. They may purchase supplies and arrange for outside services, such as trash collection or snow removal, and are responsible for the security of the building.

Apartment managers may be called leasing agents or leasing managers. They meet with tenants to handle any complaints and to provide services. Managers show apartments to prospective tenants and discuss the conditions and terms of occupancy, along with those of the lease. They may also collect the rent from tenants and issue receipts.

If you are interested in becoming an apartment manager, you must be able to get along well with people. Your responsibilities will include dealing with tenants, employees, building owners, independent contractors, and community officials. You also must have the ability to plan, initiate, and execute programs. An understanding of inventory controls, record keeping, and production controls is also helpful.

To enter this field, you will need at least a high school diploma. An associate's degree in business management would also be beneficial. Most managers start as an aide to an apartment manager in order to gain the necessary experience.

REVIEWING CHAPTER 5

SUMMARY

When evaluating housing choices, the various types of housing available, locations and neighborhoods, and the advantages and disadvantages of renting or buying need to be considered.

Multifamily housing includes apartments, town houses, and duplexes. Single-family housing includes newly built homes, older houses, and mobile homes. New homes can be custom-built, part of a tract or development, prefabricated, or factory-built. The design and materials used in the construction should be carefully evaluated. Other important considerations include the home's location, neighborhood, and what community services are available.

The decision to rent or buy depends on a number of factors. Some of these are: amount of money available, amount of space needed, type of community desired, and degree of ownership responsibility desired. Moving involves a number of steps before you can finally settle in your new home.

FACTS TO KNOW

1. Identify three different types of apartments.

2. Explain what town houses and duplexes are. How do they differ from apartments and single-family houses?

3. List the main types of single-family houses. Explain in detail the advantages and special features of one type.

4. How does the size and shape of a lot influence the design of a house? Give examples.

5. Identify three factors that are important to deciding the location of a home. Explain why each is important.

6. What are the advantages to renting a home? What are the advantages to buying a home?

7. Before signing a lease, what information should a person find out?

8. What is the purpose of getting a mover's estimate? Explain how it protects both the moving company and the person whose goods are being moved.

IDEAS TO THINK ABOUT

1. What special kinds of housing needs are met by apartments, town houses, and mobile homes?

2. What type of housing might best meet the needs of a single person? a newly married couple? a family with children? a retired couple? Explain the reasons for your choices.

3. When evaluating a community, what factors are important to a family with children? to a single person? to an elderly person?

ACTIVITIES TO DO

1. Study the real estate pages of your local newspaper for ads related to housing rentals and purchases. In each case, what are some of the factors affecting the cost? Report your findings to the class.

2. Hold a class debate on "Renting versus Buying."

Chapter 6

Buying and Financing a Home

For most people, home ownership is the largest single investment they will ever make. At one time, buying a home always meant a single-family home. But today, new types of ownership, such as of condominium and cooperative apartments, are providing more options for buyers. Each type of housing offers particular advantages and limitations. In this chapter, you will learn about these.

The rising cost of housing has made it more difficult for many people to find a home that they can afford to buy. However, there are several different ways to finance a home. It is very important to evaluate the types of mortgages available and choose the best for you. Also, there are a number of ways to reduce or offset the cost of home ownership. Perhaps you could buy a low-priced home and later use it as equity to buy a more expensive home. Perhaps you can reduce expenses by doing your own decorating or remodeling.

What is your main reason for buying a home? Do you want to buy it primarily as a financial investment? Or is the emotional satisfaction of owning your own home most important to you? Home ownership also involves certain responsibilities.

Buying and financing a home is a major commitment, but one that can also offer you many benefits and rewards.

PREVIEWING YOUR LEARNING

After you have read this chapter, you will be able to:
- Identify different types of home ownership.

- Explain the steps involved in buying a home.

- Compare the different methods of financing a home.

- Identify the different costs involved in purchasing and owning a home, including closing costs, the down payment, mortgage and interest, taxes, utilities, and insurance.

TERMS TO KNOW

commission—a fee paid to an agent.

condominium—an apartment house in which each apartment is purchased and owned separately

contingency—a possibility that is likely but not certain to happen

cooperative—an apartment house in which shares of stock are issued to the owner of each unit by the corporation, which is made up of all the owners

deed—a legal statement of ownership of property

down payment—initial payment made by a buyer at the time of purchase with the balance to be paid later

easement—a right held by a person for the limited use of land owned by another person

escrow—money held in safekeeping by a third party

title—a legal claim proving ownership of property

warranty—written guarantee of a product's performance and the maker's responsibility to repair or replace any defective parts

EQUITY SHARING

**F
E
A
T
U
R
E**

In areas of the country where rapidly rising home prices and high property taxes create large monthly mortgage payments, people are turning to equity sharing. In equity sharing, two or more people buy a home. These buyers may be an unmarried couple, friends, or even pairs of married couples who cannot afford a home on their own and are happy to own part of a house rather than none.

Equity sharing can work in several different ways. Engaged couples can pool their savings for a down payment on a home and then rent it to cover the mortgage payments until they are ready to move in. Or a widowed parent can co-invest with his or her children, and they can all live together. Often, a young couple will find an unrelated investor to share the costs, and both parties can profit. The young couple gets to live in a house that they otherwise could not afford, and the real estate investor has a tenant who will take good care of their joint investment.

Equity sharing is an affordable way to buy a vacation home as well. For part of the year, the co-owners can share living time in the house; for the rest of the year, they can rent it.

It is important when sharing equity to have complete confidence in your co-investor, for banks require both names on the mortgage. Each partner is individually as well as jointly responsible for the loan.

TYPES OF HOME OWNERSHIP

The home that most Americans have by tradition dreamed of owning is the single-family home. Since World War II, two new types of home ownership—the condominium and the cooperative apartment—have become available. These types of ownership, particularly the condominium, have become widely used. The kind of ownership you choose depends on many factors, including cost, convenience, and the amount of space you require.

Condominium Ownership

The term *condominium* is applied to the ownership of one housing unit in a multi-unit structure. Although condominium ownership was a familiar way to buy property in Europe in the 19th century, the concept did not take hold in the United States until the early 1960's. The Housing Act of 1968, which made it possible for people to buy "parcels of space" in multi-unit build-ings, encouraged this type of ownership. Today, this category includes apartments of all kinds, town houses, duplexes, and multi-plexes.

Condominiums are bought the same way that individually-built homes are bought. Except for government-subsidized condominiums, most units are bought through conventional mortgages. Taxes and equity benefits are the same as those for a detached home on its own lot. Sometimes builder-developers finance condominiums and may offer units for a lower down payment than most financial institutions will accept. As part of the purchase agreement, owners agree to pay each month a share of the cost for maintaining grounds, parking areas, and other facilities used in common.

Although condominium ownership offers many advantages, much depends on the management of the property. Under good management, there are the benefits of owning a home without the burden of

Changing lifestyles and the high cost of single-family homes have made the condominium increasingly popular as a form of ownership.

yard care, snow removal, and other maintenance jobs. If the condominium development has 200 or more units, it should have professional management. With fewer than 60 or 70 units, an elected board often does a good management job. These people, being residents, are generally not paid for their services. Buyers should find out whether residents own the common areas of the condominium. If these areas are under outside ownership, residents may have no control over maintenance of these areas, and they may not be able to vote on monthly fee increases.

Each condominium owner is responsible for his or her own financial obligations, such as mortgage, taxes, dues, and assessments. Owners are responsible for the upkeep of their unit. They are also responsible for a portion of the costs of the common areas, such as the grounds and recreational areas. If one owner cannot meet the mortgage costs or taxes, the other owners are not financially responsible. Condominiums are regulated by state law, which varies from state to state. Those financed through HUD and FHA must also meet federal standards and regulations.

Condominium ownership may involve restrictions, just as renting often does. Condominiums with a board of directors usually have restrictions on buying, selling, and subletting units. If an owner wants to sell, it is customary that the board of directors must approve of the new buyers. These regulations help protect the other owners. However, they should not be too restrictive. Condominiums financed through HUD or FHA do not permit these practices.

Cooperative Ownership

The cooperative has been in existence in this country since the 1920's, having originated in Europe during the 19th century. The first cooperative in the United States was built by the Amalgamated Clothing Workers Union in New York City, but only after World War II did this type of home ownership become popular.

There are several important differences between the ownership of cooperatives and that of condominiums. In a cooperative, the buildings and the common property and facilities are owned by a corporation. Shares of stock are issued to the owner of each unit. The number of shares is usually based upon the number of square feet in a unit. The shareholder-owner is responsible for a portion of the mortgage, taxes, upkeep, repairs, and services of the cooperative corporation. If one shareholder defaults on his or her portion of the expenses, the other shareholders must make up the difference. If enough shareholders default, the cooperative could be foreclosed. Because the shareholders are responsible for the entire cost of the corporation and are not limited to the expenses of just their unit, the financial status of applicants is very important. The board of directors has the right to refuse to allow anyone to purchase an apartment if it seems they cannot afford the costs.

Cooperative ownership is similar in some ways to condominium ownership. In both cases, the property taxes and interest on the mortgage are tax deductible. Owners must pay for taxes, insurance, and home repairs, in addition to mortgage. Co-ops are much less common than condos and are more likely to be high-rise apartments in cities. Many former rental apartment buildings in large cities have been converted to cooperatives.

Single-Family-House Ownership

Buying a single-family house is usually the most expensive form of home ownership.

New houses Houses that are new and fresh can provide real benefits in terms of both investment and comfort. The initial cost and long-term value of a house will vary. Factors affecting the value include location—whether in the city, suburbs, or country—and the construction—whether a development house, an individually built one, or a custom-built home. As the cost of land and construction rise, more and more houses are being mass-produced. This type of development and construction helps to keep a house within a price range that more families can afford.

The buyer of a new house may be able to obtain a Home Owners Warranty (HOW) from the builder. This warranty protects the homeowner from the cost of structural defects. Developed by the National Association of Home Builders, HOW is now an independent insurance company. The warranty provides a two-year guarantee for major structural defects and the wiring, plumbing, and heating systems. For the third to the tenth years, the owners are covered by an insurance policy that includes structural defects but not systems. Two states, New Jersey and Minnesota, have mandatory warranty programs. New homes with HOW warranties are accepted for FHA and VA mortgages without an inspection.

Buying land and having a house built to order on it, particularly according to an architect's plan, offers the widest range of choices in style and layout. However, because of the cost of materials and labor for building a specially-designed house, this is the most expensive type of home

The most popular type of housing today is still the single-family house. However it is usually the most expensive form of home ownership.

there is. Reason for the high cost include the use of nonstandard materials and components, adaptation of the structure to the site, and the architect's fee. Such custom-built houses usually require a larger-than-usual down payment and may also involve some payment to cover material and labor costs during the building process.

Older houses Homes that have previously been lived in, whether for ten years or a hundred, are the most common type of single-family home available. Often —depending on the original cost and the present condition of the structure—a home of this kind is a good investment.

The value of an older home depends on the condition it is in. If the house is in good condition, the value will be high. If it is not in good condition, the purchase price may be lower, and remodeling may be necessary. The best way to judge the quality of an older house is to have a contractor or an architect evaluate it.

STEPS IN BUYING A HOME

Buying a home involves certain preliminary steps before the actual purchase takes place. Some of these steps are merely customary; others are legal requirements. Knowing what procedures are involved in buying a house helps you to prepare for the legal and financial requirements.

In starting to look at homes, you should become familiar with communities, their neighborhoods, and the types of homes available. The Sunday newspaper has the most comprehensive listing of resale homes and new homes. You should also drive around the areas that interest you and make a note of the "For Sale" signs. Write down each realtor's name and phone number in a small notebook. If you drive by new developments, stop at the office and ask to be shown the model homes. These are usually furnished so that people will have an idea of how the bare

---

ALTERNATIVE APPROACHES TO OWNERSHIP

If the cost of buying a single-family house seems unreasonably high, there are a number of ways to reduce or offset that cost. Among them are the following:

—Consider a sectional or factory-built house. These houses look like conventional homes, and they are available in a wide variety of styles and plans.

—Purchase building plans, and contract with a local builder to build a house according to the plans. Be sure to inquire about local building codes and the builder's reputation.

—Buy a basic house and live there until you can accumulate some equity in it. Then you will have a down payment for a more expensive home. A basic house may have 7½-foot (2.29-m) ceilings instead of 8-foot (2.44-m) ceilings, plain cabinets in the kitchen and bathrooms, unpretentious entrances, and inexpensive roof coverings.

—Buy a duplex and rent one unit. The rent can be enough to finance your own unit, and you can deduct from your income tax the yearly depreciation, interest, and taxes on the rental unit.

—Buy a partly finished house and do the painting, lay the floor tile and carpeting, and install cabinets as time and income permit.

—Buy a basic house with possibilities for future expansion. Add rooms as they are needed and as your income can cover increased mortgage payments.

—Buy a mobile home.

A real estate agent will show you properties, provide information about the homes and their costs, and negotiate the terms. An agent will handle most of the business transactions involved in the purchase of a home.

rooms will look when lived in. On your tour of houses, make notes concerning the area, the range of prices, and floor plans for homes you like, together with room sizes, exposure, and other items of interest to you. These notes will help you in establishing your priorities and weighing alternative choices.

Finding an Agent

The sale or purchase of property is sometimes handled directly between buyer and seller. More often, the transaction is made through a real estate agent, a person who handles the selling and buying of homes.

For arranging the transaction, the agent receives a commission—usually a percentage of the purchase price. The commission is paid by the seller, but often the cost is passed along to the buyer. Buying a home by direct purchase avoids the payment of a commission. However, working with an agent gives you the benefit of the agent's knowledge of the community and its housing. The agent may also be able to advise you about obtaining a mortgage and a clear title to the property.

Homes that are for sale are usually listed with a real estate company or several realtors. You might want to talk with several agents before selecting one to help you, or you may choose to work with more than one agent. It is important to find an agent in whom you have confidence. After you have discussed what price range, type of home, and neighborhood you prefer, the agent will begin to give you information about homes that are listed for sale.

Preparing for Purchase Costs

When you decide that you are ready to buy a home, you must be prepared to do so soon after you find the home you want. This means making available the funds needed to complete the purchase. The major cost of a home is usually covered by a long-term loan, or mortgage. However, part of the cost is usually met by a down payment, which must be paid by the buyer at the time of closing. Certain types of mortgages, such as a VA mortgage, may require a small down payment or none at all. Some builder-contractors may offer mortgages based on a low down payment. FHA mortgages may also have a low requirement for a down payment. Whatever the down payment, you as the buyer must be ready to meet it. The different types of mortgages are described in a later section of this chapter.

Buying a home involves a number of costs besides the down payment and monthly mortgage payments. Such costs include the money to bind the sales agreement, any lawyer's fees, and the cost of reviewing the title and officially registering the new deed. These costs must be paid by you at the time of purchase. The real estate

---

AN EXAMPLE OF CLOSING COSTS

SELLER'S CLOSING COSTS

Preparation of deed

Deed transfer tax

U.S. document stamps for deed

Realtor's fee (often 6% of the selling price)

Prorated taxes and insurance

*BUYER'S CLOSING COSTS

Origination fee (lender's charge for processing the loan)

Mortgage insurance premium

Credit report (report on buyer's ability to pay)

Title search/title insurance premium

Appraisal fee

Survey fee (if required)

Lawyer's fee

Fee for recording deed

Homeowner's insurance (for which the original policy may be kept in escrow until closing)

Prorated payments for insurance and property taxes

Escrow fee (if charged)

Loan discount points (if charged)

Other costs according to community

*These costs are in addition to the earnest money, down payment, and mortgage costs.

agent's commission is paid by the seller, though it may be passed on to the buyer. The customary costs for buyer and seller are shown on page 116. Legislation now requires the lending agency to send the buyer a "good-faith" estimate of closing or settlement costs within three days of the time a mortgage loan is applied for. The lender is also required to present the buyer with a booklet entitled *Settlement Costs and You.* A day before the closing, the lender, upon the buyer's request, must give the buyer an accurate list of final closing costs.

Making the Sales Agreement

A sales agreement is a tentative contract between the buyer and seller indicating the willingness of both to reach a final settlement. This is the first legal document that is signed. It is usually drawn up on a standard form provided by the real estate agent. This document gives a detailed description of the property, the total purchase price, the amount of the down payment, and the date for closing the sale and delivering the deed to the new owner. Some people like to have a lawyer review the sales agreement before they sign it. It is a good idea to make note of any statements you want to discuss or question. The sales agreement remains in effect from the time it is signed until the closing of the purchase. During this interval, the buyer can investigate the title and arrange for financing.

Before signing an agreement, the buyer should find out from the seller the cost of property taxes. If buying a condominium or a cooperative apartment, the buyer should know the monthly maintenance fee and exactly what it covers. If the seller has agreed to include such extras as carpeting, draperies, lighting fixtures, and so on, this information should be written into the sales agreement. The cost of these extras is separate from that of the house and is paid in cash. If taxes, fees, or charges, such as those for water, have already been paid by the seller, the buyer must reimburse the seller. This information should be specified in the sales agreement.

At the time the sales agreement is signed, the buyer must provide "hand" or "earnest" money, which indicates that the buyer is acting in good faith and expects to make the purchase final. The amount of this binder may be a few hundred dollars or a percentage of the selling price. The money is kept in escrow; that is, it is held in safekeeping by a third party, such as the realtor, until the closing of the purchase. This money is eventually credited toward the down payment. If the buyer decides to back out of the sale for no acceptable reason, the binder is turned over to the seller. This practice is fair, because the home is taken off the market during this period, and the seller may have been prevented from selling to another person.

Investigating the Title

In buying property, it is important to know that the title is clear—that is, that there is no question about the rightful ownership. Although the title usually is clear, the buyer should not take a chance. At some time in the past, there may have been inaccurate boundary descriptions, contested wills, or claims against the property for unpaid debts. An investigation of official records can assure that the title to the property has no restrictions. In some states, it is possible to obtain title insurance to assure rightful ownership.

Although you as the buyer can look up records about the property, you may prefer to have a lawyer do this for you. A lawyer can review the title, check for any claims against it, and find out whether any easements have been granted. An easement is permission for special use of the property, such as a right to build power lines, water mains, sewers, or roads across

At the closing, the ownership of the property is transferred to the new owners. The deed is signed by both parties, the downpayment is made, and the mortgage papers are signed. Any additional costs must be paid by the buyers at this time.

PROFILE OF THE AVERAGE HOME BUYER IN U.S.	
MEDIAN AGE	35.8
HOUSEHOLD SIZE	
1 or 2	52.9%
3 or more	47.1%
MARITAL STATUS	
Single	25.2%
Married	74.8%
FIRST-TIME BUYERS	39.1%
PURCHASE PRICE	
Less than $50,000	22.1%
$50,000–89,999	40.8%
$90,000–119,999	14.7%
$120,000 or more	22.4%
MEDIAN PRICE	$75,000
AGE OF HOME	
New	22.1%
Less than 25 years	44.0%
25 or more years	33.9%
CONDO BUYERS	13.4%
ANNUAL HOUSEHOLD INCOME	
Less than $15,000	2.0%
$15,000–24,999	11.9%
$25,000–34,999	20.9%
$35,000–44,999	19.7%
$45,000 or more	45.5%
TOTAL MONTHLY EXPENSE	
$600 or less	34.9%
$601–900	31.7%
$901 or more	33.4%
DOWNPAYMENT	
10% or less	28.4%
20% or more	44.1%
MEDIAN DOWN PAYMENT	$14,100
HOUSING EXPENSE EXCEEDING 25% OF HOUSEHOLD INCOME	33.5%

Source: U.S. League of Savings Institutions

it. An easement, which is a permanent limitation, may decrease the value of the property. A surveyor should be hired to stake out the exact boundaries of the property as recorded in the deed.

A lawyer can also find out about deed restrictions and zoning ordinances that apply to the location. These may restrict changes made in existing structures or the general use of the property. It may not be desirable to buy a home near an area zoned for commercial or industrial use. On the other hand, if zoning laws are changed to allow businesses or industry, your property might increase greatly in value.

Closing the Purchase

The original sales agreement indicates the date when the sale is to be closed. At that time, the buyer and seller, together with their representatives, meet to "pass papers"— that is, to transfer the ownership of the property. During this meeting, the down payment is made, the papers for the new mortgage are signed, and the buyer receives the deed to the property. The deed contains a complete description of the property and all conditions concerning the property. The deed is the written instrument which transfers ownership. The deed must be signed and dated by both buyer and seller. Their signatures must be witnessed by a notary public, who places his signature and a seal upon the deed. The lending agency often keeps the original deed until the mortgage is paid off.

The deed The deed to real estate property is important because it identifies the owner or owners and shows the type of ownership involved. There are several different kinds of ownership available, and each has certain advantages and disadvantages. You should know about these types and perhaps discuss them with a lawyer before deciding which one best serves your purpose.

The deed for a single buyer is the simplest kind because only one owner is involved. Specifying ownership for married couples is more complicated. In times past, when the husband was customarily the sole support of the family, deeds were often drawn up to indicate that he was the sole owner. If he died, the home was left to his widow and children.

Today, particularly since many wives are employed and making a direct financial contribution to the household, both husband and wife are often listed as owners. Such ownership is known as "joint tenancy" or "tenancy by the entirety." In this type of ownership, both owners have a share in the total property, and neither can dispose of that ownership. Such ownership includes the "right of survivorship"; that is, on the death of one spouse, the property automatically passes to the surviving spouse, without probate court proceedings. However, inheritance taxes may be involved.

Another form of ownership is that of "tenancy in common." Under this arrangement, each partner or owner has a separate, partial interest in the property. That interest can be sold or transferred by one of the owners. This form of ownership is often used when unrelated people buy property—for example, when two people invest in land for development.

Insurance In preparing for closing, you should arrange to have the property insured, with coverage beginning as soon as you take over the ownership. This may be done by transferring the insurance coverage from the previous owner or by taking out new insurance. Insurance is essential, both for your own protection and that of the mortgage lender, who will require adequate coverage for the property.

Various types of home insurance are available. Perhaps the most common type is the homeowner's insurance policy. This policy includes both comprehensive coverage, which is insurance against damage, and personal liability insurance, which protects any member of the household in the case of accident and insures payment for injury to any guest, stranger, or delivery person while on the property. Comprehensive coverage provides protection against loss in the case of fire, theft, storm, or vandalism, as well as protection against damage from landslides or falling objects, and against the structural collapse of any part of the building. A comprehensive homeowner's policy is less expensive than buying the same coverage in separate policies.

It is important to review home insurance coverage regularly to be sure that it increases as the value of the property increases. Some policies automatically adjust for inflation. If improvements are made, insurance should of course be increased. Insurance rates and coverage differ from company to company. Be sure to compare the policies available so that you get the most coverage for the least amount of money. Discounts may be available if you have such protective devices as smoke alarms or burglar alarms. Cost is also based on how close your home is to a fire hydrant or other source of water, and the type of construction it has.

In addition to insurance on the real estate property, insurance on personal property is important. The amount of coverage should be related to the value of the possessions within the home. An up-to-date list of all personal possessions should be maintained.

FINANCING THE PURCHASE

Few people can afford to pay cash for a home. The amount of money needed to buy a home is more than most people have available at any time in their lives.

BASIC COVERAGE

1. fire or lightning
2. loss of property removed from premises endangered by fire or other perils
3. windstorm or hail
4. explosion
5. riot or civil commotion
6. aircraft
7. vehicles
8. smoke
9. vandalism and malicious mischief
10. theft
11. breakage of glass constituting a part of the building

BROAD COVERAGE

12. falling objects
13. weight of ice, snow, sleet
14. collapse of building(s) or any part thereof
15. sudden and accidental tearing asunder, cracking, burning, or bulging of a steam or hot water heating system or of appliances for heating water
16. accidental discharge, leakage, or overflow of water or steam from within a plumbing, heating, or air-conditioning system or domestic appliance
17. freezing of plumbing, heating, and air-conditioning systems and domestic applicances
18. sudden and accidental injury from artificially generated currents to electrical appliances, devices, fixtures, and wiring (TV and radio tubes not included)

COMPREHENSIVE COVERAGE

all perils except flood, earthquake, war, nuclear attack, and others specified in the policy

The most common practice is to pay a part of the purchase price in cash—the down payment—and to borrow money for the remaining balance. A long-term loan used to finance the purchase of a home is called a mortgage. Like any other loan, a mortgage requires the payment of interest. Interest on mortgage payments is deductible on your income tax, as are the closing costs paid at the time of purchase. The home is used as security for this mortgage loan.

A mortgage is obtained by applying for it from a savings and loan association, a bank, an insurance company, or some other lending agency. You will need to find out what institutions have mortgages available; what you must have in order to qualify; and what variations exist for the amount of the loan, the down payment, the interest rate, and the duration time for the mortgage. Your real estate agent can provide some information, but some you will have to gather for yourself.

Establishing Credit

Once you make application to a lending agency for a mortgage loan, the agency will begin an investigation of your credit rating. If you have bank accounts or charge accounts, they provide evidence of your credit rating. The local credit bureau will also have a record of your credit rating. If the credit bureau reports a poor credit rating, a buyer can expect problems with the lending agency. Anyone suspecting that a credit rating is inaccurate has the right, under the Fair Credit Reporting Act, to inspect the file at the credit office and have the rating corrected if there is an error.

Buyers seeking a mortgage loan may also encounter discrimination. If that occurs, the buyer is protected under the Equal Credit Opportunity Act. This act prohibits lenders from discriminating against an applicant for credit because of race, sex, national origin, religion, marital status, or age (minors excluded). The act also states that lenders must consider the applicant's income from public assistance programs, alimony, and child support, if these are received as regular payments.

Studying Interest Rates

Mortgage interest rates are determined by many different factors at any given time. Some of these factors are: the national economy; the economy of the area in which the house is located; the type of lender you use, such as a bank, insurance company, or an individual; the type and length of the mortgage; and your own credit rating. In general, when there is little surplus money in the economy, mortgage rates go up. When there is more money

COMPARISON OF EQUITY BASED ON
DOWN PAYMENT AND MORTAGE LOAN

A large down payment and a small loan or mortgage will give more present equity in a home than a small down payment and a large loan or mortgage do. The larger equity makes it easier to borrow if the need arises.

A mortgage can be obtained from a savings and loan association, a commercial or savings bank, an insurance company, or other lending agencies.

available for investment, mortgage rates go down. Mortgage interest rates vary from lender to lender. Therefore, it is important that you shop for the lowest interest rate and best terms available to you.

The size of the mortgage that you are able to obtain depends upon your income, the amount of money you have for a down payment, other assets you may own such as stocks or bonds, and your other debts. The more money you have for a down payment, the lower the total amount of your mortgage will be, as will be the total interest that you pay.

Monthly mortgage costs are determined not only by the amount of the loan but also by the term or length of the loan and the interest rate. The longer the term, the lower the monthly payments will be. However, in this case you will pay more for total interest over the life of the loan. The total interest paid on the loan when you have finished paying it can easily double, triple, or quadruple the initial price of your home.

To keep their interest rates comparable to other lenders and yet make more profit, lenders often charge "points" on the mortgage. Each point is equal to 1% of the mortgage loan. The points "discount" the amount of money lent to the buyer. For example, if you took out a mortgage of $60,000 at two points, the bank would actually lend you $58,800, but you would have to repay them $60,000.

Types of Mortgages

Because there are so many different types of mortgages with different features and rates, it is important to shop for a mortgage

---

Comparative Costs of Interest Rates

Let's examine the comparative costs of a $70,000 house with a $10,000 down payment and a $60,000 mortgage at two different interest levels:

Amount of Mortgage	Interest Rate	Term	Monthly Cost	Total Cost
$60,000	12½%	30 years	$640	$230,530
$60,000	10%	30 years	$526	$189,558
				$ 40,972 difference

The length of the mortgage term also strongly affects the total cost of the mortgage. Let's look at the same loans but for a 20-year term:

Amount of Mortgage	Interest Rate	Term	Monthly Cost	Total Cost
$60,000	12½%	20 years	$682	$163,606
$60,000	10%	20 years	$579	$138,965
				$ 24,641 difference

If we could increase the down payment by $5,000, leaving a mortgage of $55,000, we could further reduce the total cost:

Amount of Mortgage	Interest Rate	Term	Monthly Cost	Total Cost
$55,000	12½%	20 years	$625	$149,973
$55,000	10%	20 years	$531	$127,387
				$ 22,586 difference

By obtaining a lower interest rate, making a larger down payment, and shortening the repayment period, you can lower the total cost of a home. As you can see, the final cost of the $70,000 house ranged from $127,387 to $230,530—a difference of $103,143!

as you would for any other consumer purchase. Mortgages are available from savings and loan associations, savings banks, commercial banks, mortgage companies, insurance companies, pension funds, credit unions, and individuals. It may also be possible to take over a mortgage that is already on the home.

Today, almost all mortgages consist of equal monthly payments throughout the loan period. These payments cover a portion of the principal, the debt itself, plus the interest on the loan. During the first half of the mortgage payment period, each payment almost totally goes toward paying the interest. However, toward the end of the mortgage period, most of each payment goes toward paying the principal. In this way, the owner is able to build up equity —the portion of a property that has been paid for—and lower the outstanding debt with each payment. This method of mortgaging is called amortization. Although most mortgages made at this time are amortized, many new mortgage patterns have been developed recently.

The conventional mortgage The conventional mortgage is an amortized fixed interest rate loan, usually taken out for 15, 20, or 30 years. The monthly payments and the interest rate remain the same over the period of the loan, no matter how general interest rates fluctuate. If you have a steady income that can cover these monthly payments, but not any larger amount, then a conventional fixed-rate mortgage might be the safest type for you. Down payments are usually 20%. However, payments of 10% and even 5% may be possible if you can provide mortgage insurance.

Variable rate mortgages In the past few years, lending institutions have developed creative financing plans to make it possible for more people to buy homes. Among these are adjustable rate mortgages, graduated payment mortgages, variable maturity mortgages, and reverse mortgages.

- **Adjustable rate mortgages** have become very popular over the past few years. The interest rate on these mortgages varies as interest rates change in the economy. As a result, the interest rates may be adjusted every six months, every year, or every two to three years. ARMs usually have a cap or limit on the amount they can be increased in any one period. Also, there is usually a cap on the total percent the interest can be increased over the life of the loan. For example, the interest rate may have a cap of 2% per year and a total cap of 5% over the life of the mortgage. Adjustable rate loans benefit the lender because the interest income of the loans can keep pace with changes in the economy. Borrowers benefit by not being locked into high interest loans if the general rates go down. The initial interest rate of the ARMs is usually a percentage point or two lower than the fixed-rate mortgage.

- **Graduated payment mortgages** are designed for individuals or families with low incomes now, but who have prospects of higher incomes in a few years. The monthly payments begin low but increase each year as salaries increase, until the payments are large enough to amortize the loan.

- **Variable maturity mortgages** have an interest rate that varies just as it does with an ARM. However, the payment charges of a variable maturity mortgage remain the same throughout the loan. Instead of raising the monthly charges, the mortgage lender makes the adjustment by lengthening or shortening the term.

- **Reverse annuity mortgages** are designed for elderly homeowners who own their homes but need additional income. They are able to borrow on their equity in their house. With a reverse mortgage, once the house is appraised, the bank agrees to pay the owner a set amount each month as income. The homeowner then owes that amount plus interest. The bank is repaid when the estate of the borrower is settled.

Government assisted mortgages
The federal government encourages home financing by guaranteeing mortgage payments or helping to finance loans. These types of mortgages include the FHA insured mortgage, the VA guaranteed mortgage, and FmHA loans.

- **The FHA insured mortgage** was introduced by the Federal Housing Authority during the Great Depression. FHA provides an insurance program that protects lenders from losses on mortgage loans. In return, lenders must accept lower down payments and lower interest rates than those of conventional mortgages. FHA appraises the value

Older homeowners are able to borrow on their equity in their house with a reverse annuity mortgage.

and construction of the houses that it insures. The amount of the mortgage is based on the appraisal. Houses bought before construction is completed must be warranted to meet FHA construction standards. The homeowner is charged ½% a year on the remaining balance of the mortgage for this insurance. It is the lender, not the buyer, who receives the benefit of the insurance. It is difficult to obtain an FHA loan at this time because the amount that can be borrowed is too low to finance most houses on the market. Also, the maximum interest rate is lower than that of conventional mortgages. In addition, FHA will not permit a second mortgage on the property. FHA mortgages are usually financed through mortgage companies whose funds come from individual investors. The amount of paperwork involved as well as the low interest rates make FHA mortgages unattractive to other lenders at this time.

- **VA guaranteed mortgages** are available through the Veterans Administration for the purchase of new or older homes by eligible veterans. Most veterans can qualify, as well as the husbands and wives of any veterans who died while in the service or died from disabilities received while in the service. The VA guaranteed mortgage is similar to the FHA mortgage. However, the government guarantees the loan and the buyer does not pay an insurance cost. If the property is approved for purchase, a veteran can borrow up to 100% of its appraised value. No down payment is required unless the cost of the house is higher than the appraisal. Interest rates for VA guaranteed loans are low and similar to those of the FHA.
- **FmHA loans** are intended to aid in the financing of housing in small towns or rural areas. The Farmers Home Administration guarantees mortgages and

makes direct mortgage loans. No down payment is required, and the time for repayment may extend for as long as 33 years. These loans are financed through the Department of Agriculture. Interest subsidies are also available for low-income families to buy at prices that they can afford.

- **Other government assisted loans** are periodically made available through selected banks for low interest rate mortgage loans. These loans are designated for owner occupied housing. When these sales are announced, prospective borrowers line up outside the banks days in advance.

Second mortgages If a home buyer cannot get a first mortgage that is large enough to cover the price of the home he or she wants to buy, it is possible to get a second mortgage to make up the difference. Interest rates for second mortgages are much higher than those for first mortgages because there is greater risk for the lender. In the event of a foreclosure, the first mortgage holder must be paid first. If any money is left over from the sale, the holder of the second mortgage receives the balance.

A second mortgage can also be obtained to finance renovations, repairs, and additions to your home. This is sometimes called an equity loan.

Foreclosure

Although some provisions in mortgages may vary, others remain similar. One provision contained in all mortgages is for foreclosure, or repossession by the lender, in the event that payments are not maintained. Failure to keep up payments may occur for a number of reasons, such as prolonged unemployment, the severe illness or death of the homeowner, or marital problems leading to separation or divorce. Sometimes homeowners may find that they are not ready for the responsibilities of ownership. Foreclosed property is sold at auction. From the auction proceeds, the mortgage holders are paid first. Then other creditors are paid, and the owner receives any money that is left over. If the auction proceeds do not cover the debts, the owner is liable for the difference. If the foreclosed property was insured by the FHA, the lender is protected from loss.

SELLING ONE HOME AND BUYING ANOTHER

When a person or family decides to move to a new home, the present home must be sold. The equity gained from this sale is often used as the down payment on a new home. If the home must be sold immediately, the seller may have to set a low price. If a home does not sell before the owner has to move, the owner may have to make monthly payments on two homes until the first one can be sold.

If any of these problems arise, solutions can usually be found. For instance, if the owner must support two homes for a time, a "bridge loan" may be the answer. This is a loan based on the equity, or amount of ownership, in the present home. A good credit rating is essential in obtaining this type of loan. Some realtors offer a guaranteed home-sale plan. Under this arrangement, the realtor promises to buy, for 85% or 90% of the market price, a home that has not sold within 90 days. Another solution may be to "trade in" a home to a developer or real estate agent. Usually these arrangements are possible only in areas where real estate sells quickly.

A final option for the person who needs to sell one home in order to buy another is to include in the sales agreement for the new home a contingency clause. Such a clause provides that the purchase of the new home is conditional—that is, dependent upon the sale of the old home within a certain period of time.

CAREER C REAL ESTATE AGENT

PROFILE Real estate agents handle the selling, buying, and renting of property for clients. Realtors accompany prospects to property sites to inspect houses or apartments. They discuss the purchase price and the conditions of the sale or the terms of the lease. Agents must also be able to provide information about the community, property taxes, zoning laws, and the approximate cost of heating and cooling the home. If the client is interested in the property, the agent seeks to negotiate terms that are acceptable to both the buyer and the seller. Real estate agents also handle most of the business involved in transferring the property. They draw up the sales agreement or lease and work with lawyers and lending agencies regarding deeds and mortgage loans.

It is very important for real estate agents to develop and maintain lists of people who have property to sell or rent, as well as lists of people who are interested buyers or renters. Agents talk with prospective clients to solicit listings of properties. Many times, properties are multilisted with all the real estate agencies in the area. Realtors must continually study these lists to be familiar with what is currently available. Trade journals are reviewed for information about marketing conditions and property values.

If you are interested in becoming a real estate agent, you should be able to work well with people and enjoy it. It helps to have an outgoing personality and a good memory for names, faces, and facts. You need good verbal skills and persuasive selling skills. You must also be able to handle routine forms and paperwork. Because this field is highly competitive, you should have lots of initiative and drive.

To become a real estate agent you do not need to meet any specific educational requirements. However, some business schools and community schools offer specialized courses in real estate. Some experience in selling or business management is helpful. All states require you to obtain a real estate license by successfully completing a written test. You may also hold a brokerage license, and then you will have the title of real estate broker.

Most real estate agents are employed by realty firms. These companies may be large or consist of only a few people. Some realty firms are part of a nationwide franchise of realtors with a well advertised name. An agent might also work for a real estate developer and operate from a model home in a new development or apartment complex. Real estate agents can also be self-employed and work only as many hours as they desire. Most agents are paid on a commission basis, which makes competition very keen.

REVIEWING CHAPTER 6

SUMMARY

Buying a home is a major financial investment. In addition to single-family homes, condominium and cooperative apartment units can also be purchased.

The actual buying of a home, from making the sales agreement to completing the purchase, involves a number of steps. There are legal requirements as well as financial commitments. A real estate agent will be able to advise you, but you may also want to have the help of a lawyer for handling the title and deed.

Several different types of mortgages are available today, depending on your resources and the property that you are buying. In addition to obtaining a mortgage, you will need money for the down payment and closing costs. Long-range costs of home ownership include mortgage payments, interest, taxes, utilities, and insurance.

FACTS TO KNOW

1. Explain the meaning of the terms *cooperative* and *condominium*. How are they alike and how do they differ?

2. List the major steps in buying a home, from deciding to buy it to completing the purchase.

3. What services can a real estate agent and a lawyer provide for someone buying a home?

4. What obligations does a buyer have when signing a sales agreement?

5. Explain why a title search is important. What is a deed and why is it important?

6. Explain how the amount of the down payment, the interest rate, and the duration of the mortgage affect the eventual cost of a home.

7. Identify three types of mortgages. What are the special benefits of each type?

8. What problems might arise when selling one home and buying another?

IDEAS TO THINK ABOUT

1. If you wanted to own a home but had little money available for a down payment, what are several ways in which you could still become a homeowner?

2. Review the *Profile of the Average Home Buyer in the U.S.* on page 000. What conclusions can you make about buying a home today?

3. Do you think that a young, newly married couple should buy a house or a condominium if they can afford either one? Give reasons for your answers.

ACTIVITIES TO DO

1. Interview a local realtor to find out how active the housing market is at present. What types of homes are most popular? What types of mortgages are most common? And what is the current average interest rate?

2. Select a local real estate ad offering a house, condominium, or cooperative for sale. Figure out the monthly cost of buying it using two different types of mortgages.

Chapter 7

Space Needs for Livability

If you lived in a studio apartment with just one room, would you consider it confining? Or would you consider it cozy and easy to maintain? Some people are content with a small amount of living space while others want a lot of space to move around in. Scientists, architects, and interior designers have become more aware of people's space needs and the ways space is used. The smaller size of today's homes has led to a new concern for the efficient use of space.

What factors influence space requirements? Cost is one of the main factors—usually the larger the home, the more expensive it is. But other factors besides cost influence people's choice of space. Among these are the number of occupants and their ages, the amount of time spent in the home, and the occupants' interests and activities.

The way the rooms of a home are laid out is almost as important as the total amount of space because it affects the use of that space. The floor plan determines how traffic flows through the home and the use of space within each room. Some people prefer a room arrangement that is very open with different living areas combined or flowing together. Others prefer more privacy with complete separation of the different areas within a home. What type of arrangement do you prefer?

PREVIEWING YOUR LEARNING

After you have read this chapter, you will be able to:

- Recognize individual needs for space.

- Evaluate space requirements, especially those for disabled or elderly people.

- Analyze floor plans and traffic patterns.

- Suggest ways to expand living space.

TERMS TO KNOW

attic—a room or a space immediately below the roof of a building

basement—the part of a building that is wholly or partly below ground level

disability—a temporary or permanent mental or physical condition that is limiting in some way

entrepreneur—a person who organizes and manages his or her own business

illusion—an appearance or feeling that misleads by giving a false impression

landscape—the scenery around a particular area

space—amount of distance or area that can be measured

traffic pattern—the path people follow most often as they move around a room or from one room to another

SHOJI SCREENS

F E A T U R E

For Frank Lloyd Wright and many other modern American architects and designers, Japanese culture has been a source of inspiration. One versatile element of Japanese interior design is the shoji—a delicate, framed screen, usually made of wood strips and rice paper, which can be freestanding or made to slide along a track. In Japan, the shoji is used to define living areas of the home and to partition off spaces for sleeping, working, and entertaining. Shoji screens provide more flexibility in space definition than a permanent wall or partition because they can be opened to increase living space and then closed again to limit it. As a result, they work beautifully in the multi-use rooms that are popular in modern interior design.

The shoji, besides defining space, can also provide more flexibility. For example, screens placed between a living and dining area can be closed during small dinner parties or opened for large buffet entertaining. The shoji can also screen off a kitchen from a dining area to create a more formal look. Part of a den or bedroom can be sectioned off to provide a quiet place for study. Another practical use for the shoji is to conceal multimedia storage areas. Built-in shelves containing a stereo, television, books, and records could be neatly screened from view when not in use, to give the room a more spacious, uncluttered look. The interior panels of the screen can be made of coated rice paper, fiberglass, plastic, vinyl, or even bed sheets that coordinate with the other furnishings. The shoji is a traditional design feature that fits into today's modern lifestyles.

HUMAN NEEDS FOR SPACE

Have you ever felt that you must escape from a crowded elevator or from a room or bus filled with people? Have you ever felt imposed upon when you have had to give up your bedroom to guests who are staying overnight? Have you ever wished people around you would be quiet when you are trying to concentrate? On the other hand, have you enjoyed camping in a tent where you had little space to call your own? During a storm or other threat to your well-being, have you felt better being close to other people? If any of your answers are yes, then you are aware that the space around you is important.

Only within recent years have social scientists studied the psychological effects of space on human beings. Dr. Edward T. Hall was one of the pioneers in this field of science. He and other scientists observed the behavior of birds, fish, and animals in their natural environment. They concluded that these creatures apparently have a built-in mechanism for claiming and defending certain territorial rights as a means of survival. When territories become overcrowded or strangers intrude, their behavior becomes disorderly.

Space Needs for Individuals

Social scientists believe that human beings react to space-related needs in much the same ways that other living creatures do. People tend to be affected by conditions in the space around them. If that space is kept clean and orderly, it can contribute to a peaceful frame of mind. If physical hazards, such as toys and broken furniture, or mental hazards, such as noise, are present, they can cause stress. When food is left around, attracting insects and rats, it can lower the standard of living and contribute to poor health.

People in groups—such as in communities and urban centers—are also affected by conditions in their environment. People, like animals, react to overcrowding. Some social scientists attribute much of the crime in large cities to overcrowding, a condition which causes stress and antisocial behavior. Urban planners also recognize the importance of space for people living in cities, although they realize that the amount of space available may be less than what is desirable. In the United States, housing experts define overcrowding as more than one person per room in a home. Thus a four-member family requires a minimum of four rooms.

Most people live more happily and effectively if the quantity and quality of their space needs are met. In a home, individuals should have the right to a private space where they can be alone without intrusion of any kind. If this is not possible, a person should be able to get away to a quiet place for a short time. Everyone needs some private place to retreat to for reading, studying, pursuing hobbies, or simply daydreaming.

A desk, a comfortable chair, and some tables and lamps turn this bedroom corner into a quiet retreat for reading, studying, and relaxing.

In recent years, architects have designed windowless offices and school buildings. They claim that these buildings are more economical to heat, cool, and maintain. However, the effect of such surroundings upon people has been questioned. In one study made of computer programmers, the error rate was much higher in windowless offices. Some windowless structures have glassed-in areas with lighting and landscaping to simulate daylight. These innovations help to compensate for the missing natural light. To some people, the simulated environment is satisfactory. To others, some visual contact with the natural world is essential. Knowledge of your own feelings and preferences can help you in choosing the type of environment and the amount of space that are best for you.

SPACE REQUIREMENTS IN HOUSING

The family activities that take place within a home require three different types of areas: active areas for social interaction; quiet private areas for sleeping, reading, and studying; and work, storage, and maintenance areas such as kitchens, laundry and utility rooms, and garages. A single person does not have to be too concerned with defining these areas. However, families made up of several people should consider methods of separating these areas. This will help to prevent conflicts and insure that the activities of one person do not interfere with those of other family members.

WORK, STORAGE AND MAINTENANCE SPACE
SHARED LIVING SPACE
PRIVATE LIVING SPACE

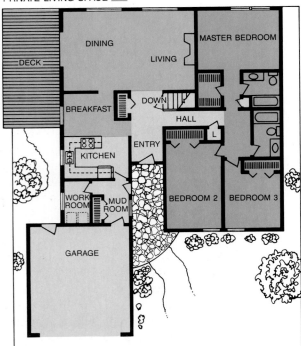

The space within a home must meet a wide variety of needs.

CHECKLIST FOR SPACE

☐ Living area should have space for at least one conversational area 10 feet (3.05 m) in diameter without traffic interference. This requires a room at least 12 feet by 16 feet (3.66 m by 4.88 m)—longer if part of the room is used for traffic or dining.

☐ Dining area should connect with the kitchen. Space should allow 3½ feet (1.07 m) all around the table for seating.

☐ Kitchen must have adequate storage space for cooking utensils, dishes, and food. Traffic patterns should not interfere with the work centers. Minimum kitchen size is 8 feet by 10 feet (2.44 m by 3.05 m). Kitchen should have its own outside entrance or be close to an entrance.

☐ Bedroom(s) should have a quiet location away from home and street noises. Primary bedroom should be at least 12 feet by 14 feet (3.66 m by 4.27 m). Additional bedrooms should be at least 10 feet by 12 feet (3.05 m by 3.66 m). Adequate closet and storage space should be provided. Clothes closets should be at least two feet (.6 m) deep.

☐ Bathroom should be adjacent to bedroom. Minimum size is 5 feet by 7 feet (1.52 m by 2.13 m). A two-story house should also have a half bathroom on the first floor.

☐ Entrance area should have space for removing coats and a coat closet.

The social areas are usually used jointly by all family members. They are the rooms for entertaining guests, serving meals, watching television, and children's play. These areas may be used both day and evening. Sometimes social rooms are very formal and are not used by families except on special occasions.

The quiet private areas of a home should be placed as far away from the social areas as possible. Sometimes bedrooms are placed in a separate wing of the home or on the second floor of a two-story house. It is preferable that bathrooms not be seen from the social areas. The number of bathrooms needed depends on the number of family members and their schedules. Probably no other area is as apt to cause space problems as the inadequacy of bathrooms. Work areas also should be located away from the quiet areas, if at all possible. Refrigerators, washers and dryers, ventilating fans, and small equipment are often noisy.

Guidelines for Room Sizes

Many studies have been done to determine the adequacy of different room sizes for the activities that take place in them and for the number of occupants. The FHA has established minimum standards for the houses that they insure. Other government and private agencies have also developed standards. Most lenders have their own standards which they use in granting home loans. Usually the standards vary depending upon the size of the mortgage requested. A more expensive house is expected to provide larger rooms than a less expensive house. For more specific information about room sizes, see the Checklist for Space.

Space for Special Needs

Many families include a member who has some type of physical disability which makes it difficult for the person to function in an average home. The blind, the deaf, the wheelchair bound, and the aged face similar problems in a typical house or apartment. Demonstration houses have been built to show how new homes can be designed specifically for people with one or more disabilities. Most families, though, cannot afford or are not able to build a new house when a member becomes disabled. They have to adapt their present home to the situation as best as they can.

Perhaps the easiest adaptions are those that can be made for the deaf. For example, signal lights can be attached to the doorbell and the telephone to indicate when they have rung. Other visual devices can be used to signal that some action has taken place. Vibrating timers that can be held in the hand or in a pocket are helpful.

The blind, the aged, and the wheelchair bound all need open areas, clear passages with handrails, and no-slip floors. There should be no scatter rugs and no unnecessary furniture or clutter in their homes. People who use wheelchairs have special space needs. One of these is ramps, which can be added to private houses. Most apartment houses, however, still have steps at their front entrances. Ramps are now required at all new public buildings.

It is usually more convenient for physically disabled people to live on the first floor of buildings. Doors should be 3 feet (.9 m) wide and hallways 4 feet (1.2 m) wide to allow wheelchairs to move through easily. Handles on doors, light switches, thermostats, mirrors, and telephones should be lowered for easy reach. Closet rods may also have to be lowered. Bathrooms should be large enough so that a wheelchair can move around easily. Toilet bowls should be higher than normal and

People who use wheelchairs have special space needs. Sinks and range tops should be lowered, and lower cabinets should be removed to accommodate the wheelchair.

have side rails for support. Wheel-in shower stalls are preferable to bath tubs and should have a seat and special guardrails. It is desirable to have handrails about 32 inches (81.3 cm) above the floor along ramps and hallways in the home.

For a person in a wheelchair, a one-wall, L-shaped, or U-shaped kitchen is preferable to a two-wall kitchen. Someone in a wheelchair cannot reach the sink and range top in the average kitchen. These should be lowered. In addition, the cabinets under the sink and range top should be removed so that there is open space to accommodate knees and wheelchair. Countertops themselves will need to be lowered, and base cabinets with shelves should be changed to drawers. The work area requires a 5 foot (1.5 m) circle in order for a wheelchair to turn easily. Modifications must consider both convenience and safety. Many of the special adaptations can be done by family members themselves. In some cases, homeowners may obtain financial help from the state vocational rehabilitation agency to make these changes.

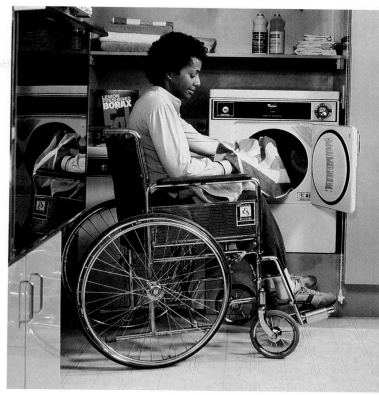

Special modifications can help the physically disabled live more independently.

FLOOR PLANS FOR MAXIMUM LIVABILITY

The actual amount of floor space in a home is less important to livability than the use made of the space available. The number of people sharing the home, together with their interests and activities, determines how floor and storage space are to be used. Since few floor plans are ideal, people often have to adjust. Good organization is especially important when space is limited or when the layout is not efficient. In such situations, an illusion of space can be created through the use of color, lighting, and furniture arrangement.

Using Space as a Whole

Most floor plans are designed to meet the basic needs of housing—cooking, eating, sleeping, personal care, and socializing. Because needs vary according to individual preference, lifestyle, and stage in the life cycle, it is important to find the layout that meets one's own particular requirements. The use of space need not be confined to the names traditionally given to areas or rooms on a floor plan—dining room, bedroom, and so forth. Instead, the space available should be looked at as a whole to see how it can be used most effectively.

Since the cost of housing space is rising, it is important to make good use of all the space within a home. As you start to look for suitable housing, consider how space can be adapted to meet your particular needs.

Providing for Social Activities

People who are sociably inclined and who enjoy entertaining at home like to have a large living and serving area accessible to the kitchen. A living area with wide openings leading to a family room or patio provides enough circulation space for large groups. People who do little entertaining may prefer to break up a large living area into at least two areas, such as a living room and a dining area. This can best be accomplished by the use of area rugs, screens, or room dividers. A family room might at times become a study or guest room or hobby center.

Some people place social and psychological importance upon having a large dining room for relaxed family meals and entertaining. Such a large space would be wasted for an individual or a couple who had no children and who did not enjoy entertaining. Instead, part of a large dining room might be used as a library or a study; as a place for viewing television, listening to a stereo, or playing an organ or piano; as a center where special hobbies are displayed or plants grown; or as a small nursery or playroom.

Providing for Quiet Zones and Sleeping Areas

Any home with several people living in it needs to have well-defined areas for both quiet and social activities. When bedroom and living-room walls are adjacent, a closet or storage wall between rooms can serve to reduce noise. It is also important to locate bedrooms so that they are not near the kitchen, or in the line of traffic between the living room and the bathroom, or close to the living room and its entrances. When you examine floor plans, you will want to keep these suggestions in mind.

A few people are fortunate enough to enjoy bedrooms with enough space for a large bed, lounge chair, television set, chest of drawers, walk-in closet, and large bathroom. This arrangement would be considered extravagant for a person living alone or on a limited housing budget. In such situations, a minimum-sized bedroom, closet, and bath would meet the budget limitations and yet provide adequate space for living.

Providing for Personal Interests and Activities

A home should provide for the development of personal interests. Musically-oriented families need floor space for a piano, an organ, or a stereo, as well as storage space for smaller musical instruments, sheet music, and records. People who enjoy reading may need a great deal of bookshelf space or even a separate study or library.

People who enjoy cooking usually prefer a large kitchen. People who do less cooking may want to use part of a large kitchen for writing, bookkeeping, hobbies, or correspondence.

Families with young children need a great deal of space for equipment and toys that are used daily. Space can usually be set aside in children's bedrooms for collections of autographs, buttons, coins, dolls, shells, or stamps. Some people have hobbies that require extra floor space, as well as storage space. Such hobbies may include ceramics, china painting, metalcraft, painting, sewing, weaving, woodworking, or photography. People who collect rare books and prints may want to display them in a study, family room, or living room.

Outdoor enthusiasts need storage space for equipment used in sports and recreation. These activities might include bad-

Space for personal interests and activities, such as hobbies and music, should be provided.

A kitchen with a large eating area provides space for informal entertaining.

A separate dining room can be used for family meals and more formal entertaining.

Children's bedrooms should have space for toys and a play area.

EXAMPLES OF TRAFFIC FLOW IN LIVING AREAS

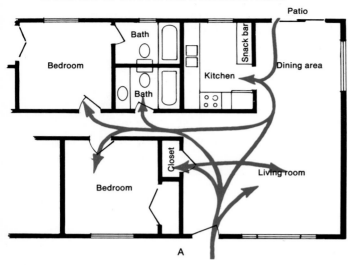

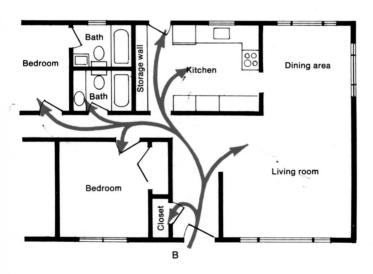

Compare these two floor plans in terms of traffic flow. What advantages and disadvantages does each plan have? How might the arrangement of furniture help to offset any disadvantages?

minton, baseball, basketball, bicycling, boating, bowling, camping, gardening, golf, hockey, hunting, ice skating, roller skating, skiing, and tennis. Some types of sports equipment can usually be stored in a garage, utility room, or basement.

Providing for Traffic Patterns

Providing efficient, convenient, and safe traffic patterns within the home will add to both safety and livability. In factories, traffic through work areas is not permitted. By contrast, in many homes, children dart back and forth through the kitchen, dining area, and living area. Such activity may cause falls, breakage of china, and damage to furniture, not to mention annoyance to others in the home. Especially in the living area, traffic interferes with conversation, study, listening to music, or watching television. Falls in the home are a very serious matter: in fact, they account for half of all accidental deaths in the United States. Many of these accidents could be avoided with better planning for traffic within the household.

To get a better idea of the effect of home traffic patterns on safety and privacy, compare the different floor plans illustrated. The plans are similar, but the traffic patterns are arranged quite differently. In Plan A, the traffic pattern crosses through the living room. Because the living room is open to all traffic, family members have no privacy in entering the home and reaching the bedrooms or bathrooms. Also, a person entering through the sliding doors between the dining area and terrace and carrying an armload of groceries must be careful to avoid bumping into the dining table and chairs.

In the kitchen, the lack of a major work center under the kitchen window is a disadvantage, since a view reduces fatigue and prevents a closed-in feeling. The kitchen also provides no space for cleaning equipment, such as a vacuum cleaner, broom, bucket, or mop. The absence of a door between the kitchen and dining area makes more cleaning necessary in the dining area and results in worn carpet along the line of traffic.

Together with its disadvantages, Plan A offers a few advantages. Plumbing for both the kitchen and bathroom is concentrated on one wall, thus avoiding the higher cost of two-wall plumbing. The bathrooms provide a sound barrier between the kitchen and bedrooms.

Plan B offers a number of advantages. The small entrance passageway allows traffic to flow easily into the living-dining area. Family members can enter the kitchen or sleeping areas without having to go through the living room by either the front or back door. The coat closet is near the front door. In general, Plan B provides a more livable home than Plan A. Minor changes in design can improve traffic flow.

Analyze this floor plan in terms of traffic flow. What advantages and disadvantages does it have? Can it be improved?

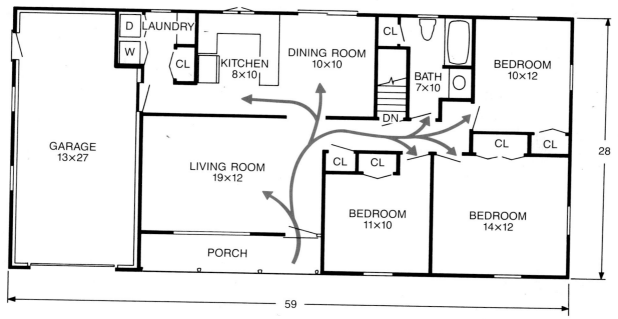

Creating an Illusion of Space

Japanese architecture is famous for its use of space. The culture and lifestyle of the Japanese people have led to an emphasis on simplicity, openness, and uncluttered space in the interior design of their homes. Even their design for small homes creates an illusion of space. The Japanese also emphasize flexibility in the use of an area. Placing a hibachi in the center of the living area, for example, transforms it into a place for food preparation and dining. Unrolling padded quilts on floors with straw matting changes a living space by day into a sleeping area by night. Movable screens, rather than fixed walls, are used as dividers within the home and add to the flexibility.

Frank Lloyd Wright, the great American architect, adapted many features of Japanese architecture in the designs for his prairie house and modern homes. Among these features were the typical openness and simplicity of interiors, relating indoors to outdoors, and the use of large window areas. Wright's influence may be seen today in the use of picture windows or full-length windows and sliding glass doors. These features, found in all types of housing, create an illusion of space.

Light, too, can work magic in creating an illusion of space within the home. Natural daylight coming through windows can be regulated by blinds, shades, curtains, or drapes to create a variety of effects. Skylights and glass walls can also give a feeling of space. Indoor lighting, both direct and indirect, can be controlled to provide brightness and shadows, thus giving a feeling of spaciousness and distance, even within a small area.

A feeling of space may also be suggested in a number of other ways. Using light-toned, wall-to-wall carpet and light-colored walls and draperies adds to the illusion of space within a home. Large rectangular mirrors without frames and indoor plants near windows can make an area seem larger than it actually is. Rooms that are not cluttered with a great many pieces of furniture and personal possessions appear larger than rooms that are overcrowded. Often, a room will appear more spacious if you remove a single piece of seldom-used furniture or meaningless accessories. Reorganizing closets, shelves, and drawers, and disposing of unused items will provide more usable space for storing items that are better out of sight.

Using light colors in a room helps to create an illusion of space.

Indirect lighting from sliding glass doors and large windows can make a room seem larger.

EXPANDING LIVING SPACE

The trend toward smaller homes, together with the need to conserve materials and energy, has emphasized the importance of utilizing living space as fully as possible. More indoor space can often be gained by converting unfinished attics, basements, or garages into space for living. Living space can also be extended by integrating indoor and outdoor areas for maximum use.

Converting Indoor Space

It is usually less expensive to gain space by converting unused areas, such as those in a basement or an attic, than by building an addition to a house. Because these areas already have a partial structure—a foundation or floor, walls, and a roof—they can be developed at less cost than for new construction. People who do some of the work themselves can further reduce the expenditure. It is usually advisable to make or to obtain from an architect rough drawings of alternate plans for the conversion.

Such drawings will allow you to weigh alternatives in both costs and benefits. Since a building permit is required for making structural changes, the plans must conform to local building codes.

Attics Unfinished attics provide a suitable space for expansion. Attics which are accessible by stairways are easier to convert than those reached by stairs pulled down from the ceiling. In the conversion of attic space, both a permanent stairway and a secondary exit (perhaps onto a roof) are required by traditional safety standards. If the attic roof is low, a section of it may be raised to provide window space, or dormer windows may be added. Skylights also offer possibilities for improving light and ventilation. The heating-cooling system may be tied into that of the rest of the house, or a separate heating-cooling unit may be added. It is advisable to install a small bathroom—if possible, one with a shower.

A basement can be converted into a recreation room to provide space for all types of activities that family members enjoy.

An attic can be transformed into a bedroom-sitting room. Dormer windows or skylights can be added for extra light and spaciousness.

Basements Converting an unfinished basement for use may cost less and be more efficient than remodeling an attic. The expense may be lower, because the basement already has a roof, floor, walls, and windows. Since the basic structure already exists, people may choose to do much of the remodeling work themselves, except for wiring and any necessary plumbing. A person skilled in the use of power tools can install insulation, paneling, partitions, storage areas, and floor and ceiling tile. Basement areas may have existing heating facilities, and they are not subject to the intense heat of most attics. It may be relatively easy, also, to tie a small bathroom into plumbing already there for laundry facilities. One problem in converting basement space for living may be the dampness often found there.

Garages Converting a garage to living space involves a choice between the convenience of another room and protection for your car. A possible compromise is to use the garage for seasonal recreation. In that case, the walls may be painted and decorated with travel posters; the floor may be painted or temporarily covered with inexpensive outdoor carpet. The tables and chairs chosen for this area should be collapsible and stackable for easy removal and storage.

A garage that is attached to the house on one or two sides may be converted easily, because the roof, floor, walls, and windows already exist. Since the garage is usually near the kitchen, the converted space can provide a multi-purpose area—family room, recreation room, hobby shop, or guest space for visiting family or friends. If the garage is being permanently converted to living space, the walls and ceiling must have adequate insulation. Carpeting for the floor should have a backing that provides both insulation and comfort. Depending on the amount of use and the climate, a heating-cooling unit may be necessary.

If the garage is part of a two-story house or is set below the level of the house, it may be possible to add space over the garage. This can be expensive, since it may involve building two or three walls, a floor, and a roof. However, the added living space obtained in this way may be very desirable and well suited to a number of uses. Careful planning is necessary to relate this new space to the rest of the house.

Converting Outdoor Space

Homes with outdoor areas have a valuable resource to develop as additional living space, particularly in warmer climates. Whether the area to be extended is large or small, open or enclosed, it can add immeasurably to the livability and to a sense of spaciousness.

Many different types of outdoor areas may be developed. In row houses and town houses, an entrance area may be created with a few steps and a small platform. Sometimes it includes a small yard for plantings, a flower bed, or a rock garden. A porch is a covered place attached to a house on one or two sides. It usually has steps and a railing and may be screened in. A breezeway is a covered area between the house and garage. A lanai, similar to a porch in size, is often level with the ground and is screened in for outdoor living.

A patio may be an outdoor extension of a family room or living room, or it may be a courtyard surrounded by one wall of the house and a fence on three sides. A deck is a wooden platform, usually extending at floor level from a family room, living room, or kitchen. A terrace is an open area, often paved with stone or brick, and adjacent to the house. A balcony is an outdoor platform entered by a door or sliding glass doors from a living area.

In planning for outdoor areas, it is important to consider how the space is to be used. If the space is intended mainly for entertaining, a large portion should be covered with a hard surface, such as flagstone, concrete, slate, or asphalt. Some provision for shade—from a roof, trees, or latticework covered with vines—will probably be needed. Trees and fences also provide privacy. It may be desirable to install lighting, as well as special facilities for outdoor cooking.

If the particular outdoor space is intended mainly as a play area for children, a soft ground cover such as grass may be desirable. Shade may be obtained from trees or fences. A fence around a patio area adds to the safety of small children. It may be desirable to have a low wall around flower beds for protection against children and animals. The wall makes weeding and flower care easier and provides a place to sit. Some paved area is useful for the riding of tricycles and playing with wheeled toys.

If the outdoor living area is to be used for family recreation, it is important that fences, walls, or plantings be included to provide some privacy. Recreation may consist of gardening, either of the formal,

A deck or patio extends the living space of a home.

flower-garden type or the growing of vegetables and cut flowers. To some people, recreation implies a swimming pool. If space is limited, a decision must be made as to the size of the pool in relation to the surrounding area. Additional space will be needed for tables, chairs, and maintenance equipment.

Many people prefer to use an outdoor area—such as a patio, deck, or terrace—as a quiet, private retreat. If personal relaxation is the goal, rather than creating an area for entertaining, play, or recreation, special attention should be paid to personal preferences in design.

Whatever the purpose of an outdoor area, plantings can be very important. They serve to establish character and to provide background interest. A choice must be made among types of flowers, shrubs, and trees, and between those that need regular care and those that need little attention. Flower gardens, whether formal or informal, tend to need regular care, whereas rock gardens, cactus gardens, and flowering shrubs require little maintenance. Some people may prefer to have little permanent vegetation but rather to enjoy seasonal bloom through the use of potted and hanging plants and container gardens.

C
A
R
E
E
R

P
R
O
F
I
L
E

LANDSCAPE ARCHITECT

Landscape architects design the arrangement of structures, roads, sidewalks, trees, shrubs, and flowers for the best use and enjoyment of people. Their projects include parks, golf courses, highways, airports, shopping malls, and other commercial and residential sites. They confer with clients, engineering personnel, and architects about the overall project.

Landscape architects compile and analyze data on a site condition, such as its soil, vegetation, rock features, drainage, and the location of structures. They then prepare a site plan for the client that shows the contour of the ground, its plantings, and the location of any buildings, roads, walks, parking areas, fences, walls, and utilities. Landscape architects inspect the construction work as it progresses to be sure that it complies with the landscape specifications. They also advise homeowners on the best way to landscape the property around their home. Landscape architects supervise the actual planting of the trees, bushes, ground cover, and grass and the construction of any retaining walls.

If you are interested in becoming a landscape architect, you need the ability to visualize spatial relationships and to work with detail. You should have an interest in drafting, engineering, and mathematics, as well as in creative design. Working outdoors and supervising others should be something you enjoy. To become a landscape architect, it is necessary to take a specialized college course in landscape architecture, similar to the one an architect takes.

You could also become a landscape gardener, someone who specializes in the planning of yards and grounds of homes. Some landscape gardeners specialize in yard care, such as mowing, trimming, fertilizing, leaf removal, and weed control, and work on a regular basis throughout the year. Training for this career can be obtained through apprenticeship programs and on-the-job experience. Vocational courses can also be helpful.

Landscape architects may be employed by an architectural firm or a land development contractor. They may also be self-employed and work on a contractual basis with clients. A landscape gardener may work for a landscaping firm or become an entrepreneur, owning and operating his or her own business in the community.

REVIEWING CHAPTER 7

SUMMARY

Space needs are often an individual matter. Some people like a lot of space to move around in; others are content with a small amount of space for living. Disabled and elderly people may have special space needs to enable them to live safely and more comfortably.

The arrangement of rooms affects the total use of space as well as the flow of traffic through the rooms. In planning how space is to be used, you should consider the specific activities and interests of each person as well as the family as a whole. Often you can create an illusion of more space through the use of color, lighting, and furniture arrangement. Space can also be extended by converting unfinished attics, basements, or garages into new living areas. An outdoor area, such as a porch, patio, deck, or balcony, can add a sense of space and livability to your home.

FACTS TO KNOW

1. Identify the three activity zones of a home.
2. List 10 items to check when evaluating room layouts.
3. What are some special housing needs for a disabled or elderly person?
4. Give examples of how people need certain types of space for their personal interests and activities.
5. Explain how traffic patterns can affect safety and privacy in a home.
6. When space is limited, what are three ways to creat illusions of space?
7. Identify three indoor areas for possible use as expanded living spaces.
8. How can outdoor space be used as additional living space?

IDEAS TO THINK ABOUT

1. Analyze the flow of traffic in the floor plan on page 139. How could the layout be improved?

2. List as many ways that you can think of to extend indoor and outdoor living space. For what purposes can each space be used?
3. In relation to the space around you —such as in high places, spaces below ground, crowded spaces, and empty spaces—what experiences have you had? Describe your feelings and reactions.

ACTIVITIES TO DO

1. Draw the floor plan for a home that you would like to live in someday. Shade the social area, quiet area, and work area with different colors. Show the traffic patterns. Check the floor plan against the guidelines in this chapter. Explain what changes, if any, should be made to improve livability.
2. Cut out pictures from magazines or newspapers that illustrate one or more of the following: multipurpose rooms, ways to create an illusion of space, ideas for converting indoor space, ideas for extending living space outdoors.

Chapter 8

Work and Storage Spaces

The old-fashioned kitchen, typical of those in rural and small town homes during the early part of this century, had a character all its own. The water from a single faucet dripped rhythmically into the sink below. The fire in the big iron stove crackled. Occasionally the water in the basin under the wooden icebox overflowed and trickled silently across the floor. Many movies and books have described the old-fashioned kitchen as being the center of family life.

By the middle of the century, this scene had changed. The kitchen looked more like a hospital clinic with its white metal cabinets, streamlined white refrigerator, and electric or gas range. The introduction of laborsaving equipment and the need for more efficient storage space spurred interest in kitchen planning.

Today, kitchens can have many different looks. They can range from a small, one-wall, efficiency kitchen to a large, family-centered kitchen where members of the household can work together or pursue individual activities.

As homes become smaller, storage is being planned more efficiently. Closets for every area of the home have become standard. Other storage areas both within and outside the home, such as a basement, attic, garage, or carport, may be provided. When choosing a home, both kitchen and storage facilities should be considered carefully.

PREVIEWING YOUR LEARNING

After you have read this chapter, you will be able to:

- Evaluate the efficiency of the work triangle and work flow in different kitchen designs.

- Compare the advantages and disadvantages of various materials used for cabinets, countertops, walls, and floor coverings.

- Evaluate laundry and utility areas according to various needs.

- Plan convenient and efficient storage areas.

TERMS TO KNOW

duct—a pipe for carrying air or liquid
laminated—composed of layers bonded together
utility area—space for cleaning equipment and supplies

ventilation—the means of admitting fresh air
work triangle—the triangle formed by a kitchen's refrigerator, sink, and range

KITCHEN SPACE-SAVERS

F E A T U R E

Kitchen space is a precious commodity. Besides being an active workplace throughout the day, the kitchen must also store more goods and tools than any other room in the house. Here are some practical and attractive ways to keep things in order and make the most of the space that you have.

Good storage need not be out of sight. Attractive ceiling racks keep pots and pans out of the way and easy to find. Wall racks hold small kitchen tools and keep them within easy reach. Wire grids hung on walls organize bulky kitchen utensils in a decorative way. Wire mesh bins hung from the ceiling make great storage containers for vegetables and fruits.

Handy new "hideaways" pull out when necessary but store out of view. A spring out table–shelf folds flat against the wall or counter side until extra work space is needed. With the use of special hinges, a hideaway shelf can hold a mixer or food processor inside a cabinet and then swing out and up to counter height when needed for food preparation. Pull out racks can hold pots and pans, lids, serving dishes, and even a garbage bag.

Small appliances used to take up a lot of counter or cabinet space. Now there are coffeemakers, can openers, electric knives, toasters, and even microwave ovens that hang from the bottom of kitchen cabinets. All of these space-savers can help you keep counter areas clear and cabinets free for other storage.

PLANNING THE KITCHEN

When you are choosing a home, you should consider how well the kitchen meets your requirements. People who are renting a home or buying an existing home have to adapt their needs to the kitchen already there. People who are remodeling a kitchen in an older home or who are building a new home have more freedom in kitchen planning. Anyone making a decision about housing should have some guidelines for judging a kitchen.

The total environment of a kitchen includes many different aspects. Among these are the general plan; the layout of the work area; floor, walls, and counter surfaces; storage areas; and lighting and ventilation. Each of these aspects is important to the use of the space as a whole. Because so much activity takes place in the kitchen, good organization and easy maintenance are particularly important.

The location of the kitchen is an important factor to consider. The kitchen should have a direct connection with the dining area. It should also have its own entrance so you do not have to walk through the living area with groceries or garbage. It is also convenient to have access to the patio or yard from the kitchen.

People differ in their preferences concerning the size of a kitchen. Some people like a small, streamlined kitchen where food preparation can be done very efficiently. Others prefer a multipurpose kitchen so that they may combine food preparation with other activities, such as laundry work, sewing, raising plants, working on hobbies, or pursuing special interests. Many people like to have enough space in the kitchen for informal family meals. Some want to have a small planning area with a telephone, a desk, and a shelf for books. Whether the kitchen is large or small, it should be a cheerful place in which to work, eat, or carry on other kinds of activities.

Families with young children may have special requirements for the kitchen. It should be possible to supervise an indoor and an outdoor play area from the kitchen. It may even be desirable to fence off a play area in the kitchen for a few years. Later, the space can be used for an eating area or an activity center.

An eating area for the family, plus a small desk for planning, adds greatly to a kitchen's efficiency.

The Work Triangle

The major work area of a kitchen is usually planned around three major appliances —refrigerator, sink, and range. Each appliance is related to a major function in food preparation: the refrigerator, to storing and mixing; the sink, to preparation and clean-up; and the range, to cooking. Together these appliances and the surface areas near them form the work triangle.

The layout of this triangle is important to its efficiency and its convenience as a work area. Kitchen engineers recommend that the sink be between the range and the refrigerator for the greatest efficiency. It is usually desirable to have the sink and the range on the same wall or on adjacent walls, because most activity for food preparation takes place between or near those two areas. A wall oven may be placed outside the work triangle because it is used less frequently than the burner surface. If there is a dishwasher, it should adjoin the sink; the side of the sink it is located on depends upon the space available and the direction of the work flow. Several feet of uninterrupted work space is needed between major appliances.

The dimensions of the triangle, as well as the layout, affect its efficiency as a work area. As a rule, the sum of the sides of the work triangle should not be smaller than 15 feet (4.9 m) or larger than 22 feet (6.7 m). In a large kitchen, the sum may be increased to 26 feet (7.9 m).

Basic Plans for Work Areas

Kitchen work areas are usually laid out in one of four basic designs. These are the one-wall, two-wall, L-shaped, and U-shaped designs. Variations of these basic designs are made with the addition of a peninsula or an island. Each type of kitchen layout has its own advantages and limitations.

One-wall kitchens The one-wall, or panel, kitchen provides an efficient work area in a small apartment or in a home with limited space. For maximum efficiency in this kitchen, the sink should be placed between the range and the refrigerator, with counter space on both sides for stacking dishes. Some studio apartments have compact, self-contained units with a cooking surface, undercounter refrigerator, sink, small oven, and wall cabinets.

Two-wall kitchens The two-wall, or corridor, kitchen is an efficient design. It provides the maximum amount of undercounter storage space for its size. However, if the kitchen has an outside door at one end and a door to the dining area or family room at the other end, traffic through the work area may become a problem. To reduce hazards and increase working efficiency in a corridor kitchen, the sink and range should be placed on the same wall. Counter space is necessary on each side of the sink and range for a work area or a place to stack dishes and cooking utensils. A kitchen 8 feet by 8 feet (2.44 m × 2.44 m) is the smallest area that will accommodate a two-wall layout comfortably.

L-shaped kitchens The L-shaped, or corner, kitchen is an efficient design because work areas are uninterrupted by traffic. In this kitchen, two adjacent walls are taken up by cabinets and appliances; the other two walls are free for doors and windows, a cleaning closet, and an area for eating. An L-shaped kitchen may include a peninsula for extra work and storage space.

U-shaped kitchens The U-shaped, or two-corner, kitchen is popular because it is compact, step-saving, and usually free of cross traffic. The sink should be placed at the inside or center of the U, at least 12 inches (30.48 cm) or 15 inches (38.10 cm) from each corner. The range should be near the dining room, and the refrigerator near the rear entrance.

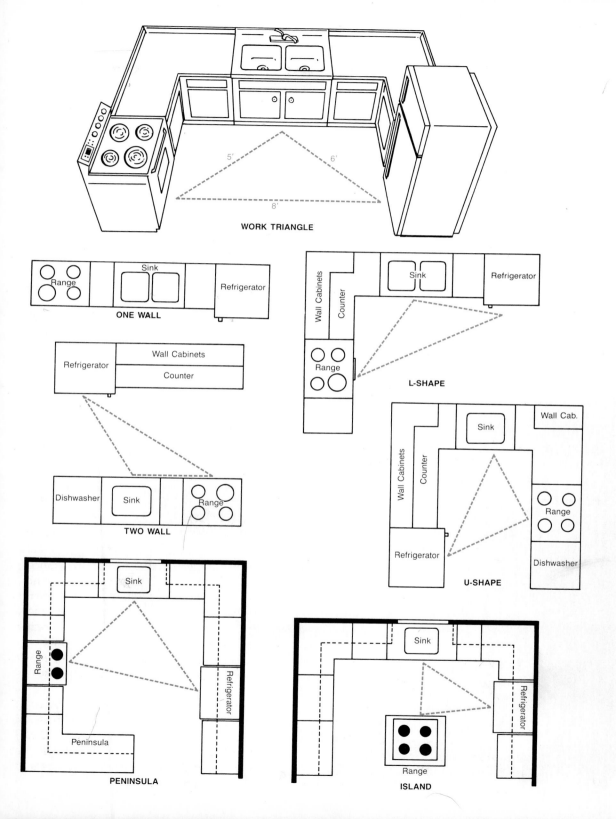

153

WORK TRIANGLE

5'

6'

8'

ONE WALL

Range

Sink

Refrigerator

L-SHAPE

Wall Cabinets

Counter

Sink

Refrigerator

Range

Refrigerator

Wall Cabinets

Counter

TWO WALL

Dishwasher

Sink

Range

U-SHAPE

Wall Cabinets

Counter

Sink

Wall Cab.

Range

Dishwasher

Refrigerator

PENINSULA

Sink

Range

Peninsula

Refrigerator

ISLAND

Sink

Range

Refrigerator

Variations in layouts If the kitchen area is large, a peninsula or an island may be included in the layout to provide additional undercounter storage and counter space for working or for eating. A peninsula is often used as part of a U-shaped kitchen. It may also serve as a divider between the kitchen and the dining area. Wall cabinets may be suspended from the ceiling over the peninsula, leaving enough room for a pass-through between the suspended cabinets and the counter top.

Large kitchens may sometimes contain an island as part of the work area. Sometimes the island contains a sink or range and is permanently installed. In some kitchens the island may be movable and used only for mixing and serving, as well as storage. Often, there is a counter for eating on one side of an island.

Layouts for special needs People who use wheelchairs or who must sit down while working often prefer a one-wall or L-shaped kitchen. Cabinets under the cooking surface and sink should be eliminated so that the person can pull up close to the work area. If the kitchen is L-shaped, an island or peninsula can be added to provide more undercounter storage space.

The Kitchen Environment

Color scheme, materials, and types of surfaces affect the appearance of the kitchen. If there is little or no natural light in the kitchen, it may be advisable to use light colors on the floor, walls, ceiling, and other surfaces. Since light colors reflect light, whereas dark colors absorb it, the use of light background colors reduces the need for artificial light.

The island provides a fifth type of kitchen layout. An island can provide storage space as well as a work and counter area.

Lighting and ventilation All kitchens require good general lighting as well as lighting over work centers. In large kitchens, windows can be a pleasant feature of the environment. In small kitchens, the need for storage cabinets may reduce the amount of wall area available for windows. Although it is desirable to have a window over the work area, it may be preferable to have windows near the table, if a choice must be made.

Few kitchens, even those in older homes with large windows, provide enough natural light. Overhead lighting, such as ceiling fixtures, fluorescent panels, or a luminous ceiling provide general lighting for the whole room. Fluorescent lights over the sink and under wall cabinets in work areas make tasks more enjoyable. A range usually has a light over the burners and in the oven.

Good ventilation is necessary in the kitchen, not only for comfort but also for controlling air pollution. An exhaust fan or a range hood with a duct will quickly remove cooking odors and smoke. Some ranges and cooking tops have special down-draft exhaust fans built right into them. In homes where outside ducts are difficult to install, a nonducted hood with activated charcoal or chemical filters may be used. These filters are easy to change and should be cleaned or replaced according to directions. If ventilation is poor, it may be possible to install either a wall or ceiling exhaust fan near the range.

Cabinets Kitchen cabinets come in a wide variety of materials: metal; solid wood, plywood, or particle board; and sheet plastic laminated to plywood. Solid-wood and plywood cabinets are available in natural wood grain, or they may be painted. Particle-board cabinets are less expensive than wood or plywood ones. Many people prefer any type of wood cabinet to metal ones because metal scratches more easily and may chip or rust.

This one-wall kitchen with an undercounter refrigerator is suitable for an efficiency apartment. The hood over the range conceals both the ventilation unit and artificial lighting. The pegboard helps to maximize storage space.

Kitchen cabinets can be factory-built or custom-made. Factory-made units come in stock sizes and a wide choice of finishes and styles. Base cabinets are 24 inches (60.96 cm) deep and 36 inches (91.44 cm) high. They are available with drawers, set-in shelves, or pull-out shelves. Wall cabinets are 12 or 15 inches (30.48 or 38.10 cm) deep and have doors. More expensive wood cabinets often have special hardware and paneling. Custom-made cabinets are built to exact specifications and are installed by skilled cabinetmakers.

When you are choosing kitchen cabinets, some features to look for are magnetic door closers, and drawers that operate smoothly on rollers without going off balance. If shelves inside cabinets pull out, they should be firm enough to hold large pans and roasters, together with small appliances. Drawers may be compartmented

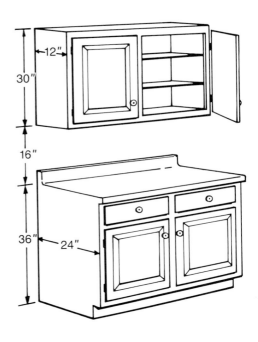

Kitchen cabinets are available in a wide variety of materials. Special features can be selected for specific storage needs. The countertops and floor can be chosen to complement the cabinets.

for cultery, flatware, and mixing and measuring supplies; bins may be provided for bread and cake, vegetables, sugar and flour; pull-out shelves may be provided for cutting and chopping, and pull-out racks for dish towels; doors may be equipped with small bins or racks for spices, or they may conceal a wastebasket or trash compactor. Basic cabinets and drawers may also be individually equipped with storage organizers available at department and hardware stores.

Walls Semigloss paint and vinyl or vinyl-coated wallpaper are the most popular wall finishes for kitchens. Other finishes, for one or more walls of the kitchen, include ceramic tile, laminated plastic, cork, brick, and wood paneling.

Floor coverings Resilient floor coverings, such as sheet vinyl and vinyl tiles, are the most popular choices for kitchen floors. These materials are easy to maintain, durable, and resistant to grease and stains. They are available in a wide variety of colors and patterns.

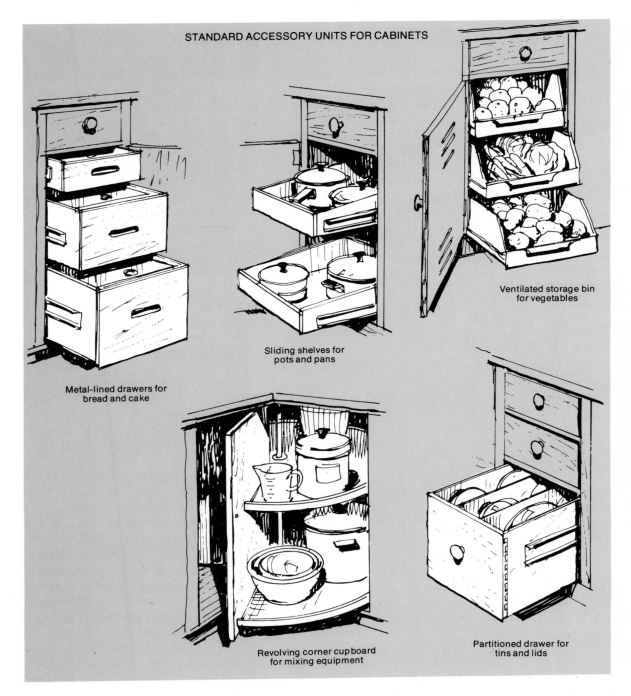

STANDARD ACCESSORY UNITS FOR CABINETS

Metal-lined drawers for bread and cake

Sliding shelves for pots and pans

Ventilated storage bin for vegetables

Revolving corner cupboard for mixing equipment

Partitioned drawer for tins and lids

Base cabinets are designed with a variety of accessory units to meet different storage needs. What purpose does each of these units serve? What other types of undercounter storage might be needed? A variety of options are available, though each addition increases the cost.

Resilient floor coverings are available in squares 12 inches by 12 inches (30.48 cm × 30.48 cm) or 9 inches by 9 inches (22.86 cm × 22.86 cm), and in rolls 6 or 12 feet (1.82 or 3.66 m) wide. Rolls make a good floor covering because there are few or no seams. However, installing rolls of floor covering is not easy for the do-it-yourself person. Also, if an area of a wall-to-wall installation becomes damaged, it cannot be repaired, whereas individual tiles can be replaced if they are damaged. Vinyl floor tiles are flexible and may be cut with large shears or a special cutting knife. There are many choices—even some with a peel-off backing, making installation fast, easy, and clean. It is always wise to keep a

Vinyl flooring and laminated plastic counter tops are easy to clean, durable, and resistant to stains.

few extra matching tiles on hand as replacements, in case of damage. Reinforced vinyl tile is less expensive than solid vinyl.

Some vinyls have a foam cushioning to lessen fatigue and reduce noise. Most vinyls with a shiny appearance are now made with no-wax finishes. While this finish remains glossy for some time, the shine will eventually wear off and need to be replaced. Transparent acrylic floor finishes, made for no-wax floors, can be applied as necessary.

Ceramic tile, quarry tile, brick, and stone are often used for kitchen floors. They may be utilized to create a natural look. Since these surfaces do not absorb shock, they have the disadvantage of increasing human fatigue. These materials are also expensive. Resilient floor coverings that simulate these natural materials are available at lower cost.

Carpeting made especially for kitchens is attractive, quiet, and soft to walk on. Despite these good characteristics, kitchen carpeting is not recommended. It stains badly, is difficult to clean, and may hold bacteria and other micro-organisms that can contaminate food and infect family members.

Counter surfaces Of the many types of countertops available, laminated plastic surfaces are the most popular and practical. A laminated surface is resistant to stains, heat, and wear. However, placing hot pans on it will damage it permanently, and the entire surface may have to be replaced. A high-density solid plastic material that looks like marble is also available. It is extremely stain resistant and easy to keep clean. Butcher-block counters are made of hardwood strips glued together. Hot pans can scorch the surface but butcher block can be sanded down and refinished. Another desirable type of counter surface is ceramic tile, which is attractive, durable, and heat-resistant. However, it is

KITCHEN SURFACE MATERIALS

SURFACE	MATERIALS	ADVANTAGES	DISADVANTAGES
Walls	Paint	Inexpensive, easy to apply; has wide color choice. High-gloss or semigloss, oil base enamel gives durability and easy maintenance.	Choice of textures limited. If a poor quality or a flat latex paint is used, maintenance is difficult.
	Wallpaper	Adds interest, establishes a color scheme; gives wide range of choices. A vinyl-coated scrubbable surface is recommended.	More expensive than paint; may be more difficult for the amateur to apply.
	Ceramic tile	Resistant to grease, acid, and scratches; easy to keep clean.	Choice of colors more limited than paint or wallpaper. Expensive, reflects more noise than paint or wallpaper.
Floors	Resilient coverings—vinyl sheets and tiles	Vinyl-coated resilient floor coverings are the most popular choices, especially if they have a cushioned backing to reduce fatigue. Wide choice of colors and patterns; easy to maintain.	Pure vinyl, rubber, and cork are expensive. Cork, unless it has a vinyl surface, absorbs grease, acids, and soil.
	Carpet	Comfortable underfoot.	Shows stains; difficult to maintain and clean.
Counters	Plastic laminates	Wide choice of colors and patterns; easy to maintain; complement a color scheme. Pattern surfaces show marks less than plain surfaces do.	Damaged if extremely hot pans are lifted from range to surface. Show cuts and stains, though most stains can be removed with chlorine bleach.
	Ceramic tile	Fairly wide choice of colors and designs; nonabsorbent and scratch-resistant.	Noisy; glassware and dinnerware shatter if dropped. Dirt accumulates in cracks. Surface not smooth.
	Butcher block	Ideal cutting surface as an insert. When used on countertops, can have a laminated surface.	Shows burns, stains, and cuts. Plastic laminate finish provides some protection.
	Metal	Moisture- and heat-resistant.	Adds nothing to color scheme. Noisy; shows scratches. Used more in institution and restaurant kitchens.

noisy as a work surface and so hard that if glassware or china is accidentally dropped on it, the item will shatter. Tile also does not provide the kind of smooth surface that can be wiped off easily and that most people prefer to work on. The grout between tiles requires special cleaning, since dirt and grease tend to accumulate there.

Ceramic glass makes a good insert material near the range because it is heatproof and provides a smooth work surface. Stainless steel counter surfaces are good to work on, too, and easy to maintain. Because of their high cost, stainless steel counters are more often used commercially than in the home. The table on page 159 evaluates various materials.

Kitchen Storage

Food, utensils, and portable appliances should be stored near the place of use. Organizing storage according to the tasks performed at the different areas will save time and energy and provide efficiency.

KITCHEN STORAGE AREAS

SINK CENTER: Food Preparation and Clean-up

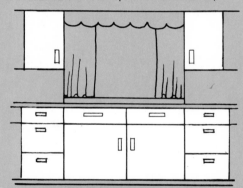

STORAGE: Detergents, cleansers; paper and cloth towels, dishcloths and sponges; drainer for dishes, and dishpan; strainers, brushes; disposal for food waste.

RANGE CENTER: Surface Cooking and Oven Use

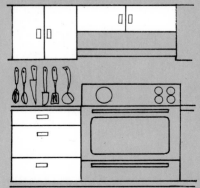

STORAGE: Pots, pans, frying pans, lids, stirring spoons, spatula, cake turner; tea, coffee; pot holders.

MIXING CENTER: Food Preparation and Mixing

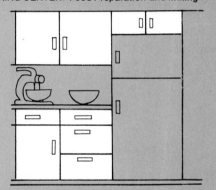

STORAGE: Mixer, blender, juicer, hand beater; mixing bowls and spoons, measuring cups and spoons, sifter; pans for cakes, pies, and bread; casseroles; spices, flavorings, sugar, flour.

SERVICE CENTER: Near Dining Area or Kitchen Table

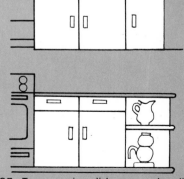

STORAGE: Trays, serving dishes; everyday dishes, flatware, and glassware; toaster, waffle iron; pitchers, teapots, and coffee pots.

A kitchen needs convenient and adequate storage space for dishes, cooking utensils, and food supplies.

PLANNING LAUNDRY AND UTILITY AREAS

The laundry area and the utility area (for cleaning equipment and supplies) are both important to the management and maintenance of the home. Each of these areas requires space for equipment and for storage. A laundry area should, if possible, have space for sorting and folding clothes, as well as a rack for drying items washed by hand.

The Laundry Area

The type of housing and amount of space available influence the kind and arrangement of laundry equipment. Some apartment buildings provide a common laundry center or facilities on each floor. Town houses may provide a small laundry area in the kitchen. In a single-family home, the laundry may be in the kitchen, basement, or utility room. Wherever space is limited, it may be desirable to have an apartment-sized unit, in which the washer is stacked above the dryer.

Even when there is a choice of laundry locations, people often have different preferences. A laundry in the kitchen may cause objectionable odors, moisture, and lint. However, that may be the most convenient location for a family with small children. A laundry in the bathroom may be convenient for a one-person household; for a family, it may interfere with the other uses of the room. A basement laundry involves many trips up and down stairs, even if there is a laundry chute from the floors above.

The placement of water, gas, and electrical outlets also affects the location of a laundry area. A washer requires access to hot and cold water and a drain. A dryer may require special electrical wiring and

A well-planned laundry area should include storage space for laundry supplies and space for sorting and folding clothes.

the venting of steam. Because of these limitations, together with lack of space, some people may prefer to use either the common facilities provided in multi-unit housing or low-cost public launderettes.

The Utility Area

Because care and maintenance are necessary activities in the home, an area should be set aside for cleaning equipment and supplies. These may include a vacuum cleaner; broom, dry mop, dustpan and brush; wet mop, sponges, and bucket; soap, detergents, and other cleaning supplies; and simple tools, such as a hammer and a screwdriver.

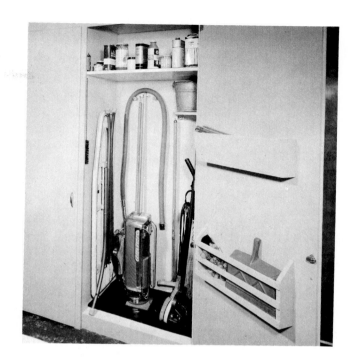

What design features in this utility closet add to its use? Where might storage of this type be located?

GENERAL AREA STORAGE NEEDS	
Entrance and Living Areas: Living Room, Family Room, and Study	**Dining Area:** or Combination Dining and Study Area

outer garments
umbrellas, boots (unless stored elsewhere)
television, video cassette recorder
card tables, folding chairs, games
books, magazines, writing supplies
stereo, cassettes, music, musical instruments
cameras, projector, screen, slides, and film
sports equipment for seasonal sports
	dishes and serving dishes used in area
	table cloths, table mats, napkins
	flatware and glassware used in the area
	flower containers, candle holders
	serving trays, if not stored in kitchen
	reading and writing materials if area also
	   serves as a study area
	hobby materials if area serves as a hobby
	   center

Bedrooms	**Bathroom and Linen Closet***

in-season and out-of-season clothing
underwear, sleepwear, and stockings
accessories and jewelry
purses, belts, ties, shoes
grooming aids and toiletries, unless stored in
   bathroom
reading materials
luggage
	sheets, pillowcases, blankets
	bath towels, hand towels, washcloths
	soap and cleaning agents
	toilet paper and cleansing tissue
	hamper for soiled clothing
	heating pad, ice bag
	shaving and grooming items if used in bathroom
	medicines (for which a cabinet is usually
	   built-in)

*If a linen closet is not provided, a storage cabinet can be bought or bedroom drawers used for sheets, pillowcases, and bath towels. Adjustable floor-to-ceiling shelves can be bought for open-shelf storage over the toilet.

A number of places are suitable as a utility area. In an apartment, this area may be a small closet. In many homes, the kitchen includes a separate closet for cleaning supplies and equipment. Larger homes may have a utility room near the kitchen. Such a room might include space for work clothes and children's outdoor play clothes and boots. A convenient location adds to the usefulness of equipment and supplies. In a two-story house, it is preferable to keep additional cleaning equipment on the second floor. In or near the laundry area, a small cabinet or shelves are needed for laundry supplies. Basements are less desirable than the first floor for the storage of household items in frequent use. Garages usually provide space for the tools and equipment needed for general maintenance and repair and for outdoor work.

What different types of storage are shown here? In what other ways might this storage space be used?

PLANNING STORAGE FOR PARTICULAR AREAS

As the size of the average home has decreased, the need for efficient storage space has increased. Most new houses and apartments have closets near the entrance, in bedrooms, in or near bathrooms, and in kitchens. Built-in units can provide additional convenience. However, too many built-ins can hinder the flexible use of space in living areas by limiting the placement of furniture and accessories. If built-in storage units are to be added, they should harmonize with the architecture of the room and the style of the furniture and decoration.

This linen closet could be built as a do-it-yourself project. What other storage needs could it meet?

Each area of the home has particular storage needs, depending on the activities there. The general storage requirements for major areas of the home are indicated on page 163. Specific needs will vary with the number and ages of people in the home and with their lifestyles and interests.

Organizing Storage

Well-organized storage is important to pleasant and convenient living. Did you ever get off to a bad start in the morning because you could not easily find your notebook, pen, or keys, and thus become late for school? The expression "a place for everything, and everything in its place" may sound trite, but following that rule helps you to save time and avoid hunting for things you need.

Determining what your storage needs are and then providing the necessary facilities will simplify your living and free you from unnecessary frustration. Here are a few suggestions for better organization, once you have provided enough space in the appropriate areas:

— Make better use of the space you have by putting things away carefully and keeping your possessions in good order.

— Take time out to sort through closets, drawers, and other storage areas. Give away items you have not used for a long time. Arrange remaining items neatly, so that you can find them easily and put them back in place.

— Visit a hardware store or the notions section of a large department store and buy closet organizers, such as hangers, garment bags, and racks for shoes and belts. Study drawer and door organizers as well, for bedrooms, kitchens, and bathrooms. Also visit the bath department for additional storage ideas. Send for mail-order catalogs and study the storage ideas illustrated. Notice the storage units pictured in magazines or described in books.

— Convert unused space in your home for storage. Analyze your space to see where drawers, racks, and shelves might be added.

Types of Storage Units

Storage units and components are available for every storage need. What you choose depends upon your storage needs, the space available, and what you can afford to pay. Alone or in combination, the storage units shown on the chart can supplement existing storage and contribute to good home management.

TYPES OF STORAGE UNITS		
Freestanding	**Portable**	**Modular or Wall Systems**
display cabinets	bins and boxes	upper bookcases
chests of drawers	baskets and bags	lower chests
hutches	metal wall racks	open upper shelves
bookcases or shelves	hampers	dressing tables
filing cabinets	trunks	desks
buffets	low chests	entertainment center
dressers	small filing cabinets	pull-out typewriter and
room dividers		sewing tables
computer table		home office area

A KITCHEN PLANNER

With kitchens being one of the most expensive rooms in the home to install or remodel, many people are turning to experts for help. Kitchen planners design the interiors of kitchens based on the needs and preferences of their clients. First, they meet with a client to discuss the proposed project, such as the layout, types of cabinets, major appliances, special design features, and total budget. Then the kitchen planners sketch a plan of the new kitchen arrangement, select samples of materials to be used, and estimate costs for the project. The plans are then presented to the client for approval.

The responsibility of kitchen planners may include the selection and purchase of the appliances, according to the client's specifications. They may also select and purchase other materials, such as the floor coverings, ceiling materials, wall coverings, curtain materials, and lighting fixtures. Planners oversee the installation of the new kitchen. They may direct the plumbers, electricians, painters, and flooring installers who are involved in the project. Sometimes clients may decide to purchase and install many of these materials themselves.

If you are interested in becoming a kitchen planner, you should have an interest in art and design. You also need to be able to get along well with people and to communicate your ideas to them.

One way to become a kitchen planner is to obtain a degree in interior design from a college or art school. You can also become a certified kitchen planner after you have had seven years of experience in kitchen design. The certification may be obtained by passing a written exam based on the kitchen industry's technical manual. The exam is given by the American Institute of Kitchen Dealers. You must provide affidavits of professional competence, consumer references, and work experience, along with samples of your work, in order to take the exam. It would also be helpful to take courses in design from a vocational or technical school.

A kitchen planner may be employed by a kitchen design firm, a kitchen cabinet manufacturer, a floor covering manufacturer, or an appliance manufacturer or store. A planner may also be self-employed.

REVIEWING CHAPTER 8

SUMMARY

Today a kitchen may be a center not only for preparing food but for a wide range of activities. The major work area of a kitchen is the triangle formed by the refrigerator, sink and range. Kitchens are designed in a variety of layouts including the one-wall, two-wall, L-shaped, and U-shaped. Variations include the island and peninsula designs.

A kitchen should provide good lighting and ventilation. Work surfaces and floors should be easy to maintain. Cabinets, countertops, walls, and floor coverings are available in a wide choice of materials.

The laundry and utility areas of a home should have space for equipment and storage. These areas may be in separate rooms or combined with other work areas, such as the kitchen. Well organized storage is important to any home. Chests, built-ins, and other organizers provide added storage space.

FACTS TO KNOW

1. What three pieces of equipment determine the work triangle? What is the maximum recommended size of the triangle?

2. Identify the four basic kitchen designs. What are the advantages and disadvantages of each?

3. In what ways may a peninsula or island be used in a kitchen?

4. List six ways that basic cabinets and drawers can be designed for special storage needs.

5. What important factors should be considered when evaluating different materials for walls, floors, and counters in a kitchen?

6. Describe three ways of including a laundry area in the home.

7. What items are usually stored in a utility area? Identify several alternate locations for this area.

8. Select one area of the home and describe in detail the items likely to be stored there and the type of storage they require.

IDEAS TO THINK ABOUT

1. Explain how the design of a kitchen can affect home management. How do different kitchen designs reflect today's lifestyles?

2. What special requirements might a disabled or elderly person need in the kitchen, laundry, utility, and storage areas of a home?

3. How can additional storage areas be created in an apartment?

ACTIVITIES TO DO

1. Draw the layout of an actual kitchen with which you are familiar. Draw a second plan to show the room remodeled for greater convenience and efficiency.

2. Visit a hardware store or department store and look at different types of storage units and organizers. Gather information about their size and price. Design one or more new storage areas for your room at home. List what you would need to purchase and the total cost of the project.

Chapter 9

Comfort, Conservation, and Safety

Flip a switch, turn a faucet, or adjust a thermostat. These simple, daily routines that provide you almost instantaneously with light, water, and heat would have astounded your ancestors a century ago. In less than a hundred years, technology has transformed the home into a controlled living environment filled with comforts and conveniences.

In recent years, however, the increased demand for natural resources has raised important and serious concerns regarding the issue of energy conservation. Worldwide resources, especially fuels, have become more scarce as needs and costs have risen. Our nation, with only 6 percent of the world's people, consumes 30 percent of the energy used in the world each year.

Through your conscious efforts and wise decisions, you can make a big difference. By learning to conserve resources, you can personally save money and protect your standard of living. And best of all, you can preserve resources for future generations.

Safety and security are other concerns that face individuals and families in their homes. Long gone are the days when homes were left unlocked. Today, each person must be aware of the need for safety and security measures wherever he or she may live.

PREVIEWING YOUR LEARNING

After you have read this chapter, you will be able to:

- Identify basic electrical and plumbing systems.

- Evaluate various heating and cooling systems.

- Describe specific methods for conserving energy and other resources.

- Take steps to improve safety and security within a home.

TERMS TO KNOW

acoustical—having to do with sound

circuit—the path through which an electric current flows

circuit breaker—a switch that automatically interrupts an electric circuit when an abnormal situation occurs

conductor—a substance that transmits electricity, heat, or sound

decibel—a unit for measuring sound

fuse—an electrical safety device that includes a strip of fusible metal that melts and interrupts the circuit when the current exceeds a certain level

kilowatt—1000 watts

outlets—points in an electrical system where electrical cords may be plugged in

thermostat—an automatic device for regulating temperature

voltage—electrical potential expressed in volts

wattage—unit of power expressed in watts

AIR POLLUTION IN THE HOME

FEATURE

Homes today are more airtight and better insulated than ever before. As a result, the air in a home tends to linger and become stale and polluted by toxic substances found in nearly every home. Asbestos and formaldehyde are two common home air pollutants that can cause serious health problems.

For many years, asbestos was a common building material. Asbestos blankets were used to insulate steam and hot water pipes. Asbestos insulation was used in ceilings and walls. Certain joint compounds, textured paint, and ceiling finishes contain asbestos, as well as flooring materials. Asbestos is harmful when its fibers are inhaled and become lodged in the lungs. This can lead to various lung diseases. The dangerous fibers can become airborne when sanding and scraping during renovation or simply by natural surface deterioration. If a hazardous condition exists in a home, professional asbestos removal contractors, using specialized equipment, must be employed. Asbestos surfaces that are still intact can be covered, sealed, or painted to stop any potential danger.

Formaldehyde is often used in manufacturing many goods found in the home. Plywood, particle board, permanent press clothing, draperies, and carpeting all contain formaldehyde in varying degrees. Health hazards occur when formaldehyde evaporates because harmful fumes are produced. These fumes can cause respiratory irritation, headaches, or an excess number of colds. By using building materials with low formaldehyde content and sealing existing surfaces with waterproof paint, dangerous emissions may be checked. Windows of newly carpeted or draped rooms should be kept open for several weeks to allow hazardous fumes to escape.

WIRING AND ELECTRICAL NEEDS

Electrical and plumbing systems are both essential in homes: there are no real alternatives to running water and electric power. These basic systems tend to be alike everywhere, because they are made up of standard components. They differ in that way from heating and cooling systems, of which many different types are available. In looking at homes, you should notice the condition of the eletrical and plumbing systems, as well as their suitability for your needs.

Electricity is a basic support system in the home. In addition to light, it provides the power for most appliances throughout the home. The wiring in all homes is subject to building code regulations. Newer homes are more likely to have adequate wiring, although there is always a danger from overloaded circuits. The major problems in wiring are likely to occur in older structures, where the wiring may be worn or unable to carry the heavy load of today's many appliances. In such a case, it may be necessary to install new wiring or to add more circuits and outlets.

Wiring systems The diagram on this page shows the major parts of a home wiring system. Three service wires, or power conductors, connected to the local utility line reach the house from either overhead or underground. They come together at a servicehead and are funneled through a hollow tube to the meter and service-equipment panel. A conductor connects the wiring system with a grounding rod, such as a cold-water pipe, that acts as a safety device in preventing fire or electrical shock. Every wiring system has a main switch which turns on and shuts off all the power. Any time that electrical work is being done, this switch should be disconnected to shut off the flow of current into the house.

The wiring system within a home is made up of circuits. A circuit consists of two or more wires carrying the flow of electricity from the supply source to the outlet and back. The main types of circuits are general-purpose circuits for lights and

Every house requires certain public services, such as overhead or underground electric and telephone wires; water, gas, and sewer lines; and perhaps a storm sewer to drain off surface water.

SERVICE CONNECTIONS TO HOUSE

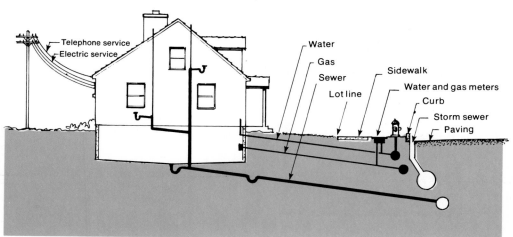

- Telephone service
- Electric service
- Water
- Gas
- Sewer
- Sidewalk
- Lot line
- Water and gas meters
- Curb
- Storm sewer
- Paving

SERVICE ENTRANCE EQUIPMENT

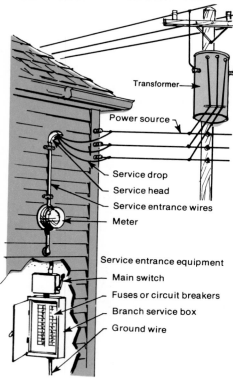

A variety of connectors are needed to link utility lines and pipes with a house.

PLACEMENT OF OUTLETS AND SWITCHES

wall outlets, small appliance circuits which provide power for portable appliances used in the kitchen and other work areas, and special purpose circuits for more powerful appliances such as electric ranges, dishwashers, dryers, and water heaters. General-purpose and small appliance circuits operate on 120 volts of electricity. Special purpose circuits require 240 volts.

Outlets are another part of the electrical system in the home. Outlets are points in the system where lamps and appliances may be plugged in. Double outlets are more convenient than single ones. Special outlets are required for ranges, dryers, and some other major appliances.

Outlets should be located at convenient places in all rooms in the house. It should not be necessary to move furniture or to string electrical cords together to reach an outlet. The National Electrical Code requires that bathroom switches and outlets be out of reach of bathtubs and showers, since contact with electricity while a person is standing in water may cause a severe shock or even death. All appliance outlets in damp areas should be grounded to prevent shock or fire. Outlets such as those on a patio are designed with covers that are kept closed except during use.

Light switches are also a part of the electrical system. The following guidelines will help you to evaluate the choice and placement of switches:

— All switches should be located on the latch side of the door for convenience.
— Switches should be placed so it is possible to light an area before you enter it. It should be possible to turn these lights off elsewhere without retracing your steps.

This living room floor plan shows a typical placement of outlets. Are these outlets conveniently located? The wall switches next to the doors turn on the desk lamp. In what ways is this a safety feature?

— Two-way switches should be located at both the top and bottom of stairs, at each door in a bathroom if it serves two bedrooms, and at kitchen and garage doors.

— Pull-chain switches may be used in closets, storage areas, and other seldom-used areas.

— Weatherproof outlets and extension cords should be used outdoors.

— "Dimmer" switches are a pleasant feature in areas where you might want to control the lighting, such as in dining areas and hallways.

— If you expect to be away from home frequently at night, set up a clock with an automatic switch device to turn lights on and off in certain areas of the house.

Safety regulations and precautions

The wiring system of the home should conform to the requirements of the National Electrical Code, local building codes, and the standards of the utility company providing the power. Among the requirements of the National Electrical Code are the grounding of outlets in damp areas and the proper location of bathroom switches. All electrical supplies should bear the UL label of the Underwriters Laboratory, a nonprofit organization sponsored by the National Board of Fire Underwriters.

Electrical systems contain a number of automatic protective devices or warning signals. When a circuit is overloaded, a fuse or circuit breaker will cut off the current. Fuses, which usually screw in like light bulbs, may have a 15-, 20-, or 30-ampere capacity. Higher "amp" fuses are for appliances like ranges or washing machines. If you have occasion to replace a blown fuse, make sure that it has the proper ampere capacity.

PREVENT ELECTRICAL ACCIDENTS

Severe shocks and burns can be obtained from electrical outlets, cords, and appliances that are used incorrectly. To prevent such accidents, follow these guidelines:

☐ Check electrical cords for broken insulation or plugs. If damaged, do not use until repaired.

☐ Do not overload outlets with too many plugs.

☐ If small children are in the family, cover outlets with safety caps.

☐ Never use electrical appliances if you are standing in water or have wet hands.

☐ Remove cords from outlets by pulling on the plug, never on the cord itself.

☐ When using appliances with detachable cords, first connect the cord to the appliance and then plug the cord into the outlet. When disconnecting the cord, remove the plug from the outlet and then disconnect the cord from the appliance.

☐ Never insert a metal object, such as a fork, inside an electrical appliance while it is connected.

☐ Always disconnect appliances before cleaning them.

☐ Use only heavy-duty extension cords with large appliances and power tools.

☐ When changing a fuse, be sure to first turn off the main power supply and stand on a dry surface.

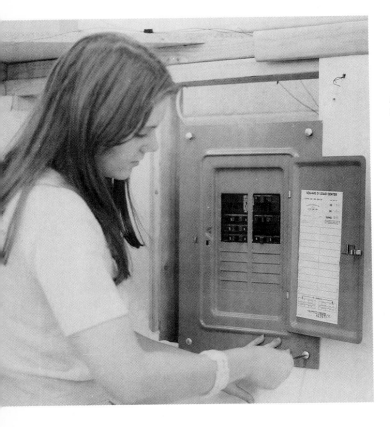

A circuit breaker can be easily reset by pressing a button or pushing a handle.

Circuit breakers, either push-button or handle type, are safer and more satisfactory than fuses. Circuit breakers, like fuses, are chosen according to the power needed. When a circuit is temporarily overloaded, the circuit breaker is activated. To restore power, a person needs only to press a button or push a handle. If the same fuse or circuit breaker continues to interrupt current, it may be necessary to add another branch circuit to the system in order to prevent overloading.

If there is too much strain on the power, certain warning signals will occur even before a fuse or circuit breaker shuts off the current. The lights will dim or the television picture will fluctuate when a major appliance, such as a toaster, mixer, or vacuum cleaner, is in use. People often add more lights and appliances without realizing how much more power is needed. The warning signals just mentioned should alert you to consult your power company—or your landlord, if you are renting—about the adequacy of your electrical system.

Conserving energy As a consumer, you should be aware of how much electric power your home uses, how much that power costs, and how you can reduce the consumption. Electricity is measured in watts, or units of power. The number of watts an appliance uses is indicated on it, just as it is on light bulbs. If a house or apartment is heated or cooled by electricity, this accounts for 70% of the cost. A water heater accounts for about 20 percent of cost. The other 10 percent covers lighting, food preparation, and use of appliances.

The water heater uses a surprising amount of energy because it is in constant use. A 40-gallon (152-l) heater is the minimum size recommended for a family of four. Two adults and two children use a minimum of 70 gallons (266 l) of heated water a day for all needs.

Appliances such as room air conditioners, ranges, refrigerators, freezers, and dryers are next to water heaters in consumption of electricity. Refrigerators and freezers have a low wattage in comparison with such items as clothes dryers, ranges, and dishwashers, but their total use of electricity is high because they run almost all the time.

Most large electric appliances have labels that rate either their energy efficiency ratios (EER) or the comparative cost to operate the appliance at a set electric rate. The higher the EER, the more efficient the appliance, and the lower the operating costs.

The following suggestions can reduce the energy consumption of appliances:

— In cooking, reduce the heat of a surface unit as soon as the contents of a utensil are hot. Keep the utensil tightly covered until the food is cooked. Be sure that pans have flat bottoms for maximum heating of the utensil and minimum loss of heat to the kitchen.

— Keep heat reflector pans clean. Replace them if they are beyond cleaning.

— Preheat the oven no longer than five minutes. Use the oven for several items at a time whenever possible. Prepare double quantities and freeze the extra servings for future use.

— To avoid opening the refrigerator, remove and replace several items at a time. Do not overcrowd the refrigerator, since efficient operation requires circulation of air.

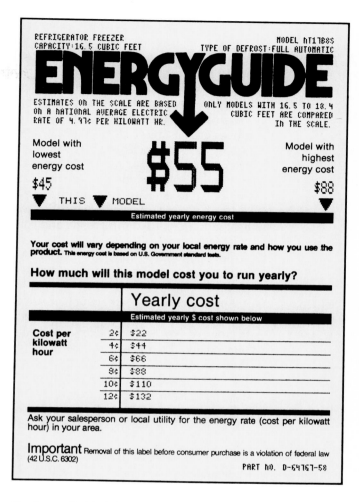

The EnergyGuide label contains information about the energy costs for a specific appliance model.

— Open the freezer only when necessary. Freezers function best when relatively full. Avoid placing the refrigerator or freezer near a range or sunny window.

— Clean the coils and back of the refrigerator and freezer, as well as the space underneath, at least twice a year. Wipe the rubber gaskets inside the refrigerator and freezer doors regularly. Replace them when they become worn.

— Keep the filters in the washer and dryer free of lint to decrease drying time. Use a rack or hangers to dry small items. Use low heat in the dryer for small loads and light materials.

— Turn off room air conditioners when the rooms are not in use. Keep filters and fins clean.

Appliances which are minor users of energy include television, dishwashers, microwave ovens, humidifers, and dehumidifiers. Energy-saving practices for these appliances include the following:

— Turn the television set off when no one is using it. Remember also that large TV's use more energy than small sets, and color TV's use more energy than black and white sets.

— Run the dishwasher only when it is full. It takes no more energy to run a full dishwasher than one that is half full. Open the door after the last rinse and let the dishes air dry. Keep the drain clean, and check the gasket around the door for wear.

— Humidifiers are needed to offset the dryness of air in certain climates or at seasons when heating systems may dry out the air in the home. Dehumidifiers are needed only in homes where the air is too humid. If either appliance is needed, the energy cost is justifiable. Buy a size recommended for the area in which it is to be used.

Energy can be saved even with electrical items that may seem to consume little energy. Although home lighting is not one of the major uses of current, some energy can be saved. Turn off lights that are not in use. Since one large bulb is more effective than several small bulbs, use the more efficient size. Flourescent bulbs use less electricity than regular or incandescent bulbs. If flourescent bulbs are to be in use for an hour or longer, it is more economical to leave them burning than to turn them off and on.

PLUMBING NEEDS

The basic home plumbing system involves the kitchen and bathroom, though it may also include a laundry or utility room and outdoor faucets. The minimum plumbing needs in a home are a sink in the kitchen and a washbowl, toilet, and tub or shower in the bathroom. If there are several people in the home, a second bath or half-bath is desirable. A laundry area should include a washer, dryer or clothesline and drying rack, and a stationary tub if possible. Outdoors, there should be at least one faucet.

Whether you are renting a home or buying one, the most important criteria for plumbing are its condition and its suitability for your needs. However, if you are building a home, economy in the layout of the system also becomes a factor. It is more economical to concentrate plumbing so that fixtures for the bathroom, kitchen, and laundry are placed on adjacent walls in a one-story house or vertically in a two-story house.

Bathrooms Space requirements for bathrooms vary according to the number of users and the space available. For a very limited space, a square tub or shower may be used. An average-sized bathroom can contain a full-sized tub, as well as a washbowl and toilet. A larger bathroom may be divided, with a wall separating the toilet and washbowl from the bath area. Sometimes space allows for two washbowls.

A PLUMBING SYSTEM   (Back-to-back kitchen and bathroom plumbing)

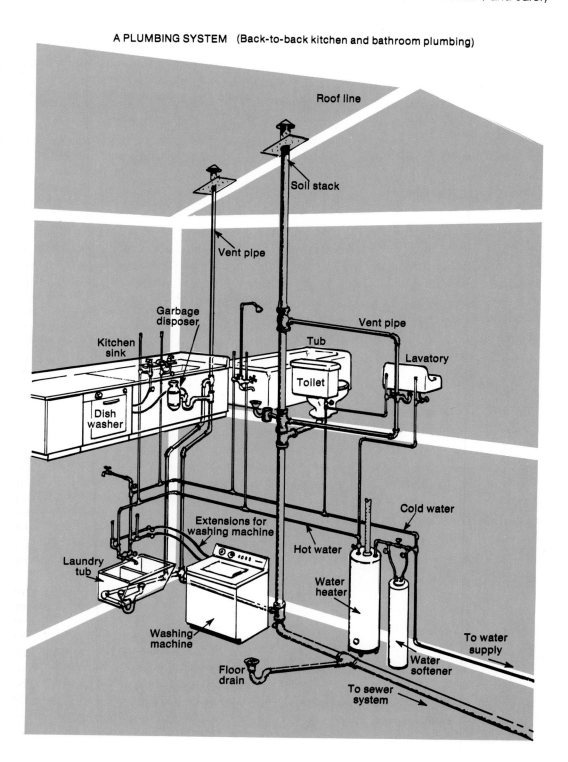

BATHROOM LAYOUTS

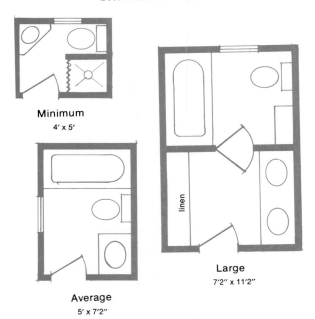

Minimum
4' x 5'

Average
5' x 7'2"

linen

Large
7'2" x 11'2"

A large bathroom will have space for a vanity with two washbowls and perhaps space for both a tub and a separate shower stall.

Toilets are available in many styles and in a wide range of prices. They are classified according to the shape of the bowl and seat. A toilet with a long bowl and seat is more expensive than a cadet type with a round seat. The most expensive type of fixture hangs from the wall for ease in floor cleaning. The more popular and less expensive type is the one-piece water container and toilet bowl that stands on the floor.

Washbowls, sometimes called lavatories, are available in many styles and prices. A washbowl may be a one-piece unit, or it may be built into a counter. A built-in washbowl and counter, with doors below to conceal the pipes and add storage space, is often referred to as a vanity. Ready-made vanities come in a variety of sizes and styles. Standard, wall-hung washbowls with towel racks at the side are preferable for wheelchair users.

For bathing facilities, many homes provide a combination of bathtub and shower. Such a combination is useful in meeting personal preferences. For that reason, if there is only one bathroom in the home, a tub with a shower fixture is preferable to either a tub or shower stall alone. If the home has more than one bathroom, both a tub and shower should be provided.

Bathtubs are available in several sizes, but the 5-foot (1.52-m) tub is the most popular. Having a handle grip at shoulder height and another within reach of a person sitting is a safety factor for older people. In a shower, a seat and a long handrail is safer for older people and wheelchair users. Slip-proof adhesive strips in the tub and shower help to prevent falls. A shower curtain is less expensive than sliding glass doors for either a tub or a walk-in shower. With glass doors, water from the shower is less likely to spill onto the floor, but the metal grooves are difficult to keep clean. For families with small children, a tub with a curtain is preferable to one with sliding glass doors, for easy access.

Prefabricated bathtubs and shower stalls of fiberglass now come in one-piece models to be set in a recessed space. They are less expensive than units needing ceramic or vinyl tiles. As a finish for a tub or shower enclosure, ceramic tiles are more durable and easier to maintain than vinyl board or tiles, but they are more expensive than the other kinds.

Kitchens The sink is the major plumbing facility in the kitchen. The most commonly used sink has a center drain and is made of acid-resistant enamel over a cast iron base. Stainless steel sinks are easier to clean, but they are more expensive. A double sink is usually preferable to a single sink, especially if dishes are washed by hand. However, the large single sink is better for large utensils such as roasters and broilers. It is also suitable for use with a dishwasher. If a garbage disposer is used, a double sink is necessary. Both a dishwasher and a disposer require additional plumbing.

Conserving water Because water is so easily available in our homes, we tend to take it for granted and use it very freely. If we had to carry water from wells and pumps, we would use less of it! Water is a resource with a limited supply; in some parts of our country, there is never enough water to meet all the needs. For that reason, we all need to know about and practice conservation measures.

What various plumbing facilities are included in this kitchen? What other plumbing might be included in a kitchen area?

The following practices can help to conserve water:

— Check faucets and toilets for leaks. A small leak can waste more water than is normally used in a day.

— Turn off the faucet while brushing teeth or shaving. Several gallons of water may be wasted in the time it takes to brush your teeth or shave.

— Avoid running water until it is hot, unless you save the water for some other use.

— A toilet is a major user of water. If a new toilet is to be installed, inquire about water-saving models.

— Adjust the water-level controls in the washing machine according to the size of the wash load.

— Water your lawn or garden only if it is necessary to save plantings. Watering in the evening allows the moisture to sink into the ground and reduces evaporation.

HEATING AND COOLING: ALTERNATIVE SYSTEMS

Today, a variety of home heating and heating-cooling systems are available. If the home you are considering—such as a rented apartment—has heat provided, the type of system used may be of less concern to you. However, if you will be paying for heating costs, and particularly if you are buying a home, the type of heating or heating-cooling system is of major importance to both cost and comfort.

Traditional Heating Systems

The central-heating system common in many houses includes the furnace and boiler, the ducts or pipes that distribute the heat, the room heating units, and the controls. Oil and gas are the fuels most often used in furnaces, though coal and wood can also be used as sources of heat.

TWO TYPES OF HEATING SYSTEMS

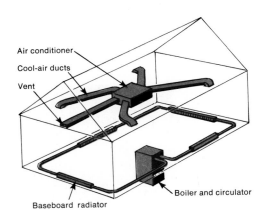

Hot-water radiation heating system
with overhead air conditioning

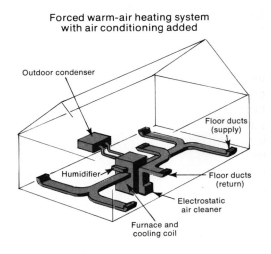

Forced warm-air heating system
with air conditioning added

Distribution systems carry heat in some form from the furnace or boiler to the various rooms. These systems are classified as hot-air, hot-water, and steam. Steam heating is seldom used today because other systems are more efficient. Hot-air and hot-water systems operate by gravity flow and forced circulation. A forced-hot-air system can be installed in homes with a slab foundation, crawl space, or basement. However, a gravity-hot-air system requires a basement.

A hot-water system provides the most uniform heat, especially when baseboard radiators are used along outer walls. In this system, water is heated in a boiler and circulated through pipes to radiators or baseboard units. A forced-hot-water system is preferable because it can be installed in homes with a slab foundation, crawl space, or basement. Disadvantages of hot-water systems are the need to drain the radiators if the house is unoccupied in freezing weather and the need to release air from pipes occasionally to prevent knocking.

Electricity provides energy for central-heating systems, for heating-cooling combinations, and for other types of heating and cooling. It also provides energy for humidity and pollution control. An electric furnace is practical in areas of the country where rates are relatively low.

Electric heating provides either hot water circulating through baseboard panels or panels with direct heat. An advantage of these panels is that they can be controlled separately, room by room. However, there is the disadvantage that they become extremely hot, and curtains made of acetate may be scorched by touching the panel. In another type of electric system, a heating cable or electric-resistance wires are embedded in the ceiling or floor. The temperature of each room is individually controlled with a thermostat.

Solar Heating Systems

Since prehistoric times, people have used the sun's rays as a source of heat. Today, technology is making it possible to concentrate and store that warmth in home heating systems. Solar heating systems can be passive or active. Passive systems use the orientation and size of windows to capture some heat. They may use masonry walls and floors to help store the heat. Active solar heating systems require heat absorbing roof panels, storage wells of masonry or water, and fans or pumps to circulate the heat through the system.

Home heating by solar energy has been accepted slowly in the United States. Key design features of homes with solar heating are site orientation, insulation, and window limitation. Solar roof panels as well as main window areas of the house must face south to collect and store the sun's warmth. In colder climates, no windows should face north and on the east and west walls windows should be limited in size. Double- or triple-glazed windows are recommended in the South to keep out heat and in the North, to prevent heat loss. Windows and doors must be well sealed, and insulation in all areas must meet strict standards. Solar heating is most commonly installed in new housing. Older homes that have the right orientation, adequate insulation, and low ceilings can be adapted to the use of solar energy, though the cost of installing the new system may be high.

Since the interest in solar energy began, few homeowners in the United States have built active solar homes. In 1978 there were only 40,000 structures with solar devices for the heating of homes or water. Each installation was custom built using nonstock materials; they were very expensive. Today over 100 manufacturers make solar heating systems. With the availability of standard parts, construction costs should be reduced, and solar heating systems will be more affordable.

A SOLAR HEATING SYSTEM

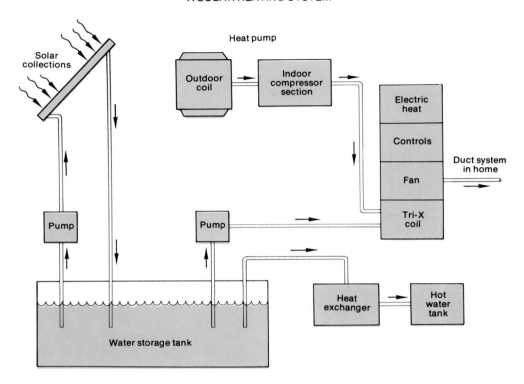

Active solar heating systems are from 50 to 80 percent efficient for heating needs, depending upon the climate, the design of the home, and the type of solar system. In most areas, another heating system is required. Any back-up system can be used, including standard furnaces heated by coal, gas, or oil. However, a heat pump is recommended as a back-up system for new homes.

Passive solar heating systems can supply from 28 to 54 percent of the heat necessary for comfort, depending on where a home is located. Over the past few years, many homeowners have added glass greenhouses or sun rooms to their homes. These sun space additions, which face south, absorb heat, look attractive—even on traditional houses, and can serve as enclosed gardens or atriums. Many of these greenhouses have been combined with thick masonry heat storage walls. The adjoining rooms are warmed by the radiation of the wall. On cloudy or cold days, the glass walls must be covered with insulating shades or draperies to prevent heat loss. Sometimes an adjustable skylight is used to prevent too much heat build-up during the summer months. Several companies are marketing sectional glass panels of different heights and sizes that can be bolted together on a foundation very rapidly. Most of these designs are very attractive.

Combination Heating and Cooling Systems

Heating and cooling systems can be combined in a number of ways. Apartments and town houses often have centralized systems. In single-family homes, combined

This home has a combination heating-cooling system whereby both hot air and cool air are circulated through vents.

Individual air conditioning units can be installed in windows or through walls.

systems for heating and cooling, or for central heating and air conditioning, are most satisfactory when they are included in the original plan. Some people prefer separate heating and cooling systems even though the cost may be higher. A combination heating-cooling system can be built into a forced-hot-water system or forced-hot-air system at the time a home is constructed, or the system can be added later. For cooling, cold water instead of hot water is circulated through baseboard panels, and cool air instead of hot air is circulated through vents.

The heat pump has become the most popular heating-cooling unit in many areas of the country, especially where winters are short. The heat pump was introduced in the 1950's, but it did not come into common use, even in southern states, for over a decade. In principle, it pumps heat from one area to another. On the cooling cycle, it becomes an air conditioner, collecting heat through vents inside the house and pumping it to an outdoor coil where it evaporates into the air. The process is reversed in the heating cycle. Heat is collected from the outdoors, stored, and then pumped through indoor vents when needed. The heat pump usually has an auxiliary system for use on cold days. Even with some heat loss, the electric heat pump operates at high efficiency in comparison with oil and gas furnaces.

The least expensive way to cool a home, especially where summers are short, is to use air conditioning units. They can be installed in windows or in a wall, though such installation is expensive. For a small home, through-the-wall units are practical and efficient. The ultimate in comfort and convenience is a total system—one that heats, cools, and purifies the air for every room in the house. The heat source can be electric heat elements, a gas or oil furnace, a heat pump, or solar heat. Temperature and humidity are automatically controlled; the air is freed of dust, smoke, and pollen. Although this total system is expensive, it is valuable for people with asthma or allergies.

Controls for Comfort

Controls that regulate heating systems or heating-cooling systems are a real convenience. They not only regulate daytime and nighttime temperatures but also can control humidity and pollution. A relative humidity of 30 to 60 percent, with a wintertime temperature of 68 degrees Fahrenheit (20°C), and a summertime temperature of 78 degrees Fahrenheit (26°C), should provide for daytime comfort. Older people need a daytime temperature of 70 to 72 degrees in the winter.

The humidity of the air within the home affects people's comfort. If the air is too dry, the skin will feel tight and itch. If the air is too moist, a person will feel tired and listless. If built-in controls are not part of the heating or heating-cooling system, a humidifier can provide needed moisture, and a dehumidifier can remove extra moisture. The humidity can also be affected by such simple steps as covering or uncovering cooking utensils or doing laundry at particular times of day.

Evaluating Heating Fuels

The traditional resources for fuel are wood, gas, oil, and coal. Each of these fuels is an effective source of heat, but their efficiency can be increased by adequate home insulation and proper controls. Because fuel costs vary in different areas of the country, it is impossible to make a simple comparison based on cost. It is possible, however, to point out certain advantages and disadvantages of each of these fuels.

Wood has always served as a source of heat for the home. Although largely replaced by gas and oil in the past hundred years, wood has become more popular again. Today, it is being used in wood-burning stoves and furnaces. Wood-burning fireplaces tend to waste heat because heat is drawn up the chimney. The chief advantage of wood, for people who have a source, is that wood is inexpensive. However, they must be willing to chop and store a supply. Two disadvantages to wood are that it requires a large storage area, and it is less safe than other heating methods due to the open flames and the very high temperature of the stove itself. Some insurance companies have raised their rates on homes with wood-burning stoves because of the increased possibility of fire. If you install a wood burning stove yourself, have it checked for safety by your fire department.

Wood-burning stoves can be used as primary or supplemental sources of heat.

Gas is a clean and efficient fuel that provides about 50 percent of our residential fuel. It comes in forms known as natural, manufactured, and bottled gas. The use of natural gas is limited to those areas reached by pipe lines. Bottled gas, which is usually propane or liquified petroleum gas, is popular in rural areas because empty containers are easily replaced. Since leaks may cause explosions, bottled gas requires the use of safety control valves to shut burners off when the pilot goes out. The different types of gas require different burner adjustments on ranges and heaters. Be sure your burner is adjusted for the type of gas that you are using.

Oil has long been the most popular heating fuel. It requires little space for handling, leaves no ash, and is currently available in adequate supply. A large amount of our oil comes from the Middle East. Costs and supplies are therefore sensitive to the actions of the countries in this area and how they affect the exporting and pricing of oil.

Coal is seldom used as a residential fuel today because it causes air pollution and smog. In addition, coal requires a large storage area within the home and someone who is able to shovel the coal into the furnace. In the 1800's and early 1900's, coal was the most common heating fuel. Many older buildings are still stained dark by the soot from the burning coal.

Electricity differs from wood, gas, oil, and coal because it is a secondary source of energy. It is obtained from primary sources, such as waterpower, coal, oil, or nuclear power. Lack of those sources or shortages of them directly affect the availability and cost of electricity. Where waterpower or natural fuels provide energy for operating generators, electricity may be relatively cheap. Where it must be produced from oil, electricity may be expensive. Electric heat offers convenience, cleanliness, an even temperature, and freedom from fumes or odors. No chimney is required. Electrically heated homes do, however, require the maximum of insulation to prevent loss of heat.

Homes with electric heating systems usually have a thermostat in each room that regulates the temperature so that rooms can be heated selectively. Timers can be installed that turn on the heat in each room automatically. Baseboard electric heat is comfortable and quiet. Heaters with fans can be noisy.

Energy Sources for the Future

The energy crisis of the early 1970's has made us aware that our present fuel resources cannot last forever and that new sources of energy will be needed. Among the future sources of energy to be developed are solar, nuclear, and geothermal energy, as well as energy from fusion, garbage and other waste, wind, and tides. Actually, the answer to future energy needs may lie not in a single source but in the use of a number of sources.

Solar and nuclear energy have gone beyond the experimental stage. Solar energy is particularly suitable for certain areas of our country that have prolonged periods of sunshine. In such areas, energy from the sun may be used to produce electricity as well as direct heat.

Nuclear energy provided over 15 percent of the nation's electric power in 1984 and is expected to provide 25 percent of our electric power by the end of the century. Uranium is the second largest source of the supply and generation of electricity in this country. The use of nuclear energy, however, involves certain hazards including the danger of accidents and the disposal of nuclear wastes. Future technological advances may help solve these problems and thus allow greater use of nuclear energy. Fusion, a clean form of nuclear power, has been under intensive study for some time. However, fusion is not expected to become a practical energy source until the 21st century.

Other more unusual ways to generate electrical power are being investigated. These include:

— **Recycling garbage and trash** This method has an added advantage: it gets rid of garbage as it provides power. However, no economically practical recycling method has been developed yet.

Energy conservation techniques can save homeowners money and help preserve our natural resources.

— **Production of methane gas from vegetable and animal waste** This method has been used experimentally, but at the present time it requires too much water to be feasible.

— **Windmills** Very large windmills of modern design have been built in some areas on an experimental basis. However, their use is limited to areas that have constant strong winds.

— **Tidal power** People have long wished to harness the power of the ocean. One method being investigated makes use of the water power of the tides. The two areas selected by the government as being feasible for this study are in Alaska and Maine. Unfortunately, both areas are remote from consumers of electricity.

— **Geothermal sources** Geysers and hot springs naturally provide geothermal energy. These sources are being used for power wherever they are available. Unfortunately, few of these sources are in large populated areas.

PLANNING FOR ENERGY CONSERVATION

The energy crisis of the 1970's showed people that the supply of many important natural resources is limited. Oil, which is made from petroleum, is the major source of home heat. Next in importance is natural gas, and then electricity, which depends upon the use of other fuels. In all these sources of energy, shortages or price increases continue to be possible.

The best way to protect our own nation's energy resources and to reduce our dependence upon imported oil—which amounts to half of our use—is to practice conservation. Even before technology made control of the home environment possible, people found ways to maintain comfort. Those living in hot climates devised many ways to keep their homes cool long before air conditioning was developed. In the South, people built homes with breezeways, verandas, and porches to shade the home and provide air circulation. In colder regions, people learned to shelter their homes from cold winds and to reduce the exposure on shaded sides.

Conservation Measures

Today, people are rediscovering old ways, as well as finding new ones, to provide for comfort and yet save energy. Among these ways are site orientation, plantings, exterior design, interior planning, and the use of insulation in construction.

Site orientation You have already seen, in the new designs for homes, that the way a house is set in terms of direction and land surface can help to conserve energy. The location of windows—whether toward or away from the sun—can make an important difference in indoor temperatures. In warm climates, large window areas often face away from the sun or are shaded by plantings and roof overhangs. In climates with cold winters, windows may be located to catch the winter sun, with only small window areas on northern exposures. Protection from cold and wind can be increased by using changes in land surface, such as setting a house against a hill, to provide shelter.

Plantings, fences, and walls In cold climates, trees can serve as windbreaks. Set close to buildings, they can offset the wind chill and help to reduce heat loss. Solid walls can also be used to protect against winds and to create sheltered areas. Walls with openings can be used in warm climates to permit the movement of air. In warm climates, people often use shade trees, tall hedges, and woven-wood or wire fences with vines to provide shade and prevent a buildup of heat inside a home. On a hot day, the temperature under a tree can be 10 or 15 degrees cooler than in the sun. A shaded roof can reduce air-conditioning bills considerably.

Exterior design In hot climates, extended roofs or roof overhangs can be used to shade window areas. In cold climates, they can provide added shelter. Shutters may be used inside and outside to control the temperature, although they are more effective on the outside. Metal and canvas awnings can be installed on the outside to shade windows, porches, and doorways. In cold or rainy climates, recessed doorways or protected entryways provide convenience and save energy.

PROVIDING SHADE FOR COMFORT AND CONSERVATION

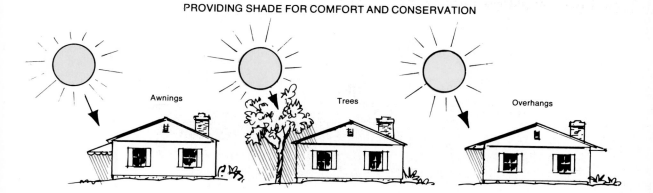

Awnings   Trees   Overhangs

Interior planning Because regions with cold winters often have hot summers, it is difficult to plan for year-round indoor comfort. This is especially true because most homes in these regions do not have air conditioning and must rely on natural ventilation. The layout of rooms to allow cross ventilation is one way to increase summer comfort, since the movement of air makes the atmosphere cooler. Fans are another means of providing air circulation. Some homes without air conditioning use large attic fans to draw out the hot air and pull in cooler air. Ceiling and floor fans, too, are effective ways of making a room comfortable. To insure safety, all floor fans should be well protected and set away from main traffic areas. Exhaust fans in the kitchen, laundry, and bathroom are a good means of drawing out warm air, even from an air-conditioned home, and of maintaining comfortable temperatures.

Windows and Doors

Windows and doors are important to the indoor environment because they let in hot and cold air. You will notice that on a windy day a great deal of air enters the house around windows and doors, even when they are closed. If you sit near a window on a cold day, you will feel chilly. People who live in the North use double-glazed windows or storm windows and storm doors to keep out the cold. Since these are expensive, people sometimes tape sheets of heavy plastic to the outsides of windows. In the South, where many homes have large windows and sliding glass doors, homes may have double- and triple-glazed windows to keep out the heat. A less expensive means of keeping out heat and cold is to cover the glass with insulated film.

If you are paying your own fuel and electricity bills, investigate the cost of caulk-

A ceiling fan to provide air circulation adds comfort indoors during hot weather.

ing windows and weather-stripping windows and doors. If this is too costly, buy a rope-like putty substance to install around the inside or outside of window frames. Look for cracks between the frames and the walls, and caulk them with a caulking tube or gun.

Draw draperies can shut out heat in summer and cold in winter. Window quilts, made of several layers of insulating fabrics, also help reduce energy loss. A track system holds the quilt tightly around the window to keep out cold air.

Insulation The way a home is built and the materials that are used can be major factors in conserving energy. The use of insulation under the roof and floors and between the walls helps to prevent the loss of either cooled or heated air. If adequate insulation has not been built in during the original construction of a home, various types of insulation can be added in order to conserve energy.

Four major types of insulation are available. Batts or blankets can be trimmed and laid in place between walls, in attic floors, between rafters, and in the crawl space below a first floor. They should have a moisture barrier to keep out dampness. Loose-fill insulation can be poured into floors or blown between inner and outer walls through holes drilled and later concealed. This type of insulation is especially suitable for existing homes that need additional insulation. The interior walls should then be painted with two or three coats of semigloss paint which acts as a vapor barrier. Foam insulation is installed by being sprayed above ceilings, between walls, and under floors, where it hardens as it dries. Rigid insulation boards are sometimes used on basement walls, foundations, roofs, and ceilings.

Insulation is graded by its ability to resist the flow of heat. This is called its R factor. The larger the R factor, the greater the resistance.

PLANNING FOR SAFETY AND SECURITY

Safety and security, as well as comfort, are important to the physical environment of the home. Safety includes prevention of fire and accidents resulting from hazards in and around the home. Security involves the protection of both people and possessions in and around the home.

Preventing Accidents

Although we do not usually think of a home as a dangerous place, a great many accidents do take place there. Every year more than 10,000 people die as a result of falls in the home; another 6,000, of fires; nearly 3,000, of accidental poisoning; and about 1,300, of accidents caused by firearms and sharp objects. Thousands of other persons suffer disabling injuries. Many of these accidents could be prevented if everyone observed standard safety precautions.

Accidents may happen in any number of ways. People fall on stairs, trip on loose rugs, or fall over items left in the line of traffic. Most falls occur when people stand on an unsteady base to reach for things on high shelves. Using a sturdy stool, a steady chair, or a safe ladder can help to prevent falls. Some people are careless about the storage of firearms, sharp objects, poisons, and medicines. If there are small children in the home, extra precautions should be taken in storing these items.

Preventing Fires

Fires in the home may begin in a number of ways. These include overheated electrical cords, overloaded circuits, clothing ignited from a flame, or hot grease spilled on a stove. Oily or dirty rags and newspapers piled up in basements, garages, or attics may ignite by themselves. Fires may start in chimney flues that have become clogged with soot. Hot coals from unprotected

A smoke detector should be installed on each floor of your home. It is especially important to have one located near the bedrooms.

fireplaces may cause fires in rugs or upholstery. People are often careless about leaving matches, candles, and cigarette lighters within the reach of children. Children may also get burned by touching hot utensils, burners, or oven racks.

Several precautions can be taken to reduce home fires. First, make sure that all appliances have the Underwiters Laboratories (UL) seal or the American Gas Association (AGA) seal. These seals guarantee that new products have met safety requirements. Keep a small fire extinguisher in or near the kitchen. Install a smoke detector in a small apartment, or several of them in larger apartments and one-story or two-story homes. These alarms detect smoldering fires as well as flames. They are inexpensive and can be installed easily.

However, they must be checked occasionally and kept free of dust. In both single-family and multi-unit homes, know where the nearest exits are in case of fire.

Controlling Noise

Noise has been shown to affect people physically and psychologically. It has been linked to stress, irritability, and the inability to concentrate. Loud noise can result in hearing loss and has even been linked to cardio-vascular disease. Noise levels are measured in decibels. Recent research indicates that even noise at a 70-decibel level can adversely affect hearing. Such equipment as dishwashers, vacuums, blenders, and garbage disposals all make noise above 70 decibels when operating.

Noise in the home results from the activities of family members, neighborhood conditions such as noisy traffic, and the operation of appliances. Noisy activities and equipment should be removed as far as possible from the quiet areas and the dining areas of the family. If you must use equipment that emits loud or shrill sounds try to do it when others are not around and when the family is not eating. You can also install acoustical tile in the kitchen and laundry areas to help reduce noise levels.

Promoting Security

In recent years, protecting the home and its occupants against intruders, theft, and vandalism has become increasingly important. People living alone should never admit unidentified strangers to the home. Doors should be locked at all times. In 40 percent of all burglaries, a door has been left unlocked. It is said that a professional burglar can steal the major valuables in a home and be gone in less than three minutes. Often homes are entered in the daytime by professional thieves dressed to look like business people. A neighbor may even watch burglars remove television sets or

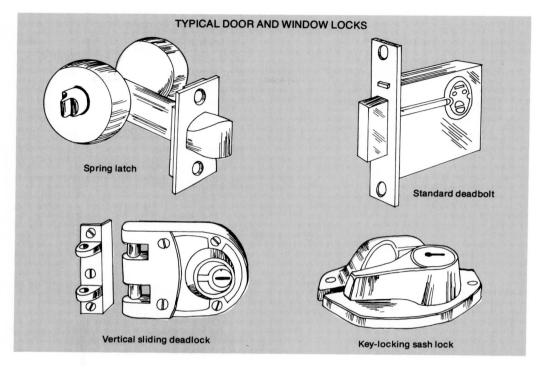

TYPICAL DOOR AND WINDOW LOCKS

Spring latch

Standard deadbolt

Vertical sliding deadlock

Key-locking sash lock

Locks are made in a wide variety of designs, to meet varied needs.

stereos from a home and think the burglars are repairmen.

Unlike thefts, which may be committed by either amateur or professional burglars, vandalism involves destruction that is done as a prank or as antisocial behavior. Vandalism may involve either single-family or multi-unit homes, and it may occur in either cities or suburbs. Its effects are frightening, and repairing the damage may be costly.

The following precautions can help to cut down on robberies in the home:

— Keep doors locked at all times. Replace spring-bolt locks with dead-bolt locks. For added protection, install sliding surface bolts at the top of doors. Place restraining rods on sliding glass doors, or use chain bolts at the top. Anyone can lift out a glass door that is not secured.

— Have a viewer inserted in the front door

so that you can see who is there before opening it. If the person is a stranger, do not open the door.

— Replace outside hollow wood doors with solid wood doors. To keep hollow wood doors from being pushed in, have them covered with a sheet of metal and painted.

— Label television sets, art works, and valuable furniture with etched markings, such as a social security number. Keep a list of your most valuable possessions to aid in identifying them if they are stolen and recovered.

— Close and lock windows when you are out of the house. Set blocks in double-hung windows so they cannot be raised high enough for a person to crawl through. Because awning-type windows and jalousie doors and windows are easy to open, they need special protection. Steel grills can be attached inside awning-type windows and jalousie doors and windows.

— If you have a dog, keep the dog in the house when you are out at night. The barking will often deter a burglar.

— Keep ladders locked up or out of sight.

— Use shades at garage windows, so that a potential intruder cannot check on the car and other possessions.

— When you go on a vacation, stop all deliveries but leave a few things—such as an old tricycle, shoes, or grill—in view so that your home will appear to be lived in. Arrange to have the lawn mowed and snow removed.

— Attach timers to lights in two areas of the house so that lights will turn off and on at different times.

— Leave a key with someone who will check your home while you are away.

CAREER PROFILE

PLUMBER

Plumbers install and repair pipes, fittings, and fixtures for heating, water, and drainage systems. They study building plans to determine the location of installations and their proper sequence. During the construction of a building, plumbers mark the position of the pipes and pipe connections, as well as the passage holes for the pipes in the walls and floors. Using hand tools and power tools, they cut openings in floors to accommodate the pipes and pipe fittings. Plumbers assemble and install valves, join pipes together with fittings, and solder or caulk joints. They also repair and install plumbing fixtures, such as sinks, bathtubs, toilets, water heaters, dishwashers, and garbage disposal units. They replace washers in leaky faucets, mend broken pipes, and open clogged drains.

If you are interested in becoming a plumber, you should have good manual dexterity and an interest in working with tools. It also helps to be able to plan sequences of operations and to analyze and solve problems. You can become a plumber by taking courses at a trade or vocational school. You can also enroll in an apprenticeship program for two to six years. Plumbers are employed by plumbing companies, plumbing supplies stores, and building contractors. You can also be self-employed and be hired by builders and homeowners on a job-by-job basis.

REVIEWING CHAPTER 9

SUMMARY

The comfort and convenience of a home depends partly on its basic systems of plumbing, electricity, heating, and cooling. Although you do not need to be an expert on these systems, you should be able to evaluate existing ones or choose new ones. You should consider the convenience of the locations of outlets and switches, the adequacy of the wiring system, the condition of the plumbing, and the operating cost and efficiency of the heating and cooling systems. Learn how to save energy when using each of the major systems of your home. Energy conservation can save you money and preserve resources for future generations.

Safety and security are important to the home environment. Take steps to prevent falls, fires, and poisoning, which are the most common types of home accidents. Precautions should also be taken to prevent robbery and vandalism of your home and property.

FACTS TO KNOW

1. Identify four major elements of a home wiring system. What is the function of each element in the total system?
2. What are some warning signals that indicate possible wiring problems in a home? Describe several safety measures related to the use of electricity.
3. Name three areas of the home with specific plumbing requirements. How can water be conserved in the home?
4. Explain in detail how one heating system works and what its main advantages and disadvantages are.
5. Describe four ways to conserve energy through the design of your home and the outdoor environment.
6. Why is good insulation important in both hot and cold climates?
7. What are the most common types of accidents in the home? What can be done to prevent each of them?
8. Identify four ways to increase security in a home.

IDEAS TO THINK ABOUT

1. Explain how home orientation and design were used to provide comfortable temperatures before central heating and air conditioning were available. Why have these methods become important again?
2. What new source of energy do you think has the greatest potential for home use?
3. List as many ways as you can for improving home construction and design to conserve energy, prevent accidents and fires, and provide security.

ACTIVITIES TO DO

1. Compare various kinds of traditional and nontraditional heating systems in the region where you live. What are the advantages and disadvantages of each system? What are the annual costs for an average-sized home?
2. Make a study of some potential source of fuel or energy for the future. What would be needed to make the use of this source practical?

YOU CAN DO IT!

Extra Storage Space

Do you need extra storage space in your home? Organize a bedroom closet by installing vinyl-covered wire racks in it. Mount adjustable shelves in a bathroom to hold towels and grooming items. Add hooks on the walls of an entryway so more coats and hats may be hung. Mount racks on a kitchen wall or its ceiling to hold cooking equipment. Purchase plastic milk crates or stacking units and use them for storing toys and games. Surround a window, door, or fireplace with floor-to-ceiling bookshelves. Organize a basement or garage with hooks and racks for storing tools and sporting equipment. Look in hardware and building supply stores for ready-made storage units, shelving units, and other supplies.

Clean up a bedroom closet with wire racks.

Install a kitchen pegboard to provide extra storage for pots and pans.

Hang a rack in an entryway for coats and hats.

Build wall-to-wall shelving to provide plenty of extra storage for books and artwork.

Store toys and games in stackable plastic containers.

Chapter 10

The Basics of Design

When you look through a home furnishings magazine, what types of rooms appeal to you? What styles and combinations do you like best? It may be difficult for you to explain your choices until you become familiar with the elements and principles of design.

The elements of design—line, form, space, pattern, texture, and color—are the tools used in decorating. The principles of design—balance, proportion, rhythm, emphasis, and harmony or unity—are the guidelines for successfully combining the different elements. By understanding certain basic ideas about design, you will be able to look at a room and determine why you do or do not like it. You will also be able to use these basics to achieve the decorating look that is most pleasing to you.

When you begin to decorate and furnish a home, you will be making decisions, just as you did when choosing the home itself. Again, it is important for you to gather information, evaluate alternatives, and make thoughtful choices.

The interior of your home should reflect your own likes, interests, and values—not look exactly like the rooms in a magazine. When your home decor reflects you, it will be a place where you can relax, feel comfortable, and enjoy your family and friends.

PREVIEWING YOUR LEARNING

After you have read this chapter, you will be able to:

- Recognize the elements of design—line, form, space, pattern, texture, and color.

- Identify the principles of design—balance, proportion, rhythm, emphasis, and harmony.

- Describe how design affects the character of a room.

- Apply the elements and principles of design to decorating and furnishing a home.

TERMS TO KNOW

balance—equilibrium of all elements

diagonal—something positioned at an angle

emphasis—a center of interest; a focal point; an area or object of importance

harmony—a pleasing arrangement of all parts

monotony—sameness; a lack of variety

proportion—size relationship of one part to another part or to the whole

rhythm—a sense of motion that flows from one area to another

scale—relative size

structural—related to the construction of an item

texture—the surface characteristics or feel of something

MAKE A SMALL ROOM LOOK LARGER

F E A T U R E

When it comes to rooms, "compact" need not mean "cramped and confined." The small rooms found in most apartments and development houses can have all the necessary elements for comfort and livability and still look spacious.

Color plays a big part in creating the illusion of space. Pale, light colors seem to push out walls and broaden floors. White, in tones from eggshell to ivory, creates the airiest look of all. Color works best when the walls, floors, and other broad surfaces—such as tables, curtains, and bed linens, are all in tones of the same color.

Utilization of wall space in small rooms should be planned carefully. Mirrored walls seem to expand the dimensions of a room. Vertical blinds can turn a wall broken up by windows into one broad surface. For convenient storage, wall-hung shelving units leave floor space free for other furniture. Some of these units have doors that drop down and double as desk tops.

The selection of furniture for small rooms is extremely important. Furniture should be smaller in size with slim, straight lines. Furniture with reflective chrome or transparent glass and plastic keeps the look light and spacious. Pieces that serve double purposes make the most of the space at hand. Decorative trunks can be used as end tables while also providing storage space. Parsons tables, available in many sizes and finishes, can serve as desks, dining tables, and accessory tables.

Track lighting is perfect for small rooms. It provides both overall and focused light while keeping floor space open for furniture.

THE ELEMENTS OF DESIGN

The elements of design—line, form, space, pattern, texture, and color—are the ingredients that can be used to achieve a variety of effects in decoration. The use of these elements is governed by a number of rules or principles of design that help to assure that the total effect is pleasing. A knowledge of when and how to use and combine the various elements will help you in decorating your home.

Line Establishes Direction

The artist working on a flat surface first establishes line direction, or motion. Some lines are dominant, and others are subordinate. In some instances lines may be so conflicting that they create confusion. In other instances lines may be so repetitive that they convey an impression of monotony, or so vibrant that they create an atmosphere of excitement.

Lines take four general directions—vertical, horizontal, diagonal, and curved. There is no limit to the designs that can be made by combining directional lines. Designers have found that lines have certain psychological associations. These include the following:

— Vertical lines that point toward the sky seem to convey an impression of dignity, discipline, and strength. In architecture, vertical lines are exemplified in tall monuments, skyscrapers, and churches; in nature, by tall trees and grasses; in home furnishings, by a tall desk, bureau, mirror, or picture.

— Horizontal lines are down-to-earth and suggest serenity, repose, and relaxation. In architecture, horizontal lines are noticeable in low contemporary buildings and ranch-type homes. In nature, the setting sun over the ocean or across a plain suggests horizontal lines. In the home, a sofa, a low chest, or a long, low bookcase emphasizes horizontal line movement.

The direction of line—vertical, horizontal, and curved—can be used to create a wide variety of decorative effects.

— Because diagonal lines are active, they seem to disturb the dignity of vertical lines and the tranquility of horizontal lines. However, they break the monotony of vertical and horizontal lines. In architecture, slanted and pointed roofs produce diagonal lines; in nature, mountain peaks and rocks suggest diagonal direction; and in the home, diagonal lines are expressed in open stairways and in some fabric designs.

— Curved lines are graceful and suggest youth, gaiety, and subtle motion. Architects make use of curved lines in arches and domes; nature uses curved lines in clouds, leaves, and winding streams. In decoration, curved lines are prominent in furniture design and window decoration.

The horizontal lines in this room add to its contemporary mood. The modern furniture is simple in design, and the accessories add interest. The room has an informal feeling in comparison to the illustration on page 201.

Form Relates to Shape

Lines help to give an object form or shape. Whereas the landscape artist works on flat surfaces to give an illusion of form, the sculptor and the furniture designer work with three-dimensional materials to create many different shapes. Chairs, sofas, tables, and lamps take many forms, in which either straight, diagonal, or curved lines may predominate.

Some shapes are more pleasing than others. Rectangular shapes are associated with masculine rooms and contemporary furnishings; oval or curved shapes are associated with feminine rooms and Victorian furnishings. When you study furniture design, you will notice that during some periods rectangular forms dominate furniture styles, and in other periods curved forms dominate.

A room is more interesting when different forms are combined. The form or shape of an object should have some rela-

tionship to its function, but need not always serve some purpose. For example, some shapes, such as large objects of art in a living room, hall, or garden may serve only as objects of beauty.

Design may be structural or functional or purely decorative. Most modern furniture depends solely upon structural lines and texture for beauty. Eighteenth-century furniture depends upon both structure and decoration, because many pieces are carved or inlaid. You will notice as you study period furniture that the structural and decorative lines are interrelated.

Fabric, too, may be structured to produce design. The warp of the fabric may be set up to produce a plain, stripe, geometric, brocade, or damask design. A plain fabric may have an applied or a decorative design, which is usually printed on the surface. It may be a natural design, a conventionalized design, or simply a geometric or abstract design, such as checks or dots.

Decorative design must be in keeping with structure and function. For example, a delicate fabric would not be suitable for a chrome or steel chair, and a heavy leather cushion would not be suitable for a chair with finely carved woodwork.

The answers to the following questions will help you to judge structural and decorative design:

— Will the structure or form serve its function? Will the chair you are considering provide comfortable, steady seating?

— Are all parts of the structural design in good proportion? A heavy chair with short, pipelike legs may sit squarely on the floor, but the legs may look out of proportion to the chair.

— Does the decoration improve the appearance of the structural form? Are the style and proportions of the decoration compatible with the basic piece of furniture? If they are not, the decoration should be omitted.

The lines in this room are primarily vertical and curved, creating a feeling of formality and gracefulness. The traditional-styled furniture has decorative details and elegant fabrics. The room has a formal look in comparison to the illustration on page 200.

Pattern and texture add surface interest and touch appeal to fabrics.

Space Provides the Setting

Space is the three-dimensional setting for decoration and furnishing. The size of furnishings and the interior design depend on the amount of space available. A small room will appear crowded if heavy furniture, bold colors, and large patterns are used. The same room can be given an illusion of space by applying the principles of design. This means selecting furniture forms in scale with the room, together with using light colors and related textures that convey distance or a feeling of space. Plain backgrounds that do not distract the eye also create a sense of space.

Pattern Creates Surface Decoration

Patterns are produced by a combination of line, form, color, and space. They provide the element of graphic design in carpets, fabrics, and wallpaper. Because of variations in the form and style of patterns, great care must be used in combining them.

Texture Provides Surface Structure

Texture, which refers to the surface structure of fabrics, coverings, and furnishings, appeals to the sense of touch as well as sight. It can be used to create a delicate and airy feeling or a heavy and oppressive feeling. Texture can be light or heavy, rough or smooth, shiny or dull, soft or firm. The same piece of furniture, such as a sofa, will look quite different upholstered in homespun, mohair, or damask. The character of a floor changes according to the texture used—tile, wood, or carpeting. Certain textures are compatible, whereas others clash.

The type and style of furniture used in a room will determine to a large extent the textures suitable for rugs, drapery fabrics, and wall finish. For example, traditional or 18th-century furniture is made of fine mahogany or walnut, often carved or inlaid. Furniture of this period looks best with rather rich textures, such as brocade, damask, velvet, fine linen, and smooth firmly-woven cotton; and with silver, brass, and alabaster accessories. French Provincial furniture and Early American furniture are often made of light and more informal woods—maple, birch, or fruitwood—which are compatible with chintz, gingham, and other informal fabrics; and with copper, pewter, and pottery accessories. Contemporary furniture may be made of light or dark wood, metal, or plastic—usually in a simple, uncluttered style. It combines nicely with rough textures and bold patterns and with wood and wrought-iron accessories.

When styles of different periods are combined, the shape of the room and the predominating style will determine the best choice of textures. All of the textures should harmonize. It might be possible for an experienced decorator to combine homespun and satin in the same room, but the amateur is more successful in combining homespun with printed cotton and satin with brocade.

Color Adds Unity and Focus

Color is the least expensive and most dramatic of all the elements of design in setting the mood and character of a room. Color can make a room appear bright or somber, exciting or dull, spacious or crowded, warm or cool. Accent colors in pictures, wall hangings, and accessories will give rhythm and emphasis to the decorating scheme and bring about unity or harmony. Color is such an important element of design that the following chapter is devoted to its characteristics and use.

THE PRINCIPLES OF DESIGN

Design principles are guidelines for achieving pleasant effects in home decoration, furnishings, landscaping, and other environments for living. The basic principles of design are balance, proportion, rhythm, emphasis, and harmony or unity. Their use is described here and further referred to in the chapters that follow.

Balance Means Equilibrium

The use of balance in the placement of furniture, pictures, or colors conveys a feeling of satisfaction and rest. When objects are out of balance—as when all the upholstered pieces of furniture are at one end of the room, or when a single bright-colored chair has nothing to balance it—the effect

How is balance used in each of these diagrams? Which one uses balance least effectively?

USING BALANCE IN DECORATION

This room contains both formal and informal balance through the furniture arrangement.

is like that of a seesaw with all the weight on one end.

Balance may be obtained by placing identical objects on each side of a center point, or by placing unequal objects at unequal distances from a center point. The former arrangement produces even balance—sometimes called formal balance. The latter produces uneven balance —sometimes called informal balance. A room looks more interesting when both types are used.

Proportion

Proportion is the size and space relationship of objects to one another and to the total look of a room. Pleasing proportions are important in arranging objects, in hanging pictures, and in arranging furniture. As a rule, unequal proportions are more pleasing to the eye than equal ones. Therefore, it is better to break up spaces unevenly in a room. A door or window

should not divide a wall equally, and a piece of furniture should not divide a space equally.

The ancient Greeks were masters in the application of the principles of design, as all their great temples and statues show. They developed a scale of size and space relationships that avoids monotony. According to the Greek laws of proportion, flat areas are to be divided unequally in the following ratios: 2:3, 3:5, 5:8, and so on. The beauty of Greek architecture depends in part on this use of unequal proportions.

Proportion cannot be discussed without mentioning scale, because the terms are similar in that they deal with size relationships. Furniture must be chosen in scale with a room; lamps, tables, and accessories grouped about a sofa or a chair must be chosen in scale with the dominant object; a picture over a fireplace must have the right proportions and be in scale with the fireplace and mantel.

This room has good proportion. Nothing looks too big or too small. Because the space is broken up unevenly, the room has interesting space relationships.

Rhythm

The design principle called rhythm is used to create motion and to carry the eye from one area to another without abrupt interruptions. Rhythm is created in a number of ways, including the following:

USING RHYTHM IN DECORATION

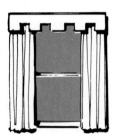

Rhythm by repetition

Rhythm by opposition

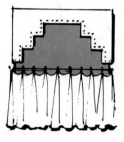

Rhythm by gradation

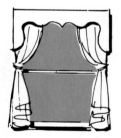

Rhythm by transition

Rhythm by radiation

How does each window treatment create a particular type of rhythm in its design?

—by repetition of lines, shapes, or color;
—by gradation, or a gradual progression of sizes in the arrangement of pictures on a wall or objects on a shelf or chest;
—by using lines in opposition or at right angles in the treatment of windows—for instance, where tailored draperies are used with a straight-edge cornice;
—by transition, or by connecting straight lines with curved lines, as in the use of curved cornices at the top of draperies;
—by radiation, in which many lines radiate from a central axis, as in a flower arrangement or in tieback curtains.

Emphasis

Usually the attention of an observer is attracted to one particular part of a room. It might be a painting around which a color scheme is planned, a beautiful rug, an interestingly arranged set of shelves, beautiful windows, or an attractive fireplace. This object or area of a room becomes the focal point or center of interest of the room. The skilled decorator knows how to use emphasis and avoid overemphasis. The amateur may create a pleasing, restful room, but may lack the skill or knowledge necessary to give a room character or to focus attention on an interesting structural feature or item of furnishing.

Overemphasis, which gives an impression of clutter, is far less desirable than underemphasis, which often conveys a feeling of simplicity. As a rule, it is advisable to focus attention upon an area of the room that is seen as one enters the room.

Harmony or Unity

When colors, lines, and shapes are properly related in a room arrangement, flower arrangement, or painting, unity and harmony will prevail. To create harmony, the artist or interior designer usually aims to express an idea in which art elements—

line, form, texture, and color—are combined. For example, the decorator may want formality or informality, ruggedness or refinement, classic simplicity or contemporary boldness. If lines, shapes, textures, and colors are coordinated according to the principles of design, the result will be harmonious. However, this does not mean that different furniture styles cannot be combined successfully. Such combinations are a further extension of the elements and principles of design.

ADDITIONAL ASPECTS OF DESIGN

Home decorating involves a number of values and principles besides the purely aesthetic ones. The character and effect of the design should be suited to the people who live in the home. If the members of a family like outdoor life and simple living, they may not be happy in a home that has a formal atmosphere or is cluttered with bric-a-brac, no matter how attractive it is.

You can create a focal point or center of interest in a room by emphasizing a piece of furniture, an accessory item, or even an architectural feature.

The artistic effect of the design should contribute to comfort and efficiency. A home should look "lived in," not like a showroom or a magazine illustration. However, this does not mean that it must look lived in to the point of presenting an untidy or unkempt appearance.

The furnishings of the home should be functional in design and arrangement. It is quite possible to become so enthusiastic about achieving an artistic effect that function is overlooked. If a living room has tables without drawers and no place for storage of records, writing supplies, or other items, it will not be conducive to efficient living. Beautiful kitchen equipment and attractive walls and windows cannot compensate for inconvenient kitchen storage or work space.

APPLYING DESIGN BASICS

In the preceding unit, you dealt with many of the questions and decisions involved in choosing a home. Now, many decisions have been made: the type of home; its size and location; and whether to rent or buy. Other kinds of decisions are still ahead. These are related to the interior of the home—namely, its decoration and furnishing. The unit that follows presents many aspects related to home furnishing and decoration. In studying these, you will be using the basics of design.

Designing the interior of a home requires coordinated planning. Although each aspect of the interior, such as carpets or draperies, is a separate component, it is also part of the total design. Selecting colors,

What elements and principles of design are used to create the pleasant appearance of this room?

patterns, and shapes that go well together results in a pleasing appearance. How closely coordinated the design is depends on personal taste, lifestyle, and resources. For a formal effect, the rules of design are used strictly; all aspects of the design are closely related; and a rather upright, precise, and finished effect is achieved. For an informal effect, the rules of design are used more freely; the various aspects of design are less closely related; and the result is relaxed or casual. For either a formal or informal design, the final appearance will be more pleasing if the furnishings and decorating are planned in relation to each other, as parts of a total design.

Planning the design for a room involves many different factors. Some of these, such as furniture, are of primary importance. Others, such as accessories, are of secondary importance and yet are essential to the total scene. The most important factors in creating the design for a room are the following:

—**The theme, character, or idea being expressed** The theme becomes the basis for the design to be developed. It is a matter of personal choice, which depends, of course, on the resources available. You may decide on the theme yourself, or you may also seek advice from professional decorators. Many large stores can provide decorating services. Because the theme provides unity to the total design, it influences other choices.

— **The style of the home itself** Sleek, modern furniture would not be appropriate for a simple, informal setting, nor would Early American furniture be very appropriate for a town house with high ceilings and tall windows. Most homes lend themselves to a wide range of styles. Whatever style you may choose to implement the theme, that style should be used consistently, in order to create a unified effect.

— **The use of design elements and principles** These factors are carried out through the choice of furnishings and decorations. Combinations of line, pattern, color, and form are all important for a total design that provides balance, unity, and emphasis. For example, the choice of a picture to hang over a fireplace may provide a color scheme and suggest fabric patterns and textures, as well as the shape of furniture.

— **The background surfaces and their coverings** These surfaces include walls, ceiling, floors, and windows. They provide the setting within which furniture, lamps, accessories, and household furnishings are arranged and used. Background materials, such as wallpaper, draperies, and carpets, should be integrated as parts of the total design. In turn, they should be appropriate for the kind of furniture, decorative items, and furnishings to be chosen.

— **The furniture, which should fulfill the purpose of the room** A living room should contain a sofa, chairs, and tables; a bedroom requires a bed and chest of drawers. Furniture is available in a wide variety of styles. Knowledge of these styles, together with the background materials and accessories, will aid you in creating a coordinated and pleasing design. Comfort, as well as style, is an important consideration in selecting furniture.

— **The lamps, lighting, and decorative accessories** Although lamps and lighting have a specific function, they can also be important items among the decorative accessories. Accessories in general help to create a sense of enrichment and to provide finishing touches to the total design. They include pictures, mirrors, art objects, hangings, plants, and flowers.

— **The household furnishings for specific areas** These include table settings of dishes, glasses, and flatware, and the linens for the dining room, kitchen, bedroom, and bath. Although these furnishings must be functional, serving their intended uses, they can also be decorative, helping to carry out a theme or add enrichment to a total design.

— Household equipment, such as appliances, needed for operating and maintaining the home Although efficiency and convenience are the major criteria in selecting these important items, they can also serve as elements of design within an area.

Combining background and furnishings in a unified design requires a great deal of careful planning. Your decisions should be based on an awareness of your own needs, preferences, and resources; on a knowledge of design; and on the wise use of consumer information. Good judgment in choosing and carrying out a theme will result in a home you will enjoy living in.

CAREER PROFILE: INTERIOR DESIGNER

Interior designers plan the interiors of homes, hotels, restaurants, offices, and institutional buildings. Designers first meet with their clients to discuss their needs, preferences, and proposed budget for the project. Then sketches are made of the proposed rooms or interiors showing the arrangement of the furniture and accessories. A color scheme also is developed. An estimate of the cost and amount of materials that will be required for the project is calculated. A designer then presents a proposal to the clients for approval.

Next, the interior designer purchases any furniture, light fixtures, rugs and carpeting, wallpaper, fabrics, and accessories directly from manufacturers. Part of the job may also include overseeing the workers who paint the walls, lay the carpeting, and install the fixtures and draperies.

If you are interested in becoming an interior designer, you need to be able to work well with people. You must be able to communicate your ideas and be sensitive to others. You also need a feeling for spatial relationships and color combinations, plus a creative imagination.

To become an interior designer, you need to take interior design, applied arts, or home economics courses at a college or specialized school. It is essential to become a member of the American Society of Interior Designers (ASID). An interior designer may be employed by a department store, a furniture store, a paint and wallpaper store, or a home furnishings manufacturer. Some designers work for private interior design firms or have their own clients and work independently from their own home.

REVIEWING CHAPTER 10

SUMMARY

The elements and principles of design are the ingredients and guidelines for interior decoration. The elements of design include line, form, space, pattern, texture, and color. A person should become familiar with the direction of lines, the forms of furniture, and the limitations of space. Pattern, texture, and color relate to the fabrics and wall and floor coverings in each room

The design principles—balance, proportion, rhythm, emphasis, and harmony—are guidelines for choosing the design elements. Balance gives a sense of equilibrium. Proportion involves size relationships and scale. Rhythm leads the eye from one area to another. Emphasis creates a center of interest. Harmony is achieved when all the principles form a pleasing design.

Designing the interior of a home requires coordinated planning. Decisions should be based on your own needs and preferences as well as the design elements and principles, in order to achieve the look that you want.

FACTS TO KNOW

1. List the six elements of design. Explain how they apply to interior design.
2. What four directions may line take in design? What effect does each direction tend to create?
3. Define the terms *structural design* and *decorative design,* and explain the difference between them. Are structural and decorative design ever used together?
4. Describe several ways that pattern and texture may be used in interior design.
5. List the five basic principles of design. Explain how each principle affects the total look of a room.
6. Explain the difference between even and uneven balance, using examples.
7. What does the term *proportion* mean? How are proportion and scale related?
8. List eight factors that should be considered when creating the design of a room.

IDEAS TO THINK ABOUT

1. Make a list of the major decisions involved in designing and furnishing a home. Which of these decisions do you consider high in priority?
2. How may a family's lifestyle be reflected in the way they have decorated their home?
3. Compare the relative importance of beauty, comfort, convenience, economy, and ease of maintenance when deciding how to decorate and furnish a home. Which of these criteria do you consider most important?

ACTIVITIES TO DO

1. Visit a furniture showroom that has model rooms decorated in different styles. Select one room for special study. What theme or character does the room express? In what ways do the decorations help to carry out this theme? Analyze the use of the various elements and principles of design in the model.

Chapter 11

The Magic of Color

Of all the elements of design, color has the greatest impact. Color can set a mood, suggest temperature, and create optical illusions. Color is also symbolic. People feel "in the pink" when they are happy and well, or "blue" when they are sad. Red may symbolize danger or excitement. Blue may create a feeling of calm or dignity. Black may be dramatic or somber.

Nature is an excellent source of inspiration for color. Think of the brilliant reds, yellows, and oranges you see when you look across at an autumn hillside. Or picture the cool and refreshing blues and greens surrounding a mountain lake.

The impact of color is as great in decorating as it is in nature. Color has the power to make a room look spacious or crowded, warm or cool, exciting or relaxing. Colors are also linked to style and fashion. Certain colors may be associated with particular periods of design and decorating. In this chapter, you will learn how to choose and use colors that will help set the style and character of your home.

First you need to think about colors and how you feel about them. What colors do you like best? What colors do you dislike? What messages do you associate with different colors? What colors and color combinations make you feel good?

PREVIEWING YOUR LEARNING

After you have read this chapter, you will be able to:

- Classify colors and identify color harmonies or schemes.

- Recognize factors that influence color choices.

- Identify starting points to use as guidelines for selecting color schemes.

- Apply the principles of design to the use of color.

TERMS TO KNOW

analogous—similar; two or more colors that are next to each other on the color wheel

complementary—completing or making up what is lacking; colors that are opposite each other on the color wheel

hue—the name of a color

intensity—brightness or dullness of a color

monochromatic—having only one color

primary colors—the basic colors from which all other colors can be made; red, yellow, and blue

secondary colors—equal amounts of two primary colors; orange, green, and purple

spectrum—band of colors reflected by light through a prism

tertiary colors—any color produced by mixing a primary and secondary color

value—lightness or darkness of a color

OLD FURNITURE: COLOR IT NEW

FEATURE

Don't throw away that old table! Save that worn-out chair! Give old furniture a whole new look with a wash of color.

Actually, the idea of coloring furniture is not new at all. Centuries ago, European peasant craftsmen painted furniture, which they handcrafted from inexpensive, mixed woods, to give it uniformity and character. With paint, they could imitate more expensive materials which they could not afford such as marble, mahogany, and bird's-eye maple.

Some of these European craftsmen came to live in the New World. Swiss, Dutch, German, and English settlers each brought to the new land their own particular furniture painting techniques. Early American country furniture was colored with paint made from vegetable matter and minerals dissolved in oil. Around 1800, milk rather than oil was used as a base, and the colors became warmer. Chests, tables, and trunks—as well as doors, walls, and floors—became alive with color, applied in a variety of ways. Sponges were used for a mottled effect, graining combs were used to simulate rosewood grain, a finger or two made dots and squiggles, and stencils were used for geometric patterns.

Today, renewed interest in American folk art has revived the craft of furniture painting. Warm, country furniture stains can be made by mixing oil-based paint with paint thinner or by dissolving fabric dyes in hot water. Traditional application techniques, such as sponging and stenciling, give newly colored furniture the look of Early American antiques.

APPROACHES TO COLOR

The subject of color can be studied from many different viewpoints. A doctor might study the effect of color stimuli upon the eyes. Experiments have shown that "eye-rest" colors—soft green, blue-green, and off-white—should be used in offices and classrooms, where there is a great deal of concentration and routine activity. Avoiding strong contrasts helps to reduce eye fatigue. For example, the contrast created by a dark-colored desk and white paper causes more eyestrain than a light-colored surface and white paper. For this reason large, light-colored desk pads or blotters are often used as a work surface.

The physicist studies color in terms of light waves. Ordinary white light contains all colors, but these are invisible to the unaided eye. Passing light through a prism separates it into the bands of the entire color spectrum. When all rays of light are reflected, a surface appears white; when certain light rays are reflected and others are absorbed, various colors appear; when all the rays of light are absorbed, the surface appears black. Applying this principle to clothing and housing, we can understand why light-colored clothing and light-colored rooftops keep out heat by reflecting light waves, and why dark-colored clothing and rooftops hold in heat by absorbing light waves.

The chemist studies how to make beautiful dyes and paints. Until the middle of the 19th century, pigments for paints and dyes came from natural sources—iron oxide, iron sulfate, tree bark, plants and roots, and berries. Now most paints and dyes are artificial and are developed in the laboratory. The chemist seeks to create permanent dyes for new fibers and paints. These dyes must be able to withstand both exposure to pollution and extreme temperature changes.

The psychologist studies the effect of color upon the emotions. Red is a stimulating color. It is often used for carpeting or for wall-coverings in nightclubs and restaurant dining rooms. It is not recommended for schoolrooms or home dining rooms, because it is too stimulating. Colors that rest the eyes are often desirable in the home, at least in certain rooms.

The artist—painter, interior decorator, and textile designer—is always experimenting with color to produce new combinations for designs, interiors, and woven and printed fabrics. The use of color is closely related to changes in art and fashion. Certain colors may be popular during an era, a season of the year, or a particular style. New combinations of colors are often used to create new fashions and designs.

As you learn about color, you too should look at it from different points of view. The more you know about color, the more skillfully you will use it and the more pleasing the overall design you create will be.

THE USE OF COLOR IN DESIGN

Color is one of the strongest elements in design. It can be used to highlight or subdue, to enlarge or reduce, to complement or contrast. Although we often use colors in informal ways, colors and the relationships among them are actually based on scientific principles. These principles influence the use of color in design.

The Classification of Color

All colors are made from three primary colors—red, yellow, and blue. These can be combined into three secondary colors: orange (a combination of red and yellow); green (a combination of yellow and blue); and purple (a combination of blue and red). Between the six primary and secondary colors are six other combinations, the

COLOR WHEEL AND SAMPLES

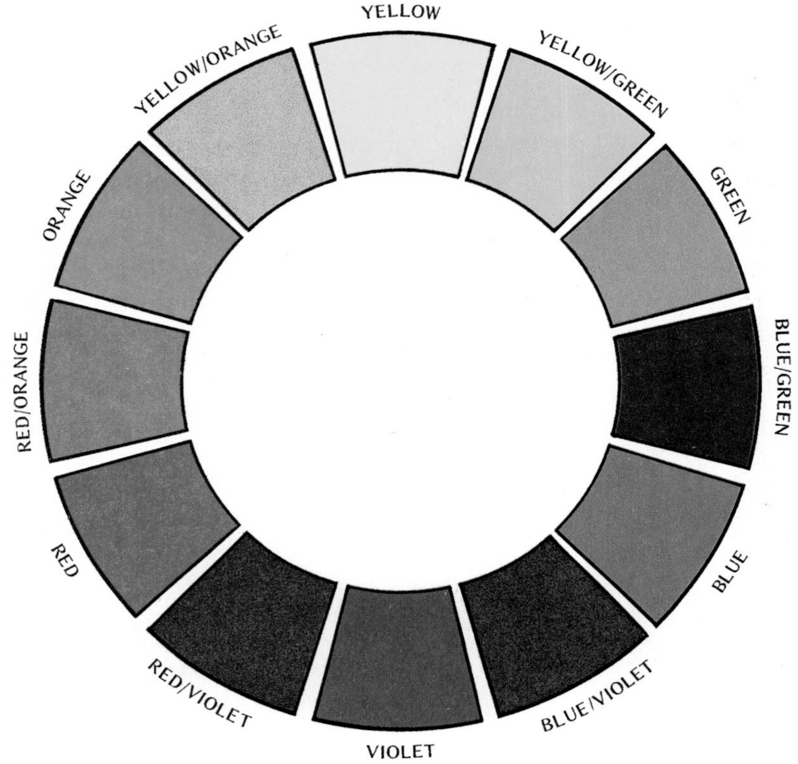

YELLOW

YELLOW/ORANGE

YELLOW/GREEN

ORANGE

GREEN

RED/ORANGE

BLUE/GREEN

RED

BLUE

RED/VIOLET

BLUE/VIOLET

VIOLET

VALUE SCALE

White

High light

Light

Middle

Dark

Low dark

Black

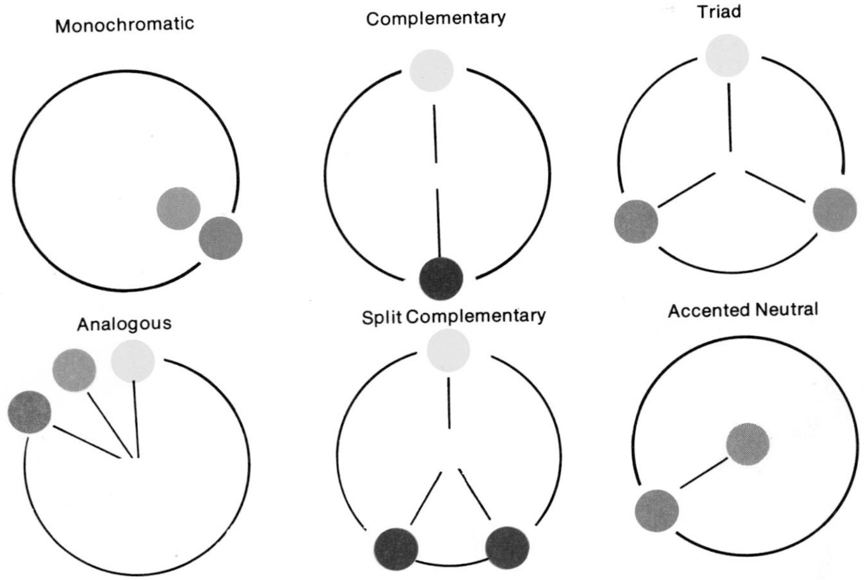

Monochromatic

Complementary

Triad

Analogous

Split Complementary

Accented Neutral

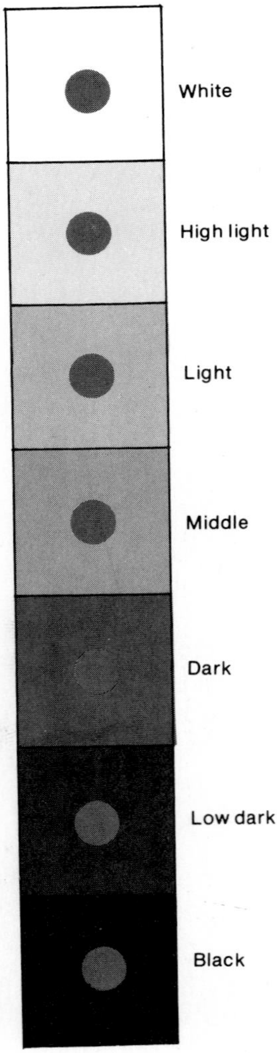

tertiary colors: red-orange, orange-yellow, yellow-green, green-blue, blue-purple, and purple-red. Together, these twelve colors make up the color wheel, which contains the full range of colors.

Another way of classifying colors is according to *dimension*. This term includes three important aspects of color—*hue, value,* and *intensity.* When you understand the meaning of these terms and how to apply the principles involved, you will be ready to use and combine colors with skill and confidence.

Hue is another word for the name of a color. We might say that red, yellow, blue, and so forth are family names for colors. A red hue can mean a red from pale pink to crimson, as well as orange-reds or purple-reds. It is important to develop an eye for color, in order to be able to discriminate between color combinations that are not pleasing and those that are really effective.

Value refers to the lightness or darkness of a color. Light color tones are called tints; dark color tones are called shades. Sky blue, shell pink, and Nile green are tints; royal blue, rose, and forest green are shades. When mixing paints, you can lighten colors by adding white, and darken them by adding black. However, you should add black very slowly, because it can change some colors very quickly.

Intensity refers to the brightness or dullness of color. Kelly green, fire-engine red, and sunflower yellow have high intensities. Although experienced decorators may use intense colors for all or several of the walls in a room, the amateur is advised to use intense colors in very small amounts, to accent a color scheme.

Standard Color Harmonies

In design, several colors may be used together to create a harmony. Harmonies may be similar or contrasting. Similar harmonies are produced from colors close together on the color wheel; contrasting harmonies are produced from colors that are separated. Similar color harmonies can be *monochromatic*—that is, produced by using one color in several values and intensities; or *analogous*—produced by using colors that are close neighbors on the wheel—yellow and yellow-green, for example. Similar harmonies tend to unify a room and give an illusion of more space. However, some contrast in value and intensity is often needed to avoid sameness.

Contrasting color harmonies can be *complementary, split complementary, accented neutral,* or *triad.* Colors which are opposite on the color wheel produce a complementary harmony—for example, red and green. When used together, in varying intensities and values, opposite colors tend to emphasize each other. This means that a light-pink wall will look pinker if soft green or even blue-green draperies are used instead of either light-blue or beige draperies. In a split-complementary harmony, a color is used with the two colors on either side of its complement, or opposite color, making three colors in all. For example, red can be combined with blue-green and yellow-green to give a split complementary harmony. An accented neutral harmony uses tints and shades of a neutral color such as beige or gray with color accents. A triad color harmony is produced by using three colors that form a triangle on the color wheel. This harmony requires a little more skill in handling if you are to avoid color contrasts that are too sharp.

Special Uses of Color

Color has magical powers. No other element of design is so effective in creating a mood, changing the size or shape of a room, camouflaging awkward-looking furniture, or focusing attention on treasured possessions. Color may serve in creating special decorative effects and in relating furnishings to setting in a total design.

Which furnishings and decorations in this room are used to create a monochromatic color scheme?

Colors have the special quality of appearing warm or cool. Colors such as yellow, yellow-green, yellow-orange, orange, red-orange, and red appear warm. Rooms where these colors are used seem inviting and cheerful. Walls painted in light values of any of these colors seem to "advance," or to give a feeling of nearness. The cool colors are purple, blue-purple, blue, and blue-green. Rooms in which these colors are used appear cool and relaxing. Walls painted in light values of these colors appear to "recede," or to give an illusion of distance.

Because colors can appear warm or cool, they can be used to offset the exposure of a room. Some designers believe that colors in rooms that face north should be chosen from the warm-color family and that background colors in rooms that face south should be chosen from the cool-color family. This practice is most successful in rooms that are always used in daylight. At night, incandescent lighting can give greater warmth to all colors. A soft turquoise or green-blue, for example, can appear almost as warm as a pale, soft yellow.

The relationship between colors can be used in decorating to conceal problems caused by awkward-looking furniture. If a large upholstered chair has poor lines, these can be made inconspicuous by using a slipcover that blends with the color of the wall behind it. On the other hand, complementary colors can be used to enhance each other. For example, a violet chair looks brighter against a wall that is yellow— a complementary color—than against a wall that is blue. Woods of brown—a very dark orange-red—look richer against walls of blue-green, a complementary color, than against walls of pink or rose.

Why is this color harmony considered analogous? Check the color wheel on page 216 for the location of these colors.

What effect is created by the complementary color scheme of this living room?

What accessories are used to provide color in this accented-neutral color harmony? How does this use of color differ from the monochromatic design on the previous page?

The Oriental rug has influenced the choice of colors throughout this room.

The delicate color scheme used here focuses attention on the heirloom bedspread.

FACTORS INFLUENCING COLOR CHOICES

Many factors affect people's selection of colors in decorating. Among these factors are personal preference, room orientation, size and layout of the room, colors in adjoining rooms, and the decorating theme.

Personal Preference

Perhaps the most important factor in choosing colors is to make sure they will please the person or people using the room. No matter how attractive certain colors seem in a magazine or in a friend's home, they must satisfy the people in the home where they are used. Some people have strong color preferences—for neutral shades, delicate pastels, or bright contrasting tones. Others may have a real dislike for certain colors. A few people, for example, do not like green, although it is a popular decorating color. Knowing people's likes and dislikes is a help in creating a successful and pleasing design.

Color in Relation to Setting

Color has the power to make a room feel warm and exciting or cool and relaxing. For that reason, the direction a room faces should be considered when selecting colors. A room with a south, southeast, or southwest exposure will have a great deal of sunlight. Therefore, it is usually advisable to use cool colors for the major areas —that is, for walls and floors. On the other hand, a room with a northern exposure will not have the warm effect of sunlight; there, it is advisable to use warm colors to offset the general coolness.

Exposure is a particularly important consideration for rooms such as kitchens, where people may spend a lot of time. Exposure is less important in the choice of colors for rooms that get little use during daylight hours. There, personal preference may be the deciding factor.

Color can also be used to influence our perceptions of space—in other words, to make walls seem closer or farther away. Dark, bright, or warm colors on the walls of a small room may create a sense of crowding or confinement. In the same room, the use of a light color for walls, curtains, and woodwork, with a lighter value of the color for the ceiling and a slightly darker value for the carpet, can give a sense of space. In a room that is cut up by nooks, chimneys, windows, and doors, using the same color on all surfaces can create a feeling of unity. This feeling can also be achieved by using a printed wallpaper with drapery fabric to match, and by painting the woodwork the same color as the background of the print.

Color can be used to enhance or offset the shape of a room. A square room can be made to appear rectangular by the skillful use of color. For example, an off-white or creamy-yellow paint may be used on three walls, and a turquoise-blue on the fourth wall, to give an illusion of length. If you do this, be sure to mix a little of the off-white or creamy-yellow paint with the blue to blend it with the predominant color. A sharp cool blue, while giving an illusion of greater distance, may be too unrelated to the white or yellow color.

The appearance of a long, narrow room can often be improved through the use of color. If one of the end walls is painted in a warm, "advancing" color, or covered with a wallpaper or drapery fabric designed with warm colors, the room will appear to have better proportions. Of course, furniture can also be arranged to offset the awkward proportions of a room.

The color of the ceiling can have an important influence on the total effect of a room. In a room with a ceiling of 8 feet (2.44 m) or less, it is advisable to paint the ceiling off-white or a tint of the color used on the walls, in order to give a feeling of height. High ceilings, such as those that are often found in older homes, are often painted a little darker than the walls, to make them seem lower. However, a dark ceiling will require more artificial light, because it will reflect little light.

The color scheme of adjoining rooms is often an important factor in selecting colors for a particular room. Since the entire decoration of a home is unlikely to be changed at one time, new colors in one room must often be keyed to those in adjoining areas. It is good practice not to use more than two or three colors in a single room or living area where rooms and halls are closely connected. It is also best not to use one set of colors in a living room, another in the hall, and still another in the dining room if these areas are adjoining. The effect would lack harmony. Instead, colors should flow from one room to another.

If a house is small, the best way to give a feeling of unity and space is to use wall-to-wall carpeting of a medium-light color in the living room, hall, and dining room. The hall wallpaper, if figured, may suggest color schemes for adjoining rooms. For a feeling of maximum space, paint the living room, hall, and dining-room walls the same color, preferably a light color. Window treatment and accessories can be used to give each area individuality or character. Be sure to study all your furnishings, in order to integrate all colors into the total color scheme.

Color in Relation to Style or Theme

Homes—and rooms within homes—often tend to be particularly well suited to a certain style, thus taking on a character of their own. This tendency can be used to advantage in decorating. If you are trying to achieve spaciousness, study styles such as the Egyptian, Greek, Japanese, or contemporary, where simplicity is the keynote. If you are aiming at dignity and formality, study rooms furnished in the Georgian period. If you like informality, study Provincial and Early American rooms.

What color harmony is used in this room? How does it help to carry out the theme and design?

How do color and design help to create a warm, cozy effect in this Early American room?

Rooms often take on character according to the way they are used. Because living rooms and dining rooms are often rather formal and impersonal, the colors there should not be too stimulating. Bedrooms, which are for relaxing and sleeping, should have designs and colors that are restful. A family room or kitchen may be more colorful, because these rooms are places for informal activities. You can be as original and bold as you please in choosing and combining the colors in a children's playroom.

Other Factors in Color Selection

Influences such as lighting and texture are often important to the use of color. Incandescent light, which tends to be yellow, may fuse its color with other colors. The result is that yellows and greens become more sharp; blue, more green-blue; and purples, almost brown. Fluorescent light, on the other hand, draws color out of furnishings. This type of lighting, which is frequently used in bathrooms and kitchens, sometimes even distorts colors. Fluores-

cent light bulbs can be obtained that do not greatly influence light reflection.

Texture, too, influences the apparent color of fabrics and other furnishings. Even though the same dyes are used for a linen or satin drapery fabric and a wool or synthetic carpet, the resulting colors often look different because the textures vary. In choosing colors, you should always bring fabric or rug swatches to the room where they will be used. There, you can judge better how the colors of the different textures will fit in with present furnishings and how they will appear in both daylight and artificial light.

STARTING POINTS FOR COLOR SCHEMES

You may find the selection of colors already determined if you move into a home or an apartment with wall-to-wall carpeting or wood paneling that would be too expensive to change. However, changing the wall color may be possible if you can afford the cost of paint or wallpaper and labor, or if you can do the work yourself. Although some factors in decorating are predetermined, there is usually some opportunity for making a few choices. The following guidelines can help you in selecting and combining colors.

Start with What You Cannot Change

If a rug or carpet is green, or if an Oriental rug has a great deal of red and blue in it, you cannot ignore these existing colors. Other colors must be chosen to coordinate with them. It will be helpful for you to start a file of ideas, based on the color scheme you are interested in. You can also go through both old and current decorating magazines to see the advertisements for carpeting, paint, draperies, and furniture, and to list special brochures to write for. After you have chosen several possible color schemes to go with your existing furnishings, you might display the clippings on a wall in the room and study them.

A painting such as ''Still Life'' by Paul Cézanne *(National Gallery of Art, Washington, DC, Chester Dale Collection)* can provide the basis for a room's color harmony.

Start with a Patterned Wallpaper or Fabric

The skillful use of pattern is a trick known to all decorators. You, too, can use it to achieve a coordinated effect. The artist who created the print will have partially solved your color problems. The print will suggest not only what colors to use but also the proportion in which to use them. Note the colors that dominate the print. You may want to wallpaper three walls of a room and paint one wall the color of the wallpaper background; then you can use draperies of the same print.

For major room areas, do not choose a color that appears in small amounts in the wallpaper or draperies, because it may be too insignificant to be effective. By holding fabric swatches and large paint cards against the print, you can find the two colors to use in the largest quantity. Then if you wish, you can pick up a third color for emphasis and use it in accessories. It is not always necessary to use a third color, especially if you use two colors in more than one value. For example, if you have a drapery print with a white background and a design that uses several values of blue and yellow-green, you can use a medium-blue carpet, light-blue walls, an avocado sofa or chairs, and white lamps. In a large room, the print can be repeated in a sofa or chair; in a smaller room, it can be repeated in sofa cushions. Additional upholstered furniture can be covered in a neutral fabric with a woven pattern.

Start with a Picture or an Heirloom

The colors in a painting, vase, wall hanging, or quilt can be used to provide interesting harmony. Use one or two of the colors in decorating the largest areas of the room, with a third for accent if desired. It is wise to gather swatches of fabric, carpet, and paint samples, and to study them in the room before making any decisions.

Start with a Favorite Color

If you have a favorite color, such as orange, it can be used as a focus in decorating. For example, you may want to select a burnt-orange carpet. Your next consideration would be the walls. Off-white or light-yellow tones, or even pale turquoise, will go with orange. By adding a very small amount of the rug color to the wall paint, you can key the carpet to the walls.

Your next step may be to find a window fabric. If you like a feeling of space, match the window fabric to the plain walls and provide pattern interest in your choice of a painting or a wall hanging for a main-wall area. This piece of art should display fairly large amounts of the two colors you have already selected. Other colors in it will then provide a key to the colors for accessories throughout the room.

Start with a Standard Color Harmony

Pleasing color combinations can be developed by following the rules for standard harmonies. Using favorite colors or a painting as a key to colors may or may not involve colors used in standard color harmonies. Unless you have a flair for decorating, it may be safer to rely on the standard combinations for guidance. Experimental color schemes, of course, can always be tested against the standard harmonies to see how much variation there is. Illustrations in this chapter show color schemes based on standard color harmonies as well as on printed fabrics and wallpaper, paintings, and heirlooms.

Use the Eclectic Approach

The term *eclectic* is used in decorating to describe a pleasing combination of different styles and periods of furnishings. Some people have the ability to ignore rules and to express independence and imagination well, whereas others prefer to follow standard rules and practices.

In the eclectic approach, unusual color combinations may be used and different styles and periods of furnishings may be combined to create a special effect. An eclectic approach is particularly useful when beautiful antiques or family treasures must be integrated into a decorating plan.

APPLYING DESIGN PRINCIPLES TO THE USE OF COLOR

The principles of design apply to the use of color as well as to the use of line, area, and shape. Each of these elements plays a part in creating the total design and assuring a pleasing effect.

Balance

If a room has two predominant colors, they should not be used in equal amounts in furnishings. Neither should all items of one color be placed on one side of a room, and all of another color on the opposite side. Two chairs of the same color may balance each other on opposite sides of a fireplace or a table. On the opposite side of the room, a color in a figured sofa may repeat the chair color, or cushions on the sofa may pick up the chair color for balance.

Proportion

Colors should be used in varying proportions. The wall area of a room, including doors and windows, represents the largest mass. The proportions of colors used on the wall area influence the total effect of the room. For example, a room will appear larger if walls, doors, and window fabric are all one color. As a rule, light and neutral colors may be used in larger proportions than bright colors. However, in high-fashion design, decorators may take the liberty of painting the walls or ceiling a strong color, or they may use a strong-colored carpet. Other decorators may use wallpaper with a large print and matching fabric for draperies and the bedspread. In general, however, large areas of vivid color or print are disturbing to people who must live with them every day.

Rhythm

Color rhythm may be obtained by repeating, in a painting or other art object, the colors that are present in a figured fabric or carpet. Try to avoid spotty repetition, which may create a disturbing staccato rhythm. Color transition from one room to another is an important part of the principle of rhythm. In a small home, for example, wall-to-wall carpeting in the living room, hall, and dining room, with related colors used in these areas, will create rhythm. Rhythm can also exist in a monochromatic harmony where walls, draperies, and furnishings are variants of one color.

Emphasis

In any decorating scheme, one or two colors usually predominate and thus provide the major emphasis. In addition, color may also be used to emphasize beautiful furniture by contrast or by repetition. A drapery fabric that uses a color which repeats the tone of the wood—cherry, walnut, maple—will emphasize the warm tones of that wood. A plain, light background will always emphasize any dark wood furniture more than a medium-colored or figured background will. Furniture that is overstuffed or awkward in shape may be de-emphasized by the use of colors that blend it with its background. The location of color within a room—as a major interest, accent, or minor focus—is also an aspect of emphasis. When colors are coordinated and conform to the principles of design, harmony and unity are achieved.

CAREER PROFILE

COLORIST FOR FABRIC COMPANY

Colorists for fabric companies develop the color formulas used in printing all types of textiles. They compare a customer's sample with a standard color card or blend pigments in order to duplicate the desired colors. After the color formulas are determined, the dyes are selected according to the specifications and properties that the customer wants. A color sequence chart is prepared to assist the printer in setting up the printing machine. After the fabric is printed, colorists inspect the fabric to be sure that specifications are maintained. They may also advise clients as to fashionable hues and color combinations for upholstery fabrics, drapery and curtain fabrics, rugs and carpeting, and other textile products.

If you are interested in a career as a colorist, you should prefer research work to working with people. You will need courses in mathematics, engineering, textiles, chemistry, and related lab work. A college degree with emphasis in chemistry and a state license are required to become a colorist.

REVIEWING CHAPTER 11

SUMMARY

Color is one of the strongest elements in design. It can be used to establish a mood, create illusions, or carry out a theme in decorating. All colors, or hues, are made from the three primary colors. These can be combined to form secondary and tertiary colors. Colors can also be classified according to value and intensity. Color harmonies may be similar or contrasting and may be categorized as monochromatic, analogous, complementary, split complementary, accented neutral, or triad. The skillful use of color can be used to solve many decorating problems.

Many factors affect people's selection of colors in decorating. Among these are personal preference, room orientation, size and layout of the room, colors in adjoining rooms, and the decorating theme. When selecting colors, you can use several starting points as guidelines. The principles of design must be applied to the use of color to assure a pleasing effect.

FACTS TO KNOW

1. Define *primary colors, secondary colors,* and *tertiary colors.* How is the color wheel organized?

2. Define each of these terms: *hue, value,* and *intensity.*

3. Describe the following color harmonies: monochromatic, analogous, complementary, split complementary, triad, and accented neutral.

4. What are warm colors and cool colors? Explain how warm and cool colors can create a mood in a room.

5. What factors can influence color choices?

6. Explain how color can be used to enhance or offset the shape of a room.

7. What starting points can you use when choosing color schemes?

8. How do the principles of design apply to the use of color within the home?

IDEAS TO THINK ABOUT

1. Compare the use of color in the two photos on page 218. What effect does each color scheme create? Why do you think these color schemes were chosen for these particular rooms?

2. What are some factors that cause color fashions in clothing and home furnishings to change? Analyze current color fashions and give possible reasons for their popularity.

3. Analyze your own color preferences in terms of favorite colors and combinations of colors. What colors do you like for your clothing and accessories? What colors do you prefer for your surroundings?

ACTIVITIES TO DO

1. Find pictures in this textbook or in magazines that illustrate different color schemes. Explain how the design principles apply to the use of color in each example.

Chapter 12

Backgrounds for Furnishings

When you walk into a room, what do you see first? In one room, it may be a particular piece of furniture, a large window, or a special painting. In another room, you may first notice the color of the walls, the pattern of the wallpaper, a beautiful rug, or a shiny tiled floor.

Walls, floors, and ceilings provide the setting for home furnishings. The colors, patterns, and textures of these backgrounds are important to the total impression of a room. Sometimes, these background areas are designed to complement the furniture and accessories in a room. At other times, a background area may be planned as the focal point of the room, capturing your attention first.

In this chapter, you will learn about many different materials that can be used for walls, ceilings, and floor coverings. Color, pattern, texture, and ease of care are important factors and should be considered, but your choice should also be based on the size and shape of the room. How will the room be used? What is the character of the room? Do you want a formal or informal effect? Do you need to reduce noise or cover up damaged surfaces? How much money can you spend on redecorating the room? Special attention should be paid to walls, floors, and ceilings because they set the stage for each room in your home.

━━━━ **PREVIEWING YOUR LEARNING** ━━━━

After you have read this chapter, you will be able to:

- Evaluate paint, wallpaper, and other types of finishes for walls and ceilings.

- Identify different rigid and resilient flooring materials and their characteristics.

- Evaluate different types of rugs and carpeting.

- Explain the relationship of wall, ceiling, and floor backgrounds to other furnishings.

━━━━ **TERMS TO KNOW** ━━━━

broadloom—carpeting that was woven on a wide loom

enamel—paint that dries with a smooth, glossy appearance

latex paint—water-soluble paint

parquet—a geometrically patterned design in wood floors

pile—yarn on the surface of a fabric or carpeting

polyurethane—a very hard, durable finish that can be applied to surfaces

synthetic fibers—fibers produced from chemicals

terrazzo—particles of marble set in cement used for floors

vinyl—any of various plastics used for coverings

SPECIAL EFFECTS WITH PAINT

Giving a fresh coat of paint to an old room can be more exciting than it seems, especially when you paint in some special effects.

Can you imagine a pretty painted rainbow arching over a child's bed? Or diagonal stripes running across the wall of a family room? These painted effects are known as *supergraphics*. First, a design is mapped out on graph paper; then it is sketched on the wall. For circular designs, a compass can be made by tying one end of string around a pencil and securing the other end to the appropriate place on the wall. Then, acrylic paint colors should be added one at a time, making sure each color is thoroughly dry before the next color is applied. The different color sections should be marked with masking tape to keep the borders clear.

Another way to dress up a wall with paint is to create a textured pattern by combing. A coat of glaze is applied over the wall's base coat. The glaze is tinted by the paint dealer to match the base coat. Then a comb, a special tool available at paint stores, is used on the glaze as it dries to create the textured pattern. With combing you can produce a wide range of effects: walls can be covered with a loose weave pattern or appear to be coated in expensive moiré satin. The paint dealer can give advice on which combing tools achieve which effects. After the glaze is dry, a protective coat of polyurethane or varnish is applied to the walls.

WALL FINISHES

The treatment of walls is important in interior design because walls provide the background for other furnishings. The design of these areas must conform to the character or decorating theme and the size and shape of the room. In addition, they must complement the furniture and accessories. Walls can make a room appear spacious or crowded, formal or informal, exciting or relaxing. Wall finishes can also be used to hide architectural defects or to emphasize good features.

Paint

Paint is one of the most popular wall finishes. It is easy to apply and maintain, and the color choices are unlimited. A wide range of colors is available as ready-mixed paint. An even greater color selection can be obtained with formula-mixed paint. Paint can be mixed by any store having a paint-mixing machine. Paint cards give the exact proportions for hundreds of colors. Colors can be thoroughly mixed in about 20 minutes. When matching the colors in draperies, slipcovers, or other furnishings, you should use a color a little lighter than the one you want to match, because the color will appear darker on the walls.

Another reason for the popularity of paint is that it is relatively low in cost. Painting walls, after the cracks and holes have been filled, is the least expensive way to restore them. Almost anyone can apply paint successfully. The introduction of the paint roller and of paint that is water-soluble caused a boom in painting by amateurs. More than three-fourths of all paint is bought by people planning to do the work themselves.

There are three major types of paints: latex, oil-base, and epoxy. Each of these is available in several different finishes, depending on the use.

A flat-finish paint is recommended for all rooms of the house except the kitchen and bathroom. A semigloss or high-gloss finish is more serviceable in rooms where there is steam or grease, because it is easier to maintain. It is also often used to cover wood trim.

People who do their own painting prefer latex because it is easy to apply, usually needs only one coat, has little odor, and dries fast. Because the paint is water-soluble, brushes and rollers are easily cleaned in water and detergent. However, spills must be wiped up immediately because the paint dries fast. If a wall has been painted previously with an oil-base paint, a special undercoat is required before latex paint can be applied. Latex paints come in a flat, semigloss, or enamel finish. They are made for either exterior or interior use. They can be used on plaster, wallboard, acoustic tile, masonry, or wood siding.

The brightly painted walls of this room offer a warm welcome.

Oil-base paint comes in flat, semigloss, and high-gloss finishes, and there are interior and exterior types. If it is too thick, it must be thinned with a special paint thinner or turpentine. Rollers and brushes used with oil paint must be cleaned with thinner or turpentine because this paint is not water-soluble. Oil-base paint holds up better in areas where walls must be washed frequently. Oil-base paint in a semigloss finish that can easily be wiped clean is usually preferred for bathrooms and kitchens.

Epoxy paint gives a durable, glossy finish that looks like porcelain or ceramic tile. It is used in kitchens and bathrooms for refinishing tile walls that have become discolored. The paint comes in two cans, with the paint in one can acting as a catalyst and in the other as a reactor. This paint must be mixed shortly before using, because a chemical reaction to solidify the paint takes place immediately after mixing. There is a special thinner to keep the paint at the right thickness for spreading. Good room ventilation is necessary during the mixing and application of this paint because the fumes are overpowering.

Latex paint and a modified epoxy paint are also available in pressurized spray cans. Spray paints can be used for painting furniture, picture frames, outdoor equipment, and other items. Most spray paints give a high gloss or enamel finish.

Special paints that have a textured finish are available for either interior or exterior use. These paints create pebbly or rough finishes that help to hide any cracks or repairs in surfaces. They can be used on

Painted walls provide a plain background for this rather formal room. The darker color of the ceiling makes it seem lower.

plaster, wallpaper, masonry, wood, brick, cement and metal. Some textured paints come pre-mixed in three finishes: fine, coarse, and stucco. Also, special sands and absorbent materials can be purchased separately to add to paint for a textured finish. One disadvantage of textured paints is that walls must be sanded to obtain a smooth finish again.

Certain precautions are important in the use of any type of paint. These include the following:

—Never paint over a dirty or greasy surface, because the paint will peel. Before painting, prepare the surface by sponging it with a detergent and wiping it dry. If there are cracks, fill them in with patching plaster. If the paint has begun to peel, scrape it off, and rub the surface with fine sandpaper until it is smooth. Wipe the surface again with a slightly damp cloth.

—Read the directions carefully before starting to paint. Work in a well-ventilated room, especially when using an oil-base or epoxy paint.

—Always use spray paint outdoors or in a confined area, such as a large box, to prevent tiny droplets of paint settling on other surfaces.

Clear Finishes

In addition to paint, which provides color in home decoration, there are products which provide a clear finish. These products are varnish, shellac, polyurethane, and lacquer.

Varnish, which is soluble in turpentine and paint thinner, comes in dull, semigloss, and high-gloss finishes. It may be used on natural-wood doors, window frames, and wood paneling. Shellac, which is soluble in alcohol, comes in a clear and an orange color. It is used as a wood sealer or as a base for paints. Polyurethane, soluble in mineral spirits, is a very hard, durable finish. It is used to protect painted or stained surfaces against scratches, spills,

and heavy wear. Lacquer, which is soluble in lacquer thinner, is used more often on furniture and wall screens than on walls. Lacquer is available in pressurized spray cans, which are easy and convenient to use. If directions are followed carefully, a very smooth surface can be obtained with lacquer. Applying lacquer with a brush is more difficult than applying paint, varnish, polyurethane, or shellac, because lacquer dries rapidly. When applying any clear finish, follow the same precautions as for paint.

Textured paint gives a new finish to the walls of this old house. Plus it hides small cracks and irregularities in the walls.

Wallpaper

Wallpaper is next to paint in popularity as a finish for walls. Wallpaper is more difficult to apply than paint. It is also more expensive, and the cost of hanging it may be high if the work is done by a paperhanger. However, wallpaper offers certain advantages, in comparison with paint:

—It is available in a wide range of designs and textures as well as colors.

—The colors in the design can become the basis for a color scheme.

—Wallpaper gives warmth to a room and affects the sense of space. For example, a scenic wallpaper at one end of the room increases distance; a design with a large pattern makes a large room appear smaller.

—The design can serve to camouflage irregular surfaces, cracks, and rough spots.

—Wallpapers are often developed with coordinated or companion designs. These can be used to create special effects in a room or to provide a pleasing transition from one room to another. Coordinated borders or narrow strips of wallpaper can be used for accents.

—Many wallpaper patterns have matching fabrics for draperies or slipcovers.

Wallpaper is available in a wide range of colors and designs. Many patterns have coordinated designs or matching fabrics.

Selecting wallpaper Because wall areas are so large, the choice of wallpaper is an important factor in decorating. Since the design of wallpaper sets the theme for the room, select a pattern or texture that is appropriate and carries out that theme. A formal living room may require a damask or brocade pattern, or perhaps a Chinese design. An Early American room will call for something less formal—perhaps small prints or stripes. A contemporary room might use a textured wallpaper, or one with a bold design.

The principles of design apply to the selection of wallpaper. If a patterned wallpaper is chosen, the pattern should be scaled to the room. Large, bold patterns overpower a small room and its furnishings. Dainty floral prints are lost in a large room. Since the appearance of a paper varies with lighting conditions, study the effect in the room by daylight as well as by artificial light.

Wallpaper offers a wide variety of patterns and textures from which to choose: floral prints, raised brocades, geometric designs, landscaped motifs, murals, and textured fabrics. It is usually best to avoid wallpaper that looks like a cheap imitation of brick, stone, or ceramic tile. Although the original, natural materials are expensive, they are preferable to the cheaper imitations and may be used in small quantities for emphasis or effect.

Today, most wallpaper is actually a vinyl wall covering which is resistant to soil, grease, and oil. The vinyl coating is backed with cloth, non-woven fabric, or heavy paper.

Most vinyl wall coverings are labeled washable or scrubbable. This means that most stains can be removed with a mild detergent and water if treated immediately. A vinyl finish is highly desirable on wallpaper for rooms that have constant use and need occasional washing, such as kitchens, bathrooms, and children's rooms.

The wallpaper and coordinated border accent the architectural lines of this room.

Some wallpaper is hung by being spread with a paste or adhesive and then applied to the wall. Prepasted wallpaper may be more convenient to use; it is soaked in water for about thirty seconds before it is hung. Some wallpaper is made with a paper backing that can be peeled off. This type may be used in small areas, such as above kitchen counters. However it may be difficult to use because it may become stuck together and hard to separate.

Most wallpaper is labeled strippable and can be removed easily by peeling the strips off the wall. Otherwise, a special wallpaper steamer must be used to loosen the paper before scraping it off. Steamers can be rented from paint, wallpaper, and hardware stores.

Most wallpaper stores will let you bring samples or wallpaper books home to see how specific designs look in your own home.

Wood paneling lends warmth to a room and can be a do-it-yourself home improvement project.

Guidelines for using wallpaper The appearance of wallpaper on the wall often seems different from that on the roll. For that reason, the amateur decorator is sometimes disappointed in the effect of wallpaper after it has been hung. The following suggestions will help to prevent problems and mistakes:

—To see the effect of a particular design, bring home a roll or strip of the paper several feet long, and tape it to a wall in the room where it may be used. (Use masking tape to avoid damaging the wall and the paper.) If you cannot obtain a roll or strip, bring home wallpaper books and study the designs you like. In either case, look at the wallpaper in both daylight and artificial light.

—Choose wallpaper designs that are in scale with the room. Large motifs or repeats will overpower a small room, and small motifs will be lost in a large room.

—Use vertical stripes to give an illusion of height and horizontal stripes to create an illusion of width.

—For an interesting effect, use figured wallpaper on two or three walls, with paint and matching drapery fabric on the other wall or walls. The painted wall should repeat the background color of the figured wallpaper.

—Avoid using scenic wallpaper or wallpapers with large repeats if the walls are broken up with doors, windows, or a fireplace.

Wood Paneling

Before the introduction of wallpaper, wood paneling was often used as a wall finish. Because it was very expensive, it was used mainly in the homes of the wealthy. Today, wood paneling is a popular covering for the walls in a den, library, family room, or recreation room. Wood panels are available in several forms, which are relatively inexpensive. These panels, which are precut and finished, can be made of either pressed wood or plywood. Panels interlock to conceal the joints. Wood panels come in a wide variety of surface finishes, including grained off-white or tinted wood and natural birch, walnut, mahogany, pine, fruitwood, maple, and oak. A less expensive grade of paneling may be used if it is to be painted.

Wood paneling is both attractive and practical. It can be used as a covering for badly damaged walls. It also helps to keep out moisture and cold air. If it is used on basement walls where there might be some dampness, sheets of insulation, which are available where paneling is sold, should be placed between the wall and the paneling, together with a vapor barrier.

Ceramic Tile and Other Finishes

Certain areas of a home are suitable for specialized materials. Ceramic tile is frequently used for bathroom walls, because it is not harmed by heat, steam, or water and it is easy to maintain. Plastic tile simulates ceramic tile, but it lacks the richness and permanence of ceramic tile.

With the greater emphasis upon integrating outdoor and indoor living areas, structural materials have become popular for inside walls. These materials include brick, either glazed or unglazed, and glass in a clear, patterned, opaque, or brick form. Sheet vinyl and cork are also used for walls.

A brick wall adds textural interest to this family-sitting-room.

CEILINGS

Most recently built homes have ceilings no higher than 7½ or 8 feet (2.29 or 2.44 m). Ceilings are usually painted an off-white or a lighter value than the walls. Plastered ceilings in new homes are not always painted. A small figured wallpaper is sometimes used on kitchen and bathroom ceilings and on the ceilings of rooms with dormer windows. High ceilings in older homes are sometimes painted a darker value than the walls, to make them seem lower.

In rooms where noise is a problem, acoustic panels or tiles are often used on ceilings. This type of ceiling can reduce noise 55 to 75 percent. Acoustic tiles come in panels, 2 feet by 2 feet (.61 m x .61 m) or 2 feet by 4 feet (.61 m x 1.22 m). They are available in finishes suitable for any room. They will not peel, chip, or crack, and they are easy to replace.

Acoustic-tile ceilings can be installed several different ways. Some tiles or panels are supported by metal grids that hang from the ceiling or rafters. Other tiles are stapled to thin wood furring strips or glued directly to the ceiling.

Acoustic-tile ceilings are easy to maintain. They can be dusted occasionally with a soft brush and cleaned with a sponge and mild detergent. Dirt does not clog the small holes in the tiles because the dead air acts as a barrier against dirt-laden air.

TYPES OF FLOORING MATERIALS

The floor and ceiling occupy the same area in a room, but people look at a floor more than at a ceiling. As the foundation of rooms, floors can serve to unite, separate, or divide areas. A solid-color, textured floor covering used throughout the living area will create an illusion of space. An area rug used over a solid-color carpet can define a dining or conversation area.

People differ in their preferences for floor surfaces. Also, floors in different areas of the home may require different treatment. A wide variety of rigid and resilient materials, as well as carpets and rugs, are available to meet these different needs.

Rigid Flooring Materials

Rigid flooring materials include hardwood, softwood, marble, flagstone, slate, brick, terrazzo, quarry tile, ceramic tile, and concrete. If you are building or remodeling a

The type of resilient flooring chosen depends in part on the structure of the floor in relation to grade level.

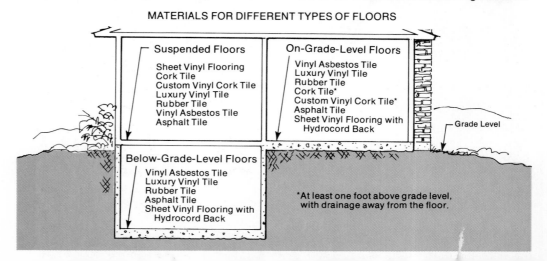

MATERIALS FOR DIFFERENT TYPES OF FLOORS

Suspended Floors
Sheet Vinyl Flooring
Cork Tile
Custom Vinyl Cork Tile
Luxury Vinyl Tile
Rubber Tile
Vinyl Asbestos Tile
Asphalt Tile

On-Grade-Level Floors
Vinyl Asbestos Tile
Luxury Vinyl Tile
Rubber Tile
Cork Tile*
Custom Vinyl Cork Tile*
Asphalt Tile
Sheet Vinyl Flooring with Hydrocord Back

Grade Level

Below-Grade-Level Floors
Vinyl Asbestos Tile
Luxury Vinyl Tile
Rubber Tile
Asphalt Tile
Sheet Vinyl Flooring with Hydrocord Back

*At least one foot above grade level, with drainage away from the floor.

home, you have a choice of materials. If you are renting or buying an existing home, you will have to use the flooring materials already there. Of course, those floors can be refinished.

Wood flooring Many people prefer wood flooring, both because the color and grain are attractive and because wood floors provide a desirable background for beautiful rugs. The wood color should not contrast too much with the rugs used on it. Dark wood finishes also show dust more than medium or light finishes. Some people like an unadorned wood floor, but such floors present a maintenance problem and provide no resistance to noise or shock. In many apartment buildings, unless wall-to-wall carpeting is used, the landlord requires that wood floors be 80 percent carpeted to reduce the noise level.

Oak is the most popular hardwood. Other hardwoods are maple, beech, and birch. Pine is the most popular softwood. A filler, usually shellac, is used on wood

What background materials in this children's room make it both pleasant and practical?

floors to fill in the pores. A semigloss polyurethane finish can be used to seal the floor. Wax helps to preserve the shine.

Wood flooring is available in a number of styles, finishes, and grades. The major types include the following:

—narrow boards fitted together by a tongue-and-groove method.

—planks or random-width boards nailed in place. Nails are countersunk, with short wooden pegs glued over them to resemble the actual wooden pegs used in colonial homes.

—parquet or wood squares, often combining several kinds of wood and set to form a geometric pattern.

—squares of laminated wood or wood chips, set at an angle to resemble parquet flooring. These squares are precut, prefinished, and grooved. Some are self-adhesive, with a peel-off backing for easy installation.

Masonry flooring Masonry floors are made of such materials as stone (marble, slate, and flagstone), heat-hardened clay (brick, quarry tile, and ceramic tile), and concrete or terrazzo. Each material has particular advantages and disadvantages. All these materials are durable, but some are very expensive.

Various forms of stone have been used as flooring materials since prehistoric times. Marble was used in the palaces and fine homes of ancient civilizations. Today it is considered a luxury material. Marble is available in many colors and grains, and it can be cut to produce simple or intricate patterns. It is used mainly in entrances, halls, and bathrooms. Flagstone and slate are produced in many areas of the country. Flagstone is especially popular for entrances, hallways, family rooms, terraces, outdoor steps, and paths. For indoor use, flagstone is usually set in cement to provide a rigid surface. For terraces and patios, it may be set in sand. Slate has similar uses,

in addition to its use as a flooring material near fireplaces. Both slate and flagstone look better when waxed.

Brick, quarry tile, and ceramic tile have, like marble, been used since ancient times. Brick can be laid to form a geometric design, similar to that of parquet flooring. It can be sealed with a low-gloss glaze. Quarry tile is highly durable, whether glazed or unglazed. Dark quarry tile holds heat well and is often used as thermal mass in passive solar rooms. A clear sealer can be applied for a stain-resistant finish. Ceramic tile is durable and easy to clean. Both natural and glazed tiles come in a vast array of colors, textures, shapes, and sizes.

Concrete and terrazzo are poured flooring substances. Many homes without basements or crawl space now have poured-concrete floors, over which carpeting or resilient floor materials are laid. Plain concrete is satisfactory for the laundry or terrace but not very decorative otherwise, unless it is painted or divided into geometric shapes. Terrazzo consists of a cement mortar which holds together either pebbles or chips of colored marble or glass. After the substance is poured and becomes hard, it is polished by machine to expose the embedded particles.

Resilient Flooring Materials
Linoleum was the first resilient flooring material. Produced by accident more than a century ago, it has now been replaced by other resilient materials. Among these newer products are vinyl, asphalt, and rubber. They are sometimes combined with other materials, such as asbestos or cork.

Resilient floor coverings in tile form have become popular because they are easy for amateurs to install. Tiles come in squares, 9 inches by 9 inches (22.86 cm x 22.86 cm) or 12 inches by 12 inches (30.48 cm x 30.48 cm), some with a self-stick backing.

Vinyl flooring is an excellent resilient floor covering for kitchens, family rooms, entrances, laundry rooms, and playrooms.

Resilient floor coverings are also available in rolls. These flooring materials vary in composition, durability, ease of maintenance, resilience, and resistance to grease stains and moisture. Various types of cement are available for securing the tile or rolls to the flooring beneath.

The advantages and disadvantages of the main types of resilient flooring materials are as follows:

—Vinyl flooring is one of the most satisfactory of all resilient floor coverings. It comes in tile form and in rolls 6 feet (1.83 m) wide. The pattern choices and color range are almost endless. Pure vinyl has good to excellent resilience if the backing is cushioned; good recovery from dents; and high resistance to grease, water borne stains, and chemicals. It is durable and easy to maintain. Some types of vinyl flooring have a no-wax finish and maintain their shine for a long period of time. If necessary, a special liquid polish can be applied to restore the luster. Vinyl flooring is relatively expensive.

—Vinyl-asbestos tile is popular with people who are doing the work themselves. It can be laid anywhere, and it can be cut with scissors to fit around curves and corners. There is a wide range of patterns and colors. The surface is durable and has excellent resistance to grease and chemicals; however, stains will leave a mark unless wiped immediately. Vinyl-asbestos tile requires a minimum of maintenance, especially if it has a no-wax finish. Like vinyl tile, it is also made with a cushioned backing to reduce shock.

—Asphalt tile is the least expensive resilient floor covering. It dents easily, shows poor resistance to grease, and is only fairly easy to maintain. The development of newer flooring materials has reduced the demand for asphalt tile.

—Cork tile is usually recommended for floors that are above grade level. It has superior resilience and noise resistance.

However, it dents easily and has poor resistance to stains, grease, chemicals, and cigarette burns. Cork tile is rather difficult to maintain, and it is not durable in areas where traffic is heavy. It is often used in rooms where maintaining a low noise level is important.

— Vinyl-treated cork combines natural and synthetic materials in an attractive form. It can be purchased in either tiles or sheets. The vinyl coating provides excellent resistance to stains, grease, and chemicals, and it assures easy maintenance. Vinyl-cork flooring is expensive. However, its attractiveness and durability make it popular for living rooms, family rooms, and recreation rooms.

— Rubber in tile and sheet form is a practical material for flooring. It has good resiliency and recovery from dents. Rubber flooring is resistant to grease and stains, but it can be harmed by strong detergents. It is relatively expensive.

RUGS AND CARPETING

Rugs and carpets provide both decoration against the plain background of a floor and comfort against the hard—and often cold—surface. They also absorb shock and noise, and they cushion falls. Rugs and carpets are available in an almost endless variety of sizes, shapes, materials, and designs. If the carpet or rugs in a room have a pronounced design, it is advisable to use solid-color draperies and little pattern in other furnishings. Because there is a wide range of choices in rugs and carpeting and because they must be replaced from time to time, you should know what is available in order to meet the needs for your home.

Types of Rugs and Carpets

Although the terms *rug* and *carpet* are often used interchangeably, rugs are of less than room size and can be removed, whereas carpeting is available by the yard,

Wall-to-wall carpeting can provide a sense of unity and a feeling of luxury within the home. Carpeting may be used in individual or adjoining rooms or throughout the home.

cut to length, and used to cover the entire floor. Because carpets are usually woven on wide looms, they are often referred to as "broadloom." Both rugs and carpets are made in a wide variety of fibers and finishes. With advances in the production of chemical fibers, special weaves, and finishes, carpeting is now used indoors in kitchens and bathrooms, and outdoors around swimming pools and on terraces, as well as in the traditional areas for living, sleeping, and eating.

Wall-to-wall carpeting Carpeting has become increasingly popular for use on the concrete slab and plywood floors of many contemporary homes, as well as on damaged hardwood floors or on any floors where added comfort is desirable. Carpeting reduces noise, absorbs shock, cushions falls (especially on steps), and acts as insulation. The material of a carpet is chosen according to performance, beauty, resilience, and ease of maintenance. Wool, which once accounted for most of the carpeting sold, has been largely replaced by synthetic fibers. One main objection to wall-to-wall carpeting is that traffic lines may show after it has been in use for some time. Because it is permanently installed, it cannot be turned around to distribute wear, as room-size rugs can, nor can it be sent out for cleaning. On-the-floor cleaning is not as thorough as that done by professional cleaners. Also, wall-to-wall carpeting is more expensive than a room-size rug because of the yardage required and the cost of installation.

Rugs Rugs provide more flexibility than carpeting in use and care, since they can usually be turned to distribute wear and they can be sent out for professional cleaning. Rugs are available in many different sizes, depending on the intended use.

A room-size rug may be woven a standard size or cut from tufted broadloom carpet in almost any size desired. It may cover an entire floor, or it may come to within 9 to 12 inches (22.86 to 30.48 cm) of the wall on all sides. A floor space of more than 12 inches around the rug is too much, unless the floor and rug are similar in color. For example, a beige rug that is a little too small may be used on a beige terrazzo or vinyl-tile floor without calling attention to a wide border, whereas a rug of the same size but in a contrasting color would appear too small.

An area rug is used to define a certain space. In room arrangements with a large expanse of floor, area rugs may be used to indicate particular areas. For instance, an area rug may define a dining area, a conversation area, or a study area. Though it may be of any shape or pattern, the shape, pattern, and color must bear a relationship to the area, furnishings, and character of the room.

Area rugs or carpet can provide either a plain background, as in this room; or a focus of color or design, as with the Oriental rugs shown on the next page.

Scatter rugs are small rugs used in an entrance hall, under a coffee table, in front of a fireplace, or in a bedroom or bathroom. It is important to choose a scatter rug with a nonskid back, because scatter rugs on slippery floors may cause falls.

Accent rugs are small rugs used to add interest. They are often placed under a coffee table or in front of a sofa or fireplace to add interest, or on top of wall-to-wall carpeting as a work of art. They may be machine-made or handmade.

Oriental rugs Handmade Oriental rugs have been valued possessions since European traders began to import rugs from the Near East during the late Middle Ages. Only people of wealth could afford to own these luxurious coverings for the cold floors of castles. Oriental rugs are still treasured, often being treated as works of art. Today, machine-made copies of Oriental rugs are available at a relatively low cost. However, these rugs should not be confused with the handmade kind.

Oriental rugs are unmatched for beauty of color and design. Although authentic Orientals are very expensive and increasingly scarce, good-quality modern reproductions are available, and at a moderate cost.

True Oriental rugs may be either hand-woven or knotted. They are imported from Asian countries, from Turkey to Japan. Certain countries or even communities may have their own characteristic designs, which have become traditional. The most valuable Orientals are made with vegetable dyes. Oriental rugs are never of a regular size, because each knot is tied by hand and no two weavers tie knots with the same tension. A skilled weaver, following a pattern pinned to the loom, may tie between 8,000 and 12,000 knots a day. The colors and designs show through on the back of the rug, and fringe appears only on the finishing ends of the rug. These rugs are becoming increasingly scarce because hand production is giving way to production by machine.

Fibers for Rugs and Carpeting

Durability is an important factor in the selection of floor coverings. The durability of carpeting depends upon the density, or closeness, of the tufts or weave; the fiber used; the twist of the yarn; and the height of the pile. Carpet fibers vary greatly in their resistance to dirt and wear. It is particularly important that areas of heavy use—such as entrances, hallways, stairs, and places where people gather frequently—have rugs or carpeting that can withstand the wear. In other areas, such as bedrooms and dining areas, rugs or carpeting made of less durable fibers may be satisfactory.

The fibers used in making carpets are of two main types—natural (including wool, cotton, sisal, straw, hemp, and rush) and synthetic (including nylon, acrylic, polyester, olefin, and rayon). Synthetic fibers now account for about 95 percent of all carpet yarns, with nylon the leading fiber. Each manufacturer has one or more trade names for these basic fibers.

Each main type of carpet fiber has special characteristics and offers certain benefits and disadvantages, as follows:

— Nylon is a durable fiber which resists abrasion, crushing, and matting. It accounts for over 70 percent of the carpet produced. Nylon yarns are of two types: continuous filament, which are woven; and staple yarns, which are cut and twisted. Continuous-filament nylon yarns are more durable and produce less pilling than staple nylon yarns, but staple yarns give a softer texture. One disadvantage of nylon is that it conducts static electricity unless an anti-static finish is applied. Nylon is moth- and mildew-resistant, and it is easy to maintain.

— Acrylic yarns look and feel like wool and produce a soft plush pile. These yarns produce less static electricity than nylon. They are not as durable as nylon, but the colors may be clearer. Carpeting made of acrylic yarns is recommended for low-to-moderate-traffic areas. Modacrylic fibers are modified acrylics popular for both mats and scatter rugs in bedrooms.

— Polyester yarns resemble wool but do not generate static electricity. Heatset polyester yarns are crush-resistant. Polyester carpet is durable and easy to maintain.

— Olefin is very durable and soil-resistant. It is used a great deal in needle-punch carpeting for outdoor and kitchen use. It is non-absorbent and mildew-resistant, and it is easy to maintain. It does not take dye as well as other fibers.

— Wool is the most popular of the natural fibers used for carpeting, though it now accounts for less than five percent of the carpeting sold. Wool wears well and has excellent resistance to crushing, but it is not recommended for use in warm, moist climates. Moths may attack wool fibers, unless a moth-repellent finish has been used.

— Sisal, straw, hemp, and rush are natural fibers used for rugs. They resist heat but are not soil- or mildew-resistant. They are intended mainly for informal settings, for seasonal use on porches or covered terraces, or for second homes such as cabins or beach houses.

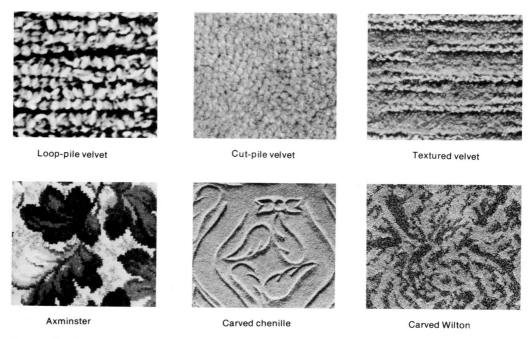

Loop-pile velvet   Cut-pile velvet   Textured velvet

Axminster   Carved chenille   Carved Wilton

The construction of carpeting is an important factor in selection. The type of construction is closely related to durability and intended use.

Construction of Carpets

Carpeting is found in an almost unlimited variety of types and textures. These variations depend on two main factors—the process by which the carpeting is made, and the way the surface texture is finished. The process of manufacture and the surface treatment are important not only to appearance but also to durability and resistance to dirt.

Three different methods—weaving, tufting, and needle-punching—are used to make carpeting. Woven carpet is produced on a loom. Good-quality woven rugs are very durable. The most familiar types of woven carpet are Wilton and Axminster. About 90 percent of carpets today are made by tufting. In this process, loops are pulled through a backing in somewhat the same way as in hand-hooking. A layer of latex is applied to the back to secure the yarns, and a second backing is bonded to the back for durability. The process of tufting is less expensive than that of weaving. In needle-punching, sheets of loose fibers are punched with many needles to raise the fibers. The fibers are then matted with an adhesive to create a felt-like effect. Carpeting made this way is most often used outdoors but is also appropriate for kitchens and play areas.

Carpets are made with many different surface textures. Most often, this texture depends on how the pile—the yarn on the surface of the carpet—is treated. In cut pile, the yarn ends on the surface are cut to form a dense finish. The finish may be short and smooth or long and shaggy. In a looped-pile surface, the yarn ends are not cut. The texture may be smooth or shaggy, depending on the type of yarn and the length of the loop. Cut pile and looped pile may be combined to give the surface a carved or sculptured effect.

Carpet Backing and Padding

Good backing on carpet can prevent stretching or wrinkling, make it more comfortable underfoot, and add years to the life of the carpet. Jute is the backing used most frequently on tufted carpeting. Some carpets have a secondary backing made of foam rubber, sponge rubber, or vinyl. With these kinds of backing, an underpadding is not needed.

For carpets without secondary backing —including woven carpets—it is often desirable to use an underpadding. Felted, rubber, or urethane padding should be used under all wall-to-wall carpeting and large woven or tufted rugs. Such cushioning extends the wear, reduces fatigue, gives resilience, and provides insulation.

The best insulator against both heat and cold is felt cushion made from animal hair.

Assembling a swatch card can help you make decisions about combinations of textures, shapes, and colors.

It should have a moth-resistant finish. Rubberized felt cushions are less expensive and feel firm under foot. Foam rubber is the most popular cushioning material. It is available in a flat or waffled surface. The flat-surface foam rubber, which is more expensive, is recommended for areas with heavy traffic. However, waffled cushioning feels more resilient. Sponge rubber, which is less buoyant than foam rubber, is recommended for cushioning under outdoor carpet.

CAREER PROFILE

PAINTER

Painters apply coats of paint, varnish, or stain to the interior or exterior surfaces and trims of buildings. One important aspect of their job is to properly prepare the surfaces before beginning to paint. They may have to smooth the surface with sandpaper or steel wool. Old paint may have to be removed with a scraper and paint remover. Nail holes, cracks, and joints must be filled in with putty or another type of filler. Only then do painters apply paint to the surfaces using brushes, rollers, and spray guns. They can create special effects by applying the paint with sponges, pieces of cloth, or other materials. They can also simulate wood grain, marble, brick, or tile by using special techniques. Some painters also hang wallpaper.

If you are interested in becoming a painter, you should like working with your hands. An understanding of color is very beneficial. You should have the patience for detailed work and be able to perceive small differences in color and texture. You should like working outdoors as well as indoors.

To become a painter, you can enter an apprenticeship program or receive on-the-job training. Many painters work independently on a full-time or part-time basis.

REVIEWING CHAPTER 12

SUMMARY

Walls are important to a room's color scheme because they establish the background for other furnishings. Paint and wallpaper are the most widely used finishes for walls. Wood paneling, ceramic tile, brick, and other materials can also be used. Usually, ceilings are painted a light color in order to reflect light. Sometimes ceilings are covered with wallpaper or acoustic tile, which helps absorb noise.

Different areas of the home may require different types of floor surfaces. Some of the more common rigid flooring materials are wood, marble, flagstone, slate, brick, and ceramic and quarry tile. Resilient floor coverings, such as vinyl flooring, are available in rolls and in square tiles. Rugs and carpets provide decoration as well as comfort and are available in a wide variety of sizes, materials, and designs. Durability and ease of care are important factors in the selection of floor coverings.

FACTS TO KNOW

1. Describe the advantages and special uses of four types of wall finishes.
2. Explain the meaning of each of these terms: latex, oil-base, varnish, and polyurethane.
3. What are the advantages and disadvantages of latex paint and of oil-base paint?
4. Explain how wallpaper can be used to solve certain decorating problems.
5. What guidelines should you follow when using wallpaper?
6. List three types of ceiling finishes. How does ceiling height influence the choice of color used on the ceiling?
7. Describe three types of rigid flooring materials and three types of resilient flooring materials. Compare the advantages and disadvantages of each material.
8. Explain these terms: wall-to-wall carpeting, room-size rug, area rug, scatter rug, and accent rug. How is each type used?

IDEAS TO THINK ABOUT

1. Evaluate the ease of care of different types of wall and floor coverings. How important is this factor for today's lifestyles?
2. Analyze the different background materials shown in the pictures in this chapter. What conclusions can be drawn about the type of backgrounds appropriate for different types of rooms? for different styles of decorating?

ACTIVITIES TO DO

1. From advertisements, gather the prices of different types of wall and floor coverings, such as paint, wallpaper, paneling, carpeting, and tile. Figure the cost of using each material to decorate a 12 foot x 15 foot (3.6 m x 4.6 m) room.
2. Visit a paint and wallpaper store, a carpet store, or a home improvement center. Note the selection and variety of materials available. Report your findings to the class.

Chapter
13

Window Treatment

Have you ever imagined what it might be like to live in a home without windows? We often take windows for granted, yet they serve many purposes. Windows are a source of light and air, as well as an architectural feature. They may offer a special view of the outdoors or face the sun for solar heating. Windows come in a wide variety of shapes, such as bay, dormer, arched, and cathedral. Their sizes may vary from narrow casements to wide picture windows, and to large glass walls and sliding glass doors.

What is the best way to decorate a window? There are as many different options for window treatments as there are types of windows. You can choose from curtains, draperies, blinds, shades, and shutters. Some windows may be left uncovered so as not to obstruct their views. For other windows, coverings may be essential to provide privacy for people in the home. If your windows are oddly shaped or poorly spaced, you can create illusions of different proportions with your choice of window treatments.

In this chapter you will learn how to make your windows as attractive as possible—no matter what size or shape they may be. You may choose to have the window treatments blend with the walls, match a chair or bed, or become the focal point of the room.

250

PREVIEWING YOUR LEARNING

After you have read this chapter, you will be able to:

* Identify basic types of windows.

* Evaluate window treatments in terms of function and decoration.

* Choose window treatments that are suitable to the type of window and to the character of a room.

* Apply the principles of design to window treatments.

TERMS TO KNOW

blinds—horizontal or vertical slats that can be tilted open or closed

café curtain—fabric curtain, attached by rings to a rod, that covers only part of a window

cornice—a horizontal molding over a window that conceals the drapery rod

draw draperies—pinch-pleated fabric panels that can be opened or closed by pulling a cord at the side of the window.

lambrequin—a shaped frame for a window

sash—the frame that surrounds the pane of glass in a window or door

sheers—curtains made of sheer or semi-opaque fabric that hang close to the window

sill—the horizontal piece at the base of a window

swag—something hanging in a curve between two points

traverse rod—a metal rod with a pulley mechanism for opening and closing curtains or draperies

valance—a short drapery heading hung across the top of a window

A WINDOW GREENHOUSE

FEATURE

If you love plants, you might consider adding a window greenhouse to your home someday. Imagine seeing plants grow and bloom in the middle of winter! A window greenhouse helps to bring the great outdoors inside your home. If well-insulated, a greenhouse can also be a supplemental source of heat for a room during winter months.

The first step in installing a window greenhouse is to choose the best available location. The window should have a southern or eastern exposure and provide three to four hours of sunlight a day during winter months. It is important to monitor available sunlight throughout the year. Since the winter sun arcs low in the sky, a building or nearby hill may not block the sun in summer but may block it in winter. If the window you really want to use does not meet all the requirements, just add a fluorescent light during the winter.

Most window greenhouses are framed in aluminum with glass or plastic panes, but all are not adequately ventilated. Without ventilation, heat buildup inside the greenhouse will virtually boil the plants. The window greenhouse should be vented on top to permit hot air to escape and to provide proper air circulation. The top vents should also be screened to keep insects out.

Although too much heat can be tough on plants, some is needed to keep them healthy. A window greenhouse with double- or triple-glazed panes will retain enough heat, even in winter, to keep your plants lush and healthy.

BASIC WINDOW TYPES

If you study the homes in your own neighborhood, you will see many different kinds of windows. You might list the various types of windows shown in this chapter and see how many of them you can find in your community. Notice what style of architecture each type of window is used with. Are any windows used with several different types of architecture?

Windows are made in a number of standard shapes and sizes. The basic window types are double-hung (single or multiple), casement (in-swinging and out-swinging), corner, dormer, bay, arched, awning, jalousie, picture, ranch, clerestory, and slanting. The type of window used in a particular home depends upon a number of factors. Among these are the style of architecture, exposure, need for light and ventilation, and desire for privacy.

Just as the type of window should conform to the basic architecture of the home, the treatment of windows in decoration

often depends upon the type of window. Various types of windows are illustrated on page 255. Special curtain and drapery rods are available for the more unusual styles of windows. Shades, blinds, and shutters can also be used on most types of windows.

STANDARD WINDOW TREATMENTS

The treatment of windows in decorating should meet several basic requirements. First, they should meet certain standards of design, and they should complement the furnishings in a room. At the same time, they should meet the functional needs for light and privacy. Some window treatments are mainly for decoration; others are mainly functional. In some situations, the window treatment selected can serve both decorative and functional purposes. Often, combinations such as draperies and shades are used to meet different needs. From the many fabrics and styles available, you must select those that suit your personal taste, are appropriate for the decorating theme, and meet the needs of your home.

Functional Treatments

The main purposes of window coverings such as blinds, shades, and shutters, are to control light, air, and temperature, and to provide privacy. These coverings can also be decorative, but that aspect is usually of secondary importance.

If you are renting an apartment, you will find that window blinds, shades, or shutters are frequently provided. If not, rods are usually provided for draw draperies. Most people like to have draw draperies or curtains, in addition to blinds or shades, for privacy and control of light and heat. If shades are used in a home, they should be raised the same distance from the window sills.

TERMS RELATED TO WINDOW AND DRAPERY LENGTHS

Blinds Window blinds have either horizontal or vertical slats that can be tilted to open or close. Blinds actually originated in China. They were brought to Europe by way of Venice, the city for which venetian blinds were named. They became popular in both England and America during the Georgian period of the 18th century.

Blinds are useful for controlling both light and ventilation. The width of the slats can vary—from wide vertical slats, to the narrow mini or micro horizontal slats. Blinds are available in aluminum, steel, plastic, and wood. Metallic or fabric finishes are also used. Blinds may be used with almost any decorating scheme. Sometimes draw draperies or stationary side draperies are used with them. They must be dusted fairly frequently and cleaned periodically with a mild detergent.

Shades Roller shades are the most common and least expensive means of shutting out light and providing privacy. Purely functional shades are made of cloth with a special finish or of plastic material.

Either may be purchased with a blackout material laminated between two layers, which allows very little light to enter the room when the shades are pulled to the sill. If dusted and cleaned occasionally with a mild detergent, cloth and plastic shades last a long time. Decorative shades may

Vertical blinds provide light control and privacy. They can be used with sliding glass doors.

Mini blinds are available in a wide range of colors, including prints and metallics.

Shades can be used alone or with curtains.

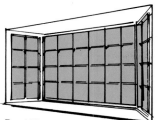

TYPES OF WINDOWS
AND HOW TO TREAT THEM

Bay Window
Special rods are available for threesided or circular bay windows so that they may be treated as a group.

Jalousie
These may be treated in the same manner as double-hung or awning-type windows.

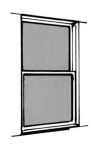

Double-Hung
This type is easy to decorate as a single window or a group of windows. Use tailored or ruffled curtains, draw or stationary draperies, café curtains on both sashes or either upper or lower sash. Cornices, valances, and swags may be used.

Dormer Window
For these traditional-style windows, use sheer ruffled curtains, tailored curtains, or café curtains. For a decorative effect, use figured wallpaper on surrounding walls. A window shade may be covered with the wallpaper also.

Awning Type
These may be treated in the same manner as double-hung windows.

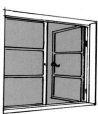

Out- Swinging Casement
These may be treated like double-hung windows, whether single or grouped.

In-Swinging Casement
The treatment must not interfere with window opening into the room. Curtains must be fastened to the window and not the frame. Draperies may be used with swinging rods. Cornices and valances are not usable.

Ranch Windows
These are long, narrow windows set high in the wall. Use sill-length draw draperies, or curtains with draperies to the sill. A valance or cornice may be used. Full-length stationary draperies may be used if a bed or chest is directly under the windows.

Other Types of Windows
An arched window may be treated like a single window below the arch. A special rod will permit a fanlike arrangement over the arch. A clerestory window is usually left plain. A slanting window may be treated with draw draperies on a special rod.

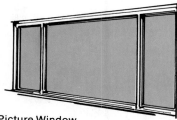

Picture Window
This may be a glass wall with sliding panes or a long window of ordinary height with stationary panes. If the view is not interesting, block it out with semi-sheer glass curtains under draw draperies. Cafe curtains are also used. A valance or cornice gives unity.

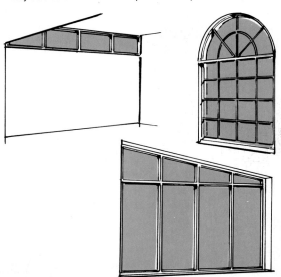

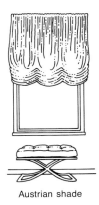

Austrian shade

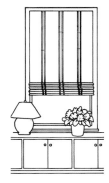

Roman shade

Balloon shade

be made from any kind of firmly woven fabric to match the wallpaper, bedspread, or upholstery in the room.

Matchstick or split-bamboo roller shades are popular in informal rooms. Sometimes they are decorated vertically or horizontally with colored yarns. An occasional dusting and sponging with a mild detergent will keep them new-looking.

Austrian, Roman, and balloon shades are more like curtains than shades because they are made of fabric. Austrian shades, which are drawn up in gathers, are rather elaborate. Roman shades, which are drawn up in accordian folds, are simpler. Balloon shades create poufs at the bottom. For adjusting these shades, tapes with rings are fastened to the back of the shade. The tapes are looped at the bottom and hold a metal rod. A cord runs through the rings and loops and pulls the shade up in folds.

Shutters Shutters are especially popular in areas where heat is intense. In the cities of southern Europe and northern Africa, heavy wooden or metal shutters are used on the outside of the windows to keep the sun off. Many Southern Colonial homes, as well as Victorian homes, also had louvered shutters outside the windows. By contrast, colonial homes in the North often had shutters inside windows to

Shutters provide privacy yet permit light to enter.

keep out the cold. In many homes today, outside shutters are merely decorative and are not meant to close. However, shutters are frequently used on the inside of windows—for one sash only or for both the upper and lower sashes. They give a decorative effect, control light, provide privacy, or hide an unpleasant view.

Decorative Treatments

Draperies and curtains are mainly decorative in purpose, though they may also be functional—shutting out light and providing privacy. Draperies, particularly, are often an important feature of design. When closed, they help to conserve energy. Curtains add interest, diffuse the light, and provide some privacy in the daytime.

Drapery and curtain styles Fashions in curtains and draperies have changed along with changes in architecture. Windows in old New England houses and Cape Cod cottages were small and required little decoration except perhaps cottage curtains. Georgian homes in both England and America placed a great deal of emphasis upon woodwork, including window frames. Draperies or curtains were frequently set inside the window frame to expose the wood trim.

The Victorian age in American architecture and design was a time of ornateness and display in decoration. The bay window became such an important status symbol that people whose homes had no bay knocked out a wall to create one. The decorative treatment of bay windows was very elaborate. By contrast, in most contemporary homes today, wooden window framing is almost eliminated, and the simple window decorations used are in keeping with today's more informal way of life. Where a picture window or window wall offers a beautiful view, draperies are often kept plain to avoid competing with the view for interest.

Draperies Draperies are generally made of a medium or heavyweight fabric, though not as heavy as that used for upholstery. They need not be lined if the fabric is heavy, firmly woven, or laminated on the back. However, lined draperies have certain advantages: they protect the fabric from sunlight, allow the draperies to hang better, shut out more light, and present a more uniform appearance from the outside. In colder regions, heavy window coverings called window quilts are used to help reduce heat loss and conserve energy. Draperies may be used alone or combined with curtains. For example, draperies are often hung on a double rod along with sheer curtains.

Draperies may be hung in a variety of ways. Two-way draperies are hung on a traverse rod which allows them to be pulled open and closed. Stationary draperies hang on either side of the window and

The sheer curtains provide some privacy in the daytime but still let in light. The draw draperies can be closed at night for additional privacy.

INFORMAL WINDOW TREATMENTS

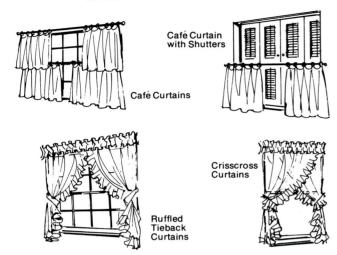

Café Curtains

Café Curtain with Shutters

Crisscross Curtains

Ruffled Tieback Curtains

TRADITIONAL AND FORMAL WINDOW TREATMENTS

Two-Way Draw Curtains or Draperies

Tie-back Drape

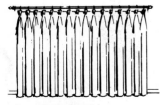

Draw Draperies on Decorative Rod

Stationary Drape

TREATMENTS FOR PROBLEM WINDOWS

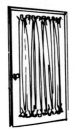

Door with Panes of Glass

cannot be closed. Draperies usually extend just above the top of the window frame. At the bottom, they may reach to the sill, to the bottom of the window frame, or to just above the floor. They may also reach to a covered radiator, low cabinet, or set of shelves. However, draperies should never dangle in the middle of a wall.

A wide variety of fabrics can be used for draperies. Brocade, velvet, taffeta, and antique satin are commonly used with traditional furniture. For more informal furnishings, such as colonial and provincial styles, chintz, printed cotton, calico, muslin, gingham, and even printed sheets are used. Draperies for contemporary rooms are usually made of plain or textured fabrics.

Curtains Curtains are made of sheer, lightweight, or loosely woven fabrics and are unlined. They may hang across the entire window, be partially pulled back with tiebacks, or be pulled back and forth on a rod. Sheer curtains, which hang close to the window, may be gathered on a rod or pleated to hang straight down to the sill, window frame, or floor. They should be twice the width of the window in order to hang well. If the fabric is very sheer, the curtains should be even wider. When sheer curtains are attached to a door or casement window, they are called casement curtains.

Café curtains were originally used for the lower sash in street cafés to provide some privacy. They are short curtains hung on a rod from rings, clips, or fabric loops. They may be used on the upper half, lower half, or both halves of a window. Sometimes they are combined with shutters.

Tieback curtains look best if they stop at the window frame or floor. Ruffled curtains may meet in the center or be crisscrossed and tied back. Tailored curtains used with draperies may stop at the sill, the bottom of the window frame, or just above the floor.

These contemporary draw draperies are made of a fabric that provides some privacy but allows light to filter through to the room.

Valances, cornices, swags, and lambrequins For a special decorative effect, separate headings may be used across the top of draperies or curtains. Such headings—including valances, cornices, lambrequins, and swags are used more often in rooms of a particular period or in older homes with high ceilings than they are in modern homes. Most newer homes have ceilings of 8 feet (2.44 m) or less, and any window decoration with a strong horizontal emphasis tends to make the ceiling seem lower. When any horizontal decoration is used at the top of windows in modern homes, it should be placed close to the ceiling.

A valance is usually a gathered or pleated heading hung on the outside rod of a double curtain rod. Simple valances or cornices covered with cloth, matching the stationary or draw drapes, may be used in large rooms. The depth of the valance or cornice should be between one seventh and one eighth of the distance from the top of the window treatment to the floor. Sometimes a valance is suspended on a rod from the ceiling, so that the pleating at the top almost touches the ceiling. Draw draperies or side draperies may be used with a valance extending all the way across a group of windows. In that case, the valance hides the curtain rod.

Swags are used in large formal rooms with tall windows and high ceilings. They may also be used in traditional-type homes with fairly large rooms and ceilings that are at least 8 feet (2.44 m) high. However, they may be too heavy in the rooms of an average-size home.

Lambrequins are shaped frames made of plywood, masonite, or heavy buckram, all of which may be covered with fabric or a vinyl plastic. Masonite and plywood frames may be painted with a solid color or have designs applied to them. Like valances, cornices, and swags, lambrequins are used most often in rather formal settings.

DECORATIVE FINISHES FOR DRAPERIES AND CURTAINS

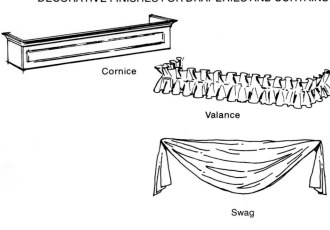

Cornice

Valance

Swag

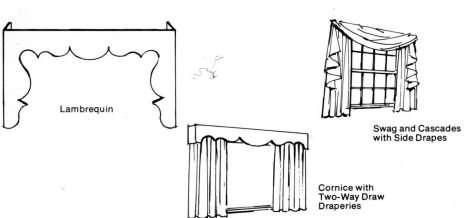

Lambrequin

Cornice with
Two-Way Draw
Draperies

Swag and Cascades
with Side Drapes

Cafe Curtains
with Valance

DESIGN PRINCIPLES FOR WINDOW TREATMENTS

The draperies, curtains, or other window coverings you choose should coordinate well with your furniture and the other parts of your decorating and color scheme. Windows, walls, and floors must have unity and provide a pleasing background. The style of architecture and the size, shape, and grouping of windows place some limits upon window decorating. Nevertheless, the pattern, fabric, and type of window treatment can all be used to enhance the character of the room. The principles of design apply to the treatment of windows, just as they do to backgrounds and the total effect you are seeking.

The basic principles of design can be of special help to you in dealing with windows that are awkwardly placed or out of proportion. Windows that are too long and narrow, too short and broad, entirely too small, or poorly spaced on a wall can be decorated to give an illusion of good proportion. A narrow window may be made to appear wider by extending the draperies over the wall at each side so that the entire window is exposed. A low window will look higher if a cornice or valance is used on the wall above, barely covering the top of the window.

Many contemporary homes have ranch-style windows placed high on the wall. This location simplifies the arrangement of furniture and provide privacy, but it does very little for the appearance of a room. Also, they are difficult to see through, and they provide little ventilation. In older homes, the small windows often found over built-in bookcases on each side of a fireplace may present a decorating problem. Bay windows and corner windows may also be difficult to treat. Several suggestions for dealing with problem windows may be found in decorating magazines or books.

WINDOW TREATMENT IN RELATION TO ROOM USE

The purpose of a room is an important factor in the treatment of windows. Windows in a living room may have a more dignified and formal treatment than those in other rooms. Floor-length draw draperies in a solid color are usually in good taste. They may contrast with the walls if the room is large, blend into the walls if the room is small, or pick up a prominent color in the wallpaper. Figured draperies are effective with solid-color walls, especially if the background of the print is repeated in

These poorly placed windows have been camouflaged with side-by-side tieback curtains that unite the two windows.

the wall color. Floor-length draw draperies make a very attractive backdrop for a living room at night.

Dining room window decorations should not contrast too sharply with those of living room windows if the two rooms are close together. A dining area separated from the living room may be treated less formally than a regular dining room.

In bedrooms the choice of window decoration is a personal matter. Many people have definite ideas about how they want their windows to look. Even young children often have their own ideas about the decoration of their rooms. If wallpaper is used, the window treatment should be simple. If the walls are a solid color, a printed drapery fabric may be desirable.

OWNER OF A DECORATOR FABRIC SHOP

C A R E E R   P R O F I L E

A decorator fabric store specializes in fabrics that are used for upholstery, draperies, and curtains. The store may also carry ready-made draperies, curtains, bedspreads, decorative pillows, window blinds and shades, and all types of drapery and curtain rods. The owner of the shop is responsible for selecting and purchasing all of the merchandise for the store. He or she must hire and supervise employees and keep business records. The owner or employees might set up window and store displays, prepare samples, and create newspaper advertisements. When dealing with customers, the owner may discuss the special features of a product, quote prices, explain credit terms, and prepare order forms. Sometimes the owner may visit customers in their homes so that they may view samples of fabrics next to their other furnishings. Many decorator fabric shops will also upholster furniture and make slipcovers, draperies, or curtains by special order. The store may have its own workshop or hire self-employed upholsterers and sewers.

If you would like to sell decorator fabrics, you should be interested in textiles, colors, and interior design. You must be able to work well with people. If you want to specialize in making items, such as slipcovers or draperies, you will need good sewing skills.

A person who organizes and manages his or her own business is called an entrepreneur. The business can be small or large. You can work out of a shop or from your own home. To achieve success in your own business, you need self-motivation, initiative, self-confidence, and you must be willing to take risks. You will probably have to work long hours, especially when the business is getting started. However, the rewards can be great, both financially and emotionally. One major advantage is that you are your own boss. To succeed as the owner of a decorator fabric shop, you can take courses in merchandising, business, textiles, and sewing construction at a college, merchandising, business, textiles, and sewing construction at a college, vocational, or technical school. Selling experience is also helpful.

REVIEWING CHAPTER 13

SUMMARY

The selection of window treatments involves knowledge of various types of windows, window treatments, fabrics, and design principles. The way a window is decorated partly depends on what type of window it is. Some window treatments are mainly decorative; others are mainly functional. Often, combinations, such as draperies and shades, are used to meet both needs.

Blinds, shades, and shutters help to control light and provide privacy. Draperies and curtains are mainly decorative, though they may also shut out light and provide privacy. Draperies and curtains may be hung in a variety of ways. Separate headings, such as valances and cornices, may be used across the top of draperies or curtains.

The choice of fabric for draperies or curtains depends upon the use of the room and its theme or character. The fabric should coordinate with your furniture and color scheme. Basic principles of design can help with problems such as awkwardly placed or poorly proportioned windows.

FACTS TO KNOW

1. Identify six basic types of windows and describe the main characteristic of each.

2. What are the special functions of blinds, shades, and shutters? What advantages and disadvantages does each have?

3. Describe Austrian shades, Roman shades, and balloon shades.

4. Explain the difference between draperies and curtains.

5. Describe each of the following types of draperies and curtains: draw draperies, café curtains, tieback draperies or curtains, crisscross curtains, and sheers.

6. Describe valances, cornices, lambrequins, and swags.

7. What types of fabrics are usually used for draperies? for curtains?

8. Explain how the basic principles of design can be used when decorating problem windows.

IDEAS TO THINK ABOUT

1. Describe several ways that functional and decorative window treatments can be used together.

2. Select eight types of windows and describe at least two window treatments that can be used for each.

ACTIVITIES TO DO

1. Study the window styles used in homes in your community. Make a list of the various types of windows, noting the architectural style of each home. What relationships do you find between the architectural design and the type of window used?

2. Compare the prices of various draperies and curtains at a variety store, a department store, and a specialty home furnishings store. Also compare the merchandise for width, hem, texture, weight, and quality of fabric. What conclusions may be drawn from the information you have gathered?

Chapter
14

Furniture Styles

If you visit a museum, you will probably see examples of different styles of furniture. Some may be very formal and elaborate, such as those from palaces or castles. Others may be plain and simple, emphasizing comfort and function, such as those from country homes. During each major period of history, people developed different styles of furniture and architecture. These styles have created a rich heritage of furniture design which we can choose from when decorating our own homes.

Today, people's preferences for different furniture styles vary widely. Some people prefer all their furniture and decorations to be of one style. Others prefer a combination of styles. You do not need to have a thorough knowledge of furniture styles in order to choose good furniture or to create an attractive home. However, some knowledge about the different periods of furniture will help you recognize good design. It will also give you greater confidence when selecting furniture for your home.

Over the centuries, furniture has evolved from four basic human needs: a place to lie down, a place to sit, a place in which to store belongings, and a surface upon which to prepare and eat food. These needs continue to be met by beds, chairs, chests, and tables —only their styles have changed.

264

PREVIEWING YOUR LEARNING

After you have read this chapter, you will be able to:
* Explain how furniture styles evolved over the centuries.

* Recognize traditional, Early American, provincial, and contemporary or modern furniture styles.

* Identify specific periods and styles of furniture design.

* Describe specific furniture pieces, such as a secretary, a highboy, and a hutch.

TERMS TO KNOW

armoire—a tall cupboard or wardrobe
contemporary—of or having to do with the present time
highboy—a tall chest of drawers
hutch—a chest topped with open shelves
pediment—a triangular shape at the top of a cabinet used as a decoration
provincial—relating to a country style of furniture that is more simple, plain, and informal

secretary—a desk topped with a cabinet with shelves and doors
stretcher—a rod or bar that extends between two legs of a chair or table
traditional—a style that is established and has been used for a long period of time
trestle—a braced frame that serves as a support

WITH ROOM TO GROW

F
E
A
T
U
R
E

Studies in child development show that infants respond to color and other visual stimuli from the moment they are born. This makes a child's room a special place—a place where the learning process begins. It also should be a room that can grow with a child's ever-changing needs.

Since children respond to color at such a young age, a child's room should be bright and fun. Colorful wallpaper borders are a great way to start. They add punch to painted walls, and motifs can be changed as the child develops—from teddy bears and ABC's to ballet slippers and racing cars. Bright accessories, such as curtains and bedspreads, are also easily changeable and serve to enliven the decor.

Most children's furniture is made of sturdy wood or plastic laminates and has clean, simple lines which withstand time and changing tastes. Smart furniture investments are those that change with the child's growth, such as cribs that convert to youth beds or settees, or changing tables that are also dressers. Bunk and trundle beds sleep two but take up the space of one. They are great for a sibling or a "sleepover" friend. In later years, a convertible sofa bed can turn a teen's bedroom into a more social place and prepares it for future use as a guest room.

Storage in a child's room should provide safe accessibility. Avoid big, wooden toy chests with hinged tops that can fall and hurt little fingers. Instead, choose plastic milk crates and open baskets which keep toys at hand and make cleanup time easy. For older children, shelving units with drop-down desk tops make good investments.

THE ORIGINS OF FURNITURE

The history of furniture closely parallels that of the home and of architecture, from prehistoric times to modern civilizations. The first bed was an animal skin or a pile of grass tossed on the hard earth. The first chair was a rock or a fallen tree; and the first chest, a hollow log or even a hole in the ground. As long as people lived like wandering hunters or herders, furnishings that were portable or available in the immediate surroundings met their needs.

With the rise of early civilizations, furniture in upright form and set on legs came into being. Excavations in Egypt and Crete, together with those in Greece and Rome, provide clues to the evolution of present-day furniture styles. In these early civilizations, the royal courts or wealthy families employed cabinetmakers to design thrones, couches, chairs, chests, and tables.

The Crusades of the late Middle Ages had a great influence on the development of furniture and furnishings in Europe. The Crusaders brought back from the Middle East goods such as four-poster beds, carved banquet tables, tapestries, rugs, and dishes made of porcelain. These refinements led to changes in ways of living. Eating was transformed to dining, as elaborate dining tables replaced boards supported by trestles. Chairs replaced benches, and a chair for the master of the house was copied from the throne chairs of ancient rulers. The master chair with arms has survived until the present time as a part of dining-room furniture.

As the Renaissance spread throughout Europe, many changes in furniture took place. For example, the simple box designed to hold the family Bible evolved into the desk. Pigeonholes and secret drawers were added to the box to contain personal records. The box was later tilted and placed on a stand so that a person could

read more easily from the Bible. An interest in writing and an increasing need for storage space turned the slant-top box into a slant-top chest or desk. As printing spread and people began to collect books, they needed a place to keep them. A cabinet with shelves and doors that could be locked was placed on top of the desk. This piece of furniture is known as a secretary.

The hutch evolved from the cupboard as a major piece of dining-room furniture. Expanding trade with the East helped to establish the custom of tea drinking in England. Shelves with hooks for cups and rails for plates and saucers were built to hold teacups, saucers, and plates. In the meantime, the board on trestles, or sideboard, which was set against the wall to hold food and dishes, evolved into a chest

The secretary provides storage space and a handy desk top for writing letters and checks.

with shelves and doors. Finally, the cupboard and storage chest were combined to produce the hutch, an important component of Early American furniture.

Other pieces of furniture also came into being because of special needs. The candlestand was needed to hold candles; tea tables held the serving pieces and dishes needed for serving tea. Because the hollow chest was not very adaptable to changing storage needs, drawers were added to make a low chest or lowboy. As storage needs increased, chests were placed on top of chests to form the chest-on-chest or highboy. Card tables came into being as people of leisure began to play card games. Leisure also provided more time for handwork and personal care, leading to the introduction of sewing tables and dressing tables with mirrors.

During the 20th century, changing needs and lifestyles have continued to influence furniture design. Lighweight, easy-to-maintain, dual-purpose, and portable types of furniture, together with modular storage and seating units, have been designed for smaller homes and our more mobile way of living.

The highboy provides extra storage space in a bedroom.

The hutch provides lots of storage space for dishes, glassware, and table linens in a dining area.

EMERGENCE OF FURNITURE STYLES

As pieces of furniture were being built to meet needs for living within the home, some nations developed their own characteristic forms and patterns of design. Fashions in furniture, as in dress, tended to be set by the royal courts, nobility, and people of wealth. The most elaborate designs were developed at the French court during the 17th and 18th centuries. English furniture of the 17th century was heavier and simpler in style than French furniture.

During the 18th century, English cabinetmakers introduced a number of furniture styles. The new furniture was simple yet elegant in design, with delicate carving and decoration. These styles set a standard of design that has seldom been equaled.

In both France and England, the custom arose of identifying furniture styles by the name of the ruler at the time, such as Louis XIV, Queen Anne, and so on. These styles are often referred to as "period furniture" —that is, the style used during a particular reign. People who are very familiar with furniture design can identify the period of almost any piece of furniture.

In the past four centuries, a great many styles and periods of furniture have appeared. In addition to European styles, new furniture designs appeared in America. Together, these styles provide a heritage of design, which is the basis of home furnishings today. The most popular styles of furniture used at present can be divided into three major groups—traditional, Early American and provincial, and contemporary or modern.

Traditional styles Most traditional furniture today is based on the classic designs of the 18th century. These graceful styles were made of fine woods such as walnut and mahogany. Inlay, veneering, and delicate caving were special features. Fabrics included brocades, damasks, satin, and fine velvet. Traditional furniture styles include Queen Anne, Chippendale, Adam, Hepplewhite, and Sheraton.

Early American and provincial styles At the same time that classic designs were being used in the palaces and mansions of England and France, simpler types of furniture were also being made. These designs were usually found in country homes and were made by hand from oak, pine, and maple. Although often copied from more elaborate designs, country furniture was basically simple and intended for informal settings. Two major examples of this type of furniture are Early American, used in colonial homes, and provincial, used in rural France.

Contemporary or modern styles Changes in technology during the 20th century have made many new types and designs of furniture possible. Modern materials include laminated wood and plastics that can be molded into almost any shape. Fiberglass, plasticized fabrics, aluminum, chrome, and other metals are used to make furniture of creative and striking design. Woods such as pine, maple, teak, mahogany, and rosewood are used with little, if any, ornamentation.

Early American-style furniture fits into the decorating theme of this family room.

ENGLISH FURNITURE,
17th AND EARLY 18th CENTURY

Jacobean Dower Chest

William and Mary Highboy

Queen Anne Highboy

The Jacobean Period

Jacobean furniture, named after King James I of England, ran from 1603 to 1688. Furniture was very large and rectangular in shape. Most pieces were made of oak and often had spiral-twisted legs. Intricate patterns were carved into chests and along the edges of tables and chairs. Drawer pulls usually took the form of acorns. Long tables with heavy legs and gate-leg tables, with sides that can be raised and supported by legs that swing out, are characteristic of this period.

The William and Mary Period

William of Orange and his wife Mary ruled England from 1689 to 1702. Furniture during this period was less massive and more graceful in form than Jacobean. From the china cupboard developed the first highboy, a chest set on a table. Many pieces were finished with veneering or other surface decoration, and fine tapestries were used for upholstery.

The Queen Anne Period

Queen Anne, Mary's younger sister, ruled England from 1702 to 1714. The Queen Anne style of furniture depended upon curves rather than the straight lines of the William and Mary period. Chairs were graceful and often armless to accommodate the ladies' full skirts. The backs of chairs were slightly curved at shoulder height and had a center splat or panel.

One of the main characteristics of this furniture period was curved or cabriole legs with club feet and shell carvings. Highboys and cabinets had carved broken-curve tops or broken pediments. Graceful brass drawer pulls and key plates enhanced the walnut and mahogany woods. Drop-leaf tables increased in popularity as well as tilt-top tables with plain tops or raised and carved piecrust edges. Upholstered wing chairs of this period are still popular today.

Chippendale Furniture

Several furniture styles became popular during the reigns of George I, II, and III. This period is sometimes referred to as the Georgian period. It became known as the golden age of furniture, and mahogany became the principal wood. Four names are connected with furniture during this period: Chippendale, Adam, Hepplewhite, and Sheraton. Chippendale is probably the most famous.

Thomas Chippendale, a creative designer and master craftsman, lived from 1718 to 1779. Many of his designs featured elaborate carvings, especially on the splat backs of chairs. Chair legs ended in claw and ball feet. As trade with China increased during this period, there was a strong Chinese influence in Chippendale's designs. Chair backs were filled in with Chinese fret or latticework. Legs resembled several bamboo rods bound together. Tables also had intricate carvings. Cupboards and cabinets had paneled and latticed glass doors. These were usually topped with a carved broken-curve pediment and a center decorative knob. Beautiful brass hardware added a distinctive finish to all cabinet pieces.

Adam Furniture

The Adam brothers were primarily architects during the period from 1762 to 1794. Catering only to the wealthy, they designed all the decoration of a house including the furniture, although they actually made very little furniture themselves. Instead of wood-paneled walls, they used plaster in delicate tones and decorated ceilings and walls with raised plaster moldings. Their furniture style was straight, small in scale, and decorated with classic designs such as medallions, urns, shields, and rosettes.

Hepplewhite Furniture

George Hepplewhite constructed much of the furniture for Adam interiors and may have also designed some of it. Chairs had oval or shield-shaped backs and straight, slender, tapering legs. Hepplewhite's other pieces included many different styles of tables, sofas, secretaries, rolltop writing desks, and four-poster beds with light delicate posts. He designed in mahogany and satinwood, frequently decorated with inlays and veneers.

Sheraton Furniture

Thomas Sheraton, who lived from 1751 to 1806, wrote a book on furniture design which influenced many other designers. Sheraton's pieces were very rectangular in shape compared to Hepplewhite's curved designs. Chair backs were rectangular with vertical balusters or supports. Legs were straight and tapering. He often built secret compartments and concealed drawers in furniture pieces. He is also known for his Pembroke table which has two drop leaves.

The furniture in this room reflects the traditional styles of the late 18th century. It might have been used in a house of Georgian, Southern colonial, or Federal style.

Victorian Furniture

The Victorian period, named after Queen Victoria who ruled from 1837 to 1901, featured very ornate and elaborate designs. Typical Victorian furniture was dark rosewood or mahogany. Chairs and sofas had curved wooden frames that were carved with roses, leaves, and fruit. Many were upholstered with thick pile fabrics. Other designs included dressers and washstands with marble tops and elaborate drawer pulls, what-not stands, tufted love seats, and scroll wall brackets. Rooms were crowded with cabinets and display cases, heavy draperies and window hangings, and many ornately patterned rugs.

French Provincial Furniture

Furniture styles during the Louis XIV, Louis XV, Louis XVI, and Empire periods were very elaborate. The term *provincial* refers to furniture made in the provinces —that is, the country—in contrast to formal court styles. Original pieces of provincial furniture were usually made by local craftsmen, and each cabinetmaker varied the style slightly. Local woods—such as fruitwood, oak, ash, elm, and chestnut —were used in place of imported woods.

Upholstered or solid wood chairs had rather low graceful backs and straight tapering or curved cabriole legs. Gingham or homespun materials were used for upholstery and arm pads. One of the best-known pieces of French provincial furniture was the armoire, a large clothes cupboard for the bedroom. Another characteristic piece was a hutch, with shelves and drawers, for the kitchen or dining room.

TRADITIONAL-STYLE CHAIRS

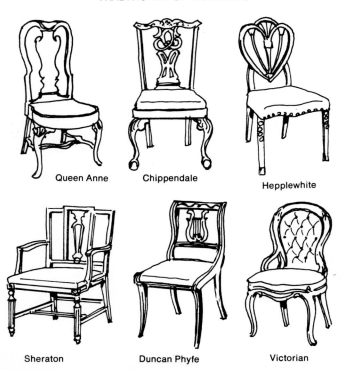

Queen Anne   Chippendale

Hepplewhite

Sheraton   Duncan Phyfe   Victorian

Early American Furniture

The furniture styles in America followed very closely those of Europe except that they were a number of years behind European styles. The Early American or Early Colonial styles of 1620 to 1725 coincided with the Jacobean, William and Mary, and Queen Anne styles of England. Early Chippendale styles were also copied until the American colonies broke their connections with England at the time of the Revolution and turned away from English influences in favor of American designs.

Although wealthy American families were able to import furniture until the Revolution, country dwellers made furniture from native woods and copied traditional styles. Original pieces and reproductions of them are treasured possessions in American homes today. Among the most valued pieces are the hutch, dry sink, Empire sideboard, ladder-back chairs, Windsor chairs, and four-poster and spool beds.

The Dutch, Swedish, and German colonists of the Middle Colonies also copied the designs of their homelands. Among the most charming pieces of Early American furniture are those of the Pennsylvania Dutch. They painted chests, cupboards, and chairs with hearts, tulips, roosters, and other peasant motifs, as reminders of their former homes. Swedish colonists painted on their furniture the designs of leaves, vines, and flowers that offset the long winters of their northern homeland.

Shaker designs, another Early American type, originated as a truly American style. The Shakers were a religious group who came to this country from England during the Revolution and established communities from the east coast to Kentucky. The Shakers, who had strict rules for living, were simple in both their dress and their ways of living. Their furniture was known for its fine craftsmanship.

Duncan Phyfe Furniture

As trade with England was cut off during and after the Revolution, Americans saw the need for producing their own furniture. Duncan Phyfe, a cabinetmaker who immigrated from Scotland to New York in 1790, became famous as a furniture designer. He brought to America the traditions and designs of fine English furniture and combined them in a new style. His designs were influenced by Sheraton in England, and later by French styles based on the classical designs of Greece and Rome.

Phyfe's favorite decorations were swags, eagles, pineapples, and acanthus leaves. He used rich damasks, brocades, satins, and floral silks, as well as glazed cotton with small designs. The styles developed by Duncan Phyfe marked a change from an informal to a more formal design in American furniture. Duncan Phyfe furniture blends well with both Early American and traditional styles.

AMERICAN 18th- AND 19th-CENTURY DESIGN

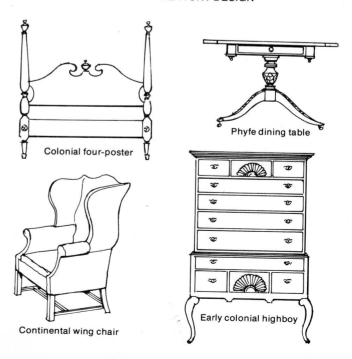

Colonial four-poster

Phyfe dining table

Continental wing chair

Early colonial highboy

ENGLISH FURNITURE	AMERICAN FURNITURE	
Jacobean William & Mary	Early American	17TH CENTURY
Queen Anne Chippendale Hepplewhite Sheraton	Windsor Colonial Wing	18TH CENTURY
Victorian	Duncan Phyfe	19TH CENTURY
	Modern	20TH CENTURY

Modern and Contemporary Styles

By the turn of the 20th century, a reaction against ornate Victorian furniture had begun. William Morris, a craftsman, helped to inaugurate a handcraft movement that resulted in a furniture style called Mission Oak. Morris also objected to the mass-produced furniture of the machine age. His trademark is the Morris chair, ancestor of today's recliner. Mission Oak furniture was popular well into the 20th century and was often used in bungalows. Designs were simple and boxy with leather upholstery and flat brass trim.

The style of furniture known as *modern* originated in the 1920's. It was closely related to the International style of architecture. The modern movement is associated with a school of design in Germany, called the Bauhaus Institute, which was founded after World War I. The first president of the school was Walter Gropius, who became a leader in developing modern styles. The new designs represented a whole new concept of furniture based on simplicity and function. The Paris Exposition of 1925 encouraged the spread of modern furniture design all over the world. Swedish designers began to set new standards for the design of furniture, ceramics, glass, and textiles. Later Danish, Finnish, French, Italian, and American designers followed the trend. Among the outstanding designers of modern furniture are Marcel Breuer, Ludwig Miës van der Rohe, Eero Saarinen, Charles Eames, Finn Juhl and Gio Ponti.

This contemporary room features a sectional couch for versatility in room arrangements. The tables, lighting, and accessories reflect designs of the 20th century.

MODERN- AND CONTEMPORARY-STYLE CHAIRS

Eames

Wegner

Saarinen

Breuer

In America, Frank Lloyd Wright and Henry Hobson Richardson were among the early pioneers of modern housing and furnishings. In the mid-19th century, Michael Thonet designed a simple bentwood chair that is still popular today. This lightweight, easy-to-handle chair became his trademark. It was copied in kitchen and dinette sets and in restaurants throughout the United States.

Changes in technology during the 20th century have made many new types and designs of furniture possible. Modern furniture materials include laminated wood and plastics that can be molded into almost any shape. Fiberglass, plasticized fabrics, aluminum, chrome, and other metals are used to make furniture of creative and striking design. In recent years, there has been a revival of rattan and wicker furniture, often combined with other materials such as bamboo, wood, or plastic. The natural materials of wicker and rattan blend well with the simple, uncluttered lines of most modern furniture.

This contemporary room includes such modern classics as the Barcelona chair designed by van der Rohe, as well as a conventional upholstered sofa.

The use of modern styles has been accompanied by a number of novelty designs. For example, some furniture is inflatable, so that it can be deflated and moved easily. Other contemporary designs will be more enduring. Modular furniture that is versatile and functional is suited to a lifestyle based on convenience and mobility. It can be arranged in a variety of ways to fit different spaces and to meet different needs. Other types come unassembled and are put together at home. Only time will tell which of these designs are passing fads and which will remain as contemporary classics.

Alternative Styles

In addition to the major formal and informal styles of furniture, there are a number of less common yet interesting designs. Mediterranean furniture, which combines Italian and Spanish designs from the time of the Renaissance, has recurring popularity. The forms are rectangular, and the decoration reflects the Moorish influence in Spain. Rectangular pieces may have the pointed Gothic or rounded Moorish arch, geometric carving, brass or wrought-iron strapwork, and nail studding. Mediterranean furniture is not designed for small rooms. Even in large rooms with high ceilings, too many pieces of it can be overpowering. Because of their interesting design, a few pieces in this style can provide an interesting accent in a room.

Art deco furniture was made in the 1920's, 1930's, and early 1940's. Designs featured simple geometric shapes, smooth surfaces, and flowing lines. Among the most popular pieces were tables topped with blue mirrored glass and bedroom sets with flowing waterfall designs. Tiered bookcases and overstuffed chairs were also common. Most art deco furniture was made of wood, but wicker, bamboo, and steel were also used. Many interesting accessories in pastel ceramic and glass are from this period.

Mediterranean-style furniture fits well in homes with large rooms or open interiors and high ceilings.

FURNITURE DESIGNER

CAREER PROFILE

Furniture designers are responsible for designing individual pieces of furniture for a manufacturer or sometimes for their own businesses. They confer with production, marketing, and sales personnel to discuss design suggestions. Then they create sketches of possible designs—sometimes an entire coordinated line of furniture—to show to a design committee, company officials, or their own customers. Scale drawings of each approved design must then be drawn. Designers also prepare the specifications—the dimensions and perhaps the type of wood and upholstery fabric—to be used in the manufacturing of each piece of furniture.

If you are interested in becoming a furniture designer, you must have creative and artistic talent. You need a background in art history, furniture construction, color and design, and textiles. A degree in art or design is needed to enter this field. Furniture designers are employed by furniture manufacturers. A few become entrepreneurs and specialize in custom designs.

REVIEWING CHAPTER 14

SUMMARY

Furniture designs have changed over the centuries due to changing needs and lifestyles. From simple boxes with lids, chests have evolved into dressers, chests of drawers, desks, bookcases, and other storage items.

Three types of furniture—traditional, Early American or provincial, and modern or contemporary—are widely used in our country today. Traditional furniture styles include Queen Anne, Chippendale, Adam, Hepplewhite, and Sheraton. Early American and provincial styles are based on simpler types of furniture that were used in colonial homes and in rural France. Modern and contemporary styles feature simple, uncluttered lines and such materials as laminated wood, plastic, and metals. Other furniture designs include Victorian, Mission Oak, Mediterranean, and art deco.

FACTS TO KNOW

1. What was the earliest form of a bed? a chair? a chest?

2. Describe the evolution of the hutch, the dining table, or the desk.

3. What does the term *period furniture* mean?

4. List the three major styles of furniture that are popular today.

5. Describe the main characteristics of traditional style furniture of the 18th century. What woods, fabrics, and design details were used?

6. Explain how Early American and provincial designs differ from traditional styles. What are the main characteristics of Early American and provincial furniture?

7. What are some features of modern furniture design? What types of materials may be used?

8. Identify the main characteristics of five different furniture periods or furniture styles.

IDEAS TO THINK ABOUT

1. Explain the effect changes in housing have had on furniture design during the past 30 years.

2. Compare the major design characteristics of furniture identified as: Queen Anne, Chippendale, Hepplewhite, Sheraton, and Duncan Phyfe.

3. What factors or values influence people's preferences in furniture styles? What are your favorite furniture styles, and why do you like them?

ACTIVITIES TO DO

1. Using photographs or drawings, prepare a display of modern and contemporary style furniture. Describe materials used and identify designers, if possible.

2. Visit a museum or historic home in your community or region to study its architecture and furnishings. Prepare a report of your visit, describing the home in terms of concepts from this chapter.

Chapter 15

Selecting and Arranging Furniture

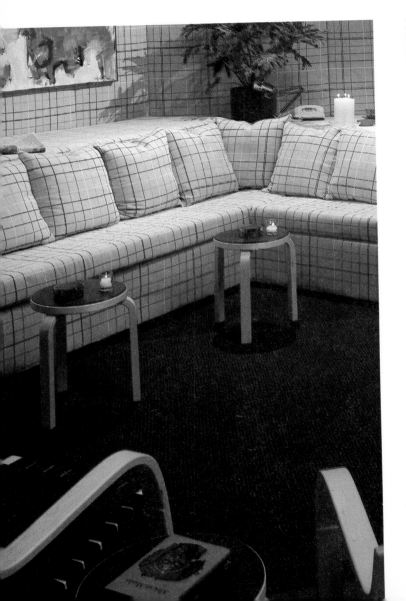

Furnishing a home is a major financial investment. In addition to furniture, a household needs rugs or carpeting, lamps, window treatments, accessories, linens, and appliances. However, furniture represents the largest expenditure—about two-thirds of the average home furnishings budget. As a result, most people cannot furnish their first homes with all new items at once. Instead, a first home may be furnished with pieces that you have assembled, restored, or refinished yourself. Whether you buy new or used furniture, you will make better selections if you know something about the construction of furniture and the materials used. Furniture varies widely in quality and durability.

Once you have acquired your furniture, the next step is to arrange it, in the best way possible. This is important to both the appearance and the function of a home. Sometimes the architectural features of a room—its size and shape and the placement of doors and windows—makes the arrangement of furniture difficult. When arranging furniture, apply the design principles of proportion and balance. Always consider comfort, convenience, and personal enjoyment. And if you are dissatisfied with one arrangement, just move your furniture around and try another.

PREVIEWING YOUR LEARNING

After you have read this chapter, you will be able to:

- Suggest different ways to acquire furniture.

- Evaluate furniture in terms of construction and materials.

- Follow guidelines for arranging furniture.

- Select appropriate furniture for different areas.

TERMS TO KNOW

buffet—a piece of dining room furniture on which food may be served, with shelves or drawers for storage

foyer—an entrance hallway

improvised—made out of something conveniently on hand

inlay—to set pieces of wood or stone into a surface to make a design level with the surface

Lucite®—a type of clear plastic

sectional—furniture that can be divided into sections

sofa bed—a sofa that opens up to form a bed

studio couch—a backless couch with removable back cushions that can serve as a single bed

template—a pattern used to form an accurate shape

MULTIMEDIA CENTERS

F E A T U R E

Advanced technology of this century has brought about a growing trend for home multimedia centers—a place in the home where family and friends watch television, take in a movie on a videocassette recorder (VCR), listen to a stereo, see home movies, or play a video game on a home computer.

Whether an entire room is devoted to the media center or just part of one, storage space for the various electronic components is the primary concern. Shelving units must be deep enough and wide enough to fit the equipment easily. The media center must provide good ventilation because the equipment generates heat, and it should have adequate storage for tapes and records. The cords and cables should be kept out of sight yet accessible to make necessary repairs. Finding storage units that adapt perfectly to your needs may not be easy. Custom-built or do-it-yourself shelving may prove the best solution.

If space allows, an entire room such as a family room or den could be devoted to multimedia use. The selection and arrangement of furniture should be practical. Sturdy, modular pieces in a durable fabric make great choices: they seat a number of people and may be rearranged depending on the focus of the room. Large floor cushions can provide additional seating. Add a sofa bed, and the room can become a guest room. Put a home computer atop a desk, and the room doubles as a home office or study area.

ACQUIRING FURNITURE

Of all the furnishings for a home, the furniture itself is usually the most expensive. Often, furniture represents two-thirds of the home-furnishing budget. The other one-third usually goes into carpeting, draperies and curtains, linens, dinnerware, and labor-saving equipment. Because of the high cost of furniture, decisions about it should be made with great care.

It is often desirable to acquire furniture slowly, over an extended time. Cost, of course, is a major factor. In addition, a person's tastes and lifestyle may change. The stage of the life cycle also influences the need for furniture. First homes are often simple, and an informal lifestyle may require a minimum of furniture. However, it is usually wise to make a decision about the style or period of furniture you prefer, so that pieces added separately will be appropriate. By deciding on a decorative theme for your home, you can follow a long-term plan for acquiring furniture.

Furnishing a First Home

A first home may represent a real challenge —to provide furnishings that are adequate and comfortable, but at a low cost. Some people receive pieces handed down from relatives and friends. Others obtain inexpensive, used furniture from garage and tag sales, auctions, and thrift shops. Furniture that is unfinished or unassembled can be purchased at discounts. Or you can improvise furniture from building materials.

Buying unfinished furniture Unfinished furniture is sold in budget, medium-priced, and luxury lines. It is available at stores selling only unfinished furniture, at lumberyards, at some department stores, and by mail order. You can find listings in the yellow pages of the phone directory. The widest choices of unfinished furniture are Early American, contemporary, and Mediterranean styles. Lower-priced furniture is usually made of pine, a soft wood, and more expensive furniture is made of maple or sometimes cherry or oak, which are hardwoods. Quality construction has dovetailed joints in drawers and slide rails under the drawers, reinforced corners in tables and chairs, and screws instead of nails. Lower-priced furniture is usually glued and nailed together. If you get unfinished furniture, buy the best grade you can afford, as well as high-quality finishing materials.

Buying and assembling furniture Furniture known as KD's (Knocked-Downs) comes in boxes, ready to be assembled with few or no tools. Tables and bookcases that can be assembled with only shelves and spindles have been available for some time. Many pieces are designed as modular units for use in vertical and horizontal arrangements. Now almost any item of furniture can be bought in a box and put together with a minimum of effort. Some more complicated pieces require basic carpentry skills. The savings in buying KD's can amount to as much as 40 percent, of

Furnishing a first home may be a challenge because of the high cost of furniture.

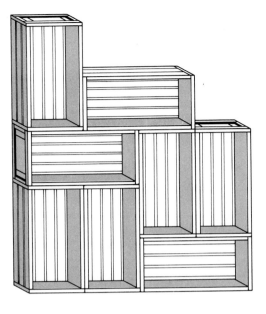

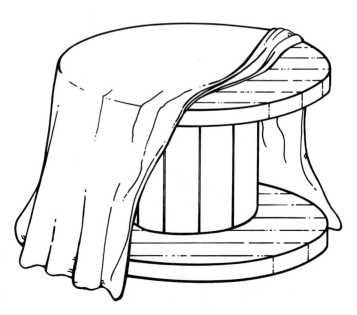

Buying unfinished furniture and creating improvised furniture are ways to furnish a home at a lower cost.

course depending upon the quality of the item. Before buying ready-to-assemble furniture, ask to see a model set up. Find out how much work is involved in putting it together, and make sure that it will meet your needs when it is assembled.

Buying used furniture Used-furniture stores often have furniture with good lines but with damaged surfaces. Some of these pieces can be stripped down to the wood grain and finished by various methods so as to look new. A bed headboard or footboard can be refinished and used with a set of springs and a mattress for a bed. A small dining table can be restored and used for serving or cut down to become a coffee table. A mirror can be removed from a used dressing table and hung on a bedroom wall. The lower part of the dressing table can be used as a desk. Detachable seats on dining or occasional chairs can be recovered, and the wood parts can be refinished or painted. A person skilled in sewing can slipcover overstuffed furniture to make it look like new.

Making improvised furniture A person with time, interest, and talent can make a number of pieces of furniture fairly quickly from building materials and hardware attachments. For example, a dining, coffee, or study table can be made from a standard-size flush door by attaching legs that are available at hardware stores or lumberyards. A modern sofa can be made from a narrow flush door by attaching legs, a rack at the back, and covered foam-rubber cushions for the seat and back. Bookcases can be made from narrow boards that are stained, varnished, or painted, and held up by ordinary bricks or glass bricks at the ends (and in the center also, if the boards are long). Wood or metal trays can be fastened to campstools to make small coffee tables. A kneehole desk can be made by anchoring a wood panel on two low filing cabinets. A coat of paint gives the combination unity. Wrought-iron wall brackets, old or new, can be used to hold up shelves made of plastic, wood, or glass. These can be used for books, plants, a small collection, or a shelf under a mirror.

A satisfactory and attractive table to seat four to six people can be made by placing a four-foot (1.22-m) circle, cut from masonite, on a card table. In order to anchor the masonite circle, turn the table upside down on the circle. Center the table and outline the edges with chalk. Glue a narrow strip of wood a foot long in the middle of each of the four chalk lines to hold the top in place. Cover the table with a round fringed cloth. If the cloth is a light color, the masonite top should be painted white.

Furnishing a Permanent Home

When you were considering housing and whether to rent or buy a home, you learned that people often move several times before choosing the place where they want to live permanently. Until that time, it may be easy to get along with simple, informal furnishings. However, getting settled in a more permanent home may require spending money on additional furniture, often of better quality.

Furniture that is bought for a permanent home is often chosen for a specific space. If a theme or design for the interior has already been decided on, it should be followed in the choice of new items. Furniture added at this time should be appropriate with existing pieces and with the interior of the home.

The range of quality in furniture is very wide. You should get to know what the standards for good quality are. Many of these are described in the following section of this chapter, which discusses the construction and materials used in making furniture. Because furniture is expensive, you should use special care in shopping for it. The following guidelines will help you:

— Set a limit on what you can spend. Then look for ways to obtain the maximum

When buying furniture, examine it carefully for sturdiness and good workmanship. Be sure it has the right dimensions for your living space.

in quantity and quality for that amount. If you finance part of the purchase, find out the terms of financing and what the total cost, including interest, will be.

— Take advantage of the furniture sales traditionally held in February and August. Watch for special sales at other seasons.

— Become familiar with nationally advertised brands and the types and styles of furniture that each company specializes in.

— Visit discount stores, factory outlets, chain department stores, other department stores, and local furniture stores. Compare cost, appearance, brand, and construction of furniture in the different outlets.

— Avoid "bait" sales, such as fire sales or liquidations, and advertising that may be deceptive. If you do get caught in a bad furniture deal, report it immediately to the Better Business Bureau or your Chamber of Commerce.

— Study labels and guarantees. If you have questions, ask salespeople to help you.

— Avoid impulsive buying or being persuaded against your will by a friend or salesperson. After you have found an item you like, have the store hold it for a few days before making your final decision.

— Take a tape measure with you when shopping to check sizes.

— When you buy chests, tables, desks, and dressers, lean against the piece or press on it with two hands to make sure it rests firmly on the floor.

— Open and close drawers and doors to check for smooth operation and a snug but not tight fit.

— If the back of the furniture is to be

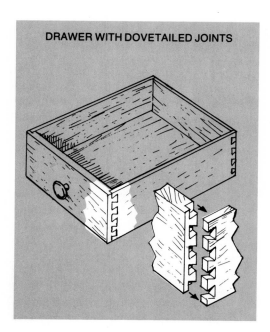

DRAWER WITH DOVETAILED JOINTS

FURNITURE CONSTRUCTION AND MATERIALS

In terms of construction, furniture is divided into two main groups: case goods and upholstered furniture. The term *case goods* includes chests, tables, desks, bookcases, dressers, serving tables, and buffets. *Upholstered furniture* includes chairs, sofas, sofa beds, couches, and beds. In addition, there are wooden chairs, called occasional chairs, which are used throughout the home.

Case Goods and Chairs: Construction

All furniture should be built well enough to carry out its function. For example, all pieces should stand firmly on the floor. For the sake of appearance, most of the features of construction should be hidden. If all joints, bracing, and screws were visible, furniture would lose its visual appeal. Construction techniques differ among producers, but certain kinds of joints and methods of support in assembling case goods and chairs are commonly used by all manufacturers of good furniture. It would be wise to check on these.

The exposed surfaces on the top, front, and sides of case goods should have the same grain and finish. If the back of an item such as a desk is to be visible, it should match the other exposed surfaces. The label will show the kind of wood used. Plywood is commonly used for unexposed surfaces on the back and underside of furniture. In better furniture, the back is set into the sides, glued, and then screwed in place. The surface is also stained and rubbed smooth. In inexpensive furniture, the back may be flush with the sides, nailed in place, and left unfinished.

The construction of furniture, as well as the surface finish, varies according to quality. Well-made furniture usually has certain

placed where it will show, make sure that it is finished.

— Sit in chairs. Lean back in them to check for stability and comfort.

— Make sure that large pieces, such as sofa beds, have rests or casters at the base so the furniture can be moved easily.

— Find out the type of construction in upholstered furniture, including framework, springs, webbing, and filling. Read the label and ask questions if you are in doubt.

— Note the matching of patterned fabrics in upholstered furniture and the evenness of the welting or cording. Be sure that cushions with prints or stripes can be reversed and still match the sofa back. Be sure to ask for protective arm covers of the same fabric to prolong the wear of upholstered pieces.

— Consider maintenance, and find out about special care some items may need.

— Buy furniture that will be flexible enough to use in another home.

CONSTRUCTION FEATURES OF FURNITURE

Mortise and Tenon Joints

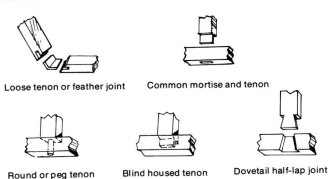

Loose tenon or feather joint   Common mortise and tenon

Round or peg tenon   Blind housed tenon   Dovetail half-lap joint

Corner Joints

Plain corner butt   Lap butt   Lock joint   Plain mitre joint

Dovetail Joints:

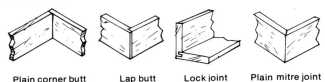

Open dovetail   Secret or concealed dovetail   Notched

Dowel Joints

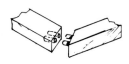

Grooved dowel   Glue dowel   Corner or corresponding dowel

Glue Joints

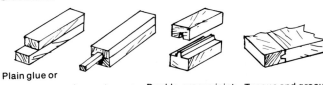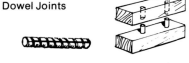

Plain glue or rub joint   Loose-tongue   Double-groove joint   Tongue and groove

joints and supports, including dowel, dovetail, mortise and tenon, and tongue and groove. Corners are usually braced with screwed-in blocks or metal braces. In better furniture, drawers have dovetailed joints at the front and usually at the back. In most medium- and high-priced furniture, there is a dust panel under the drawer. This gives added strength and helps to keep out dust. If a drawer is to slide easily, it must have a center runner or two side runners. Hinged parts, such as doors, should be flush with the framing and firm enough to open and close with no pressure. Hinges should be firm. Table leaves should have overlapping grooves to make them flush with the table when they are raised into place. Inexpensive furniture often lacks these various desirable features.

Contemporary designs in case goods may omit pulls, knobs, and handles, and instead use a groove as a pull for drawers and doors. If pulls, knobs, or handles are used, they should be spaced evenly and firmly for good balance in operation. Their size, shape, and texture should be in harmony with the piece of furniture.

Wooden chairs come with or without arms, and with wood, cane, rush, or removable upholstered seats. Seats for armless chairs are 15 to 16 inches (38.1–40.64 cm) deep. Armchair seats are 18 to 20 inches (45.72–50.8 cm) deep. A chair back should extend at least 17 inches (43.18 cm) above the seat to support the shoulders. Some chair backs are contoured for greater comfort. Whatever the design or shape of the chair, it must be rigid enough to withstand hard use. The legs may or may not have stretchers for support, but they should be braced under the seat with corner blocks or metal bracing. To test a chair for comfort, strength, and ease of handling, you should sit in it, lean against the back, and lift it.

Case Goods and Chairs: Materials

The material used in tables, chests, and chairs must be strong enough to support a heavy load. Wood and metal are the most common materials, though in recent years plastic and combinations of materials have also become popular. Each of these materials is used in a great variety of finishes and designs.

Furniture woods and wood finishes

Furniture woods are classified as softwoods, including pine, spruce, fir, and redwood, and hardwoods, including walnut, mahogany, oak, gum, maple, birch, beech, and cherry. Gumwood, which is less expensive than other hardwoods, can be stained to resemble almost any other kind of wood. Gumwood is often stained and used for the backs of chests and insides of drawers in order to reduce cost. Plywood is also widely used in making furniture. Plywood is produced by pressure-bonding several thin sheets of wood together and alternating the directions of the grain. This

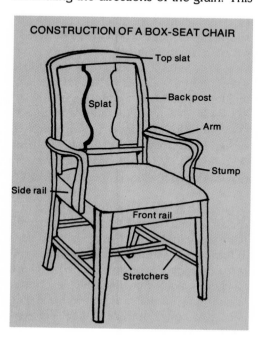

CONSTRUCTION OF A BOX-SEAT CHAIR

- Top slat
- Back post
- Splat
- Arm
- Stump
- Side rail
- Front rail
- Stretchers

process prevents warping and also permits the shaping of chair seats and backs. The surface can be veneered or given a plastic finish resembling wood grain. Legs are made of solid wood.

In the manufacture of furniture, leftover material, such as wood shavings, chips, and other particles, may be combined with an adhesive and pressed firmly into shape to produce particle board. Particle board is used for many kitchen cabinets and a great deal of inexpensive furniture. A plastic finish simulating any type or color of wood grain can be adhered to the surface. Particle board is generally satisfactory. However, if you buy a product made from particle board, be sure that drawers and doors are not warped and have no gaps.

Carved decorations for furniture are often hand-done by skilled craftsmen. Sometimes simulated carvings are plaster-molded, then stained and varnished, and finally glued to furniture to look like real carvings of wood. It is easy to distinguish these decorations from real carving: the edges of the design are rounded, and there is no sign of wood grain. Such decorations may become broken through hard use.

The surface of furniture is sometimes treated to create a special visual effect or to provide added durability. A number of different finishes are used for these purposes, including the following:

— Veneers, inlays, and lacquers. The great furniture makers of Georgian England designed furniture that was light in scale and that used new methods of decoration—veneering, inlay, and lacquer. A veneer is made of several fine layers of wood (three, five, or seven) bonded together and then cemented to form solid wood. Veneering is used to improve the appearance as well as the strength of furniture. For example, gumwood may be veneered with walnut or mahogany. A veneer may be applied to a

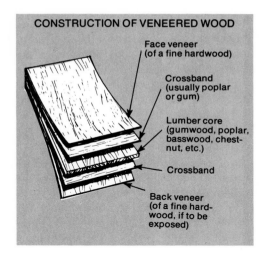

CONSTRUCTION OF VENEERED WOOD

Face veneer (of a fine hardwood)

Crossband (usually poplar or gum)

Lumber core (gumwood, poplar, basswood, chestnut, etc.)

Crossband

Back veneer (of a fine hardwood, if to be exposed)

wood surface as a continuous piece or in sections, in such a way that the grain of the wood forms a pattern.

Inlays of contrasting or exotic woods, metals, or mother-of-pearl can be set into either veneered or solid surfaces. Lacquering—a type of painting with a smooth, hard surface—became popular with the importation of Chinese lacquered furniture. Red and black are popular colors for lacquer.

— Bleached and distressed woods. Some woods, such as maple, birch, and oak, are naturally light in color. Walnut and mahogany can be artificially bleached to a light blond color. Although bleached woods darken slightly with age, they lack the distinct grain found in darker woods.

"Distressed" wood has been chemically treated to produce age marks, scars, and insect holes that make it resemble old wood. Sometimes the distressed surface is not authentic looking.

— Laminated plastics. Plastic veneers designed to resemble any wood grain are sometimes cemented to solid wood for the tops of tables, desks, and chests. The resulting surface is resistant to dents, scratches, water spots, and stains. Because

of its durability, this finish is popular for furniture in areas of the home that receive hard use, as well as in hotels, motels, hospitals, and offices.

Finishes on any wood surface should be judged in relation to the beauty of the finish and the amount of care required. Although a painted or lacquered finish is often attractive, surface scratches are visible and are difficult to repair. An oil finish was long associated with handmade reproductions of traditional furniture. Although oil does protect the wood, the finish has to be restored frequently. In addition, water and heat marks show on an oil finish. Traditional varnish finishes show scratches, and alcohol or perfume spills cause white marks to appear. New "superfinishes" are available that resemble any wood grain. These finishes include synthetic varnishes, polyurethane coatings, catalyzed lacquers, epoxies, and vinyls. All of these finishes are resistant to abrasion and discoloring.

Metals and metal finishes Metals are used for a number of different types of furniture. Metal frames combined with upholstered cushions and glass or plastic surfaces are appropriate for indoor or outdoor use. The most suitable metals include aluminum, wrought iron, chrome, and stainless steel. Because aluminum is rustproof, resistant to weather, and light in weight, it is popular for folding chairs that have plastic webbing. Wrought-iron furniture will rust outdoors unless it is coated with a rustproof paint. If wrought-iron furniture begins to rust, file or sandpaper the surface until it is smooth, and then use a rustproof paint for refinishing it. Chrome tubing used in furniture construction is smooth and durable, but the designs are limited because chrome is rigid. Stainless steel is durable and tarnish-proof. It is available in a limited choice of colors and designs. A very expensive material, it is used mainly in modern furniture of a severe and formal design.

Furniture is available in a wide variety of materials. Among these materials are vinyl and aluminum, plastic bonded to steel and fabric, welded and wrought iron, molded plastic and chrome, banana-leaf fiber, and canvas over steel rods. In what types and styles of settings would these various items be most appropriate? What are some other examples of materials used for furniture?

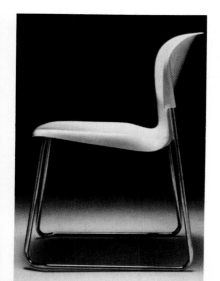

Alternative materials In addition to wood and metal furniture, wicker and plastic furniture are also available. The term *wicker* does not refer to a particular material, but to furniture or other objects made from the inner core of reeds, woven into shapes. Some wicker is closely woven; other types are relatively open in weave. The two most popular materials used in wicker furniture are willow and rattan. Wicker made of willow does not require a finish. However, wicker made of rattan must have a protective coat of varnish or lacquer.

Rattan is used in furniture in several ways. The inner core of rattan is the strongest and least brittle of reeds for weaving into wicker. The solid fibrous material under the bark is used for furniture frames. When you buy wicker furniture made of rattan, look for smooth surfaces, neat and firmly wrapped joints, mitered corners, and recessed screw heads and fasteners that are countersunk. Sit on chairs, love seats, and sofas to make sure the legs rest firmly on the floor. Look for a firm structure under the seat cushions. Chests, tables, and other pieces of furniture should be uniformly woven and rigid.

Wicker furniture fits in well with a natural or casual theme. Willow and rattan chairs, sofas, and love seats usually have loose cushions that can be covered to fit into any decorating scheme. Some types of rattan furniture come in styles formal enough to be used with traditional furniture. The surface of wicker furniture requires only occasional dusting with a soft brush or wiping with a damp sponge.

Bamboo, which is similar to rattan, is also used in furniture. Designs with bamboo are limited, because it is not as flexible as rattan. Bamboo has a hollow core and may split when nailed. Cane, which is

Wicker furniture is available in a variety of styles and pieces. It can be used in both informal and contemporary settings.

made from thinly split strips of the outer bark of rattan, is used to weave chair seats and backs and to wrap the joints of rattan furniture. It may also be used in love seats and as decorative panels on the doors of furniture.

Several types of plastic are used in making furniture. Tables made of lucite, a clear plastic, give an ultramodern effect. Colored plastic is used for tables, plant stands, wall shelves, and chairs. Plastic may also be combined with wood or metal. In considering plastic furniture, look for smooth edges and for surfaces protected against marring.

Upholstered Furniture: Construction and Materials

Beneath its soft surface, upholstered furniture has a complex construction. The frame must be strong, because of the weight it carries. Most upholstered furniture has springs and webbing for support and padding for comfort. Chairs, sofas, and couches are covered with attractive upholstery fabrics. Mattresses and box springs are covered with heavy fabric for protection.

Chairs and sofas An upholstered chair or sofa consists of a wooden frame, an interlaced webbing stretched over the seat and back frames, a set of springs, and a padding and cushioning product covered with upholstery fabric. All of these materials may vary in quality. Chairs and sofas are usually constructed in the following ways:
— Frames. The framework of a chair or sofa should be made of kiln-dried hardwood to prevent warping and to keep screws or tacks from coming loose. Softwoods such as pine and poplar are often used in less expensive furniture. All seat corners should be braced with triangular blocks screwed to the frame to make it rigid. In less expensive furniture, blocks are often glued and nailed in place, and particle board may be used for the frame.

— Springs. Coil springs are used in heavy upholstered sofas and chairs with deep seats. The coil count, or the number of spring coils per chair or sofa, is not as important as the quality of springs and the way they are distributed for comfort. However, all coil springs must be firmly tied with twine to the webbing where the webs crisscross. Ends must be securely knotted to prevent the springs from interlocking.

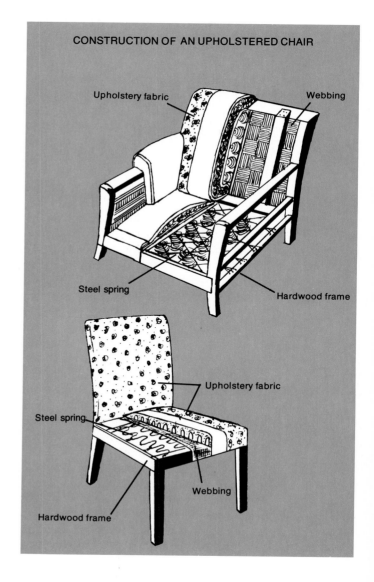

CONSTRUCTION OF AN UPHOLSTERED CHAIR

Upholstery fabric

Webbing

Steel spring

Hardwood frame

Upholstery fabric

Steel spring

Webbing

Hardwood frame

A layer of burlap is stretched over the coils. Then a layer of padding—felted cotton, horsehair, foam latex, or polyurethane foam—is placed over the burlap. A closely woven fabric is stretched over the top to keep the springs and padding in place. Finally, the upholstery is attached to the sofa or chair.

The trend toward lighter furniture forms led to the production of a flat spring with a zigzag-type construction. It is used in light-weight chairs and sofas with separate cushions.

—Cushions. Sofas with loose seat-cushions may have one long cushion or two or three shorter ones. Some people prefer a completely upholstered back with little if any tufting, because a smooth back is easier to keep clean and to slipcover or reupholster. Alternatives to a smooth back or tufted back are cushions either loose or semiattached at the back. Loose back cushions will wear longer if they can be reversed in all directions. T-shaped cushions are attractive, but they can be reversed only from one side to the other. Semi-attached cushions fastened to the back tend to sag after use. For most quality furniture, cushions are made of polyurethane foam or latex foam and held firm with a fitted zippered cover.

—Upholstery. Nylon and wool fabrics with a firm weave resist snags and abrasions and are easy to clean. Cotton, or cotton blended with polyester or acrylic fibers, will also wear well if firmly woven and treated to resist spots, stains, and grease. Pile fabrics include velveteen, corduroy, and velvet. Smooth, firmly woven fabrics include damask, brocade, tapestry, chintz, needlepoint, ticking, sailcloth, and twill. Bouclé, monk's cloth, antique satin, and similar materials that tend to snag are not recommended for upholstery.

Vinyls are a popular covering for upholstery in areas of the home that receive hard use. Vinyls, which are water-, stain-, and abrasion-proof, need little care. They come in many grades, colors, and surface finishes.

Leather is also used for upholstering sofas, chairs, and foot stools or ottomans. However, smooth leathers and suedes are very expensive and require special care.

Sofa beds and studio couches Sofa beds and studio couches are dual-purpose pieces of furniture that serve as a place to sit in daytime and to lie at night. Sofa beds are more expensive and much heavier than studio couches. Sofa beds come in traditional, Early American, and contemporary styles. They look like regular sofas, but they are much heavier to move. A sofa bed that is 60 inches (1.5 m) long opens into a double bed, and one 96 inches (2.4 m) long opens into a queen-size bed. Over-sized chairs and love seats that open into single beds are also available.

A convertible sofa bed comes with seat cushions that have to be removed before the bed is opened. A tug on a handle at the back of the seat causes the sofa to unfold and a self-contained innerspring mattress to rest on a bar. Some models permit the bed to remain made up while closed, but not all models provide for the extra bulk. At least 8 feet (2.44 m) of floor space is needed to open a sofa bed.

In buying a sofa bed, you should look for one that meets the need for comfortable seating and has a firm fabric covering, neat welting or cording, and matched designs in the fabric. The specifications for hidden construction will be in the manufacturer's catalog. Ask the salesperson if the frame is made of hardwood with corner blocks screwed in place and if the joints are double-dowel. Open and close the sofa in the store to make sure that you can handle it with ease. The springs should move quietly and easily. Sit on the sofa when it is closed and lie on it when it is open to be sure that it feels comfortable.

Both a sofa bed and a covered foam sofa can provide sleeping space by night and seating during the day.

A studio couch is not quite as wide as a single bed. Removable wedge-shaped cushions make it look like a sofa without arms. Although style choices are limited, a studio couch has some advantages over a sofa bed. It is cheaper, and if used by only one person, it can be made up as a bed and covered with a boxed slipcover. Most sofa beds must be opened and made up, but a studio couch requires only removing the cover and cushions.

The newest type of dual-purpose furniture is sofas or chairs that simply unfold into beds. A sofa can sleep two people; a chair unfolds to sleep only one person. Made out of covered foam, these pieces are lighter in weight than traditional sofa beds and usually are less expensive. They are popular for use in dens and family rooms to provide extra sleeping space for guests.

Mattresses and springs If you have to skimp on other home furnishings in order to buy a good mattress and set of springs, you should do so. Because about 85 percent of body weight is distributed between the shoulders and the hips, a mattress without adequate support will sag in the center and cause backache. A satisfactory night's rest is essential to your comfort, health, and disposition. Buy a familiar brand of the best quality you can afford. The National Association of Bedding Manufacturers recommends that a bed be 6 to 10 inches (15.24–25.4 cm) longer than the occupant and provide a width of 38 inches (96.52 cm) for each person. A traditional double bed provides only 27 inches (68.58 cm) for each person. Queen-size beds and extra-length single beds are rapidly outselling traditional double and single beds.

Bedsprings come in three types: covered and padded coil springs, uncovered coil springs, and flat springs. The covered and uncovered coil springs give 4 to 5 inches (10.16 cm–12.7 cm) more height to the bed than flat springs do. Covered box springs outsell uncovered springs. Uncovered springs collect dust, and if there are rough edges, sheet corners will catch and tear. In either type, a double-cone coil will give greater support and resilience than a single-cone coil. Flat springs cost much less. They tend to sag under heavy weight, but they are quite satisfactory for children.

Mattresses are available with inner springs and with foam—either foam latex

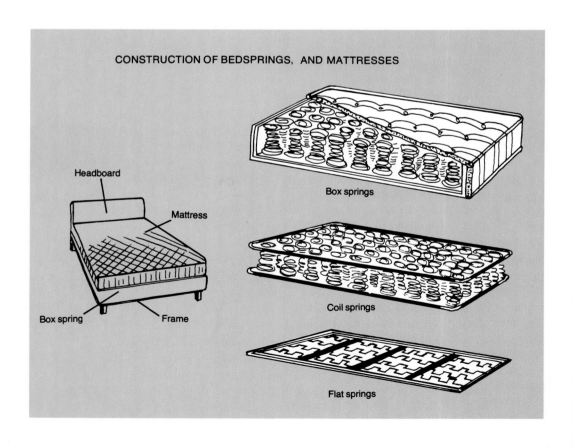

CONSTRUCTION OF BEDSPRINGS, AND MATTRESSES

Headboard

Mattress

Box spring   Frame

Box springs

Coil springs

Flat springs

or polyurethane foam. Innerspring mattresses are covered with a fabric padding of cotton, felt, or polyurethane foam and a heavy ticking. The number of coil springs, the type of construction, and the quality of the springs used are important. Strong tempered steel makes the best springs. Innerspring mattresses may have individually cloth-pocketed or wire-tied coils. A standard double-bed mattress usually has about 800 coils.

Foam mattresses are from 4½ to 6 inches thick (11.43–15.24 cm) and should be used over a high-quality box spring for comfort. The compression-resistance factor, or density, is important in buying a foam latex mattress. A compression factor of 25 represents a firm mattress, and one below 17 indicates a low-quality product. A polyurethane-foam mattress is lighter in weight and less expensive than one of latex foam. Because of its light weight, it tends to shift under the pressure of body weight or during bedmaking. A good mattress, whether innerspring or foam, will have a firm 26-ounce (728-g) ticking to cover the construction and hold the mattress in shape. Edges and fastenings should be reinforced so that the mattress will not sag if people sit on the edge of the bed. Look for handles at the side of the mattress for turning it and for metal or plastic ventilation panels.

Water beds are made of a frame, a heavy-duty plastic container for water, and a waterproof liner between the bed and the frame. A device may be added to warm the water. The biggest selling point of water beds is that they conform to body curves and provide good support. Newer designs have baffles within the plastic container to prevent the water from shifting as a person moves. These newer designs require less water, so they are not as heavy as earlier designs. Also, the danger of leakage has been reduced.

ARRANGING FURNITURE

In moving to a new home, people seldom buy a whole new supply of furniture and household furnishings. Instead, most people use the furnishings they have and try to fit them into the new setting. If possible, a plan for the interior design—backgrounds, window treatments, furniture, lighting, and accessories—should be made in advance. If there is to be redecorating, with painting, wallpapering, or refinishing floors, it can be done more easily before the furniture is in place. Any redecorating should be planned to integrate the present furniture with the new interior in a pleasing design.

The architectural features of a room —the size and shape; the style and placement of windows, doors, and perhaps a fireplace or a wall with sliding glass doors —influence furniture arrangement. Furniture arrangement is simplified when a room has good proportions and walls long enough to accommodate major pieces of furniture, including a sofa and large bookcases in a living area, and beds and long chests of drawers in a bedroom. When rooms are small, there is less freedom in arranging furniture.

Guidelines for Arranging Furniture
The arrangement of furniture must meet many criteria. Among these are function, efficiency, safety, beauty, and enjoyment. The following suggestions will help you to arrange furniture effectively:

—Study the physical structure of each room and decide on the main center of interest. This might be a painting over a fireplace, a picture grouping over a sofa, a display cabinet, or windows.

—Decide on the best place for the major items of furniture in each room. Group minor items, such as small tables and chairs, in relation to major items.

—If a room is large, consider how it can be

separated into two or three areas. A living room might have one area for conversation, another for reading or studying, and one for watching television.

—Study the flow of traffic in a room so that furniture will not be in the way and traffic will not interrupt conversation or activities such as watching television.

—Alternate wood and upholstered furniture for pleasing balance. Too much wood furniture or too many upholstered pieces on one wall will be monotonous.

—Place wood as well as upholstered furniture away from windows where the sun shines in for long periods. The sun will blister wood, and fade and rot fabrics.

—Avoid placing vertical pieces, such as a secretary or a highboy, between tall windows unless the furniture on the wall opposite can balance this arrangement.

—Avoid placing any large piece of furniture, such as a bookcase, at an angle in the corner of a room.

—Give a poorly proportioned room an optical illusion of good proportion. For a long narrow room, use a horizontal furniture arrangement at the distant end. Or break the room into areas by using open bookcases, low chests, or long tables as room dividers. Lengthen a square room by using a long horizontal arrangement on one or two sides.

—Before buying any new furniture for a room, draw a plan of the room to scale on graph paper. Indicate the size and placement of doors and windows. Then cut out templates, scaled to the floor plan, for each piece of furniture. Experiment with a number of different arrangements for the furniture to find the most satisfactory one.

This 14 by 20-foot (4.26 x 6.1 m) living room can be arranged in several different ways. In A the room seems larger because the arrangement is more open. In B the long chest divides a study area from a conversation and TV-viewing area.

VARIATIONS IN FURNITURE ARRANGEMENTS

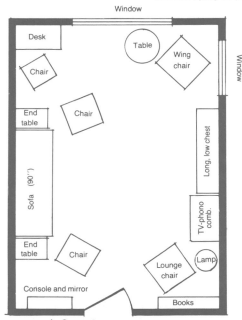

A. Open Space Arrangement

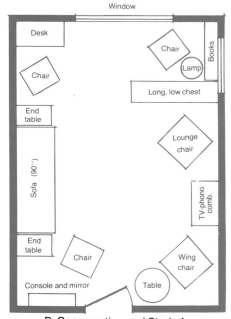

B. Conversation and Study Area

Furniture for Individual Rooms

Before you begin to decorate and furnish each room, you should make a plan for it. If you already have some furniture, the plan will help to integrate those pieces into new surroundings. A plan will also show what new items, if any, are needed, or what present ones should be refinished, re-covered, or replaced. A plan can also show priorities for adding and replacing. Knowing what you need first and what can be postponed allows you to spread the necessary buying over several years.

The entrance An entrance area is a convenience because it helps to keep traffic and dirt out of the living area. It also serves as an introduction to the home. A small entrance, or foyer, requires no more furniture than an attractive mirror and a small shelf held up by wall brackets. A somewhat larger foyer can accommodate a mirror, table and chair, and a floor plant. New homes and apartments, where every square foot of floor space is measured in terms of cost, often omit an entrance hall or foyer. There, it may be possible to give the illusion of a foyer by using a chest, bookcase, sofa, or chair to create a separate area.

The living room or living area The living room usually represents the largest area in the home. For that reason, it may require the most furniture, too. Here, especially, a long-term plan for additions is necessary. In a first apartment, the living area may include a sofa bed or studio couch that is used for sleeping. In a later home, this piece may be used in a living room or family room, thereby permitting that area to serve as a guest room. A plan for the design of the room and for adding new items assures that any purchase—a sofa, chair, tables, draperies, or lamps —will fit in well with the present furnishings.

Before starting to arrange a living room, you should decide on a center of interest. It may be an attractive window grouping, a fireplace, or possibly a view from a large window. Another possibility for a focal point is a sofa with a picture grouping above it. Still another might be sectional wall units with open shelves for a special display.

A seating arrangement of a sofa and chairs is needed to provide a conversation area. A sofa and chair grouping should permit six persons to carry on a conversation with ease. In a large room, two conversation groupings might be better than one large circle, especially if traffic would have to pass through that circle. Sectional seating units provide great flexibility for arranging a living room or family room. Depending on the number of sections, you can design an L-shaped or U-shaped conversation area that can seat several people.

The furniture is arranged for a conversational area that can seat at least six people.

Top left: A bookcase serves as the center of interest in a room that blends old and new styles. Top right: The black marble fireplace and wood paneling dominate this evenly balanced, formal room. Bottom left: Here, two centers of interest — the fireplace and the picture window — are unified by a curvilinear sectional sofa. Above: A sofa and picture collection provide the focal point of an Early American room.

The living room shown in Floor Plan A illustrates a good arrangement of furniture. The two windows on one side provide a center of interest. The sofa and chairs form a good arrangement for conversation and livability. This size room might appear crowded if space for a dining area had to be set aside. The living area of Floor Plan B is flexible enough to include a dining area as well as a conversation area.

A living room should if possible include a table or desk as a place for writing or study. Lamps and other lighting fixtures should provide both general background lighting and direct light for specific activities like

INFORMAL ARRANGEMENTS OF FURNITURE

Floor Plan A.   12' x 16'

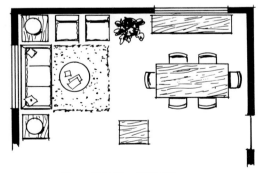

Floor Plan B.   14' x 20'

The Plan A living room becomes a guest room when the sofa is opened into a queen-size bed. Plan B shows a combination living-dining area that is both pleasing and functional.

reading. Lamps should be distributed around the room. Enough table space should be provided to allow for a decorative object, plant, or flower arrangement. Space is also needed for people to set glasses or plates of refreshments on.

Entertainment and recreational activities in a living room may require special seating and storage arrangements. A table with chairs around it provides a place for playing games or cards. A television set in a living room should be placed where it can be seen by four or five persons at one time without disturbing furniture. A stereo set and records or tapes may require special pieces of furniture for placement and storage. Both upright and grand pianos can create problems in arrangement. If possible, a piano should not be placed on an outside wall because of dampness and changing temperatures. If a room is long and narrow, a spinet or upright piano is sometimes placed at a right angle to the wall to serve as a room divider. If this arrangement is desirable, a textured mesh fabric or low folding screen can be used to cover the back of the piano. A small grand piano should be placed with the long side parallel to the wall in an area where the pianist can face people in the room.

The dining room or dining area The arrangement of furniture in a dining room is usually less flexible than in a living room. The table is usually near the center of the room, to allow space for chairs around it. The size of the table depends on the number of people in the household. A table with leaves that can be inserted and removed provides flexibility. A drop-leaf table also provides flexibility. A storage piece such as a buffet or hutch contains linens and items for setting the table or serving food. This furniture is usually set against a long wall.

When living and dining areas are combined in one room, the dining area should

VARIATIONS IN DINING ROOM LAYOUTS

A   (10' x 14')   B   (8' x 12')   C   (10' x 14')

Dining tables are not always centered in the room. The table in dining room A is placed in a bay window; in B, at right angles to a wall; and in C, in a corner window.

be near the kitchen for efficiency. All items to be used in this area should be stored nearby and out of traffic lanes. There should be provision for adequate lighting in the dining area, such as an overhead light or a wall-mounted light. If it is desirable to separate the dining and living areas, a sofa or buffet can serve as a divider as well as a storage space for dinnerware and table mats or cloths. A bookcase may also be used as a divider, since a dining area often serves as a study area too.

Bedrooms A comfortable bed has priority over other furniture in the bedroom. A night table or low chest should be placed at each side of a double, queen-size, or king-size bed. The tables should be large enough to hold several items, such as a lamp, a clock-radio, and a book or magazine. Tables with a drawer and lower shelf are preferred because of their greater storage space.

When twin beds are placed parallel to each other with a space between the beds, one larger table with a lamp can be used between them. If twin beds are placed at right angles in the corner of a room, a square table with a shelf can be placed in the corner to hold a lamp and other items. A corner table flanked by beds provides only a surface area, but the space beneath it can be used for storage.

Convenience as well as comfort is important in planning a bedroom. Here, convenience means storage space—drawers, shelves, and a place to hang clothes. In addition to space for clothing, storage is often needed for cosmetics, jewelry, and other personal items.

Some people like wide twin chests set together; others prefer a dresser and a tall chest of drawers. Many people like to have a mirror over a chest or dresser and also a full-length mirror on a door near the dressing area. If space permits, it is good to have a small lounge chair or rocker, as well as a straight chair, in a bedroom. A person often wants a private, comfortable place for getting away from the activities in a living area or for use during an illness. Often, parents like to have a large bed-sitting-room as a quiet retreat. The sitting area should have two comfortable chairs and perhaps a small television and a desk.

Although not all homes have a guest room, most have a room or area that may serve as a guest room. It may be used more often for other purpoes, such as a family room, study, or activity area.

A child's room should be planned for change as the child grows. Chests, desks, and shelves may be bought in units, with more units added as needs change. Storage space is important if a room is to appear orderly. Some young people like to have a large bulletin board over a desk for displaying personal items.

When you are planning a bedroom furniture arrangement, begin by placing the head of the bed or beds against the longest wall space. Some bedrooms may have two long walls for alternative arrangements. Remember to leave a space of at least 18 inches (45.72 cm) around a bed for making it up, with extra space allowed between twin beds. Place chests or bureaus near closets for convenience. For good daytime lighting on a mirror, place the mirror on a wall adjacent to a window. A wall lamp on each side of a mirror or tall, slender lamps on each end of a chest of drawers will provide better light than low lamps. If a bathroom has a counter and a well-lighted mirror, bedroom lighting is less important.

Multi-purpose furniture In choosing furniture, many people prefer kinds that serve more than one purpose and are easy to move about. Among these kinds are sectional, modular, collapsible, and dual-purpose furniture. Sectional wall units can be assembled for bedroom or living-room storage. Dressing-table and desk units are available as sectionals. Tables with drop leaves are versatile in both placement and use. They can seat six or eight people for a meal. When the leaves are down, two people can eat at the table, or it can be used for other purposes. A low chest can provide storage space as well as a place for setting a lamp and some small items. Modular and sectional seating units can be arranged in a variety of ways to provide flexibility. A sofa bed or studio couch may serve two purposes—for sitting during the day and evening, and for sleeping at night.

A larger bedroom has space to create a sitting area for reading or relaxing.

Planning on Paper

Moving furniture about by trial and error to find a good arrangement can be time-consuming, tiring, and exasperating. Planning on paper will save time and energy, and it will usually produce satisfactory results. Using ¼-inch graph paper, make a scale drawing of the room you are decorating. If you are arranging your present furniture, measure each piece and cut out templates to scale. If you want to experiment with templates for new furniture, use templates like those illustrated for the pieces you need. By planning on paper, you can learn what furniture arrangements are possible in a room and which one will meet your needs best.

STANDARD SPACE NEED FOR CLEARANCE AND AREA GROUPINGS

Living Room

Space between coffee table and sofa or chair	1'6"
Space before chair or sofa for legroom when person is seated	1'6" to 2'6"
Chair or bench space in front of desk or piano	3'
Study area: desk, chair, lounge chair, and ottoman	5' × 8'
Bookcase or secretary with flanking chairs (chairs 6 inches away)	2' × 7'
Space for card table and four chairs	8' × 8'
Corner grouping: 2 lounge chairs and corner table	6' × 6'
Corner grouping: 2 chairs, love seat, coffee table, and end table	7' × 9'
Fireplace grouping: 2 lounge chairs, love seat, and 2 lamp tables	5'3" × 9'
Conversation grouping: chair, average-size sofa, coffee table, and end table	6'6" × 9'
Conversation grouping: long sofa, 2 end tables, 2 lounge chairs, and coffee table	6'6" × 14' plus

Dining Room

Space between table and wall or buffet	2'8" to 3'
Space for occupied chair beyond table	1'10" to 3'
Space around chairs at table for serving	1'6" to 2'

Bedrooms

Space at each side of bed for making bed	1'6" to 2'
Space between twin beds	1'6" to 3'
Space between chest of drawers and bed	3'

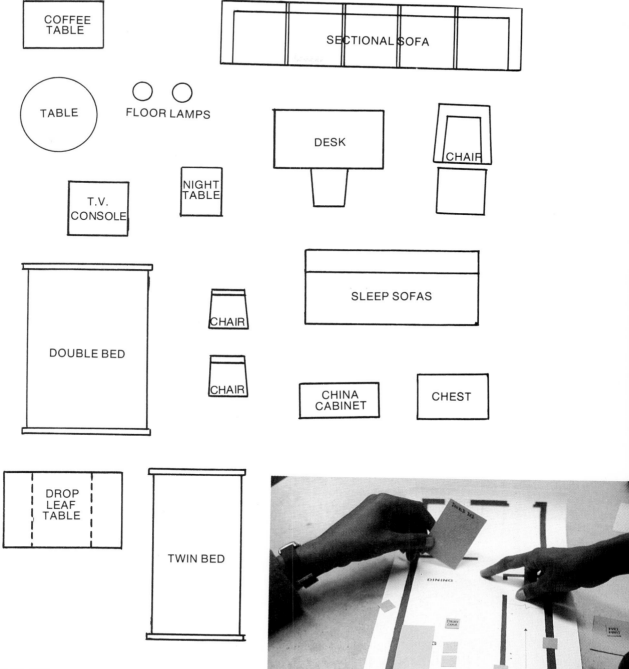

COFFEE TABLE

SECTIONAL SOFA

TABLE

FLOOR LAMPS

DESK

CHAIR

T.V. CONSOLE

NIGHT TABLE

SLEEP SOFAS

DOUBLE BED

CHAIR

CHAIR

CHINA CABINET

CHEST

DROP LEAF TABLE

TWIN BED

DINING

TEMPLATES
Scale: ¼ inch equals one foot

P
R
O
F
I
L
E

Upholsterers recover, repair, and rebuild upholstered furniture such as sofas and chairs. They remove the outer covering, padding, and webbing from the seat, arms, back, and sides of the furniture piece. Upholsterers retie the springs and replace any that may be defective. Then they replace the webbing and padding. The new upholstery fabric must be measured and cut to fit the furniture. Upholsterers operate commercial sewing machines to stitch the various sections of the fabric together before tacking it to the wood frame. They may sew or tack decorative trim, such as braid or buttons, to the fabric or the frame. Cushion covers must also be cut and stitched. Upholsterers may also repair the wood frame or refinish the wood surfaces that are left exposed after the piece is covered with the upholstery fabric. Some upholsterers assist customers in their selection of upholstery fabric and order it for them from sample books.

If you are interested in becoming an upholsterer, you must learn about fabrics and upholstery methods. You should like working with your hands and doing detailed work. The ability to apply mathematics to practical problems, such as computing dimensions, is essential. You should have good manual dexterity for working with hand tools.

To become an upholsterer, you can enroll in an apprenticeship program for two to six years. You can also take specialized courses at vocational schools, enroll in an adult education program, or obtain on-the-job training. Upholsterers may work for furniture manufacturers, furniture stores, or decorator fabric shops. Or they may be self-employed and work on a job-by-job basis for local interior designers, fabric shops, or individual customers.

REVIEWING CHAPTER 15

SUMMARY

Furnishing a first home may be a challenge because of the high cost of furniture. Unfinished, unassembled, and used furniture can usually be purchased at a lower cost than new furniture. Furniture pieces can also be improvised.

A knowledge of furniture woods, construction, finishes, and upholstery fabrics is helpful when shopping for furniture. Chests, tables, and chairs should stand firmly and be well braced. Upholstered furniture should have strong frames and be covered with firmly woven fabrics. Sofa beds and studio couches provide places to sleep as well as to sit. It is important to invest in a good mattress and set of springs for your bed.

When arranging furniture, put the major pieces in place first. Study the traffic flow and group furniture for different areas. To save time and energy, plan your arrangement on graph paper, using templates for each furniture piece.

FACTS TO KNOW

1. Describe four different approaches to acquiring furniture for a first home.

2. What are some advantages and disadvantages of buying used furniture, unfinished furniture, and knocked-down furniture?

3. List guidelines to follow when shopping for furniture.

4. Explain how you can evaluate the quality of chests, tables, and wooden chairs.

5. Describe three different types of special finishes that may be used on wooden furniture.

6. What characteristics should you look for when evaluating upholstery fabrics?

7. Describe three different types of multipurpose furniture. What versatility do they offer in a home?

8. What are *templates?* How can they be used when planning furniture arrangements?

IDEAS TO THINK ABOUT

1. Why are decisions about furniture so important when furnishing and decorating a home?

2. Describe possible differences in furniture requirements for people at various stages of the life cycle.

3. How do you account for the popularity of sectional and modular furniture in today's homes?

ACTIVITIES TO DO

1. Using templates, plan the furniture arrangement for a one-bedroom apartment.

2. Develop a long-range plan for purchasing the furniture for a home that you would like to have one day. What items would you buy first? What items would you buy later on? How might items be used differently as more pieces are acquired?

Chapter 16

Lighting and Lamps

Lighting, as we know it, is a fairly modern concept. Scarcely a century ago, people scheduled their lives by the sun. Candles, oil lamps, and eventually gaslights extended daytime activities after the sun went down. The invention of electricity did even more to revolutionize lifestyles. However, for many years electric lighting was functional but not very decorative. Until well into the 20th century, a ceiling light was the most common form of general lighting. Today it is only one of many different sources of light that are used in homes.

In this chapter you will learn about the different types of lighting that are needed in the home. They may be bright or soft, direct or indirect, functional or decorative. Lighting can also provide interesting patterns of shadow and light or accent a special object or area. Its main function may be to prevent eye strain or to provide safety and security.

Today, lamps and lighting fixtures are important not only as sources of light but also as part of a home's entire decorating scheme. They should harmonize with the room in color, shape, size, and texture. By experimenting with different sources of light, you will find the combination of lighting that is most suitable for your home and the many activities that are done there.

After you have read this chapter, you will be able to:
* Describe the function of different types of lighting.

* Identify incandescent and fluorescent lighting and their advantages.

* Plan lighting for a room.

* Follow guidelines for selecting lamps.

======= TERMS TO KNOW =======

chandelier—a branched lighting fixture suspended from the ceiling

cove—a trough for concealed lighting at the upper part of a wall

diffused—spread out over a large area

fluorescent light—light produced in a sealed glass tube which contains mercury vapor and has a coating of fluorescent material on the inside which glows brightly

footcandle—a unit of measure for illumination; the amount of light that a candle throws onto a surface that is one foot away

incandescent light—light produced inside a glass bulb by a filament that is heated by electricity until it glows

luminous—throws out or gives off a steady light

opaque—does not allow light to pass through

soffit—the underside of an overhang

translucent—permits light to pass through

NEW LIGHTING TRENDS

**F
E
A
T
U
R
E**

Good lighting can highlight a room to its best advantage. It can create a special mood, as well as provide the proper illumination. Modern lighting techniques place emphasis on creating dramatic effects, and lighting fixtures have become more art form than household necessity.

There are new styles of standing floor lamps that send illuminating arcs across walls and ceilings, dapple floors, and form romantic pools of light. Akari lanterns are light sculptures handcrafted of paper and bamboo that emit a soft glow. Striplights, traditionally seen atop mirrors in movie stars' dressing rooms, now come in chrome, brass, or various colors. They can be attached to ceilings as well as walls, and sometimes are placed behind baffles to give reflective light.

Canister lights have cylindrical-shaped "cans" of various sizes and are used to create "uplighting." This spreads the light upward to dramatize a sculpture, painting, or textured pattern on the wall. Torcheres, torch-shaped floor lamps, also provide uplighting in a most elegant way.

Portable spotlights can sit on the floor or can be attached to walls and ceilings to highlight architecture, furnishings, and special room accessories. Track lighting is now available with color-corrected fluorescent bulbs, providing energy-saving soft lighting. And, for a substantial price, you can purchase the ultimate in lighting effects—a "light sculpture" which creates flickering, multicolored lighting flashes inside a glass sphere!

THE FUNCTION OF LIGHTING

The purpose of artificial lighting is to supplement natural daylight. At night, it becomes the only source of light. Lighting should illuminate all areas of the home for safe movement, for specific activity needs, and for aesthetic or decorative needs. These needs are met by three different types of lighting—general illumination, local lighting, and accent lighting.

General illumination is background lighting which is sufficient for safe movement and for conversation. General illumination is needed to supplement table or floor lamps for all activities. To avoid fatigue from glare, you should supplement a single lamp in a dark room with additional illumination in the form of low-wattage overhead or wall lights or floor or table lamps. The additional lighting may be either direct or indirect.

Local lighting is the lighting required for such activities as reading, studying, sewing, and working at a sink, range, or work table. Local lighting may be provided by table, floor, and pole lamps; a wall fixture over a special study or work area; a fixture suspended from the ceiling; or special lights in the ceiling over a particular area.

Accent lighting refers to lighting focused on a particular object or area to create a center of interest after dark. This type of lighting, which usually illuminates only a small area, is provided by spotlights or focused lights.

INCANDESCENT AND FLUORESCENT LIGHTING

Incandescent and fluorescent bulbs are the principal types of lighting in homes today. The incandescent light, with a fine filament inside a glass bulb, served as the main type of lighting from the late 19th century until the mid-20th century, when fluorescent lighting was introduced.

HISTORY OF THE LAMP

One of the first lamps was a wick dipped in grease. The holder was made of stone.

The candle was a great improvement over fat and oil fuels. Candles were expensive and could only be afforded by the rich.

The pioneer "Betty" lamp burned fish oil. The crescent-shaped arm fitted into loops of the linked chain. This made it possible to raise or lower the lamp.

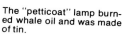

The "petticoat" lamp burned whale oil and was made of tin.

The discovery of kerosene and the invention of a glass chimney made possible a greatly improved lamp.

The gaslight lamp was the last improvement before electricity became the popular form of lighting.

Incandescent light bulbs come in a wider range of choices than fluorescent lights do. They are available in tube shapes resembling fluorescent tubes, bulbs resembling candles, round or pear-shaped bulbs, mogul (extra large) bulbs, and bullet lights. Incandescent bulbs may be clear, slightly frosted to provide more light in relation to wattage, or frosted to soften the light. When bulbs are entirely enclosed, as in ceiling fixtures or fixtures over mirrors or work surfaces, a clear light will provide more light than frosted lights of the same wattage. However, clear lights give too much glare in lamps used for reading. Incandescent lights come in tints as well as in clear or frosted types. There are also long-life incandescent bulbs, which may last three times as long as ordinary incandescent bulbs. Since these bulbs are more expensive and provide less light than regular bulbs, they are recommended mainly for hard-to-reach places.

Fluorescent lights usually come in long tubes. The wattage determines the length of the tube. For example, a 20-watt tube is 2 feet long (.61 m), a 30-watt tube is 3 feet long (.91 m), and a 40-watt tube is 4 feet long (1.22 m). A 40-watt fluorescent tube provides more light than a 100-watt incandescent bulb. Fluorescent bulbs last longer than incandescent bulbs, produce less heat, and use less energy. However, fluorescent bulbs are not flattering to the skin when used over mirrors. To obtain a more flattering light, use deluxe warm white fluorescent tubes.

Lighting can be controlled in a number of different ways. Dimmer switches are often used in dining areas, to subdue or brighten the light. Dimmers can also be used with fluorescent lights. Timers may be attached to indoor and outdoor lights so that they come on and go off automatically at set times. A better control for outdoor lights is a photocell that responds automatically to the degree of light the year round. These lights automatically come on at dusk and go off at daybreak, without having to be adjusted as days change in length.

Incandescent bulbs are available in a wide variety of shapes, sizes, and designs.

Fluorescent bulbs require less energy than incandescent bulbs.

MEETING HOME LIGHTING NEEDS

In planning the lighting for a room, it is important to consider the activities to be pursued there. Some areas and types of activities require only general illumination; others require lighting for more localized purposes. Light is measured in terms of footcandles, and the number of footcandles needed varies with the activity. For example, card-playing requires only 10 to 20 footcandles, but prolonged study and reading requires 100 to 200 footcandles. Lighting needs for various activities, in terms of footcandles, are indicated on the chart. Because the effectiveness of lighting depends on many factors, the number of footcandles cannot be correlated with the wattage of individual lights. Other factors affecting the footcandles as registered on a light meter include the lightness or darkness of the ceiling, walls, floor, and furniture; the extent of general background lighting; and the amount of direct lighting on the activity area, such as desk, card table, or work space.

When the lighting for your different visual needs is sufficient, your eyes will be healthier, you will experience less eye strain and fatigue, and you will be able to pursue an activity for a longer time. If you are choosing lamps for any kind of close work, be sure to look for those approved

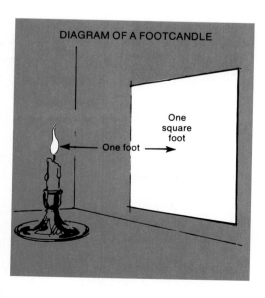

DIAGRAM OF A FOOTCANDLE

One foot
One square foot

LIGHTING RECOMMENDATIONS		
VISUAL TASK		MINIMUM FOOTCANDLES ON TASK AT ANY TIME
Reading and writing	Books, magazines, newspapers	30
	Handwriting, reproduction and poor copies	70
	Music scores, simple	30
	Music scores, advanced	70
Study desks		70
Sewing	Dark fabrics (fine detail, low contrast)	200
	Prolonged periods (light to medium fabrics)	100
	Occasional (light-colored fabrics)	50
	Occasional (coarse thread, large stitches, high contrast of thread to fabric)	30
Kitchen activities	At the sink	70
	At the range	50
	At the work counters	50
Laundry duties	At the washer-dryer	50
	At ironing board	50
	At ironer	50
Grooming	Shaving, make-up, grooming; on the face at mirror locations	50
Table games	(such as a card table, table tennis)	30
Handcraft	Rough sawing and benchwork	30
	Sizing, planing, rough sanding, glueing, veneering, medium quality bench-work	50
	Fine bench work, fine sanding and finishing	100

LUMINOUS CEILING PANEL

CORNICE & RECESSED LIGHTING

VALANCE LIGHTING

COVE LIGHTING

SOFFIT LIGHTING

is not advisable unless the ceiling is smooth, because the light will emphasize irregularities. It also requires a fairly high ceiling.

Recessed lighting is set into the ceiling to provide either diffused light or concentrated light for special areas. These fixtures may be round or square and covered with glass or plastic. Recessed lighting can be very effective in creating special effects.

Valance and cornice lighting are similar in design. However, valance lighting may be focused toward either the ceiling or floor over the full width of the drapery, whereas cornice lighting can be focused only downward onto the drapery. In both installations, lights are set behind a decorative board mounted at the top of the window. Being concealed within the framework, they provide indirect light. If the windows are a focal point of the room, these types of lighting are very effective.

Soffit lighting is used under an overhang to light display cabinets, bookcases, paintings, mirrors, and wall niches. These lights are directed toward the wall or downward. Some bookcases and display cabinets are available with built-in lighting.

Light Fixtures

Light fixtures can be attached to the ceiling or the wall. The wiring for the light may be part of the electrical system, such as for a ceiling light, or there may be a cord for the fixture that can be plugged into an outlet. Simple ceiling fixtures can be used in any room to cover an overhead light. A chandelier is a branched lighting fixture that is suspended from the ceiling, usually in a dining room. The bottom of the chandelier should be about three feet (.9 m) from the top of the dining table. Other types of hanging fixtures can be used in high-ceiling living areas, hallways, or entryways. Some hanging fixtures can be raised or lowered for added flexibility. Wall-mounted lighting fixtures can vary from traditional candle sconces to contemporary lights on swivels or extending arms.

Track lighting fixtures can be installed on a ceiling or wall to provide versatile lighting for different areas in a room. The fixtures, which are available in a variety of sizes, shapes, and finishes, can be positioned in different locations along the track and swiveled at different angles. Portable canister-type spotlights and floodlights that rest on the floor can be used for accent lighting.

A chandelier can be used in either a formal or informal dining area.

Tract lighting fixtures can provide a variety of lighting options within a room.

Lamps and Lamp Shades

Moveable lamps can sit on tables or on the floor. Lamps are used to provide local lighting for various activities, such as reading and playing games. They can also provide general illumination for a room. Sometimes lamps are chosen primarily for decorative purposes.

Lamps come in a wide choice of styles, shapes, and materials to fit both traditional and contemporary settings. Classic, or formal, lamp shapes include columns, cylinders, urns, and rectangular shapes. Materials used in these styles of lamps are porcelain, crystal, silver, bronze, marble, and pottery. Informal lamps may resemble oil lamps, brass candlesticks, glass bottles, or pottery jars. These styles may be made of copper, brass, pewter, wood, clay, and wrought iron. Some floor lamps include a small tabletop in wood, metal, or glass.

Contemporary lamps take many sleek and imaginative forms, from sculptured shapes to balls or blocks of wood, glass, metal, or plastic. Modern floor lamps include tubular pharmacy lamps and large arch lamps which extend for several feet across a room.

Lamp shades should be in keeping with the shape and size of the lamp on which they are used. Lighting needs and the types of shades on other lamps in the room are also important factors in selecting shades. Materials for translucent shades include parchment, shantung, taffeta, embroidered batiste or organdy, and textured or patterned fabrics. Shades of fluted

Shown here are three typical styles of lamps: an informal pottery-base lamp, a classic porcelain urn, and a functional metal and plastic study lamp. What type of shade is used for each lamp?

paper treated to be heat-resistant are used in informal areas.

Shades of a heavy plasticized paper resembling parchment are translucent and may be used alone or covered with fabric. Shades used for close work should be translucent or capable of giving a good soft light. Shades in study lamps can be less translucent and even opaque so long as there is sufficient background lighting and the light is reflected directly on the activity. Opaque or nontranslucent shades are used on hanging and decorative lamps such as tole lamps. Shades made of Tiffany-type glass are sometimes used on table lamps and pull lamps. Shades for outdoor use should be washable.

GUIDELINES FOR CHOOSING LAMPS

Lamps are designed in a wide variety of types and sizes, as well as styles. In planning the lighting for your home, find out what types of lamps are available to meet particular needs. The following guidelines may be helpful:

— Provide enough lamps—and lamps of different types—to achieve balanced lighting and to supply all areas with light.

— Check each room to find out where you will need light to supplement general illumination. Because the living area has a greater variety of activities—talking, reading, writing, needlework, card- and game-

A traditional-style floor lamp provides area lighting plus table-top space for small accessories.

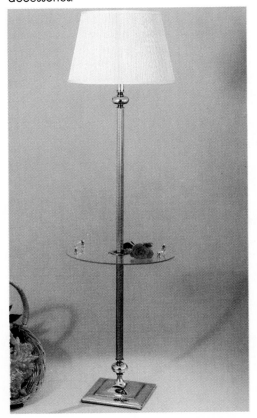

Adding a riser to the top of a lamp adjusts the height of a poorly proportioned lamp. With a riser added, the lamp will require a larger shade.

ADJUSTING LAMP HEIGHT

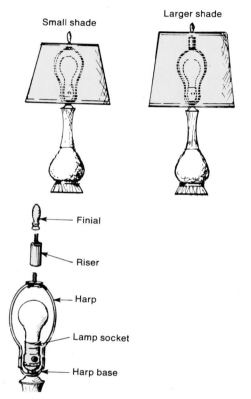

playing, watching television, and enjoying music—the need for special lighting is greater there than in any other area of the home. Each bedroom should have a lamp for a single bed or between two single beds. It is desirable to have a lamp on a table on each side of a double or other large-size bed. Sufficient lighting is needed at the grooming area, either in a bedroom or bathroom. A light on each side of a dresser is recommended in a bedroom, and a soffit with two 60- or 75-watt bulbs is recommended over a bathroom mirror. A dining room needs lighting over the table, either a pull light or a chandelier.

— Choose lamps according to function. The sketches on this page indicate the height of lamp that should be used for various activities. If you observe these rules and check the footcandles of light that you are receiving for each activity, you can avoid eye strain and fatigue.

— Adjust the height of poorly proportioned lamps. A lamp base can be made to look taller by using a riser, and a larger shade may be used if a taller harp is substituted. A riser and a harp are shown in the illustration.

Small lamps can provide an adequate amount of light for reading.

— Avoid color contrast. All lampshades in a room should be nearly the same color, whether they are made of fabric or other material. Although fashion sometimes calls for colored or fancy shades, those that are cream to off-white in color provide better light. If colored or patterned shades are used, they should be used in a furniture grouping where the shade becomes part of a unit.

— Avoid a glare. When you work or read for a long period under only a bullet-type light, the glare, together with the contrast between the light on your reading and the darkness beyond, will cause eye strain. An additional light will reduce the glare.

— Choose good structural and decorative design in lamps and lighting fixtures. Structure relates to the form or shape as well as the texture of the material, such as metal,

This modern floor lamp provides directly focused light.

wood, glass, pottery, or leather.

—Choose a style of lamp to complement your decorating theme. With traditional or 18th-century themes, the choices include classic designs which may be plain or decorated. Early American and provincial furnishings, which are less formal, often use simpler versions of traditional shapes. Contemporary rooms call for lamps that are structurally interesting, with little ornamentation.

—Choose the right-size shade. When you shop for a new shade, take with you the measurements of the present shade, including the diameter at top and bottom and the depth from top to bottom. Lampshades are usually drum- or slightly cone-shaped. Shades for floor lamps should be 16 to 18 inches (40.64 cm–45.72 cm) in diameter and shades for reading lamps should be 16 inches (40.64 cm) at the lower diameter. Shade sizes for other lamps will vary according to the lamp base.

ELECTRICIAN

C A R E E R   P R O F I L E

Electricians plan, install, and repair wiring, electrical fixtures, and control equipment. They do this in homes, stores, offices, schools, and other types of buildings. Electricians prepare sketches that show the location of all wiring and equipment by following the blueprints or diagrams prepared by the architect or building contractor. All concealed wiring is installed before the floors, ceilings, and walls are completed. Electricians connect light fixtures, switches, relays, and circuit-breaker panels. They also connect appliances, such as electric ranges or dryers, and install the ground leads which are insulated electrical conductors that prevent electrical shocks. They must be sure that all their installations and repairs conform to local electrical codes and specifications.

If you are interested in becoming an electrician, you should like working with your hands, solving problems, designing systems, and making repairs. High school courses in math, physical science, and drafting are helpful.

To become an electrician, you can take courses at a vocational or technical school. A three- or four-year apprenticeship program or other type of on-the-job training is required in order to obtain a license. Electricians may work for power companies, building contractors, and lighting firms or be self-employed.

REVIEWING CHAPTER 16

SUMMARY

Lighting can be both functional and decorative. General illumination is used as background lighting and for supplementing special lighting. Local lighting is required for activities such as reading, studying, sewing, and working at a sink or work table. Accent lighting is used to illuminate a special object or area.

Incandescent and fluorescent bulbs are the main types used in homes today. Certain lights, including ceiling fixtures and lights over sinks, are usually built-in. Additional types of built-in lighting are luminous ceiling panels and cove, recessed, valance, cornice, and soffit lighting. Some alternatives to built-in lighting are portable spotlights and track lighting.

Lamps and lamp shades come in a wide choice of shapes, styles, and textures. The style of lamp should complement your decorating theme. Usually, light-colored shades are preferable, and a shade should be the right size and proportion for the lamp.

FACTS TO KNOW

1. Identify the three different types of lighting and give an example of each.
2. What is the difference between incandescent and fluorescent lighting? What are the advantages and disadvantages of each type?
3. Explain the term *footcandle*.
4. Describe the following types of built-in lighting: luminous ceiling panels, cove, recessed, valance, cornice, and soffit.
5. What types of lighting can be used as alternatives to built-in lighting?
6. Why are most lamp shades made of translucent material?
7. Explain how risers and harps may be used to change the height of lamps.
8. List at least five guidelines to follow when choosing lamps for your home.

IDEAS TO THINK ABOUT

1. Why is lighting sometimes described as direct or indirect? Give specific examples of both types of lighting.
2. Study the illustrations in the text for various types of lighting. Give reasons why each type of lighting was used in its location.

ACTIVITIES TO DO

1. Using magazines, catalogues, and newspapers, collect illustrations of as many different types of lighting and lamps as you can find. Group them according to the three basic types of lighting and display them on a bulletin board.
2. Using a floor plan for a one-bedroom apartment, list activities that would take place in each room. Then make a lighting plan for each room indicating type of lighting, design or style, and amount of light provided.

Chapter
17
Interior Enrichment

Colorful wall decorations have been found in caves dating from prehistoric times. Since the beginning of civilization, people in many parts of the world have used the walls of their homes to display art. These works of art, like those of later cultures and civilizations, provide a record of human history.

Today, people still decorate the walls of their homes with paintings and different types of accessories. Some are purely decorative; others, such as clocks, lamps, and candleholders, may be functional as well as decorative. Tabletops and shelves are decorated with photographs, sculptures, bowls, books, flower arrangements, and many other objects. Mobiles or plants may be hung from the ceiling, pillows and cushions may be tossed on a sofa or floor, and an indoor tree or decorative screen may be set in the corner of a room.

Accessories help bring a home to life and make it a personal expression of you and the other people who live there. Without them, a home would lack warmth and individuality. You can display a favorite collection, a hand-crafted creation, a special gift, or a work of art. It is your way of creating a room that reflects your interests, activities, and preferences—a reflection that makes your home unique.

PREVIEWING YOUR LEARNING

After you have read this chapter, you will be able to:

• Evaluate and select pictures and mirrors for wall decoration.

• Follow guidelines when hanging pictures.

• Select accessories to complement a room.

• Choose plants and flowers to accent your home.

TERMS TO KNOW

abstract—having little or no resemblance to an actual object or scene

crewel embroidery—needlework done with yarn and embroidery stitches

etching—a print made by transferring a drawing or design from a metal plate

lithograph—a print made by transferring an inked image from a flat surface

mat—a border around a picture between the picture and its frame, sometimes serving as its frame

medium—technical method of artistic expression

needlepoint—needlework done with yarn that completely covers the supporting canvas

plaque—a flat ornamental piece used for decoration

sconce—a fixture consisting of one or more candlesticks which can be hung on a wall

shadow box—a shallow case used for displaying objects

silk screen print—a print made by forcing dye through unsealed areas of a screen

INDOOR TREES

Trees make dramatic additions to any decorating scheme. Their beauty and grace can brighten an empty corner, frame an entryway, or perk up a drab foyer.

**F
E
A
T
U
R
E**
While any tree can grow indoors under the proper conditions, choosing the right tree for your home's conditions is important. A tree's growth rate and mature size must first be considered. Small trees (under 25 feet, or 7.6 m, when mature) with slow growth rates (less than a foot a year) make the best indoor trees. They can be maintained easily for a long period of time by pruning them regularly to keep them within the confines of the room. A little research and the advice from people at a nursery can help you choose the right kind of tree. Growth can be helped along with the appropriate fertilizer and grow lights.

Trees bought from a nursery can be a sizable investment, depending on their type and height. Protect your investment by making sure that your purchase is from a reputable nursery. Check trees and plants in the nursery for signs of bug infestation. Ants are a sure sign that more destructive aphids are around. Look for scars on stems and branches. A few scars are normal as shedding is part of the growth cycle, but more than a few per plant indicate that a plant is unhealthy. Be sure that the tree is not root-bound in its container; roots that stick up from the soil or out of the drainage holes show improper planting.

MEDIUMS FOR ENRICHMENT

Once the backgrounds, furniture, and lighting of a room are completed, the process of decorating may seem to be done. If you look carefully, however, you will see that the room still looks somewhat bare and un-lived-in. Something is still missing in the design. What the room lacks is the visual enrichment provided by pictures and objects of art. Some of these items, such as paintings or block prints, are purely for decoration. Others—such as vases, ash trays, or bookends—are mainly functional. Such items as family photographs and treasured possessions can also add visual interest and personal character to a room.

A wide variety of art mediums are appropriate for decoration. You may have experimented with drawings in charcoal, pastels, and pen-and-ink or with painting in watercolors, oil, or acrylics. Other types of art include etchings, made from metal or wood engravings; lithographs, which are prints or watercolors reproduced by the process of lithography; and block prints, silk screen, and stencil printings. In recent years, photography has become an important type of art. Ceramic tiles, plaques, and découpage are other art mediums. Needlepoint and crewel embroidery are also considered art. A number of types of art may be combined in a large room. Combinations must be chosen more carefully if the room is small.

PICTURES AS DECORATION

The term *picture* may refer to several different types of art, including oil paintings, watercolors, etchings, lithographs, photographs, and framed needlework. Certain types of art tend to create a special effect in decorating. Watercolors, pastels, etchings, and pen-and-ink drawings are delicate in feeling. Acrylic paintings are a little heavier, and oil paintings are even more imposing. Photographs are a separate category.

ENRICHMENT MATERIALS

WALL	FLOOR	SURFACE	CEILING
Pictures	Plant stands	Bowls	Hanging baskets
Plaques	Fireplace needs	Vases	Bird cages
Clocks and barometers	Floor lamps	Clocks	Mobiles
Hanging shelves	Pedestals	Figurines	Pull-lights
Shadow boxes	Tall plants	Sculpture	
Mirrors	Cushions	Terrariums	
Wall brackets	Pictures on easels	Books	
Sconces		Book-ends	
Lamps		Candle holders	
Needlepoint pictures		Boxes	
Crewel embroideries		Plants	
Macramé Hangings		Flower arrangements	
Woven Hangings		Other art objects	

Selecting Pictures

Pictures should be selected with consideration for their subject matter, color, and size. Some pictures may give a formal feeling, such as landscapes or floral arrangements in elaborate frames. Other pictures may be more informal or even humorous in mood. These are suitable for more casual rooms, such as family rooms, kitchens, bedrooms, or bathrooms. Subject matter of pictures range from landscapes and outdoor scenes to American folk art and still life paintings of flowers or fruit. These types of pictures often coordinate with the color scheme of the room. Portraits, especially those done in oil, tend to dominate a room. They are usually hung over fireplaces or pieces of heavy furniture.

Abstract designs and modern art are usually used in contemporary settings. Abstract paintings are often very large and bold. Their direction of line and their colors can be used as focal points in rooms. Abstract paintings may be combined in arrangements with other modern art forms made from sculptured glass, plastic, or wood. Although modern designs are usually out of place in traditional and Early American rooms, they can be used very effectively in eclectic rooms which mix different periods of furniture.

Original paintings by well-known artists can be very expensive. However, works of newer artists can be purchased for lower prices at art shows and fairs. You may also find original works in thrift shops and secondhand stores. Many reproductions of high quality are now available. Posters can also be used to decorate the walls of family rooms, bedrooms, or eating areas.

In addition to pictures many different objects can be used as accessories. Here the informal grouping adds a nice touch to this room.

This painting with its carved frame is appropriate for a traditional room.

Framing Pictures

An appropriate frame is important to the total effect of a picture. The frame should set off the picture, rather than compete with it for interest. Some pictures require a mat to separate the picture from the frame.

Photographs may be framed in a narrow frame with or without a mat. Watercolors, pencil, and pen-and-ink sketches, etchings, wood-block prints, and lithographs are usually framed with a mat and a narrow frame. Mats may be made of special mat board or fabric. The color and texture should harmonize with the picture.

If you have a picture to be framed, a reliable dealer will make suggestions for the frame and let you hold up various picture moldings beside the picture before making a decision. You can also purchase a frame and mat at an art store specializing in picture framing and frame the picture yourself. Frames that snap together are available in a wide variety of sizes. Clear plastic box frames can be used as "frameless" holders for prints and photographs. There are special frames available for large or unusually sized posters.

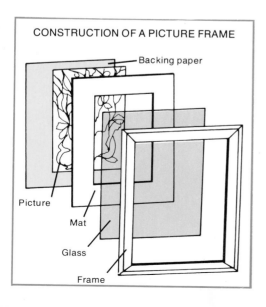

CONSTRUCTION OF A PICTURE FRAME

- Backing paper
- Picture
- Mat
- Glass
- Frame

A focal point in this contemporary room is the abstract painting.

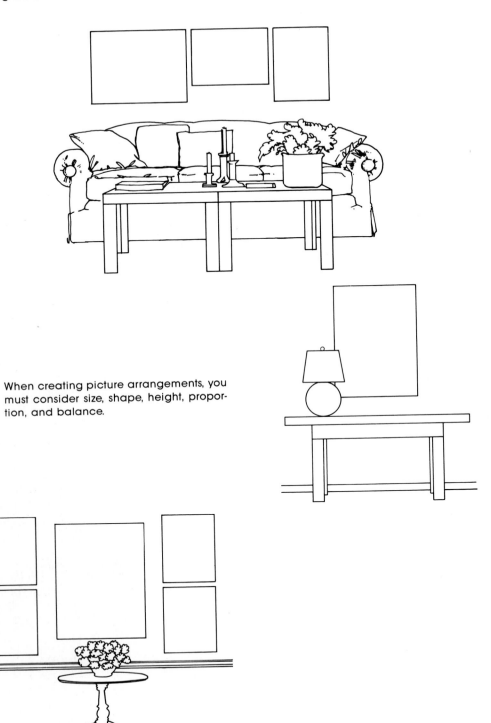

When creating picture arrangements, you must consider size, shape, height, proportion, and balance.

Hanging Pictures

Where you hang pictures and how you group them is as important as the choice of pictures. The size and shape of a picture should conform to the area in which it is hung. For instance, a large picture requires a large wall space, vertical pictures require a vertical wall space, and horizontal pictures require adequate horizontal wall space.

If you are uncertain about grouping pictures or about the size of a picture in relation to the wall space, cut out brown wrapping paper the size of a single picture or the sizes of pictures to be used in the group. Arrange the shapes on a large table or floor and study the effect. If you like the effect, use a soft lead pencil to mark the outside edges of the pictures. This procedure will eliminate guesswork and avoid unnecessary holes in the wall. If you should make unnecessary holes, they can be filled with patching plaster.

The following guidelines are helpful for hanging pictures:

—Hang a large picture on an important wall at average eye level. On this basis, the center of a large picture should be about 5½ feet (1.68 m) from the floor. Pictures over mantels may be exceptions to this rule. The height of the ceiling and of furniture beneath or near the picture also influences the level at which it is hung.

—In grouping a number of pictures together, keep an imaginary line around the outside, so that the arrangement will have unity. Use no more than one large grouping of pictures in a room.

—Be sure that good proportion exists between a picture or group of pictures and the furniture below it.

—Avoid hanging pictures against figured wallpaper, unless the pictures are matted or the subject is strong enough to hold its own against the wallpaper.

—To prepare a picture for hanging, place the eye screws on the back of it about a fourth of the way down. Insert picture wire through the eyes of the screws, pull it fairly taut straight across, and fasten it securely. When the picture is hung, it will lie flat against the wall, instead of tilting away from the wall.

—Use cloth-base hangers or small picture hooks for small pictures, and large picture hooks for large pictures. Two picture hooks placed an inch or more apart will give a large picture or mirror greater support and keep it hanging more nearly level. Very large pictures may have to be hung with a special toggle insert for adequate support.

Use the same guidelines whether hanging framed art or other objects.

The paintings and photographs on this wall are unified by their subject matter—the owner's affections and interests. Such a display is appropriate for a study or bedroom.

A mirrored wall will create an illusion of added space in a room.

Mirrors are both functional and decorative.

MIRRORS

A beautiful ornamental mirror can be the focal point in the decoration of any room. If there is a small foyer or a defined entrance to a living area, a mirror placed over a small table or a shelf suspended from the wall adds interest and gives an illusion of greater space. A large mirror at the end of a room makes the room seem larger. A bedroom, bath, or dressing room should have a full-length door mirror so that you can check your overall appearance. A mirrored wall gives the illusion of added space, especially good for a small room.

The location of a mirror, like that of a picture, should be in proper relation to other furnishings. The shape should be in proportion to the wall space around it. The style should be chosen to fit into the decorating theme of the room. Chippendale, Adam, and convex Federal mirrors are suitable for traditional rooms. Shapes that are similar but simpler are appropriate for Early American rooms, as are round, oval, and rectangular mirrors with wood frames. Unframed mirrors look best in contemporary rooms.

THREE-DIMENSIONAL DECORATIONS

Beautiful and functional objects, as well as pictures and mirrors, can be used as accessories to complete a room setting. Large objects, such as lamps or clocks, can be a focus of interest. Small objects, such as collections of fine items, should be displayed as a group.

Grandfather clocks can be new designs or antiques.

Clocks

Clocks are made to hang on the wall, stand on the floor, or rest on a table or shelf. Wall clocks include banjo clocks, schoolhouse clocks, cuckoo clocks, and many other types. The grandfather clock is the most familiar type of clock that stands on the floor. Clocks and barometers are sometimes matched and hung on opposite walls or side by side.

Hanging Shelves

Hanging shelves and shadow boxes are often used to display collections such as figurines, teacups, spoons, small wood carvings, or special seashells. Scrollsaw wood brackets are often used with Early American furnishings. They may hold a clock, a bowl or plant, or art objects in keeping with the size of the room. Candle sconces, plates, and plaques may also provide wall interest.

Hanging shelves can be used to hold books or accessories.

Surface Accessories

Interesting decorations for tables, mantels, shelves, and other surfaces add character and personal meaning to a room. These decorations include books and bookends; bowls, boxes, vases, and candleholders; glass, metal, or wood sculptures; and objects of brass, copper, or silver. The texture, color, size, and shape of these accessories should be in scale with the surface on which they are displayed and in harmony with the room. Often, people combine books and art objects on bookshelves for variety and interest.

Accessories can be arranged on tables, shelves, bookcases, and mantels to add character and interest to a room.

CRAFT WORK

Decorations that are made by hand provide a special kind of enrichment in the home. Often, such objects are ones that have been made by you or a member of your family. In that case, the personal creativity adds a special interest and meaning.

Craft work in the home may be the product of special talents, such as weaving, making pottery, and wood carving. More often, it involves sewing or handwork, such as embroidery or needlepoint. These activities, too, depend on special skills that are developed through long use. Braided rugs or chair seats, pillows or panels of crewel embroidery, chair seats of needlepoint, handsewn quilts, and woven or knotted hangings add charm and personal character to a room. Craft work should be in harmony with the decorating theme. It is used most often in informal settings.

Hand-made objects add a personal warmth and charm to a home.

HOUSE PLANTS

Living plants can provide an attractive accent, as well as a contrast to inanimate objects in a room. Plants that are well chosen and cared for can give the feeling of extending a room into the outdoors, especially if the plants are arranged near windows. Some people prefer the convenience of artificial greenery. If artificial plants are used, they should look natural and be kept clean.

Growing plants successfully depends upon the proper soil, the right exposure, correct feeding and watering, and the appropriate kind and size of container. Most house plants thrive in soil which is a mixture of ⅓ sand, ⅓ leaf mold or peat, and ⅓ garden soil. Succulents and African violets require a special soil mixture.

Most flowering plants require a great deal of sunlight. However, African violets and begonias grow well in curtained sunny windows, in a bright north window, and even under artificial light. Plants vary greatly in the amount of humidity they require. If the bottom leaves turn yellow and the stems look soft, a plant is probably being watered too much. If the edges of the leaves turn brown, the plant may not be getting enough water. A nursery salesperson can advise about soil, exposure, watering, and nourishment when a plant is purchased.

Among the most popular house plants are vines such as ferns, philodendron, coleus, wandering Jew with green or purple leaves, and English and Swedish ivy. These plants thrive in subdued light or under artificial light. They are often used in

Plants help to bring a feeling of the outdoors inside a home.

hanging baskets and floor planters, because they cascade gracefully over the container. These arrangements are also attractive on porches, lanais, and balconies.

A small indoor tree may be used to accent a corner of a room, frame a large picture window, or fill an empty space. Most trees require some natural sunlight in order to thrive.

The best pots for most plants are terra-cotta or clay. These are porous, have drainage holes, and are available in all sizes. Plastic and glazed-pottery pots are nonporous, so that water is slow to evaporate. When using these pots, place a layer of pebbles in the bottom of the container to provide drainage and avoid over-watering. Before filling a clay pot with soil, soak it until it is well saturated. Otherwise, the moisture intended for the plant will be soaked up by the pot. When the roots of a plant become crowded, separate the plant into smaller ones or transfer it to a larger container.

Select plants according to the amount of sunlight in a room. Some require a great deal of light; others will grow in subdued light.

Arrange fresh flowers in a pitcher, basket, or bowl for a colorful accent in a room.

FLOWERS

Flower arrangements add color, design interest, and freshness to any room. They may be as simple as a bouquet of wild daisies in a pitcher, or as formal as a traditional floral design.

Growing your own flowers requires space for a garden and time for tending it. There is a special satisfaction in arranging flowers you have grown yourself. However, it is also possible to buy cut flowers to use for decoration. Most supermarkets have seasonal flowers available at relatively low cost. A few flowers, mixed with laurel or lemon leaves, can become a cheerful bouquet.

Dried and artificial flowers can also be used to provide decorative interest. You can either buy attractive dried flowers or make your own by following the directions in books on the subject. Arrangements of dried flowers, nuts with wired stems, cattails, sea oats, and wheat are most suitable for a rustic decorating theme. Artificial flowers are available in a wide variety of arrangements.

Containers

A flower container and any accessories to be used should be appropriate for the color, size, and shape of the flower arrangement. They should also be in keeping with the character of the room. Containers without surface decoration are preferable, because decoration would compete with the flower arrangement. Containers in soft greens, earth colors, and off-whites will complement most arrangements. If colored containers are used, some of the flowers should repeat the color of the container. The container should also be chosen in relation to the space in which it is to be used and to the height and size of the flowers. Low containers are usually best for coffee- and dining-table arrangements. Tall containers should be used against a vertical wall area or on a low chest or table where height is needed to complement a picture or a piece of furniture.

In addition to regular flower vases, you can use round or oval bowls, baskets containing waterproof containers, glasses, teapots, pitchers, tureens, and decorative bottles. Flower holders in different shapes and sizes made of glass, metal, or plastic can be used to help hold the stems in place. Crumpled chicken wire and a florist's material called Oasis can also be used to hold the arrangement.

CAREER PROFILE

FLORIST

Florists design and arrange flowers and decorations. They may use natural or artificial flowers and foliage for their arrangements. To form corsages, bouquets, wreaths, and sprays, florists wrap flower stems with floral tape before wiring or pinning the flowers together. To create centerpieces, they arrange flowers in a variety of containers, using different materials to hold the stems in place. Florists may grow some of their own flowers and plants in greenhouses, or they may purchase all of their flowers and plants from wholesale suppliers.

Florists meet with customers to plan floral arrangements for weddings, anniversaries, birthdays, open houses, and other special events. They may travel to places of worship, restaurants, catering halls, homes, and office buildings to supervise the decorations for these events. Florists also help customers select plants that can be grown indoors and that are most suited to the available lighting. Some florists contract with restaurants, office buildings, and shopping centers to supply and maintain their indoor plants and flowers throughout the year.

If you are interested in becoming a florist, you need artistic skills, a creative imagination, and an interest in flowers and plants. An art background is helpful to your understanding of color and line and to applying the design principles to arrangements. Good eye–hand coordination and manual dexterity are also helpful.

To become a florist, you can take specialized courses in horticulture at colleges or vocational schools. You can also gain on-the-job experience by working for a florist. Florists can work for wholesale suppliers, retail florists, nurseries, or garden shops. They can also own and manage their own floral business.

REVIEWING CHAPTER 17

SUMMARY

Pictures and other kinds of accessories enrich the design of a room. Some of these items, such as paintings, are purely decorative. Others, such as vases or bookends, are also functional. Accessories can also add beauty and a personal character to a room.

Pictures may be in many different mediums, such as oil paintings, watercolors, pastels, pen-and-ink drawings, etchings, lithographs, silk screens, needlework, and photographs. Certain guidelines should be followed when hanging and grouping pictures effectively. Mirrors, clocks, and hanging shelves can also be used for decorating walls. Surface accessories include bowls, boxes, books, candleholders, and sculptures. Craftwork, such as embroidery or needlepoint, adds special charm and interest to a room. Plants and flowers can also be used to decorate interiors. They provide colorful accents and freshness to any room.

FACTS TO KNOW

1. Why are pictures and accessories important to the decoration of a room?

2. Identify various types of art mediums that pictures may be made of.

3. When grouping pictures together, what guidelines should you follow?

4. At what height should most pictures be hung?

5. Describe several ways of using mirrors as accessories.

6. What are some examples of three-dimensional accessories? Where can they be used in rooms?

7. List at least four functional objects that can be used as accessories in rooms.

8. Describe several different ways that plants and flowers may be used in decorating. What special qualities do plants and flowers add to a room?

IDEAS TO THINK ABOUT

1. Explain the relationship between the style and subject matter of a picture and the decorating theme of a room.

2. What types of craftwork can be used as decorations or accessories? With what setting and style is each type most appropriate?

ACTIVITIES TO DO

1. Collect a large number of illustrations from magazines and catalogues of accessories. Divide them into categories according to the style for which they are most appropriate—traditional, Early American or provincial, and contemporary. Which ones, if any, are suitable for more than one setting? Prepare a bulletin board display with the illustrations.

2. Bring to class an example of some type of craftwork that is used as a decorative accessory. Explain the technique that was used to make the craftwork. Where is it used in your home? Was it made by you or a member of your family?

Chapter 18

Household Furnishings

Many advertisements for household furnishings show a "total look" for tables, beds, or bathrooms. Beautiful illustrations in magazines and catalogues feature coordinated patterns, colors, and styles. Some represent the work of famous designers, so that now there are designer labels on household furnishings as well as on clothing.

The past 30 years has brought a revolution in household furnishings. The trend toward more casual living and informal entertaining has created a demand for products that are easy to care for and multipurpose. Many products for the home that were primarily functional, such as sheets, are now purchased for their decorative effect as well.

Patterned sheets and comforters are meant to be displayed in the bedroom, not hidden under a bedspread. Colorful towels and shower curtains often become the focal point of bathrooms. Table settings are offered in a multitude of styles and materials—from pottery and plastic to china and crystal. Today's household furnishings combine beauty, function, and ease of care.

Most furniture, because of its expense, is used for many years. However, without buying new furniture, you can change the look of your dining area, bedroom, and bath by selecting new colors and patterns for your linens and table settings.

PREVIEWING YOUR LEARNING

After you have read this chapter, you will be able to:

- Evaluate household textiles according to fiber content, yarns, weaves, and finishes.

- Select bed linens, bath linens, and table linens according to one's needs.

- Identify different types of dinnerware, flatware, and glassware and the advantages and limitations of each.

- Explain how to care for dinnerware, flatware, and glassware.

TERMS TO KNOW

china—fine porcelain dinnerware
comforter—a bed covering filled with a batting or fiberfill that supplies warmth
crystal—clear, colorless glass of superior quality
flatware—knives, forks, and spoons
muslin—plain, woven cotton fabric that is coarser than percale
percale—a fine, closely woven cotton fabric

place setting—a table service for one person
porcelain—a hard, nonporous, translucent material made from fine white clay and feldspar fired at high temperatures
silver plate—a coating of silver on metal
stainless steel—an alloy of steel, chromium, and nickel that will not rust or corrode
thermal—designed to prevent the loss of body heat

THE VERSATILE SHEET

Sheets may be one of the best decorating buys. Available in seemingly limitless colors and patterns, this once plain household staple has become an inexpensive decorating tool for every room in the home.

In living rooms, sheet slipcovers that you make yourself can revive old sofas, loveseats, and chairs. Choose sheets that work well with the rest of the decor, such as graphic prints for modern settings or florals and mini-prints for traditional ones. Matching or coordinating sheets can be transformed into curtains or shades. Pillow shams that are stuffed are easy-to-make throw pillows. An added advantage to using sheets is that they are washable and easy to change.

In dining areas, use matching or coordinated sheets for chair cushions, tablecloths, and curtains. Sheets with borders make nice café curtains for kitchens. Add matching placemats and even appliance covers for a coordinated look.

With all their versatility, it is easy to see why sheets can make a bedroom something special. Bed linens now coordinate in spectacular ways, with matching sheets, comforter, dust ruffle, and pillow shams. An extra sheet or two made into curtains or a dressing table skirt can tie the whole room together.

HOUSEHOLD TEXTILES

Our heritage of fibers, fabrics, and yarns dates from before the beginning of civilization. People in prehistoric ages depended upon animal skins or grasses for bedding and clothing. In time, people discovered that certain natural fibers could be woven into cloth. Flax stems were long enough to be woven directly; wool and cotton had to be stretched out and twisted into yarn before being woven. Silk from a cocoon formed one continuous thread.

Many scientists sought to imitate silk fibers and fabrics because of their high cost. The first synthetic or manufactured fiber was produced in 1924 and was named rayon. This early rayon was strong, but it snagged and pulled out of shape. Another synthetic fiber, acetate, was more satisfactory, but it melted if touched with a hot iron. Both rayon and acetate are made by treating fibrous material, such as wood pulp, with chemicals.

Just before World War II, nylon was developed through a chemical process. It is stronger than silk, light in weight, and dries quickly. However, nylon does have some disadvantages. During the 1950's, many additional synthetic fibers were introduced for use in clothing and home furnishings. These fibers included acrylic, polyester, and triacetate. Each synthetic fiber has specific characteristics or properties, and fiber research continues to improve these properties. Refer to the chart on page 343.

Generic names are used to classify groups of fibers with similar composition. In addition, fiber manufacturers have trade names for each fiber that they produce. These names are registered and protected by law. For example, polyester is the generic name for one group of fibers. The trade name for DuPont's polyester is Dacron®. Fortrel® is the trade name for Celanese's polyester and Kodel® for Eastman's polyester.

During the 50's, many new finishes appeared which added crispness or softness

Sheets, comforters, and dust ruffles are available in coordinated patterns.

Colorful tablecloths, place mats, and napkins with a permanent press finish are easy to care for.

or made fabrics resistant to moths, mildew, soil, and wrinkles.

No fiber meets all needs; each has its special properties. Some fibers are warm, and others cool; some are absorbent, and others nonabsorbent; some are strong and wear-resistant, while others are weak and snag easily; some keep their finish, and others must have the finish restored after laundering; some fibers produce very sheer fabrics, and others produce fluffy warm fabrics. However, it is now possible to create blends for almost any desired result. For example, a blend of cotton and polyester may keep much of the absorbency of cotton, but have the strength and nonshrink quality of polyester. Knowing about the different fibers and their qualities will help you in choosing household textiles. Their appearance, use, durability, and care are important factors in the look and upkeep of your household.

Yarns

Certain properties of fibers allow them to be stretched out into yarns, which in turn can be woven into fabrics. Wool has tiny scales that interlock; cotton has a natural crimp that makes the fibers cling together. The simplest yarn is made up of a single thread, or filament. Silk and synthetic fibers are single-filament yarns. Other fibers, such as wool and cotton, must be spun, or twisted, to become yarn. When two or more yarns are twisted together, they are called ply yarns. The type of yarn used affects the texture and durability of fabrics.

Sometimes yarns are cut and twisted to produce different surface effects. Among these novelty yarns are the following:
— core-and-effect yarn, in which a second yarn is twisted around a core yarn to produce loops and different surface effects in fabrics such as bouclé, where random loops appear on the surface. Such fabrics are not good for upholstery, slipcovers, or bedspreads, because they snag.
— slub yarns, which are alternately tightly and loosely twisted to produce an irregular yarn, used in such fabrics as shantung and antique satin. Fabrics with these yarns are not recommended for upholstery, slipcovers, or bedspreads that receive hard use.
— nub yarns, which look as though they have been tied in knots at intervals. Fabrics of these yarns are not recommended for upholstery, slipcovers, or bedspreads that receive hard use.

Weaves

The way in which yarns are woven affects not only the appearance of a textile, but also the texture, absorbency, and durability. Weaving is done in a wide variety of traditional patterns and designs. The weaves most commonly used in household textiles are as follows:
— The plain weave is the simplest weave of all. This is the regular lacing of filling yarns over alternate warp yarns. This is a durable weave, but its durability depends upon how tightly the yarns are spun and how closely they are woven. Percale and muslin for sheets and pillowcases and many fabrics for slipcovers and curtains have this weave.
— The basket weave is similar to the plain weave, except that two or more filling

The texture of fabrics is determined by the types of yarns used and the way in which the yarns are woven.

FIBERS USED IN HOME FURNISHINGS

GENERIC NAME	TRADE NAME	CHARACTERISTICS	MAJOR USES
NATURAL FIBERS			
Cotton		Strong, absorbent, comfortable, durable, dyes easily, blends well, easily laundered, wrinkles and shrinks unless treated, will mildew.	Towels, sheets, blankets, curtains, draperies, place mats, upholstery, rugs.
Flax (linen)		Strong, absorbent, comfortable, dyes well, easily laundered, wrinkles unless treated, will mildew.	Tablecloths, draperies, upholstery.
Wool		Resilient, warm, absorbent, dyes easily, blends well, flame-resistant, water-repellent, can shrink with heat and moisture, can be damaged by moths and other insects, usually dry-cleaned, sometimes washable.	Carpets, blankets, upholstery.
Silk		Natural luster, strong, smooth, absorbent, dyes to brilliant shades, weakened by sunlight, usually dry-cleaned, sometimes washable.	Draperies, upholstery.
MANUFACTURED FIBERS			
Acetate	Ariloft, Avron, Celanese, Chromspun, Estron.	Luxurious feel, absorbent, good drapability, wide range of colors and lusters, resilient, flame-resistant, inexpensive, heat sensitive, subject to fading, damaged by acetone.	Curtains, draperies, upholstery, fiberfill for pillows and quilted products.
Acrylic	Acrilan, Bi-Loft, Creslan, Orlon.	Soft, warm, lightweight, resilient, retains shape, quick-drying, resistant to moths and sunlight, may pill or collect static electricity, heat sensitive.	Blankets, carpets, rugs, draperies, upholstery.
Nylon	Anso, Antron, Cantrece, Caprolan, Crepeset, Enkalure.	Very strong, quick-drying, lustrous, resilient, abrasion-resistant, blends well, resistant to moths and mildew, may collect static electricity, may gray or yellow with age, heat sensitive.	Curtains, draperies, bedspreads, upholstery, carpets.
Polyester	Dacron, Encron, Fortrel, Kodel, Trevira.	Wrinkle-resistant, strong, abrasion-resistant, little stretching or shrinking, blends well, easy to dye, quick-drying, retains heat-set pleats and creases, low absorbency, may pill or pick up lint, easy to wash.	Curtains, draperies, sheets, tablecloths, carpets, fiberfill for various products.
Rayon	Avril, Coloray, Enkaire.	Absorbent, soft, easy to dye, very versatile, economical, may wrinkle or shrink unless treated, weakened by long exposure to light.	Curtains, draperies, sheets, blankets, bedspreads, tablecloths, slipcovers, upholstery, carpets.
Triacetate	Arnel.	Wrinkle- and shrink-resistant, can be permanently pleated, dyes easily.	Draperies.

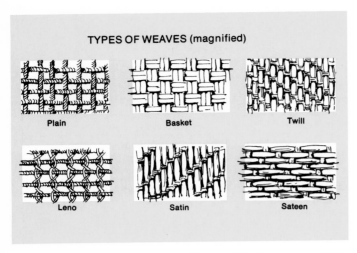

TYPES OF WEAVES (magnified)

Plain Basket Twill

Leno Satin Sateen

These drawings show the magnified detail of various weaves.

yarns regularly interlace two or more warp yarns. The most familiar household textile with this weave is monk's cloth. The basket weave is not a durable weave and is not recommended for slipcovers, but it is satisfactory for table mats and draperies.

— A corded weave is also a variation of the plain weave. In a corded weave, heavy warp yarns are interwoven with fine filling yarns, or heavy filling yarns are interwoven with fine warp yarns. Since warp and filling yarns are not evenly balanced, a corded weave is less durable than a plain weave. Rep, poplin, and faille are examples of household textiles with this weave.

— A twill weave is the interlacing of filling yarn over groups of warp yarns in regular progression to give a diagonal effect. This is an extremely durable weave, used in denim, gabardine, and many drapery and slipcover fabrics.

— A herringbone weave resembles a twill weave, except that the diagonal surface effect is reversed at regular intervals, producing a herringbone effect. It is also a durable weave and is used in fabrics for slipcovers and draperies.

— A leno weave is produced by lacing filling yarns through warp yarns with a chain-like twist. Curtain marquisette is an example of this weave.

— A satin weave is identified by floating warp yarns that pick up light reflection to give a lustrous effect. During the weaving process, a filling yarn goes over one warp yarn and under a number of warp yarns, with each row of filling yarns interlacing progressively. Silk, rayon, and acetate satins are examples.

— The sateen weave is identified by floating filling yarns, which seem to reflect less light than floating warp yarns. During the weaving process, a filling yarn goes under one warp yarn and over a number of warp yarns, with each row of filling yarns interlacing progressively. Cotton sateen is an example.

Finishes

Chemical and physical finishes are applied to cloth to improve its appearance. Among the most familiar standard finishes are dyeing; direct printing by rollers; flock printing, or direct printing with an adhesive capable of attracting and holding minute flocks or filaments; silk-screen printing (similar to hand stenciling); sizing for a firmer appearance; napping to produce a surface fuzz, which holds air cells and produces warmth; mercerizing, especially for cotton, to produce luster and strength; crease resistance to decrease wrinkling; and finishes for shrinkage control.

In addition to the above finishes, household fabrics may be given certain special finishes. Bedding and draperies for hotels may be given flame-resistant finishes. Bedding and draperies may also be given anti-odor and anti-perspiration finishes. Stain- and spot-resistant finishes are given many fabrics for household use. Finishes are also given to reduce static and to resist moths and mildew. A permanent-press finish is popular for sheets and drapery fabrics. Permanent press may be the result of a chemical finish or the result of blending a polyester fiber with cotton or other fibers.

Finishes tend to change the properties of fibers to some extent. Crease-, stain-, and spot-resistant finishes decrease absorbency in cotton and linen. Some finishes, such as napping, may weaken the fabric if the process is not carefully controlled. Many finishes require special care in dry-cleaning, washing, drying, and ironing.

SELECTING BED LINENS

Because proper rest is essential to a person's well-being, textiles for the bed should be chosen with special regard for comfort. However, appearance is also a consideration, since the bedcovering is a major factor in the room's decoration. Changes in the size of beds, with queen-size and king-size often replacing the standard-size double bed, have made the dimensions of bedding an important factor.

Sheets and Pillowcases

Sheets and pillowcases are most commonly made of percale and muslin, but satin and flannel are available. Percale sheets are finer, cooler, and lighter in weight than muslin sheets. They are made of long-staple, firmly twisted cotton yarns and are more closely woven than muslin sheets. Muslin sheets are very durable, but the fabric is coarser and heavier than percale.

Acetate satin sheets are luxurious in feel, but they do not stay in place and are not easy to launder. Cotton flannel sheets have a napped surface and provide extra warmth. They are becoming very popular, especially in colder climates.

Sheets made of a blend of cotton and polyester with a permanent-press finish are very convenient to use because they do not wrinkle after washing or drying. A blend of 65 percent polyester and 35 percent cotton is the most common used. Cotton increases softness and absorbency, and polyester increases wrinkle resistance. Therefore, the more polyester, the greater resistance to wrinkling; however, a lower percentage of cotton reduces the softness, absorbency, and coolness.

Thread count refers to the number of threads woven vertically and horizontally in one square inch of sheet before shrinking. A heavy muslin sheet may have a thread count of from 112 to 140, and a

Some fabric designs are created during the weaving process. Other designs are printed onto the fabric by circular rollers, screen printing, or other methods.

Bed linens are available in a variety of sizes. Read the labels carefully when making a purchase.

STANDARD SIZES FOR BED LINENS				
TYPE OF BED	FITTED SHEET[1]	FLAT SHEET	BLANKET	SPREAD
Crib	27″ X 52″	42″ X 72″	40″ X 60″	
Youth	33″ X 66″	63″ X 108″	54″ X 72″	
Cot	30″ X 72″	63″ X 108″	54″ X 72″	59″ X 100″
Day	33″ X 75″	63″ X 108″	66″ X 90″	
Twin[2]	39″ X 75″	72″ X 108″	72″ X 90″	81″ X 110″
Twin (long)[2]	39″ X 80″	72″ X 120″	72″ X 90″	81″ X 120″
Double[2]	54″ X 75″	81″ X 108″	80″ X 90″	96″ X 110″
Double (long)[2]	54″ X 80″	81″ X 120″	80″ X 90″	96″ X 120″
Queen	60″ X 75″	90″ X 120″	100″ X 90″	105″ X 115″
Queen (long)	60″ X 80″	90″ X 120″	108″ X 90″	105″ X 120″
King	72″ X 84″	100″ X 120″	108″ X 90″	114″ X 120″
King (wide)	78″ X 84″	108″ X 120″	108″ X 90″	
Hollywood[2]	78″ X 75″	108″ X 120″	108″ X 90″	120″ X 120″
Hollywood (long)[2]	78″ X 80″	108″ X 120″	108″ X 90″	

[1] Sizes given in this column are for standard innerspring mattresses.

[2] Fitted sheets with special boxing are available for foam-rubber mattresses.

percale sheet may have a thread count of from 180 to 200. A fine percale sheet may outwear a heavy muslin sheet, because the long-staple, firmly twisted yarns of the percale sheet are more flexible and resistant to constant friction and folding.

Size Sheets are available in a number of sizes and styles. A fitted bottom sheet must be chosen to fit the mattress properly. A sheet that is too tight will cause the mattress to buckle, and the sheet will wear out faster because of strain. A sheet that is too loose will wrinkle and become uncomfortable. Fitted bottom sheets are designed to fit the standard 7-inch (17.8 cm) innerspring mattress. Special fitted sheets are available for thinner mattresses.

Top sheets are flat and should be 24 inches (61 cm) longer than the mattress. The extra length provides for tucking it under the mattress at the bottom and folding it over the blanket at the top for protection from soil.

Sizes of sheets are indicated in torn sizes, not in hemmed sizes. Allowing for shrinkage and for bottom and top hems, a sheet with a torn size of 108 inches (274 cm) will actually be somewhere between 96 and 98 inches (244–249 cm) long when finished. The chart of recommended sizes indicates the size of sheet required for various types and sizes of beds.

Pillowcases should fit over the pillow with ease and be 4 to 6 inches (10–15 cm) longer than the pillow. Cases for standard-size pillows are 20 × 34 inches (51 × 86 cm); for queen-size pillows, 20 × 35 inches (51 × 89 cm) and 20 × 38 inches (51 × 97 cm); and for king-size pillows, 20 × 40 inches (51 × 102 cm) and 20 × 44 inches (51 × 112 cm). It is desirable to use a zippered covering for the pillow before covering it with the pillowcase. Since such a covering can be washed, it protects the freshness of the pillow.

Design In recent years, colorful designs on sheets and pillowcases have made them an important decorative element in bedrooms. Sheets are often coordinated with comforters, blankets, dust ruffles, pillows, curtains, and towels. Sheets can be used to create coordinating tablecloths, slipcovers, and wall coverings, as well as curtains and draperies. An adjoining bathroom can be decorated with coordinating sets of bath linens.

Blankets

Cotton, wool, and acrylic fibers are used for making woven blankets. Nonwoven blankets are made of nylon flocking bonded to each side of a polyurethane foam core. Cotton blankets are used as covers in the summer; they may be used as sheets in cold climates in the winter. These blankets are usually a blend of 65 percent polyester and 35 percent cotton. The yarns are teased to produce a nap, enabling the blanket to hold pockets of air for softness and warmth. Blankets made of acrylic fibers or polyurethane with nylon flocking are warm and lightweight. Wool blankets are also lightweight and warm. When given shrink- and moth-resistant finishes, they are washable. However, wool blankets are more expensive than blankets of most other fibers.

Thermal blankets are loosely woven with either a basket or leno weave. Sometimes the filling yarns are slub yarns, which are soft and irregular in appearance. The loose weave, together with the soft and irregular yarns, traps air in pockets and makes the blanket warm, especially under a lightweight bedspread.

Electric blankets are convenient to use, because the warmth can be controlled. The price of an electric blanket is based upon the quality of the fabric used, the number of temperature controls, and the length of the guarantee. Expensive electric blankets have preheat settings and a setting that adjusts automatically as the room temperature changes. There are dual controls for standard double beds and queen-size and king-size beds. Less expensive electric blankets have fewer settings. All electric blankets are machine washable if they carry the AC-UL listing. Blankets must be washed at cool temperature settings, with delicate tumble action. They should be removed while slightly damp, shaken well, and hung up to dry.

Comforters

A comforter is a bed covering that is filled with batting or fiberfill for added warmth. It is often used as a combination bedspread and blanket. The outer cover is usually made of the same types of fabrics as sheets are: percale, satin, or flannel. Today, most comforters are filled with either polyester fiberfill or down, which is soft fluffy feathers from geese or ducks. The filling and the outer cover are then stitched together, either in widely spaced vertical rows or in a rectangular pattern. Comforters may be bought separately or as part of a coordinated set with matching sheets, pillowcases, and dust ruffle.

Bedspreads

Bedspreads are available in three styles: throw, fitted, and coverlet with a dust ruffle. A bedspread should hang evenly all around the bed and be long enough to tuck over pillows, unless pillow shams are used. Many different types of fabrics are used for bedspreads, including firmly woven, loosely woven, tufted, and quilted. Bedspreads may be finished with fringe, scallops, or ruffles, and they may have a separate dust ruffle. Always read the label for the recommended method of care.

A colorful quilt, whether an heirloom or a new design, becomes the focal point of this bedroom.

SELECTING BATH LINENS

Towels, window curtains, and shower curtains are often made as coordinates. Towels for the bathroom include bath, hand, and fingertip towels and bath sheets. Washcloths and tub mats are part of the bathroom ensemble. Towel sizes are shown on the chart on page 351.

The fabric for towels is made of terry or a loop weave for absorbency and softness. A terry weave is a plain ground weave. A third set of yarns is loosened during weaving to produce loops. Sometimes one side of a towel is sheared or the loops are cut to give a soft velvet effect, and the loops on the opposite side are left uncut for greater absorbency. Bath towels are more absorb-

Bright colors create a sense of luxury in a bathroom. What decorative touches are used to enhance this bathroom?

STANDARD SIZES FOR BATH LINENS

Bath Towels	22" X 42" and 24" X 44"	Fingertip Towels	11" X 18"
Hand Towels	15" X 25" and 16" X 26"	Bath Sheets	35" X 65" and 36" X 68"
Wash Cloths	12" X 12"	Tub Mat	21" X 32" and 22" X 34"

ent if the fiber content is from 84 to 86 percent cotton and 16 to 14 percent polyester. The cotton is used for the loops to provide absorbency, and the polyester is used for the backing to give strength and constant size. A sculptured effect may be produced by shearing sections and leaving loops between them. A two-tone design, with one color predominant on one side and another color on the opposite side, also produces patterns. Printed designs on terry cloth are less desirable, because they soon look faded. The size and thickness of towels are a matter of preference and cost. Thickness and closeness of pile add durability, but they also increase the cost.

Bath towels should be laundered in warm to moderately hot water, but never in extremely hot water. If dried in a dryer, they should be removed before they are bone dry. If they are dried on a clothesline, they should be shaken well when almost dry to fluff up the loops and make the towels more absorbent.

Shower curtains are made in two different sizes. A stall shower requires a curtain 6 feet wide and 6½ feet long (1.83 m × 1.98 m), whereas a combination shower and tub requires a curtain 6 feet wide by 6 feet long (1.8 m × 1.8 m). For a fabric shower curtain, a plastic liner should be used for protection against wetness.

A bathroom can be given a new updated look with coordinated linens and shower curtain.

SELECTING TABLE LINENS

The fabrics used on dining-room and kitchen tables should be both functional and decorative. A table covering serves a number of purposes. It sets the theme for the occasion, provides a background for tableware, establishes or ties in with a color scheme, reduces noise, and protects the table finish. The table cover should complement the table setting. Dinnerware with a strong design looks best against a plain or textured background. If the dinnerware is of a solid color and the glasses and flatware are plain in design, there is more opportunity to use patterned tablecloths and mats.

Traditionally, linen has been the fabric preferred for table coverings. A beautiful linen cloth, with or without a design, provides a luxurious background for table settings. Today, linen tablecloths are used mainly for holidays such as Thanksgiving and other special occasions. The desire for convenience has made coverings of wash-and-wear materials and even vinyl or other plastics popular. Vinyl and plastic coverings also provide protection for the table surface. For linen or cotton tablecloths, it is usually desirable to have a padded covering under the cloth to protect the surface of the table. As an alternative to tablecloths, tables may also be used uncovered, with a mat under each place setting. In this case, the wood of the table surface provides the background. Place mats range from delicate embroidered ones that accompany fine china to heavy woven cotton or plastic mats for everyday use.

STANDARD SIZES FOR DINING TABLES AND TABLE LINENS

TABLE SIZE	CLOTH SIZE
30" X 48" rectangular	52" X 70"
40" X 72" rectangular	68" X 90"
40" X 84" rectangular	68" X 104"
40" X 106" rectangular	68" X 126"
30" X 30" square	52" X 52"
36" X 36" square	54" X 54"
30" to 48" round (diameter)	42" to 70"
30" X 48" oval	52" X 70"
40" X 64" oval	68" X 90"
40" X 84" oval	68" X 104"

Place mats help to protect the table surface and also accent the dinnerware.

SELECTING DINNERWARE

The term *dinnerware* applies to dishes, all of which were made from clay until the introduction of plastic dishes in the mid-20th century. Many different types of dinnerware are available. The kind of clay and other ingredients, the kind and number of glazes, the firing temperatures, and the method of decoration determine the type of dinnerware produced—pottery, earthenware or stoneware, ironstone, porcelain, or bone china.

Types of Dinnerware

Dishes made of pottery have a natural charm for informal settings. Pottery is made of coarse clay fired at low temperatures. It is quite durable. However, if the surface glaze is chipped, the porous body absorbs liquids and discolors. Earthenware is made from a finer clay than pottery and is more durable. The pieces are fired at higher temperatures and for a longer period of time. Stoneware is more durable than earthenware, because it is made of finer clay and fired at even higher temperatures. Ironstone is the name for a very durable type of earthenware. Some high-grade earthenware and stoneware may be as expensive as porcelain.

China, which is more correctly known as porcelain, is made from a very fine white clay and feldspar, a crystalline mineral substance. This combination makes a very hard clay. After being fired at temperatures up to 2600 degrees Fahrenheit (1427°C), it produces a hard, nonporous, nonabsorbent material. Two glazes are applied, and each glaze is fired at the same high temperature. After the second firing, artists apply designs by hand in color or in 24-karat gold. The pieces are again fired, so that the decoration is fused with the china.

The individual place settings of china, crystal, and silver create a formal setting for a dinner party or holiday celebration.

Porcelain is easily distinguished from other dinnerware, because it is translucent when held up to the light; it has a clear, bell-like tone when tapped; and on a broken piece, the color is the same throughout. One type of porcelain, known as bone china, contains fine bone ash instead of feldspar. The ash is mixed with fine clay to produce a white, translucent body with a soft, clear glaze. Porcelain produced by American manufacturers is noted for its resistance to chipping and breaking, and the glaze is highly resistant to scratching and dishwashing detergents.

Dinnerware may also be made of plastic. One type of plastic used in dinnerware is melamine. Melamine was developed during World War II to provide the Navy with unbreakable dishes for use on ships. Today plastic dishes are competitive with pottery and china for all but formal meals.

Melamine is nonporous, and it resists chipping and breaking. Designs are imprinted on a melamine base with paper foil, infused into flat discs. The flat substance is then molded into plates. Cups and saucers come in solid colors, because it is too difficult to build designs into deep curves and ridges. Plastics may be washed in a dishwasher, but they are not oven-proof. They have low resistance to scratches and stains.

On better grades of melamine, an extra layer of glaze on the inside of cups gives added resistance to stains, and a tougher glaze in the curing process on all pieces increases resistance to surface scratches. High-quality melamine dishes are expensive in comparison with the type of pottery or china dishes a family might buy for general use. If breakage is no serious problem,

Stoneware

English bone china

Porcelain

it is often advisable to buy attractive pottery or earthenware.

The term *ovenware* is used to describe serving dishes that you can bake food in as well; they go directly from oven to table. Ovenware may be made of earthenware, glass-ceramic, or heat-resistant glass. Glass-ceramic is actually glass that is converted to hard ceramic by a special process in order to make it ovenproof. Heat-resistant glass, such as Pyrex®, is commonly used for pie plates and baking dishes. Some ovenware can go directly from the freezer to the oven without breaking. However, for other types it is important that the frozen food be partially defrosted before the container is placed in the oven. Or you can place the container in the oven before turning the oven on to allow for a gradual change in temperature.

In microwave ovens, almost any type of container can be used except metal. Special plastic cookware, designed especially for use in microwave ovens, is now available. However, many of these pieces are expensive. Always refer to your user's manual for specific directions concerning the various types of containers to use in your specific microwave oven model.

Before selecting dinnerware, you should consider what type will best serve your needs and is most suitable for your lifestyle. Fine china is often used only for special entertaining. Less expensive dishes are suitable for everyday use. Few people today buy dinnerware in full sets. It is unnecessary to buy soup bowls, fruit dishes, and all kinds of service platters unless you really have use for them. Instead, many people buy place settings with four or five basic pieces: dinner plate, dessert plate, bowl, and mug or cup and saucer.

Guidelines for Selecting Dinnerware
The following guidelines will help you in selecting dinnerware:

—Do comparison shopping to become familiar with types and brands of dinnerware.

—Buy from well-established stores.

—Examine the surfaces of pottery, earthenware, and especially plasticware for defects such as rough edges, bulges or indentations, pits, and uneven glaze.

Molded plastic

Earthenware

—Examine cup handles for comfort in holding and for firmness at the joints.

—Choose colors, textures, and designs that harmonize with the color scheme and character of the dining area.

—Buy serving dishes and other extra dishes only if they are needed.

—It is wise to buy one extra place setting and an extra cup or two in case of breakage.

Caring for Dinnerware

The following guidelines will help you keep your dishes in good condition:

—Rinse the food from cups and dishes as soon after use as possible. Certain foods and liquids may cause stains. If cups become stained from tea or coffee, remove the stains with a mild chlorine bleach.

—Never use any kind of abrasive on dinnerware, because it will remove the protective coating and increase the tendency to stain.

—Make sure that dishes are dishwasherproof before you place them in the dishwasher. Use the kind of detergent recommended by the manufacturer. Unless fine porcelains are marked as dishwasherproof, wash them by hand to protect the colors from fading. Use a rubber mat in the dishpan to prevent chipping.

—Hang cups on hooks only if you are careful in reaching for and replacing them. Otherwise, stack them carefully no more than two deep.

—Never place dishes in an oven unless they are marked as ovenware. China will yellow and crack or break; plasticware will melt or warp out of shape; non-ovenproof glassware will break. When buying table or serving dishes, ask whether they can be used in a microwave oven.

—To store china plates, place felt pieces, or even paper napkins cut in circles, between the plates to prevent scratches.

—Buy or make a set of covers to place over dishes not in frequent use.

SELECTING FLATWARE

The term *flatware* refers to the implements (knives, forks, spoons, and serving pieces) used in eating. The first of these to be invented was the knife, which was developed from the flint knife. The flint knife made it possible for prehistoric people to kill animals, take the skins for clothing, and cut the meat for food. The stemmed gourd used for dipping evolved into a ladle and eventually into a spoon. Forks were developed later. With the introduction of tea into England in the 1600's, teaspoons became popular. Silver spoons were expensive and so highly prized that it was a special tribute to newborn babies when godparents presented them with a silver spoon. From this practice came the expression "born with a silver spoon in his mouth."

In the American colonies, only wealthy plantation owners and sea captains could afford to own sterling silver. Flatware made of pewter and tin was more commonly used by the colonists. The patriot Paul Revere, who was originally a dentist and coppersmith, was one of the earliest silversmiths in America. Silver bowls copied after Revere's design are a popular gift today. Until well into the 19th century, brides were given silver coins from which to have their flat silver handmade by silversmiths.

Pure silver is so pliable that it can be drawn into a thread as fine as silk. For any practical use, silver must be combined with another metal. Sterling silver is 925 parts silver and 75 parts copper. Sterling has been symbolic of quality since the 1200's, when highly valued silver coins were called *easterlings*. The name was later changed to *sterling*.

Because of the high cost of sterling silver, chemists began to experiment with ways to produce silverware for the average person's budget. In 1742 an English silversmith who was repairing a copper knife for a client happened to touch a little silver with the hot knife. Noticing that the two metals fused, he began to experiment with fusing large sheets of thin silver to heavy sheets of copper. The method could be used on flat surfaces but not in hollowware pieces such as teapots, coffeepots, and bowls. All exposed surfaces had to be treated by hand, which proved to be a tedious process. In 1840, silver-plating by electrolysis was invented. By this method, hollowware as well as flat silver can be immersed in a solution of silver cyanide and bars of silver. Control of the electric current allows a silver plating of any thickness to be deposited on the less expensive and harder metal to give a dull or glossy silver finish.

In recent years, stainless steel flatware has become appropriate for all but very formal table settings. Stainless steel is made of a special steel alloy of iron, chrome, and nickel that resists rust, peeling, and tarnish. It can be made into the same designs as silver and silver plate.

The five-piece stainless steel place setting shown at lower left consists of a knife, fork, salad fork, teaspoon, and soup / cereal spoon.

Guidelines for Selecting Flatware

The following guidelines will be helpful to you in buying flatware or hollowware:

—Buy from a reliable dealer. Prices are comparable for established brands.

—Consider cost in relation to use, design, and care. Sterling silver has become so expensive that many people buy silver plate or stainless steel instead. Patterns for silver plate are similar to those for sterling. Patterns for stainless steel are simple and are particularly suitable with contemporary designs in dinnerware.

—Feel the pieces for weight, balance, and ease of handling.

—Buy place settings, including a knife, fork, salad fork, and teaspoon, in multiples of four so that you will eventually have a service for eight. An extra teaspoon for each place setting will provide teaspoons for both beverage and dessert.

—Buy extra pieces according to need. A sugar spoon, butter knife, pickle fork, and serving spoons may be the next needs.

—Choose a pattern that will harmonize with your dishes and glassware.

Caring for Flatware

The following suggestions will help you in caring for silver and stainless steel:

—Using silver regularly will help to retard the tarnish. The tiny scratches from frequent use will gradually blend together to give a soft patina.

—Wash hollow-handled knives by hand, because the moisture and heat of a dishwasher might melt the cement that joins the blade to the handle. If silver dries with water marks, wipe it with a soft towel.

—Polish silver one piece at a time with a regular silver polish, not do a mass cleaning in a chemical bath. The chemicals may harm the silver, especially plated silver. To avoid the need for polishing, wipe foods such as egg and mustard off immediately.

—Keep flat silver in a tarnishproof box or drawer. Wrap seldom-used pieces and hollowware in tarnishproof cloth or paper for storage.

—Stainless steel is much easier to care for than silver. It is tarnishproof and resists stains and scratches. If washed by hand, it should be rinsed in hot water and thoroughly dried to eliminate water marks.

SELECTING GLASSWARE

Glass is produced in two main ways—by blowing and by pressing. Different types of decoration provide variation. Fine products of crystal glass are made in many countries, including Ireland, Britain, France, and the Scandinavian countries. The first glassworks in our country was started in Pennsylvania shortly before the Revolution by Henry William Stiegel, a German immigrant. Stiegel made the first American cut glass and fine decorative glass. The first pressed-glass tumbler was made at Sandwich in Massachusetts in 1827. The original formula for Sandwich

When loading a dishwasher, take care to place dishes and glasses so they will not touch. This will help to prevent chipping of the edges during the vigorous washing action of the water.

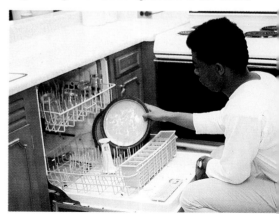

glass has been lost; as a result, Sandwich glass made between 1827 and 1888 is highly prized by collectors. However, it was not until the early 1880's that table glassware was made in America in any quanity.

Today, many types of glasses are available. These range from the traditional crystal and pressed glass to plastic glasses and thermal tumblers that keep liquids hot or cold. Glasses are also available in various sizes for different purposes.

Types of Glassware

The following terms are used to describe various types of glassware:

— Crystal is fine, clear, colorless glassware. When tapped, crystal rings like a tiny bell. Cut crystal is made by cutting a design into glass with a revolving abrasive wheel.

— Etched crystal is made by covering the background with a waxy substance and cutting a design into the wax with special tools. When the crystal is placed in an acid bath, only the cut portions are eaten away. Then the wax is dissolved, and the glass is washed and polished.

— Painted crystal is produced by applying gold, platinum, or enamel and then firing the metal until it is fused into the glass.

— Pressed glass, which is made in molds, resembles crystal, but it is less clear and the edges are somewhat rounded. It is much less expensive than crystal.

— Frosted glass is produced by sandblasting the surface to give a finish resembling frost.

— Bubble glass is made by forcing air bubbles into molten glass.

— Hobnail glass is made by pressing small bumps evenly over the surface.

— Milk glass is an opaque white glass that is made by adding chemicals to produce a milky effect.

— Iridescent glass is rainbow-colored glass made by the use of silver or bismuth.

Guidelines for Selecting Glassware

When selecting glassware, you should, if possible, assemble a place setting of dinnerware, flatware, and glassware in the store to find out how they look together. Experiment with a number of combinations until you find one that pleases you. The glassware should fit in with the color scheme and style of the dinnerware and the dining area. Often it is desirable to have simple, durable glassware for everyday use and a finer type for special occasions.

Glassware, like dinnerware, should be bought in place settings. A place setting consists of a goblet or tumbler for water, a sherbet glass, a dessert/salad plate, and usually glasses for iced beverages and for fruit juices. Decide whether or not you want water glasses and sherbet dishes with stems or with flat bases. Stemware is very pretty, but it also breaks more easily.

Check the quality of the glass by holding it to the light to check for imperfections. Feel the top and lower edges to detect uneven spots. It is wise to be cautious in selecting colored glass. Beverages may take on strange colors in tinted glasses.

Caring for Glassware

The following suggestions will help you in taking care of glassware:

— If you wash glasses in the sink, place a rubber or cloth pad on the bottom of the sink and on the drainboard. Wash glassware in clean, moderately hot soapy water before washing dishes. Rinse with hot water, and dry with a lintless towel. Clean cut glass with a soft brush and in soapy water, rinse well, and dry by hand.

— Never place ice-cold glasses in hot water, because they might break. Rinse them first with lukewarm water.

— Rinse glasses that have held milk or iced coffee served with cream soon after use to avoid cloudy marks.

— If you use an automatic dishwasher, rest the glasses where they will not fall over. Be extra careful in stacking stemware. Since some detergents make glasses washed in a dishwasher appear cloudy, use detergent sparingly.

— Note the hardness of the water if you use an automatic dishwasher. Hard water leaves a film that dishwasher heat may bake on. A weak vinegar or lemon solution will dissolve a film or remove stains if they have not been on too long.

— Never stack glasses inside each other. Store them with the rim up. Storing them with the rim down may cause germs to collect. If tumblers become stuck, avoid prying them apart. Pour cold water into the inner glass to contract it, and rest the outer glass in lukewarm water for a few minutes.

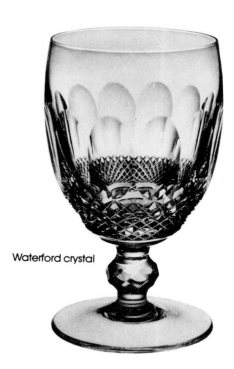

Waterford crystal

Crystal with platinum rim

Iridescent crystal

Etched crystal

TABLE DECORATIONS

Special decorations are often used on a table to add visual appeal and a focus of interest. The term *centerpiece* is misleading, because decorations are not necessarily placed in the center of the table. It may also be at one end or side, or even spread about the table. Many things are suitable for use as table decorations—an art object, a piece from a collection, an arrangement of shells, driftwood, cattails, vines, dried or artificial flowers, a plant, formal and informal flower arrangements, and others. Preparing table decorations offers many possibilities for creative design and personal expression. It is interesting to change designs frequently and in keeping with the season or a special day. The design should be suitable for the table covering and tableware to be used. Whether the setting is informal and everyday or festive and more formal, attractive decorations enhance the setting and add to everyone's enjoyment.

MEALTIME ENVIRONMENTS

Mealtime is a social occasion—a time for sharing ideas and the day's events—as well as a time for eating. All cultures and civilizations have developed certain customs and rituals related to food and eating.

The customs related to mealtimes in our society have changed greatly in recent years. At one time the members of a family ate together several times a day. Today, with differing schedules and many activities away from home, having all the members of a family together at mealtime is less often possible. Television, too, has changed mealtime customs. People often want to watch television while eating. Doing this means that mealtime is no longer a social occasion and that there is less communication among people within the home.

Another change that has affected mealtimes is the growing trend of eating out at fast-food restaurants that serve hamburger,

Choose table decorations that complement your tableware patterns. A centerpiece can help to set the mood for a meal.

For these families, the evening meal is a time to gather together and share the day's activities.

chicken, and pizza. Although these restaurants have quick service and tasty food, the atmosphere does not encourage relaxed eating and the exchange of conversation.

Providing a pleasant environment for eating is one way to offset the trends toward isolation and lack of communication. Enjoying good food and conversation in a

pleasant and relaxed setting is a happy experience. The sociability of mealtimes is itself a kind of entertainment. For these reasons, mealtimes today are more important than ever for bringing people together and providing relaxation in people's busy lives.

Experiments have shown that the environment in which we eat can affect our

A cookout can celebrate a holiday or a visit. It can also provide a change of scene for the family at home. The informality of outdoor eating encourages welcome relaxation.

physical and mental health and attitudes, values, and general well-being. A dining room or semi-separated dining area provides an opportunity for great versatility in meal service. Many dining tables can be expanded to seat eight people. If not, the table can serve nicely for buffet meals. Changes in home design have provided new settings, too, for meals. In addition to the traditional dining area, or the kitchen table for more informal gatherings, meals are often served in other areas, particularly outdoors—the balcony, terrace, deck, porch, patio, or backyard. The casual style of such meals provides a special opportunity for relaxation and enjoyment.

Wherever meals are served, an attractive setting adds pleasure to the occasion. The meal may be a barbecue in the yard, a buffet breakfast, or a late-evening gathering of friends. The important thing is to make the table setting attractive, to serve good food, and to create an atmosphere for having a good time. Holidays offer wonderful opportunities for enjoying family members and friends. Family gatherings on certain holidays have become traditional, a way of maintaining ties and keeping in touch with one's own heritage. The serving of meals, which is both essential to life and a symbol of sharing and hospitality, is one of the most important aspects of home life. And the setting for those meals—a pleasant area and an attractive table—can contribute to mealtime enjoyment and happy living within the home.

BUYER FOR LINEN DEPARTMENT

Buyers are responsible for selecting and purchasing the items that are sold in their department or store. They base their selections on the demand for specific merchandise, fashion trends, their clientele, and their own experience. They must decide the specific colors, sizes, and quantities of each item that they order. Buyers may travel to market, where manufacturers' showrooms are located, serveral times a year. Some travel to foreign countries to buy their merchandise. Or they may order their selections from manufacturer representatives that visit their store.

Buyers set the prices of items, keep track of inventory, and decide when to reorder an item or to reduce its price. They authorize the payment of invoices and the return of merchandise to manufacturers. Buyers also conduct staff meetings with the salespeople to keep them up-to-date about new merchandise and to motivate them in their selling job. In larger stores, buyers meet with merchandise managers who oversee several departments and assist buyers in developing budgets and prices. Buyers also work with display artists, who arrange window and department displays, copywriters, who write advertisements and catalogue copy, and stock clerks, who count and tag the merchandise before it is put on the shelves or racks. In a small store, the buyer may be responsible for all these tasks.

If you are interested in becoming a buyer, you must like working with people. You need good verbal skills to deal effectively with customers, staff, and suppliers. You also need writing and math skills because much time is spent on paperwork and dealing with numbers. You must adapt easily to constantly changing conditions. As a buyer you must be able to pay careful attention to the day-to-day activities within your department while, at the same time, making decisions about future merchandise that will not be in the store for several months. To be a buyer of household linens, you need a special interest in fashion, fabrics, and home furnishings. Plus you need a lot of energy because buyers work long hours and often must be at the store evenings, weekends, and holidays.

To become a buyer, you will need a home economics, merchandising, or business degree from a college, junior college, or technical school. Many department stores and chains have special training programs for buyers. As a buyer for a linen department, you may work for a department store or a specialty store. Or you can become an entrepreneur and open your own store that specializes in selling household furnishings, such as linens and tableware.

REVIEWING CHAPTER 18

SUMMARY

Household furnishings include the linens for bedroom, bath, and dining and the table settings of dinnerware, flatware, and glassware.

In order to judge household linens, you need some knowledge of fibers, weaves, and finishes. The characteristics of different fabrics affect their appearance, durability, and care. Sheets, pillowcases, blankets, comforters, and bedspreads are available in a wide variety of sizes and patterns. Towels are made of terrycloth for absorbency and softness. The fabrics used for tablecloths and placemats can range from elegant embroidered linen to quilted cotton to vinyl. Today, ease of care is a quality most consumers want in household linens.

The quality of dinnerware—whether bone china, porcelain, or pottery—is determined by the clay, glazes, and firing temperatures used. Flatware is available in sterling silver, silver plate, and stainless steel. Types of glassware range from traditional crystal and pressed glass to plastic and thermal tumblers.

FACTS TO KNOW

1. List four natural fibers and two properties of each.

2. Name an outstanding characteristic of each of these fibers: acetate, nylon, polyester, and acrylic.

3. Identify five fabric weaves. Describe each one and give an example of its use.

4. What types of fabric finishes contribute to easier maintenance?

5. What fabrics are used for sheets, for blankets, for comforters, and for towels? What are one or more characteristics of each fabric?

6. Explain the difference between pottery and porcelain.

7. What types of dishes are ovenproof? What kinds of dishes can be used in microwave ovens?

8. Explain what is meant by the terms *sterling silver, silver plate, hollowware,* and *stainless steel* in relation to tableware.

IDEAS TO THINK ABOUT

1. List several factors that may influence your choices of household linens and tableware.

2. Compare the relative advantages and disadvantages of different types of bedding.

3. Analyze the effect more casual lifestyles and informal entertaining have on the types of tableware and table settings used today.

ACTIVITIES TO DO

1. Visit a store that sells household linens. Compare different sheets, pillowcases, and blankets in terms of quality, fiber content, and care instructions. Also compare the prices for different sizes of bedding: twin, double, queen, and king. Check to see if any linens are on sale and what the savings would be if you bought them.

Household Equipment

Have you wandered through the appliance department of a store recently? If you have, you were probably amazed at the huge selection of appliances that are available. Changes in people's lifestyles have created needs for new types of equipment and more variety in appliance models. To meet these needs, manufacturers are producing different types of appliances with multiple options. Today, you can purchase an appliance for almost any cooking or cleaning task that you do. Some are multipurpose, such as the toaster oven and refrigerator-freezer. Others are highly specialized to perform such tasks as popping corn, making ice cream, and cooking rice.

Advances in technology, such as those with microchips and microwaves, have revolutionized household equipment. Today, appliances can work automatically or at the touch of a button. New technology has made it possible to install a home computer system that can be programmed to set off an alarm clock, open draperies or shades, raise the thermostat, start the coffeemaker, and cook breakfast—all before you have gotten out of bed!

With all the many types and models of appliances available, decisions about equipment for the home have become more complicated. Many factors should be considered. What appliances do you really need? What options would be beneficial?

PREVIEWING YOUR LEARNING

After you have read this chapter, you will be able to:

- Follow consumer guidelines when buying household equipment.

- Evaluate the basic models of major appliances and the additional available options.

- Compare the features and limitations of different portable appliances.

- Demonstrate how to use and care for household equipment.

TERMS TO KNOW
---

appliance—a piece of equipment designed for a particular use and operated by gas or electric current

compactor—an appliance that compresses or squeezes things together

convection oven—an oven with fans that circulate heated air at a high speed

defrost—to free from ice

disposer—an appliance that gets rid of food by grinding it to a very fine consistency

microwave oven—an appliance that cooks food with tiny waves of energy that make food molecules vibrate, producing heat to cook the food

option—a choice or alternative

processor—equipment that causes a series of changes or actions

range—a cooking stove with burners or heating elements and an oven

MICROS IN APPLIANCES

F
E
A
T
U
R
E

Many of the appliances in homes today are "intelligent" machines. Washers, for example, use soap and water at different temperatures for different periods of time to clean and spin-dry different types of clothing. The computer age has ushered in the use of microprocessor chips, or micros, that make it easier and cheaper to design and build even "smarter" appliances.

New refrigerators, dishwashers, clothes dryers, and microwave ovens are being manufactured with silicon-chip micros. These allow microwave ovens to sense when a roast is done, dryers to shut off when clothes are dry, and refrigerators to buzz when their doors are left open too long.

Video tape recorders, telephone answering machines, and automatic dialers all rely on micros to control their different motors and switches. Cameras with automatic focus and exposure use microelectronics to measure the distance to an object and available light.

It may be possible one day to control appliances with your voice, thanks to micros. Electric kettles, irons, and toasters may all be switched on or off by verbal commands.

Under the control of a micro, it eventually will be possible to cook an entire meal automatically. Oven, grill, and heating rings will all be switched on at just the right time for a three-course dinner to be prepared by six o'clock!

BUYING HOUSEHOLD EQUIPMENT

Appliances are expensive, and buying a number of them for the household is a major investment. For that reason, you should shop carefully to obtain maximum value and use. Prices for basic models are fairly standard. As the number of options increases, however, the initial cost, the cost of operation, and the cost of repairs increase. The service and durability of appliances depend largely on careful use and maintenance. For all these reasons, you should have certain basic information about buying and using the equipment for your household.

In addition to the appliances themselves, you should be sure that what you choose fits into the space available. For example, refrigerators and refrigerator-freezers vary considerably in height. Before buying any appliance, measure the height, width, and depth of the space required for it. At the store, ask the salesperson for the measurements of the appliance. Color also is a consideration in selecting appliances. If you have no appliances, the colors in your kitchen, together with your own preferences, can be a guide in deciding on a color. If you already have one appliance, such as a range, you may want to buy other appliances in a matching color.

The following suggestions will help you in selecting, using, and caring for household equipment:

— List your equipment needs, whether for initial purchase or replacement. Number the list according to priority—what must be bought first, second, and so on.
— Compare the features and cost of comparable models by different manufacturers.
— Study consumer magazines with articles on labor-saving equipment, to become familiar with brands and models.
— Inquire about delivery, installation, warranties, and service availability and cost.

— Make sure that purchases carry the UL seal indicating they have met minimum standards of safety.
— Buy from an established dealer. Record the name and telephone number of the store where the equipment was purchased, as well as the date and the name of the salesperson.
— Fill in and return warranty cards, so there will be no questions about receiving services guaranteed in the warranty.
— File instruction sheets or booklets for all equipment in a large folder, and store the folder where it will be available.
— Keep the surfaces of all appliances clean. Burned grease, acids, sharp objects, rough scouring substances, and strong detergents cause damage. A mild detergent and a soft cloth wrung out of warm suds will keep most enamel surfaces clean.

BUYING MAJOR APPLIANCES

Certain appliances, such as a range and refrigerator, are essential to a household. In rented homes, these appliances are usually provided. If you buy a home, you may buy them from the previous owner. If not, or if you buy a new home, you will need to acquire them. Although it is always possible to buy equipment secondhand for short-term use, new appliances are preferable for long-term use.

Ranges, Wall Ovens, and Microwave Ovens

Lifestyle, cooking needs, and cost are major factors in the choice of a range. The power or fuel used is also a consideration. Natural gas is not always available, but when it is, it may be less expensive than electricity. The heat loss from gas burners is greater than from electric burners. However, gas burners respond more quickly than electric burners. Flat-bottom pots and pans that fit the size of the burner will increase the efficiency of either range.

Electric and gas ranges are available in either drop-in or freestanding models.

Many different types and combinations of burners and ovens are available. Some people prefer surface burners set in a counter, with a separate eye-level wall oven. Others prefer a freestanding gas or electric range with one or two ovens or a combination or separate microwave oven. A ceramic-glass top looks attractive and is efficient, but it heats more slowly than exposed burners and requires careful cleaning. Most people still buy the traditional range that includes burners and an oven in one appliance.

Gas and electric ranges come in similar styles and burner arrangements. The most popular width is 30 inches (76 cm), although 40- and 21-inch models (102 cm and 53 cm) are available. Freestanding and drop-in models can be moved like other home furnishings, but built-in ranges, ovens, and surface burners cannot be moved. In a two-oven range, one oven may be a self-cleaning or a microwave oven. An eye-level oven makes stooping unnecessary, but a short person may have trouble lifting utensils in and out of it.

A number of safety features have been built into both gas and electric ranges. Burners have been moved back, and controls put out of the reach of small children. Two-step controls further insure safety. The pilot in gas ranges has been replaced with an electric-spark ignition for safety and fuel conservation.

Options In choosing a range, you may want to consider options or alternatives, in addition to the basic model. The most popular options are as follows:
— A built-in rotisserie, which automatically rotates meat for even roasting and brown-

ing. Consider carefully how often you would use this feature and whether it would be worth the extra cost.

—Built-in range ducts, which eliminate the need for a separate hood and fan.

—Interchangeable cooktops with plug-in grills that provide for indoor barbecuing, surface frying, and making pancakes. Consider how often you would take time to use these and which of your present appliances already provide these services.

—Lift-up surfaces and cover-ups. The entire surface of some ranges can be lifted so that the burners can be cleaned more easily. Some ranges have lids to cover burners when not in use. Consider how often you would want to cover the burners and how great a problem cleaning them will be.

—Removable oven windows and doors, which make oven-cleaning easier.

—A self-cleaning or continuous-cleaning oven. The self-cleaning oven cleans by intense heat of up to 1000 degrees Fahrenheit (538°C). All soil is reduced to a fine ash that can be easily wiped away. The disadvantages are higher initial cost, tying up the oven for one or two hours, and using a lot of energy. A continuous-cleaning oven is less expensive, stays clean, and uses no extra controls. It has a special porous ceramic coating with an irregular surface that absorbs spills by a catalyst action. However, it has less efficient cleaning. In both types of ovens, the racks must be cleaned by hand.

—A convection oven. This is a conventional oven that has fans which circulate the heated air at a high speed. The oven's temperature is usually more consistent throughout a convection oven so foods cook faster than in a conventional oven. Meats are browned more evenly and quickly, and the juices are sealed in.

Use and care of ranges and ovens

When you buy a range, oven, or microwave oven, you will receive a user's manual. Read the directions in the manual carefully before you turn on the appliance. The following suggestions will help to keep equipment in good condition:

—Place utensils on burners of the corresponding size. Placing small utensils on large burners heats up the kitchen and

One option is to purchase a separate cook top and one or two wall ovens. One oven could be either a convection oven or a microwave oven.

wastes energy. Placing large utensils on small burners may damage the surface finish of the utensil because of the built-up heat.

—Use a long-handled bottle brush to clean corners under the burner areas that are difficult to reach by hand.

—Never use harsh scouring powder or steel-wool pads on chrome trim.

—Use a special cleaner for ceramic-glass tops to avoid scratches.

—Clean an ordinary oven with a commercial oven cleaner.

—Never use a commercial oven cleaner on self-cleaning or continuous-cleaning ovens. Occasionally wipe a continuous-cleaning oven with a dampened cloth.

Microwave ovens can be built into the wall, mounted under the cabinets, or stand on the counter top.

In a microwave oven, a magnetron tube produces microwaves that are absorbed by the food. The activity creates heat within the food to do the cooking. The food heats, but the oven and kitchen remain cool. Foods can cook in a quarter of the time needed in a conventional oven.

Microwave ovens come in wall and countertop models or as part of regular ranges. Some can be mounted under a kitchen cabinet. Automatic touch controls are computerized to defrost foods, cook several different dishes at the same time, and shut off the oven. Ordinary microwave ovens do not brown food, but browning elements are available in some models. All microwave ovens must meet certain safety standards to avoid microwave leakage. Before you buy one, compare the safety features and other options of different models.

The following suggestions will help in using a microwave oven:

—Use only cooking materials made of recommended materials. For most ovens, these include glass, ceramic, paper, and plastic. Do not use metal utensils or aluminum foil unless directions specifically permit their use.

—Keep the door tightly closed during operation.

—Avoid having soil build up on the door seal, door surface, or oven frame.

—Never use abrasives for cleaning the oven. To clean the oven, turn it off and wipe inside with a damp cloth.

—Before activating a self-cleaning oven, remove all utensils and use a spatula to remove pieces of food burned onto the bottom of the oven.

Use and care of microwave ovens

Since their introduction in the early 1970's, microwave ovens have become increasingly popular. They greatly reduce meal preparation time, and they use much less energy than standard burners and ovens.

Refrigerators, Refrigerator-Freezers, and Freezers

Refrigerators and freezers have had fewer changes in design in recent years than most appliances. An exception to this is the side-by-side refrigerator-freezer. Many people prefer the convenience and efficiency of this design. All refrigerators are available in a wide range of colors. Wood-paneled doors that match kitchen cabinets may be installed.

When buying a refrigerator or refrigerator-freezer, compare the various models available for functions, initial cost and operating cost, and use of energy. Over the life expectancy of the appliance, the purchase price represents 29 percent of the total outlay; the servicing, 6 percent; and the cost of operation (energy), 65 percent. Among the options available are an ice-maker for a constant supply of ice cubes; a door dispenser that provides ice water, ice

STANDARD REFRIGERATOR AND REFRIGERATOR-FREEZER MODELS

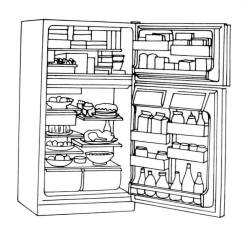

cubes, or crushed ice; a choice of manual defrost or automatic-cycle defrost; and, in combination models, the top, bottom, or side-by-side location of the freezer.

The simplest and least expensive refrigerator is a one-door model with a lower storage compartment for food and an upper compartment for making and storing ice and storing previously frozen food. This model cannot quick-freeze food, because the lowest temperature is 15° Fahrenheit (-9.4°C). Disadvantages of this model are that frozen food should not be kept more than a week and the freezing unit must be defrosted manually. However, this model uses less energy than others.

Many people prefer a combination refrigerator-freezer because of its convenience. Combinations are available in three styles—with the freezer located above the refrigerator, below the refrigerator, and beside the refrigerator in a side-by-side model. In all combination models, the freezing section will quick-freeze foods and

Top of the line models may include a door dispenser for beverages and ice, an automatic ice maker, and an ice cream maker. Some models will beep if the door is left open.

keep them frozen as long as a separate model of freezer will. The refrigerator compartment may be of either the manual-defrost or frost-free type. The frost-free type must be disconnected periodically for cleaning. The side-by-side combination is available in larger sizes and has the largest freezer capacity. Other choices are models 1½ to 3½ feet high (.46 m to 1.07 m), which are used mainly as an office accessory for ice and beverages. Under-the-counter models are used mainly in small apartments.

Use and care of refrigerators and refrigerator-freezers When your refrigerator or refrigerator-freezer is delivered, read carefully the directions for use and maintenance. Other suggestions for care are as follows:

— Make sure that the appliance stands evenly. Most large appliances have disks near the base to adjust for an even position. There should be space at the back of the appliance for air to circulate.

— Set the controls at the medium range and adjust them upward or downward as necessary.

— Check the door seals for firmness. If a

The location and amount of space available are important in choosing a freezer. How much floor space would each of these models require?

EnergyGuide labels on appliances rate the energy efficiency ratio of the appliance or list an average cost to operate the appliance for one year.

fresh dollar bill placed between the seal and the edge of the door does not pull out easily, the seal is adequate.

— Never permit more than ¼ inch of frost to accumulate on non-frost-free models. The build-up of heavy frost requires more energy for cooling.

— For energy efficiency, keep the freezer section full, but permit air to flow through the refrigerator section.

Use and care of freezers Separate freezers are made in both upright and chest styles. They are about equal in popularity. Each type is made in a number of sizes. To determine the size you need, plan for 6 cubic feet (0.17 cu m) per person. Which type you choose depends on your particular requirements. The chest type requires more floor space, stores larger and bulkier packages, and requires periodic manual defrosting. The upright requires less floor space, keeps packages visible, and has no-frost models available.

Before you buy a separate freezer, decide whether you will keep enough frozen foods in it to justify the extra cost of a separate appliance. A refrigerator-freezer with a large storage capacity may be adequate if you market every week. However, if you have a large garden, you may want the added storage space provided by a separate freezer.

In shopping for a freezer, you should be aware of certain features that add to the convenience. These include a signal light to indicate loss of current, a counter-balanced lid on a chest-type freezer, rollers or casters for mobility, and removable baskets and adjustable shelves to aid loading and cleaning.

The following suggestions will aid in the use and care of a freezer:

— Avoid placing a lot of food in the unit at one time for freezing. In storing frozen food, quick freezing is important, but overloading makes that impossible.

— Defrost the freezer when more than ¼-inch of ice forms. Pack frozen items together in a box or heavy container so they do not melt during the cleaning process.

— Clean the condenser as indicated in the manual at least once a year.

— In case of a power failure, do not open the freezer door. Food will stay frozen for two days. Never refreeze food that has become unfrozen.

Washers and Dryers

Among the factors influencing the choice of washer and dryer are laundry needs, the space available, installation requirements, the availability of service, and cost. Washers operate on ordinary household current, but most electric dryers require a 240-volt line. Gas dryers, of course, need to be connected with a gas line. They should have electronic ignition rather than pilot. The floor on which a washer and dryer rest must be level, or the leveling devices on the washer and dryer must be adjusted enough to level the equipment. For safety, there should be an automatic stop for unbalanced loads, so that the appliances will stay in place. In addition, washing or drying action should stop when lids or doors are opened, and it should not start automatically when the door is closed.

Most washers have regular and delicate wash cycles, plus controls for small, medium, and large loads; cold, warm, and hot temperatures; and time settings. Optional features are automatic detergent, bleach, and fabric-softener dispensers; and cycles for soak, prewash, permanent press, and knits. An automatic cold-water rinse will save energy. Small separate tubs or baskets for a miniwash are available with some washers. Remember, though, that the more options the equipment provides, the higher the initial cost and the cost of operation and servicing will be.

Among the types of models available are

Special models of washers and dryers can stack one above the other and fit into a closet, pantry, or bathroom of an apartment or townhouse.

Washers and dryers are available in a variety of styles, sizes, and capacities. Some people prefer a gas dryer; others an electric dryer.

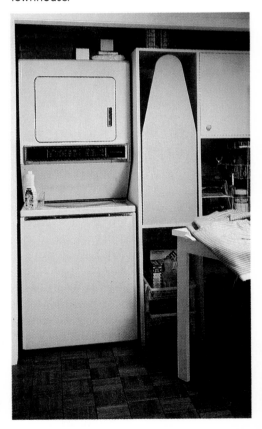

automatic full-size washers, a combination washer and dryer, and a small washer and dryer stacked or set side by side. A washer may be permanently installed or portable. The water action may be by tumbling or agitation. Front-loading models work by tumbling, and top-loading models work by agitation.

The size of laundry equipment required depends upon the number of people in the household. The washer for a family of three or four people should have a capacity of at least 8 pounds (3.6 kg) of dry wash. A 15- to 20-pound capacity (6.8 kg to 9 kg) is recommended for homes with three or more children.

All dryers have controls for adjusting time and temperature. A more accurate type of control is a dryness-sensing device that shuts off the dryer according to degree of dryness rather than time. It is desirable to have a cooling-down period to reduce wrinkling and an air-fluff tumbling action to remove lint. Some dryers have a signal that rings at intervals to remind a person that the clothes are dry.

Use and care of laundry appliances

The following suggestions will aid in the use of laundry equipment:

— A washer should be located near the water heater to avoid heat loss.

— Sort laundry items according to color, fabric care, and degree of soil. For each type, use the appropriate temperature.

— Pre-treat grease spots and stains. Polyesters and cottons absorb grease that may be impossible to remove if washed or dried at high temperatures.

— Avoid overloading a washer, or soil will not be removed properly and detergent may cling to items.

— Use the correct amount of detergent. The recommendations on packages are based on a 5- to 7-pound load (2.3 kg to 3.2 kg) of dry clothes with average soil, average water hardness, and an average

What purposes are served by this utility area?

water volume of 17 gallons (64 L) of water for a top-loading washer and 8 gallons (30 L) for a front-loading machine. More detergent will be needed for hard water and deep soil, and less will be needed for soft water and light soil. Front-loading washers require low-sudsing detergent.

— If there is no automatic cold-water-cycle rinse, turn the control manually to a cold rinse to conserve energy.

— A dryer should be vented to the outdoors by the shortest and straightest route possible.

— The lint trap of a dryer should be easy to reach and must be kept clean.

— To minimize wrinkling, avoid overloading the dryer, and remove items as soon as they are dry.

— Since a dryer uses a great deal of energy, hang small, quick-drying items on a rack and place shirts and dresses on hangers while still damp to finish drying.

Dishwashers

Dishwashers are available in built-in, portable, and convertible models. A built-in dishwasher with front loading is more convenient than the top-loading type, but it requires more floor space for mobility when the door is open. A convertible model is preferable to a strictly portable model; while appearing to be built in, it can be moved, yet it is out of the way. Racks in the unit should operate smoothly and adjust to contain large items. A booster unit, which raises the water temperature if the heater thermostat is set below 120° Fahrenheit (49°C), may be helpful. The wash cycles commonly include wash and rinse, plus rinse-hold, pre-rinse, soak, super-scrub, and gentle. The cost increases as more cycles are added. Be sure the motor mechanism is well insulated to reduce noise.

Use and care of dishwashers The following suggestions will aid in the satisfactory use of a dishwasher:

—Scrape and soak utensils, and rinse dishes before loading them into the dishwasher.

—Do not place very fine crystal or china in a dishwasher. The crystal may chip due to the washing action, and colors on some china may fade.

—Avoid placing small, delicate items where they may move about and become chipped or broken.

—Place metal items away from detergent cups to avoid chemical markings.

—Use the kind and amount of detergent recommended in the manual.

—Use a rinsing agent if the water is hard in the area where you live.

A dishwasher, whether portable or built-in, is an important convenience, especially for a large family.

Food Disposers

If you live in multi-unit housing, you should check to be sure that food disposers are permitted before you buy and install one. Disposers are of two main types—batch-fed and continuous-fed. The batch-fed type will not operate until the cover is in place, and it shuts off when the cover is lifted. This type is considered safer if there are children or older people in the home. The continuous-fed model operates only when the switch is on.

Disposers vary in the amount of insulation for noise control and in the grinding capacity. Stringy vegetables and the rinds of oranges, lemons, and grapefruit can cause problems in the machine because they tend to bounce around unless cut in small pieces. Most grinders take chicken bones, but they cannot grind heavy bones or corn husks unless they have heavy-duty motors and high-bulk cutters.

Be sure that you can locate the switch to turn the disposer off in case food jams. *Never reach for anything in the disposer with your hands.* Turn off the motor, and use a long-handled fork or tongs to unclog the grinder. Never allow rubber bands, string, glass, plastic, or cutlery to fall into a disposer.

Trash Compactors

Trash compactors reduce the bulk of household trash. They are available in freestanding and built-in models in several sizes. If space permits, an under-counter compactor with toe control to tilt the container is desirable. The odor problem can be reduced by using a built-in deodorizer or a charcoal air filter. If the sanitation pickup in your community is frequent, a trash compactor may not be necessary. Also, there may not be enough space for a compactor in the kitchen.

A food disposer and a trash compactor are useful appliances. Study the directions carefully before using these appliances.

BUYING PORTABLE APPLIANCES

In addition to the major appliances needed for a household, there are a number of portable appliances that are desirable. Some of these, such as irons, serve a specific purpose and are a necessity. Others, such as blenders, are a convenience and time-saver. Which of them you decide to buy depends on your resources, household needs, and storage space. Often, these items are bought individually over a period of time.

Mixers, Blenders, and Processors

Mixers and blenders are somewhat alike in design, but they perform different functions. A mixer has beaters that are used to combine ingredients, such as those for cake batter or cookie dough. The blades in a blender are designed for cutting or, on fast speed, for whipping. A blender will purée cooked vegetables for soups, chop cooked meats for spreads, and mix fruit or milk beverages.

Mixers are available in two styles—a stand mixer with a base, and a hand-held

These appliances do time-consuming tasks quickly and easily.

model without a base. A stand mixer can do more operations than a hand-held model, because the base gives it stability. For example, a stand mixer can be used to mix bread dough. Stand models may also have attachments such as juicers. If the mixer is to be used only occasionally and if storage is a problem, a hand mixer may be a wise choice.

When buying a mixer, look for the following features:

—a speed-selector dial that is easy to read
—beaters that are easy to plug in, remove, and clean
—a ball-bearing turntable that operates smoothly
—a self-regulated motor that maintains an even speed
—a high-powered motor and a dough-hook attachment if much bread is to be mixed.

In using a mixer, follow exactly the recipe directions for speed and timing. Use a rubber spatula for scraping; a metal spatula can damage the beaters and cause an accident. After using the beaters, soak them and wash them thoroughly. Wipe off the mixer and cord before storing them.

A blender should have at least several speeds, to meet different cutting, chopping, and blending needs. The container should open at both top and bottom for removing the contents and cleaning. The container should be resistant to heat and cold. It should fit securely on the base.

In using a blender for chopping, add only a small amount of food at once. Time the chopping carefully, since many foods quickly turn to a paste. Because liquids increase in volume when blended, fill the container only half full for thick mixtures and two-thirds full for thin mixtures. For best results, the liquid should cover the blades. Always pour the liquid portion of a recipe into the blender first. Make sure the blender is firmly in place on the stand before you turn on the motor. Rest your

hand lightly on the cover while the blender is operating. The motor must be at a complete stop before you remove the cover or scrape the sides of the container. It must also be stopped before you remove the container from the stand.

Food processors are a very versatile type of equipment. Most processors do the same operations as mixers and blenders, and other operations in addition. These include grinding, slicing, shredding, and other functions, depending on the model. Some models offer a variety of disks, each performing a different function, plus accessories such as dough blades, citrus juicers, and pasta makers. Compact models are smaller in size, easier to clean, and lower in price, yet they perform most of the same tasks as larger models.

New compact versions of mixers and food processors are convenient, easy to use, and lower in cost than standard models.

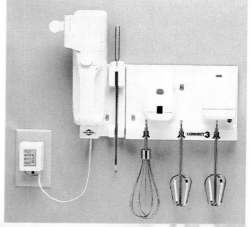

Toasters and Toaster Ovens

Toasters are available in 2- and 4-slice models. Radiant controls automatically adjust to any type of bread—thick or thin, fresh or dry, light or dark—and toast evenly on both sides according to the dial setting. Slices are raised automatically. In selecting a toaster, look for an easy-to-clean exterior and undertray and for handles that are heat-resistant and easy to lift.

A toaster must be cleaned regularly. To do this, unplug the toaster, release the crumb tray, empty out the crumbs, and wash and dry the tray. Do not shake the toaster to remove crumbs. Clean the exterior surface by wiping it with a damp cloth. Never immerse the toaster in water. If toast becomes stuck in the toaster, unplug the toaster before removing the slices.

A toaster oven can do the jobs of both a toaster and a small oven. It can toast bread, heat food, and bake small amounts of food. Some models include a broiling unit which can be used for cooking meats. Toaster ovens are especially convenient to use, instead of a full-sized oven, when preparing food for only one or two people. Some models can be mounted under kitchen cabinets to save counter space. A toaster oven must be cleaned regularly. Follow the instructions in the owner's manual.

Frypans and Slow Cookers

The electric frypan is a versatile appliance that will fry, pan-broil, roast, simmer, and bake foods. Some frypans can be purchased with an element that converts them to a broiler or a slow cooker. The buffet-style models are attractive serving pieces. Many people like the accurate temperature control, as well as the ready convenience, of this appliance.

Slow cookers are also popular, and for a contrasting reason—that they cook very slowly, at a low heat. Slow cookers are particularly suitable for cooking meats such as pot roasts that require a long, slow cooking to become tender and flavorful. Some cookers have separate heating and crockery cooking units; others are made as one single unit.

To use a frypan or slow cooker, plug the heat-control end of the cord into the pan or cooker before plugging the other end into the wall outlet. Follow carefully the directions for adding food and cooking it. Always turn the heat control to OFF before removing the cord. Allow the pan to cool before cleaning.

Irons

A self-cleaning spray/steam/dry iron meets every ironing or pressing need. Look for an iron with a cord long enough for flexibility, a smooth side plate with button slots, an easy-to-fill water opening, and an easy-to-read gauge. Observe how easily the steam and cleaning valves operate and how comfortable the handle is. Compare available models according to operation and cost.

For spray and steam irons, use the type of water recommended by the manufacturer. Distilled water is usually recommended, because the minerals in hard water might plug the holes. Empty the water reservoir after each use. Always store the iron in an upright position. Note directions in the manual for cleaning the sole plate if it becomes sticky and for restoring the smoothness of the plate.

Vacuum Cleaners

Vacuum cleaners are available in several types, ranging from canister and upright models to electric brooms and portable hand-held cleaners. A canister vacuum cleaner, which operates by suction, is most suitable for cleaning wood floors, upholstery, and draperies. The upright cleaner, which operates by both vibration and suction, is often preferred for cleaning carpeting. It should have controls to adjust to all types of pile, and the bristles should be long and firm enough to penetrate the pile and pull out dirt. Some canister models have a carpet attachment that operates similarly to an upright cleaner.

Other attachments include a floor and wall brush for removing dust from wood floors and walls; a long-handled tool to remove dust from difficult-to-reach areas; a dusting brush with long, soft bristles; an upholstery nozzle; and a flat tool for reaching into crevices. Additional points to look for in any type of cleaner are a handle that is comfortable to hold, dust receptacles that are easy to replace or empty, and wheels that provide smooth mobility.

An upright electric broom can be used for sweeping floors and carpets, but it is not meant for heavy cleaning. Small, hand-held cleaners are very convenient for cleaning car interiors or small areas in a home, or for quick cleanups of crumbs and dirt. Some models are cordless and rechargeable; others have one or more accessories.

A vacuum cleaner will pick up all kinds of small objects. However, it is wise to pick up pins and sharp objects before cleaning, since these might damage the motor of the cleaner. The dust bag must be emptied regularly, since the cleaner loses efficiency when the bag or tank is too full or when hair and lint accumulate in the brushes. Disposable bags are easy to insert and remove. It is important to use a bag designed especially for the cleaner.

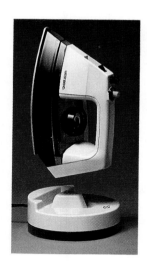

With all the many types of portable appliances on the market, it is important to decide which ones will best meet your needs.

Attachments include a floor and wall brush for removing dust from wood floors and walls; a long-handled tool to remove dust from difficult-to-reach areas; a dusting brush with long, soft bristles; an upholstery nozzle; and a flat tool for reaching into crevices. Additional points to look for in any type of cleaner are a handle that is comfortable to hold, dust receptacles that are easy to replace or empty, and wheels that provide smooth mobility.

A vacuum cleaner will pick up all kinds of small objects. However, it is wise to pick up pins and sharp objects before cleaning, since these might damage the motor of the cleaner. The dust bag must be emptied regularly, since the cleaner loses efficiency when the bag or tank is too full or when hair and lint accumulate in the brushes. Disposable bags are easy to insert and remove. It is important to use a bag designed especially for the cleaner.

Cleaners that have brushes and belts must have these items replaced periodically. The filter in a tank-type cleaner should be cleaned or replaced at intervals. If the hose of a canister cleaner becomes clogged, attach one end to the blower outlet, hold the other end to the suction inlet, and run the motor until the hose is clear.

CAREER PROFILE

APPLIANCE REPAIR SPECIALIST

Appliance repair specialists are experts at repairing household appliances, such as refrigerators, ranges, food processors, and vacuum cleaners. They examine equipment for any defective or malfunctioning parts. They refer to inspectors' checklists or the symbol markings on appliances for identification of the specific parts for a particular model. Sometimes they must take an appliance apart in order to replace or repair the defective part. Repair specialists use a variety of hand tools including screwdrivers and soldering irons. They may have to file or bend parts to remove burrs or to improve the alignment and fit of corresponding parts. When touching up defects in surface enamel, they use a paintbrush or spray gun. Some repair specialists work on appliances in factories or workshops; others travel to customers' homes to do repairs.

If you are interested in repairing appliances, you should enjoy working with your hands and using various tools. You need good eye-hand coordination and manual dexterity. You can enter this field by enrolling in an apprenticeship program or through on-the-job training. Appliance repair specialists may be employed by appliance manufacturers or appliance stores, or they can be self-employed.

REVIEWING CHAPTER 19

SUMMARY

Because buying appliances for a home is a major investment, you should shop carefully in order to obtain maximum value. Major appliances are available in many different models and have numerous accessory features. Some people prefer freestanding ranges, while others prefer separate burners and wall ovens. Microwave ovens are becoming very popular. Refrigerators are available as one-door styles and as combination refrigerator-freezers. Dishwashers, food disposers, and trash compactors provide extra convenience when cleaning up after food preparation. Washers and dryers are available in several styles and sizes.

Portable appliances include mixers, blenders, processors, frypans, toasters, irons, vacuum cleaners, and a number of other specialty appliances. Both major appliances and portable appliances will give you better service and last longer if you carefully follow the instructions for their use and care.

FACTS TO KNOW

1. What consumer guidelines should you follow when purchasing appliances?
2. Describe various types and models of ranges. What are the advantages of each?
3. Explain the differences between self-cleaning and continuous-cleaning ovens.
4. What are some advantages and disadvantages of microwave ovens?
5. Compare the features of the four basic refrigerator and refrigerator-freezer models.
6. What factors influence the choice of a washer and dryer?
7. Describe the function of each of the following portable appliances: mixer, blender, processor, frypan, slow cooker, toaster, and toaster oven.
8. What appliances can be used for cleaning?

IDEAS TO THINK ABOUT

1. What are some factors that affect the choice of household appliances?
2. Identify some reasons why food disposers and trash compactors have become popular. What benefits do they offer? How essential do you consider them?
3. List the following portable appliances in order of importance to your own needs and preferences: mixer, blender, processor, frypan, toaster, slow cooker, toaster oven. Give reasons for your choices.

ACTIVITIES TO DO

1. Using consumer reports, compare different brands and models of a major appliance and a portable appliance. Share your findings with the class.
2. List the major appliances appropriate for each of the following households: a single person, a family of four, a family of seven, and an older couple. Explain your selection of styles, sizes, and options.

YOU CAN DO IT!

Low-Cost Furnishings

By using your own skills, there are many ways to furnish your home inexpensively. Create a decorative skirted table by covering a round plywood table with a floor-length cloth. Build a simple bookcase by using bricks or cement blocks to support the wooden shelves. Sew a group of pillows to toss on a couch or stack on the floor for extra seating. Build a desk by placing a wood door across the top of file cabinets. Drape fabric over a rod for a quick and easy window treatment. Renew used furniture with spray paint, or purchase unfinished furniture and stain or antique it yourself.

Cover a round plywood table with an attractive cloth.

Build a simple bookcase with bricks, cement blocks or tiles.

Sew colorful pillows for relaxing on or for extra seating.

Bring old furniture back to life with new paint or stain.

Create a simple swag by draping fabric over a rod.

Stain or antique unfinished furniture to match other furniture pieces in your home.

Chapter

20

Regular and Periodic Maintenance

Proper maintenance is essential to the upkeep of a building. Schools, hospitals, factories, and office buildings have regular maintenance schedules. Sometimes experts are called in to study these schedules, observe workers, and suggest better methods. How can you apply these same strategies to your own home?

A regular maintenance schedule will enable you to accomplish household tasks more efficiently—you will save both time and energy. By spending five minutes each day straightening your room, you will not have to spend two hours on Saturday putting away everything from the entire week.

Household tasks should be shared with everyone in the home, and cooperation among family members is very important. Each person should help keep the home neat as well as perform specific tasks such as vacuuming or folding laundry. In this way, no one has to shoulder the entire burden of housework.

Many articles and books have been written about improved methods and shortcut strategies for accomplishing household tasks. Reading these can help you improve your efficiency or solve specific maintenance problems.

PREVIEWING YOUR LEARNING

After you have read this chapter, you will be able to:

- Explain the importance of establishing a cleaning and maintenance schedule.

- Use timesaving techniques for daily and weekly tasks.

- Select the proper equipment and cleaning products for major cleaning tasks.

- Provide for seasonal maintenance and repairs.

TERMS TO KNOW

caulking—material used to fill seams, cracks, and joints so they will not leak
detergent—a synthetic, water-soluble cleaning agent
flashing—sheet metal used to waterproof the angle between a chimney and a roof
maintenance—the upkeep of property or equipment

putty—a substance, with the consistency of dough, used to fasten glass in sashes
weather stripping—strips of material used to cover the joints of a door or window and the threshold or sill so as to keep out rain, snow, and cold air

SODIUM COMPOUNDS

**F
E
A
T
U
R
E**

If you read the labels of today's "super" cleaning products, you will find that they use sodium compounds as their active ingredients. Sodium, a silver-white metal, is extremely unstable and combines readily with various other elements to form substances common in every home. It is very handy to have around.

Sodium bicarbonate, for example, is simple baking soda. It can remove stains from china, clean teeth, deodorize drains, make jewelry sparkle, clean refrigerators and tiles, and can even be used to eliminate stomach aches caused by gas. It can be used to make bubbly drinks, help biscuits rise, relieve pain from bee stings and light burns, and extinguish flash fires.

Sodium carbonate, better known as washing soda, comes in handy for washing certain types of floors, cleaning traps and drains, cleaning gas burners, and washing greasy pots and pans. It can also be used as a water softener—a great laundry aid for hard water areas.

Sodium bypochlorite is an old friend called "household bleach" or chlorine bleach. It is made of water, washing soda, and chloride of lime. Besides being an effective laundry bleach for fabrics, it can serve as a disinfectant. It can be used to remove stains on bathtubs, sinks, enamelware, tiles, and woodwork. It is also a very effective mildew remover for use in bathrooms and basements.

Sodium perborate bleaches are safe for most fabrics. However, they should not be used in hot solutions with heat-sensitive fabrics. Sodium perborate crystals, used straight or dissolved in water, are great stain removers for washable and nonwashable materials.

HOME CARE AND MAINTENANCE

Proper cleaning and upkeep of the home are important to its appearance, efficiency, and livability. The most effective method for doing these tasks is to set up a schedule, so that cleaning and maintenance are done regularly. This approach actually makes these tasks easier, since dirt that has gathered for a long time is much more difficult to remove.

The need for cleaning and upkeep varies with the number of people in the home and with their ages. The tasks involved for one or two adults differ greatly from those for a family with a number of children. The time available for these tasks also affects the way they are scheduled. The housekeeping routine of a full-time homemaker will differ greatly from that of the homemaker who is also employed outside the home. Whether the housekeeping is done in the early morning, during the day, in the evening, or on weekends, it must be done to keep the home a pleasant and efficient place to live in.

Daily Responsibilities

If you make a list of daily housekeeping activities and study it objectively, you will be surprised to see how many practices you can initiate to make housekeeping easier. Here are a few suggestions:

—Keep dirt out by keeping entrances clean and by placing a rug outside and inside the doors to wipe shoes on.

—Remove muddy, sandy, or wet shoes at the entrance, and place them on newspaper or a sheet of plastic.

—Make a practice of hanging up or putting away clothing as it is removed.

—Hang towels neatly over a rack after using them. Do not stuff damp towels in the corner of a rack, because they will not dry and will soon smell sour.

—Turn the bed down to air and fluff up the pillows when you get up. Decide whether it is more efficient to make the bed before or after breakfast.

—Be systematic about refolding newspapers; replacing books, magazines, and writing materials after they are used; emptying wastebaskets; keeping toys picked up; and putting dishes where they belong.

Picking up items and putting them away after you are finished with them, keeps a room neat and attractive.

TYPES OF CLOSET STORAGE

Built-in storage units in clothes closets are valuable for keeping clothing and accessories put away yet easily available.

—Use screens at open doors and windows, and caulk around loose window frames and sashes. Both measures will help to keep out dust, dirt, and insects.

—Arrange utensils and food near work centers for efficient use.

—Set the table for breakfast the night before rather than putting dishes away at night and getting them out in the morning.

—Use a tray or serving cart to carry dishes to the sink area after meals.

—If you do not have time to wash dishes before leaving the house in the morning, rinse and stack them and wipe off the counters.

—Assign jobs, such as setting and clearing the table, washing dishes, and other chores, so that everyone will share responsibility for these daily tasks.

—Prepare main courses and desserts for more than one meal at a time. Freeze or refrigerate them until you are ready to use them.

Weekly or Biweekly Tasks
Marketing, washing, ironing, mending, and general cleaning may be done once or twice a week, depending upon the size of the family. The use an area receives, the amount of dirt in the air, and the available time will affect the frequency of cleaning.

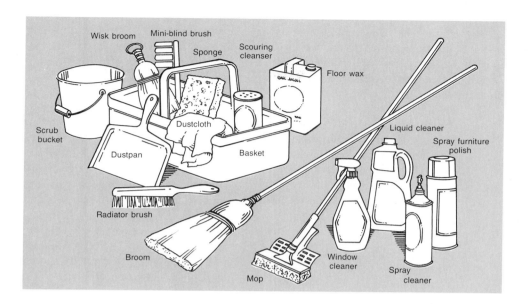

Wisk broom
Mini-blind brush
Sponge
Scouring cleanser
Floor wax
Scrub bucket
Dustcloth
Liquid cleaner
Spray furniture polish
Dustpan
Basket
Radiator brush
Broom
Mop
Window cleaner
Spray cleaner

Here are a few suggestions for reducing the time spent on weekly or biweekly jobs:
—List all the items you use for floor, furniture, and bathroom care, and store them conveniently. You may want to keep the following items in a cleaning basket ready to carry with you when you clean: dustpan, whisk broom or brush, sponge, dustcloths, furniture polishes, and cleansers.
—Dust wood furniture, vacuum-clean or brush upholstered furniture, and dust exposed wood floors before using the vacuum cleaner on rugs.
—Organize laundry supplies conveniently in the laundry area.
—Separate clothing items before washing so as to avoid time-consuming mistakes. Do not mix white and dark-colored clothes. Avoid washing dark socks with items that shed lint.
—Set aside items needing mending, and mend before laundering.
—Remove items that require no ironing from the dryer before they are completely dry to prevent any wrinkling. Fold them for storage or place them on hangers. Buy as many items as possible that require little or no ironing.
—Keep on hand a well-stocked supply of frozen and canned foods and staple items. Then menus can be easily adjusted to changed weather conditions, unexpected guests, or other changes in the number of people present or in the time available for meal preparation.

Occasional or Seasonal Cleaning

Years ago it was customary to give the house a thorough spring cleaning and, almost as thorough, a fall cleaning. Those were the days when housecleaning was a real chore. Rugs had to be taken up, hung on the clothesline, and beaten with wire or reed rug-beaters. Curtains were washed by hand and stretched on curtain stretchers. Floors were scrubbed with a scrub brush and waxed and polished on hands and knees. The coils on bedsprings were tediously dusted by hand. Blankets were washed, rinsed, wrung with a hand wringer, and then stretched over the clothesline to dry. Basements and attics, bulging with heirlooms and junk, added to the burden of the annual or semiannual cleaning. When housecleaning was over, the family was exhausted, but the homemaker's sense of pride and satisfaction compensated for the effort.

This type of spring and fall house-cleaning has gone out of date, along with the carpet beater and curtain stretcher. New equipment, such as vacuum cleaners and floor polishers, have reduced the drudgery of many cleaning tasks. New wash-and-dry curtain fabrics, blankets, and throw rugs, together with washers and dryers, have made laundering easier. Certain tasks, such as cleaning closets, may still be done seasonally as clothes from the past season are stored and those for the next season are brought out for use.

Today most homemakers prefer to rotate cleaning tasks rather than have the entire house torn up for several weeks. By concentrating on one room a week or doing one major task, such as washing windows, each week, one can keep the house clean with a minimum of confusion.

The housekeeping jobs usually done on an occasional or seasonal basis include cleaning and waxing floors, waxing furniture, shampooing or dry-cleaning carpets, washing walls and woodwork, cleaning wallpaper, washing windows, and cleaning window shades or blinds. Using labor-saving equipment or hiring help for certain tasks can reduce the effort involved.

Some tasks, such as oven cleaning, washing windows, and vacuuming draperies, need to be done only occasionally.

MAJOR CLEANING TASKS

Knowledge of the proper methods and materials for major cleaning tasks helps in doing them and having them turn out well. Whether or not you are doing the work yourself, you should know the principles involved and the equipment and materials to be used.

Maintaining Floors

Maintaining floors is one of the hardest household tasks. Always, some dirt is brought in from outdoors, and more is produced from food spillage, lint, hair or fur, and dust. The task of caring for floors is complicated by the fact that a home usually has several types of floor surfaces —wood, vinyl, ceramic tile, and others. Each type has special cleaning requirements. In addition to cleaning, floors need to be protected against wear. For most floors, waxing provides the best surface protection. Some waxes are cleaning agents as well.

Floor waxes are classified as solvent base and water base. Solvent-base wax comes in paste and liquid forms. Since it contains a cleaning fluid, the wax cleans as it polishes. Solvent-base waxes smell like dry-cleaning fluid, and they usually require polishing. Water-base wax is usually marketed in liquid form, and it is usually self-polishing. Water-base liquid waxes dry either with an abrasion-resistant luster or with a somewhat dull finish that requires buffing. Either water- or solvent-base wax can be used on wood, vinyl, flagstone, smooth brick, slate, and sealed terrazzo.

Kitchen floors need to be swept, vacuumed, or washed regularly. Some no-wax vinyl floorings keep their shine without waxing.

Cleaning and waxing floors You can clean and wax floors in one simple operation with a liquid solvent-base wax. This method is especially recommended for wood and vinyl-coated flooring that need waxing. Use the following steps:

—Vacuum-clean or dust the floor surface well. Wipe up sticky spots with a damp cloth.

—Place pads under the polisher brushes on a special polisher attachment, or use a hand applicator on a handle.

—Pour or spray a small amount of wax on the floor and spread the wax evenly. Begin in a corner and work toward a door. The dirt will dissolve and adhere to the pads. Replace the pads as they become soiled.

—After the wax is dry, buff the surface with an electric or hand polisher. Some new types of wax do not require polishing.

—If you use a paste wax, apply a very thin coat of paste. It is better to use two thin coats than to use one heavy coat. Polish after each application.

If a water-base wax is used, two operations are necessary. It should never be used on worn wood floors because the water may penetrate the wood and cause dry rot. The floor must be clean for waxing. Use the following steps for this type of wax:

—Vacuum-clean or dust the surface thoroughly.

—Use any recommended detergent for scrubbing well-sealed wood floors, tile, or stone. Use as little water as possible, and wipe up the water immediately after loosening the soil. Rinse with a mop wrung from clear water, and let dry before applying wax. If the old wax is difficult to dissolve, add a little ammonia to the water.

—Pour or spray puddles of wax on the floor, and spread a thin film evenly with a mop used only for this purpose. Allow at

Vacuum cleaners are available in upright and canister models. An electric broom or portable vacuum is convenient for quick sweeping.

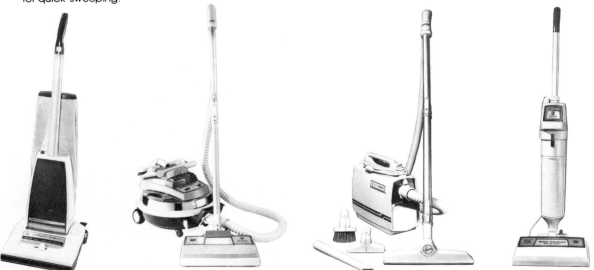

least twenty minutes for the wax to dry.
— Buff with an electric polisher or soft pads attached to a long-handle brush. Buffing between waxings will help to maintain a lustrous surface.

Shampooing or Dry-Cleaning Carpet

Rugs and carpet may be kept fresh and clean by home cleaning methods if directions are followed and if the surface has not accumulated too much soil. The easiest product to use is a foam cleaner in a spray can. If a liquid shampoo is used, it is important to avoid soaking the carpet. Acrylic nylon, and olefin fibers will not readily absorb water, and the excess water will soak into the background and cause the backing to deteriorate. Oversoaked wool carpet will take a long time to dry, and the wool or the backing may shrink in the drying. The surface foam does the cleaning and leaves the soil in suspension

A scrubber-polisher mechanizes the hard work of maintaining floors.

on the carpet, ready to be picked up with a vacuum cleaner.

The following procedure should be used for home on-the-floor cleaning of rugs and carpets:
— Move as much furniture as possible out of the room. Push large pieces, such as pianos and sofas, out from the wall.
— Vacuum-clean the rug or carpet thoroughly, preferably with a heavy-duty, agitator-type vacuum cleaner. Clean the edges of the carpet or rug with the crevice attachment or with a stiff brush before using the vacuum cleaner.
— Using a small brush or sponge, go around the edges of the rug or wall-to-wall carpeting with the shampoo or dry-cleaning preparation.
— Apply the shampoo or dry-cleaning substance to an area between 2 and 3 feet square (0.2 and 0.3 sq m) as directed on the label. Work the cleaning agent into the fibers of the carpet with a sponge, brush, or electric shampooer. If you are using a liquid detergent in an electric shampooer, switch off the flow of liquid as soon as the detergent begins to foam, and continue to agitate until most of the foam disappears.
— After completing the previous operation, let the carpet dry. Then vacuum-clean the carpet and the edges thoroughly.
— Move the furniture back into place, and put small pieces of blotter or aluminum-foil pads under all pieces. This is to avoid the possibility of rust or soil deposit on the rug from the bottom of the furniture. When the carpet is thoroughly dry, remove the pads, and brush up the flattened pile with a stiff brush.

Washing Walls, Ceilings, and Woodwork

The frequency with which walls should be washed or cleaned depends on the amount of dirt in the air and the number of people moving about in the house. In areas where there is heavy industry, walls may have to be washed once a year or oftener. In rural areas or in clean cities, a washing every two years is enough. With complete air conditioning or an air-filter system, walls stay clean for a long time.

A few precautions will reduce the amount of soil on walls. Before turning on the heat in the fall, clean the registers if you have a hot-air furnace, or the radiators if you have a hot-water furnace. Otherwise, the accumulation of dirt that has gathered throughout the summer months will be blown through the house as the heat begins to circulate.

Washing walls is hard work, and it must be done carefully. Some people leave walls so streaked after cleaning that the streaks are difficult or impossible to remove. If walls are allowed to become too soiled, it is not possible to wash them satisfactorily.

The following suggestions will help to make wall-washing successful:

—Assemble the necessary supplies—mild detergent, a bucket for the detergent solution, a bucket for clear water, two large sponges, drop cloths or old sheets to protect the floor, and a ladder or step stool.

—Read the directions given on the label of the detergent box for mixing and using the detergent. Experiment behind a large piece of furniture until you are successful in washing and overlapping an area.

—Begin at the bottom and wash toward the ceiling to avoid streaking the walls. (It is possible to wash from the top down if you do not let the water run down on the soiled wall.) Wash with a rotary motion, covering an area about 2 feet square (0.2 sq. m) at one time. Rinse with a sponge wrung from clean water. Overlap the clean area as you progress. Change the water as it becomes soiled.

Be sure a ceiling is washable before you apply water to it, since some ceilings are finished with a water-base whitener. Also, some ceilings have a rough plaster finish that is difficult to wash. Ceilings are a little difficult to reach, but the procedure for washing them is the same as for walls.

Woodwork is less difficult to wash, because it usually has a semigloss surface.

Cleaning Wallpaper

Certain wallpapers are washable and truly scrubbable. Vinyl-coated wallpapers can be washed like painted walls. Other so-called washable papers—those with a vinyl finish—must be washed with care. Wallpaper cleaners that resemble play dough are satisfactory on most wallpapers. These cleaners will remove only soil and not grease. If a grease spot is fresh, it can be removed by making a paste of fuller's earth or powdered chalk and dry-cleaning fluid.

Cleaning Window Shades and Blinds

Blinds should be pulled down flat and dusted with a soft absorbent cloth when dust shows on the surface. The tapes should be brushed before the slats are dusted. Once or twice a year (more often in industrial areas) the slats should be washed one at a time with a mild detergent solution and a soft cloth. Old bath towels or pieces of knit cotton underwear cut into convenient sizes make good cleaning cloths. Hold one side of the blind with a small cloth while cleaning the opposite side, since wet hands may streak the slats.

Vinyl-coated and cloth window shades can be dusted and washed in the same manner as walls. Wash them on a large table or counter surface, making sure that the surface is clean. Avoid using too much liquid if you use a detergent solution, and overlap the clean area as you progress. Paper shades cannot be washed, but they can be cleaned fairly well with wallpaper cleaner.

SEASONAL MAINTENANCE

People who own their home have the responsibility for general maintenance, while for those who rent a home, general maintenance is the landlord's responsibility. Whoever is responsible, there are certain tasks that should be done every spring and fall, to avoid costly services and repairs.

Spring checklist The following items should be checked in the spring, as preparation for the summer and winter to come:

—Observe the condition of paint on brick, clapboard, shingles, or stucco, as well as on window and door frames. Note the condition of caulking or putty around the windows, as well as the condition of brick pointing and mortar between the bricks.

—Note the condition of wood porches and steps.

—Replace storm windows and doors with screens. Check windows for loose locks.

—Check any need for insulation or repairs in the roof.

—Examine walls and ceilings for signs of leaks.

—Check for water leakage in faucets and flush tanks.

—Examine the heating system for necessary repairs.

—Check air conditioners or central air conditioning.

—Look for signs of termites or mice.

—Examine trees and shrubs for winter damage. Spray, trim, and fertilize outdoor plants; replace any if necessary.

If you as the homeowner cannot make the necessary repairs yourself, consult the yellow pages of the telephone directory for professional services. If you want quick service, do not wait until late in the season.

Outdoor maintenance is as important as indoor maintenance.

If you rent your home, make a list of any needed repairs and give it to the landlord or manager.

Fall checklist The following items should be checked in the fall, as preparation for winter.
—Check the furnace. If it is gas, check the pilot light and clean the burner if necessary. If it is oil, fill the tank. Check water levels in hot-water containers.
—Check the chimney in relation to the furnace or fireplace.
—Examine the roof and the flashing around the chimney for possible leaks.
—Cover the outside of air conditioners if they are not to be used until spring.
—Turn off outside water pipes that are likely to freeze.

—If necessary, replace screen windows and doors with storm sashes. Clean and repair the screens; then hose, dry, and store them in a dry place. Cover them to keep them clean.
—Check for loose caulking or weatherstripping at windows. Caulking tubes are available and as easy to use as squeezing toothpaste out of a tube.
—Remove, clean, and store fabric awnings. Fiberglass, plastic, and metal awnings may stay in place.
—Clean leaves from gutters and down-spouts, and note the need for any repairs. Consider installing mesh guards for gutters and wire cages for down-spouts, to keep them free of litter.
—Examine walks and drives for hazards that may cause falls.

CAREER PROFILE

CARPET INSTALLER

Carpet installers measure, cut, and lay carpeting to size. First, carpet padding is cut to the specified size and tacked in place on the floor. Then, metal strips are nailed around the entire edge of the area. The installers stretch the carpet over the metal strips, which hold the carpet in place without any tacks. If sections of the carpet must be attached, the installers sew them by hand or glue them using a special iron. Care must be taken when cutting and trimming carpet around corners, across openings, and down stairways. Some carpet installers also lay other types of flooring, such as sheet vinyl or vinyl tiles.

If you are interested in becoming a carpet installer, you need physical stamina and manual dexterity. You should not object to doing repetitive and routine activity. You can obtain experience from on-the-job training as a carpet installer's helper or apprentice. Sometimes vocational courses are available. Carpet installers may be employed by carpet or flooring stores. Many are self-employed and work on a free-lance basis for several stores.

REVIEWING CHAPTER 20

SUMMARY

Having a home of your own includes the responsibility for cleaning it. If you own your home, you have the added responsibility of maintaining it in good condition. A regular maintenance schedule will help you be more efficient.

Certain tasks, such as meal preparation, washing dishes, and putting things away must be done daily. Other tasks, such as laundering and general cleaning, are done weekly or biweekly. You can help reduce the need for cleaning by following certain practices, such as providing rugs at entry doorways on which to wipe shoes.

Some cleaning is done only occasionally, such as cleaning floors, carpets, walls, woodwork, shades, and blinds. Certain tasks need to be done every spring and fall to avoid costly repairs. If you cannot do all the maintenance yourself, you can hire professional services to do it.

FACTS TO KNOW

1. Explain why proper maintenance is essential to both a home and its occupants.

2. List four household maintenance tasks that must be done every day.

3. Suggest ways that housekeeping can be made easier on a daily basis.

4. What types of tasks should be done on a weekly or biweekly basis?

5. Why is intensive seasonal cleaning not done in most homes today? In what other ways can major cleaning be accomplished?

6. What supplies and equipment are required for cleaning and waxing floors? shampooing or dry cleaning carpet?

7. Describe the proper procedure for cleaning painted wall surfaces.

8. List five items that should be checked in the spring and five items that should be checked in the fall.

IDEAS TO THINK ABOUT

1. Why is home maintenance accomplished faster and more efficiently when a systematic approach is used?

2. Why is it desirable for all members of a home to participate in its maintenance? Under what circumstances might it be essential for a family to share such responsibility?

3. Describe the degree of order and cleanliness you want in your home. What are you willing to do to make this possible?

ACTIVITIES TO DO

1. Develop a plan for daily, weekly, and occasional maintenance for a one-room apartment and a six-room house. How will the tasks, schedule, and equipment needs differ?

2. Analyze your own home environment in terms of daily, periodic, and seasonal maintenance. What tasks are included in each category? Who does them? To what extent is responsibility for maintenance shared? What do you contribute?

Chapter 21

General Home Repairs

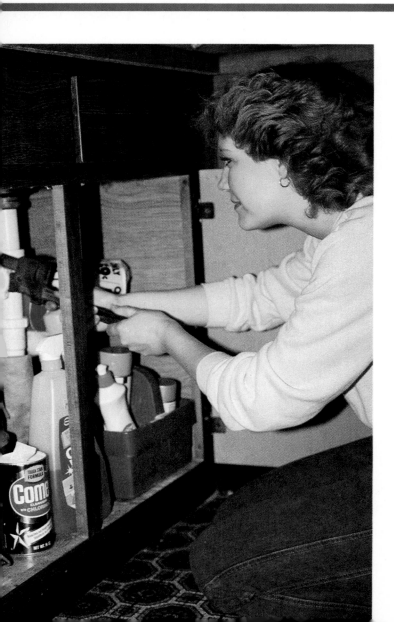

In a home there are many different types of repairs that need to be done from time to time. If you are handy with tools you can save money by doing some of these repairs yourself. Many carpentry and plumbing jobs are not difficult if you have the time, the interest, the skills, and the proper tools. The amateur carpenter can loosen a window that sticks; the amateur plumber can open up a clogged drain. With experience, you can learn to do more involved repairs or home improvements. However, it is always important to follow directions carefully and to observe safety procedures whenever you are doing home repairs.

Restoring old pieces of furniture can save you money and give you a great deal of satisfaction. If you own any antiques, you may want to restore the original finish. Or, you can buy second-hand furniture, strip off the old finish, and stain or antique it. Many people are so successful in restoring old furniture that they are able to decorate their home, with charm and individuality, very economically.

Hopefully, this chapter will inspire you to do some simple home and furniture repairs. There are many illustrated reference books that give specific instructions for all types of home repair and improvement projects. You can also take courses at an adult or community school.

PREVIEWING YOUR LEARNING

After you have read this chapter, you will be able to:
- Observe safety rules when working with tools.

- Recognize and use the appropriate tools for specific repairs.

- Identify common problems involving furniture, woodwork, and plumbing.

- Perform simple furniture, woodwork, and plumbing repairs.

TERMS TO KNOW

adhesive—a substance used to stick or glue things together

auger—a drilling tool for boring holes

epoxy—a strong adhesive compound

joint—a place where two parts are joined

pumice—a lightweight rock used in powder form for smoothing and polishing

shim—a thin, often tapered, piece of wood or metal used to fill in space between things

trap—a bend in a drain or sewer in which the water forms a seal to prevent the passage of sewer gas

REPAIRING CERAMIC TILES

F E A T U R E

Although ceramic tiles are durable and stain-resistant, they can sometimes become loose or damaged, making replacement necessary. To replace a tile, begin by first scraping out any remaining grout along the loose tile's edges, using the corner of an old chisel or other pointed tool. Next, make a deep X in the tile with a glass cutter, and using a small chisel and hammer, crack the tile. (Hit tile lightly to avoid loosening other tiles.) Then, chip out the tile carefully, working from the center outward. When all pieces are removed, chip away any cement that is loose or sticking out, and brush or vacuum the surface clean.

If there are sizable gaps to be filled where the old cement is missing, use a mastic adhesive to fix new tiles to the wall. If the cement is intact, a thin coat of silicone rubber adhesive can be used. After the adhesive is applied to the back of the replacement tile, press the tile into place against the wall. Push just hard enough to keep it level with the surrounding tiles. Use toothpicks (two per joint) to keep the spaces around the tile even. When the adhesive is set, remove the toothpicks and fill the joints with grout. Clean excess grout from the face of the tile with a damp sponge, being careful not to pull the new grout from the joints.

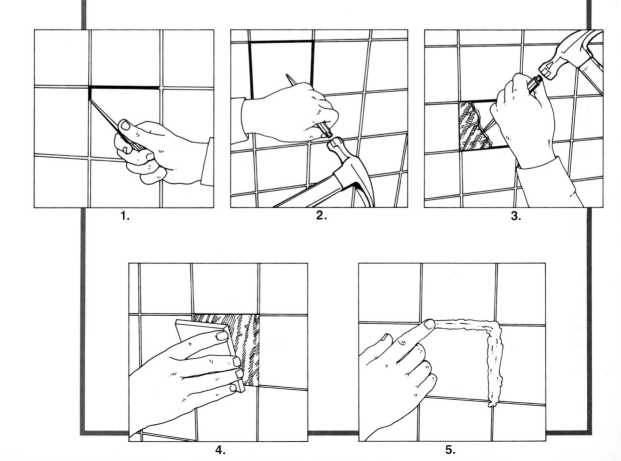

1.　　　　2.　　　　3.

4.　　　　5.

RULES FOR SAFETY

Using tools requires that you follow certain rules for safety. Fewer accidents would happen at home if the basic rules of safety set up by industry were observed. If you are working with power tools, it is even more important to be careful.

The following suggestions will help to protect you when you do repair work:

— Wear proper clothing. Avoid long sleeves, exposed shirttails, ties, or any loose clothing that can catch in tools. Wear heavy leather shoes rather than cloth shoes, which provide no protection from falling objects.

— Keep tools clean and in good repair. This means keeping handles free of oil or moisture, sharp edges sharp, handles tight, and drill bits properly installed.

— Keep tools in place when not in use, and keep sharp edges turned away from your reach.

— Provide for proper grounding of power tools. This is especially important when you are working in damp areas. A grounded receptacle has three prongs instead of two.

— Make sure that surfaces on which you are using power tools are firmly anchored.

— Turn off power tools before laying them down or replacing any part.

— Wear safety goggles when grinding stone or metal, or using any power tool.

— Work in a well-ventilated room.

BASIC TOOL REQUIREMENTS

The tools needed for most home repairs are indicated in the diagram on page 406. If tools are to be convenient for use, they must be stored in an accessible place and kept in good condition. In addition to tools, the repair shelf should contain small jars of nails, screws, and picture hooks of assorted sizes; picture wire; fine sandpaper; mending tape; and adhesives.

A number of household repairs depend on the use of adhesives, or glue. Success in using any glue will depend upon selecting the right glue for the job and following directions carefully. If joints are to be firm, they must be clean, snugly fitted, clamped, and allowed to dry for the specified time and temperature. Some of the most common glues are as follows:

— White polyvinyl acetate   This is a popular all-purpose white glue sold in plastic squeeze bottles under several trade names. It is easy to use, and dries clear. Joints must be clean and held together under pressure for 20 to 30 minutes for preliminary contact. Thorough drying requires 24 hours. These glues can be used on paper, fabric, cardboard, cork, leather, and wood.

— Casein glue   This is a powder that must be mixed with water and used at a heavy wood joints. It can be used at low temperatures, and it tends to fill in between the joints if they do not fit snugly. It is not as waterproof as plastic-resin glue.

— Plastic-resin glue   This is a powder that must be mixed with water and used at a room temperature of 70 to 80 degrees Fahrenheit (21–27°C). Joints must be closely fitted and clamped tightly for five or six hours. The glue is very strong and also waterproof.

— Epoxy adhesive   This adhesive comes in two parts, including a resin and a catalyst, and in clear, white, or metallic finish. The adhesive, which should be used soon after it is mixed, is very strong. This adhesive has many uses, from repairing drain pipes, masonry, cracked radiators, and rotted wood to repairing fine china, marble, and glass. The surface must be thoroughly clean and dry, and the adhesive should be used at room temperature or higher.

Improvements in glues make it difficult to describe all possible types. As a rule, the manager of a hardware store can recommend the best glue for a specific need.

BASIC TOOLS FOR HOME REPAIRS

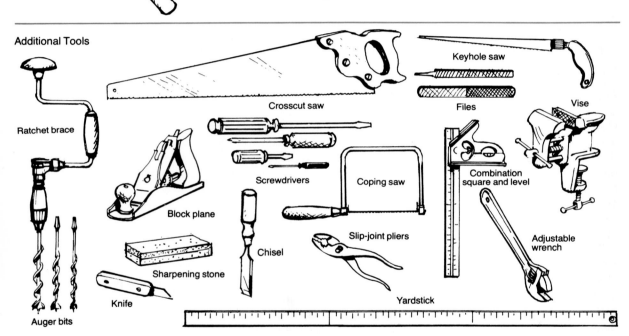

Beginner's Tools

Hammer

Pipe wrench

Pliers

Hand drill

Flexible rule

Bits

Small screwdriver

Medium screwdriver

Awl

Additional Tools

Ratchet brace

Crosscut saw

Keyhole saw

Files

Vise

Block plane

Screwdrivers

Coping saw

Combination square and level

Sharpening stone

Chisel

Slip-joint pliers

Adjustable wrench

Knife

Yardstick

Auger bits

Tools are essential for doing home repairs. Many jobs can be done with the basic beginner's tools. Additional tools. are often a help, and certain repairs may require specific tools.

RESTORING FURNITURE

Because furniture is very expensive to buy or replace, being able to do repairs or restoring can be a great saving. It is a help to be able to do simple repairs, such as covering scratches. Learning to refinish furniture, either second-hand or inherited pieces, can bring even greater rewards, since you can obtain quality furniture at low cost and also have the finish you want.

Making Minor Repairs

If you look around your home, you probably can find many minor repair jobs, such as removing scratches, dents, and holes in furniture; tightening joints in chairs and tables; easing drawers that stick; and restoring the surface on marble-top tables and chests. These jobs take little time or skill, yet they help to keep furniture in good condition. You can also save money by doing the repairs yourself.

Hiding scratches If a scratch is only surface-deep, repairing it is simple. A walnut meat can be rubbed over a scratch on most dark woods. Iodine can be "painted" over a scratch in mahogany by using a little cotton on the end of a toothpick. Light shoe polish or crayon can be used on light woods. The excess stain must be rubbed entirely away. Special furniture wood-stain sticks are available at paint stores for treating deeper scratches. After a scratch has been stained, ordinary furniture polish will blend it into the surface finish.

Raising dents You can raise minor depressions in wood by moisture and heat, using the following steps: (1) Remove the furniture polish from the dented area with a dry-cleaning fluid or turpentine. (2) Cover the dent with several thicknesses of a soft thin cloth (a piece of old sheet will do) slightly dampened. (3) Place a flat metal cap from a small can or bottle over the spot, flat side down. (4) Hold an iron over the top for a minute to swell the wood. Repeat if necessary, and then polish the entire surface.

Filling Holes Holes in furniture may be caused by cigarette burns or sharp objects. These are more difficult to mend than scratches or dents. To fix them, use the following procedure: (1) Scrape the hole clean with a sharp knife, and rub it with fine sandpaper or steel wool. (2) Wipe off the residue with a soft cloth dampened with dry-cleaning fluid or turpentine. (3) Fill in the hole with a plastic-wood filler, available at any paint store, that matches the raw wood in color. (4) Touch up the filled hole with clear varnish or shellac, and rub it smooth with pumice and linseed oil. (5) Wipe off excess oil with turpentine, and polish the entire surface. If the hole is not very deep, thin layers of clear varnish can be built up until the surface is even.

Loosening drawers that stick If drawers stick mainly in damp weather, the solution

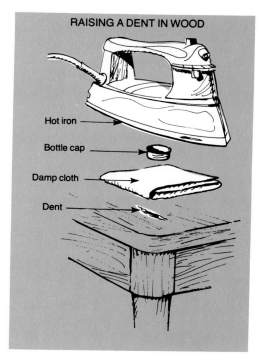

RAISING A DENT IN WOOD

Hot iron

Bottle cap

Damp cloth

Dent

The steam created by this process will often make the wood swell back into shape.

is simple. Remove the drawer, and wipe the dust or grease off with a dry-cleaning fluid. Rub the sides with paraffin or candle wax. If the wood has absorbed a lot of moisture, it may be shrunk by placing the drawer over a radiator or register long enough to remove the excess moisture. If the drawer sticks badly, place medium-grade sandpaper over a block of wood, and sand the areas that stick. If the front of the drawer must be lifted to close all the way, press a few thumbtacks under the front edge.

Removing stains on marble Marble is porous, and therefore any sticky or colored liquid, or even water, will mark it. Marble should be kept clean with a soft cloth wrung from a very mild detergent preparation, rinsed, and then dried thoroughly. If the soil is deep, a brushing with a nonabrasive detergent may be necessary. The surface should be thoroughly rinsed with clear water. If stains remain, apply a special stain removal preparation available in paint stores.

Fixing loose table or chair legs If a chair feels wobbly when you sit in it, the trouble may be in the chair rungs or in one of the three-cornered blocks that support the chair legs at the corners of the seat. If a rung is loose, it must be further loosened and removed. The surfaces must be sanded smooth before the rung is replaced. To reset the rung, it must be glued, clamped, and allowed to dry for 24 hours. If a clamp is not available to hold the rung in place while drying, a heavy cord can be tied around the legs and a stick inserted at one part of the cord to act as a tourniquet for tightening the cord.

If the triangular block is loose under the seat of a dining-room chair, or under the top of a small table or desk, the block must be removed and both the contact surface of the block and the chair frame must be sanded smooth. After the glue is applied, screws larger than the original ones should be used to hold the block in place. If these are not available, place a match stem with a little glue on it in the hole first, or insert plastic wood and allow it to harden before inserting the screw.

Restyling and Refinishing Furniture

Often you can find in a secondhand store sturdy furniture with good lines that you can restyle and refinish. Even the amateur can remove a mirror from an old-fashioned dresser and, with a little refinishing, have a good-looking chest of drawers. It is often fun to visit shops selling antique and secondhand furniture and to bargain for a piece of furniture that can be restyled or rebuilt.

Furniture may be treated in a variety of ways. You may want to preserve but freshen the existing finish. If it is in poor condition, you will need to remove the old finish and apply a new one of the kind you prefer.

Preliminary steps Before attempting to refinish the surfaces of a piece of furniture that needs restyling, do all the necessary furniture surgery first. No two pieces will require the same restyling, and no two people will have the same idea about restyling even the same piece. After a piece is restyled, it can be refinished in a variety of ways.

Work in an area that is well ventilated and has a floor covering that will not be harmed, preferably outdoors or in a well-ventilated basement. If you work in the house, protect the floors with several layers of newspaper.

Varnishing a good surface If the surface of a piece of furniture is in good condition, you can brighten it with a new coat of varnish. To do so, take these steps: (1) Repair the surface; then glue and screw loose parts as described on page 405. (2) Remove the old glossy finish with a commercially prepared product available at a paint store. (You can do this with repeated applications of turpentine and sanding, but it is more work.) (3) Wipe the surface clean with turpentine or denatured alcohol. (4) Apply a satin-finish furniture varnish, which gives a hand-rubbed appearance. You may want to use two thin coats on two successive days for a more durable finish. Avoid using varnish in damp, muggy weather, because the wood is then moist and the polish takes a long time to dry.

Removing old finish If the finish of the furniture is not in good condition, it can be removed and a new finish applied. To remove the old finish, proceed as follows: (1) Use a commercially prepared paint remover—preferably a syrup-like nonflammable liquid. (2) Avoid getting the liquid on any part of the body, especially the eyes. Keep a bucket of clear water nearby and rinse off remover immediately if it touches the skin. (Change water often.) (3) Apply the paint remover with a brush and let it stand the length of time stated in the directions before trying to remove the finish. (4) Scrape off loosened varnish with a putty knife, and wipe the residue onto newspaper. Loosen the varnish in crevices with an old toothbrush or a stiff stencil brush. (5) Clean the surface with turpentine, denatured alcohol, or a fairly strong detergent. (Avoid using too much liquid, and wipe the surface dry.) Repeat the operation until there is no trace of the original finish. Repair dents or holes as directed earlier.

Staining furniture If a darker or richer color is desired on furniture, prepared stains can be used full strength or diluted with a recommended solvent to give a natural wood or wood-color finish. The old finish must be removed down to the raw wood, and the wood must be clean and dry. Test the stain first on the underside of the furniture to make sure the new stain is the color desired. If it is too strong, dilute it, and remember that the color of the furniture will darken if a shellac, oil, or varnish finish is added.

This old table will have a brand-new look after the original finish is removed, and it is stained and refinished.

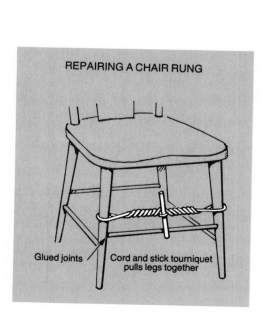

REPAIRING A CHAIR RUNG

Glued joints   Cord and stick tourniquet pulls legs together

Furniture finishes Every furniture expert has a favorite finish, among which are rubbed oil, satin-type varnish, and antique. These may be applied as follows:

— **Rubbed oil and pumice** (1) Prepare the surface by removing the old finish and cleaning the surface as described earlier. (2) Apply a thin coat of shellac (clear type on blond woods and orange type on dark woods), and allow to dry as directed. (3) Make a thick paste of pumice and linseed oil in a deep saucer. (4) With a soft pad, rub the paste over the surface until the wood feels slightly warm from friction. (5) Wipe off the excess oil with denatured alcohol. (6) Apply a rather thin coat of shellac, and let it dry. Repeat several times, finishing with a final oil-and-pumice rubbing. Finally, rub with a soft cloth until an even patina is obtained.

— **Varnish** (1) Give the surface one or more applications of the oil finish described above. Wipe off all traces of oil. (2) Using a special satin-finish furniture varnish, apply a thin coat, and let it dry overnight. This varnish will withstand heat. (3) Apply a second coat for a more durable finish, and let it dry 24 hours or longer before placing anything on the surface.

— **Antique** You may apply an antique finish to furniture without removing the original finish. (1) Repair dents, holes, and loose joints as described earlier. (2) Remove the surface gloss with a commercial preparation or by using turpentine, fine steel wool, and sandpaper. (3) Check the entire surface to make sure there is no gloss or dirt that might cause the paint to crack. (4) Select a kit that will produce the color you want. The kit will contain a white or a colored base, a glaze, and a satin-finish varnish. (5) Apply the base coat, and allow it to dry thoroughly for 48 hours. (6) Spread on the glaze, and with a cloth, sponge, or brush, streak or dab the glaze. (Practice on an old smooth-surface board until you have the effect you want.) (7) Wipe off the glaze to follow the grain of the wood. You can handle edges and joints better if you cut a two-by-three-inch (5 x 8 cm) rectangle of cardboard and hold the cloth over it as you pull it over the wood or up and down from the edges or the joints. (8) Apply a clear satin varnish for a resistant finish.

REPAIRING WOODWORK

With a little patience and time, you can learn to be your own carpenter, at least for simple jobs. You can ease a window or door that sticks, reinforce loose screws, and plane a door.

Easing windows that stick Wood windows stick because they have swelled from dampness or because the edges are sealed with paint. If the window is swollen only slightly, place a cloth-covered wooden block along the edges and tap it with a hammer. Raise the sash, and lubricate the frame with candle wax or soap.

If windows stick after painting, insert a broad, stiff putty knife between the window sash and the frame and tap it lightly with a hammer. Or hold the blade of a hatchet along the lower edge and tap it with a hammer. Twist the knife blade or the hatchet slightly after each tap. Raise the window, and scrape off the rough edges with a chisel. Work from the outside of the house. If the window is badly stuck, the molding on the inside may have to be pried off with a chisel, sanded, and then moved out slightly.

Easing doors that stick A door may stick if the weather is damp or if the hinges work loose. First, open the door wide and tighten all the screws that hold the hinges in place. If the holes are loose, remove one hinge at a time and glue in wood plugs, or simply place a wood matchstick in the hole

EASING A STUCK WINDOW

REPAIRING A DOOR

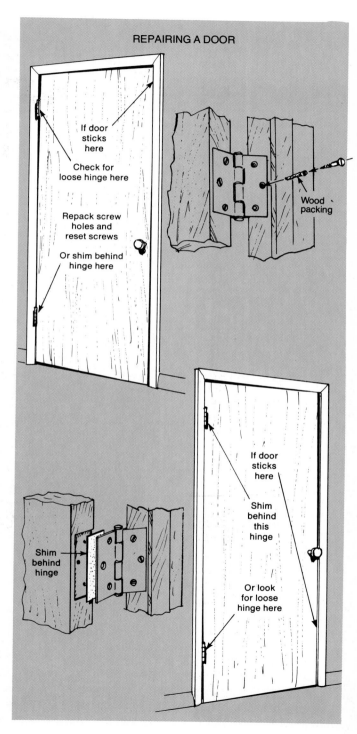

If door sticks here

Check for loose hinge here

Repack screw holes and reset screws

Or shim behind hinge here

Wood packing

Shim behind hinge

If door sticks here

Shim behind this hinge

Or look for loose hinge here

to give the screws a better grip. If the door still sticks, slide a sheet of typing paper faced with carbon paper along the edge of the door to detect the location of the trouble area. Sand the area, and rub wax along the edge of the door. If the door sags at the top or bottom, one hinge may be recessed more than the other (the hinge diagonally opposite from the sag). Unscrew and remove the troublesome hinge from the door-frame side and insert a cardboard wedge.

If the door still sticks, it may be necessary to plane down the wood on one surface. Never remove a door and begin planing any surface of it until you have tried the previous solutions.

When a new carpet is installed in a room, the doors may need to be trimmed. Mark the bottom of each door at the spot where the greatest binding occurs. Remove door and use a smoothing plane to shave off the wood along the bottom edge of the door.

REPAIRING PLUMBING

In case of an emergency with plumbing, it is not always possible to secure the immediate services of a certified plumber. Therefore, it is wise—even if you are a renter—to know at least where the shutoff valves are in case a washer gives way and water begins to overflow on the floor. As a rule, there are valves under a sink, washbowl, and toilet that can be turned to shut off the water until help arrives. Sometimes these valves are in the basement. There are also valves for the bathtub, although they may not be visible. If they are not in sight, they are enclosed either inside a wood panel at the faucet end of the tub or on the wall of an adjoining room or hallway, if the tub fits between two walls. Look for these shutoff valves, as well as the main water-control valve, because they are important in making plumbing repairs.

Fixing a clogged shower head If a shower head produces a stream instead of a spray, it needs to be cleaned or replaced.

A leaky faucet can waste gallons of water. Replacing the washer is an easy task and will conserve water.

Remove the shower-head face and clean the holes with a wire or coarse needle. Soak it in a solution of ammonia and water, and scrub the inside with an old toothbrush. Replace the face of the shower head. If the flow is not improved, a new shower head is needed.

Repairing a running flush tank The flush tank back of the toilet has three control valves: (1) the flush valve at the base of the tank, on which rests a rubber tank ball; (2) an inlet or float valve, which lets in water until the tank is full; and (3) the shutoff valve below the tank. When the toilet is flushed, the flush valve opens and the water in the tank runs through the toilet. When the tank is empty, the rubber ball rests in place, acting as a stopper until the tank fills. A metal ball on a rod connected with the inlet valve, or tank float, rises as the tank fills again. At a certain water level, the float causes the inlet valve to close automatically.

A number of things can happen to cause poor functioning of the toilet. If the tank fills too slowly, there may not be enough water pressure or the rubber ball may not be centered on the flush-valve seat. To relieve this condition, test the shutoff valve to make sure there is a maximum flow of water. If there is a sufficient flow of water, the trouble is not at the shutoff valve; it may be in the tank ball at the base of the flush tank. Therefore: (1) Turn off the water supply at the shutoff valve or tie the tank float up to prevent the tank from filling, and flush out the water. (2) Examine the position of the rubber ball on the flush-valve seat. If it is not centered, the rod holding it may have to be straightened. (3) Check the condition of the rubber ball, and if it is worn, replace it. (4) Clean the exposed flush-valve seat with a steel-wool pad, and if the rod holding the rubber ball is in poor condition, replace it. (5) Fill the flush tank, and make sure the rubber ball falls into position.

If water continues to overflow, lift up the float with your forefinger, and if the noise stops, the rod holding the float may have to be bent slightly downward, or the float may have a leak, making replacement necessary. To check for a leak, unscrew the float and shake it.

If the water keeps running, the trouble is in the float, or inlet valve. The overflow constantly runs out through an overflow pipe, and this water loss can run up water bills. Call a plumber at this point, unless someone in the home is adept at mechanics. This operation involves disassembling the valve-inlet section by removing two thumbscrews, or pins, to release the entire float-arm mechanism. The stem and plunger can be lifted so that the washer at the end of the plunger is exposed. If it is rusty, the unit should be replaced.

Opening a clogged drain If a sluggish drain in a toilet, washbowl, bathtub, or sink is attended to before it clogs up, the job will be simplified. Grease, coffee grounds, and particles of food will clog a kitchen drain; hair, lint, or greasy creams will clog up a washbowl or bathtub drain. Most trouble arises in the built-in metal drain stoppers in modern fixtures. These metal stoppers in a bathtub or washbowl can be twisted and lifted out. After pulling off hair and lint, you can clean out the grease by soaking the stopper in an ammonia solution.

Most mild stoppage in a sink or toilet can be cleared up by plunging with a force cup, which is a bell-shaped rubber cup about 5 or 6 inches (13–15 cm) in diameter attached to a wood handle. (1) Fill the sink or toilet with 3 or 4 inches (7–10 cm) of water. (2) Center the cup over the drain, and hold the handle with both hands for the maximum pressure. (3) Force the cup downward, and release it with a jerk to create a suction action. (4) Repeat 10 or 12 times to break up foreign matter and to release it down the drain.

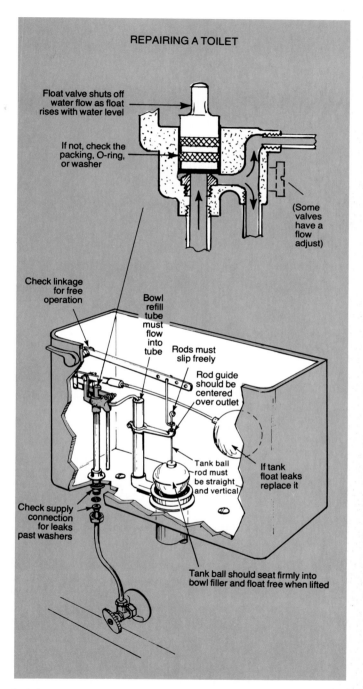

REPAIRING A TOILET

Float valve shuts off water flow as float rises with water level

If not, check the packing, O-ring, or washer

(Some valves have a flow adjust)

Check linkage for free operation

Bowl refill tube must flow into tube

Rods must slip freely

Rod guide should be centered over outlet

Tank ball rod must be straight and vertical

If tank float leaks replace it

Check supply connection for leaks past washers

Tank ball should seat firmly into bowl filler and float free when lifted

Certain problems involving the shutoff valve or the flush valve and tank ball of a toilet can be solved according to the directions given here.

If the trouble continues, use a commercially prepared drainpipe cleaner. Since this is highly poisonous material, injurious to the skin and to the porcelain finish, the instructions must be carefully followed. If the problem is not corrected, a steel auger or snake will have to be used. This is usually the time to call a plumber, because few people either own an auger or want to undertake this job.

A sink drain is often clogged at the trap, or U-shaped pipe under the sink. Place a bucket under the drain below the sink. Using a wrench, loosen the trap plug, or nut, very carefully to avoid stripping the threads. For some drains, the U-shaped pipe will have to be removed. Force a heavy wire or bent coat hanger through the drain pipe or U-shaped trap in both directions to force out the foreign matter. Reassemble, and turn on the hot water full force. If the drain is still clogged, it will be necessary to use an auger or a snake. This is usually a plumber's job.

Repairing loose bathtub caulking
When bathtubs are set in place, the edges along the tile wall and floor are caulked. If the caulking becomes loose, the water from the shower will run between the walls or through the floor and damage the ceiling in the room below. This is an easy repair job. Purchase a tube of caulking compound at a hardware store. Loosen the cracked caulking, wipe away the residue, and squeeze the compound in the open crevices to fill them completely. Read and follow carefully the directions on the container to obtain the best results.

CAREER PROFILE FURNITURE REFINISHER

Refinishing worn, damaged, or old furniture is the specialty of furniture refinishers. They may also apply a stain or painted finish to new, unfinished furniture. Refinishers prepare an item for finishing by removing all knobs, hinges, or upholstered sections. The old finish is removed by using a solvent to soften the surface and then an abrasive, such as a brush, steel wool, or sandpaper to rub it off. Any nicks, depressions, holes, or cracks in the wood can be filled with plastic or wood putty. Refinishers may also brush bleaching acid over the wood's surface to restore it to its natural color. Next, refinishers brush or spray successive coats of stain, varnish, lacquer, or paint on the item. Finally, the furniture is polished and waxed to highlight the wood grain.

If you are interested in becoming a furniture refinisher, you should enjoy working with wood and hand tools. You need the ability to distinguish differences in color and texture plus the patience for meticulous detailed work. You can take courses in furniture refinishing at a vocational or adult school or can receive on-the-job training. You can work for a furniture company, a furniture refinishing shop, or be self-employed.

REVIEWING CHAPTER 21

SUMMARY

A few basic tools will enable you to do most home repairs. It is important to always follow safety rules, especially when using power tools. Before undertaking any repair, you should consider whether you have the ability for a particular task or whether expert help is needed.

Many people gain satisfaction from restoring old furniture. You can learn to remove scratches and dents, fill holes, remove stains, loosen drawers that stick, tighten joints in tables and chairs, as well as refinish furniture. These skills will enable you to restore antique or secondhand furniture at great savings.

With simple carpenter skills, you can ease a window or door that is stuck, reinforce loose screws, and plane a door. A clogged shower head, a noisy flush tank, a clogged drain, and loose bathtub caulking can all be repaired if you have the time, the ability, and the proper tools.

FACTS TO KNOW

1. Describe five safety procedures to follow when doing repair work.
2. Name at least six basic beginner's tools that can be used for home repairs.
3. What benefits can be obtained by repairing or refinishing furniture?
4. List four minor furniture repairs, and describe how to do one of them.
5. After removing the old finish from a piece of furniture, what new finishes can be applied?
6. What may cause wooden windows and doors to stick?
7. What steps should be done to ease a door that sticks before planing down any surfaces?
8. Identify several plumbing repairs that an amateur can do with the proper tools. What plumbing problems require the work of a plumber?

IDEAS TO THINK ABOUT

1. Explain why the cost of repairs is a good investment for homeowners. How does the condition of property affect its value?
2. Who is responsible for doing repairs in a home that is rented? Where can this information be obtained if you do not know?

ACTIVITIES TO DO

1. List the basic tools on page 406. Place a check (√) by each one you have used. Place a star (*) by each one you can use skillfully. What conclusions can you make about your readiness to undertake home repairs?
2. In your own home, locate the main shutoff valve for water, the control valve for hot water, and the regulating valves for sinks, washbowls, and toilets. Also locate the main electrical switch and gas intake valve. Why is this information important to occupants of the home?

Chapter
22

Home Improvements

The do-it-yourself boom is growing larger. Magazines feature special projects that can be done in just a weekend or for under a hundred dollars. Adult and community schools offer special courses that teach skills such as tiling kitchen counters or reupholstering furniture. Being able to do many of your own home improvement projects can save you considerable money and also enhance your living space.

Fast drying, odorless, water soluble paints, along with paint rollers, have made the job of painting much easier. Prepasted wallpaper and self-adhesive floor tiles are easy to apply and lay. If you can sew a straight seam, you can make shirred or café curtains. Even fabric shades are easy to make with special kits or pull tapes.

Who does home improvement projects depends in part on whether you rent or own your home. If you rent, the responsibility for improvements belongs to the landlord. However, in some cases a tenant may undertake redecorating projects or renovations. If you own your home, you can change it in any way you wish. You are limited only by the time, skill, money, and incentive needed to do the task.

Before starting any project, always read the directions and follow them carefully. Use the proper equipment and tools to make the job as easy as possible. Your skills will increase with practice and experience.

PREVIEWING YOUR LEARNING

After you have read this chapter, you will be able to:

• Identify home improvement projects that you would be capable of doing.

• List the supplies and equipment needed for specific projects.

• Describe the steps involved in painting, applying wallpaper, laying floor tiles, and making fabric curtains and shades.

• Evaluate a remodeling project in terms of skill, time, energy, and money needed.

TERMS TO KNOW

contractor—one that makes a business arrangement to erect or remodel buildings

float—a tool used for smoothing a surface

grout—a material used for filling spaces between tiles

plumb line—a weighted cord used to determine a vertical line

selvage—an edge of fabric or paper that is meant to be cut off and discarded

sizing—a material used for filling the pores in surfaces such as plaster, paper, or textiles

solvent—a liquid substance that can dissolve another substance

BATHROOM RETREATS

F E A T U R E

King Fahd of Saudi Arabia went to the wilds of Canada to find a seven-ton slab of red granite for his royal bathtub. Why? Because bathrooms today are fast becoming *the* special room of the house. Taking their cue from the Japanese, who have always considered the bath more than just a place to wash, designers have turned bathrooms into places to relax, reflect, and indulge in private moments.

You needn't go to Canada to find luxurious bathroom fixtures. The marketplace has exploded with a variety of products for every taste and purpose—from antique clawfoot tubs to extra fancy whirlpool baths complete with speaker phones, massage pillows, four-speaker stereo systems, and foldaway tables. Some toilets are imitations of old-fashioned pull-chain types, others are sleek and modern. Ceramic tile, always popular because of its easy maintenance, comes in nearly limitless colors, sizes, and patterns. Redwood and cedar offer new alternatives to tile surfaces.

When planning to redo a bathroom, start by considering its use. Is it a master or guest bathroom? Will it be used by one or possibly two at a time? If two, try to plan for a double sink arrangement. Choose a decorative style that works best with the space that you have. Keep in mind that soft, pastel colors create a soothing atmosphere, brights a more upbeat one. White and neutral-colored bathrooms are most flexible for decorating. You can easily change their look with new wallpaper, linens, and accessories.

PAINTING WALLS, CEILINGS, AND WOODWORK

The type of paint you choose and the equipment needed depend on the task you are doing. Before buying them, check with the salesperson to be sure they will serve your purpose. If you are having paint mixed, it is important to be sure of the color desired. Stores often provide paint cards so that you can try the colors against the walls in your home.

Estimating the Quantity of Paint

The paint for one job should all be bought at one time, to avoid any variations. Before buying the paint, you should estimate the quantity needed. This depends on the size of the area to be painted. Determine as closely as possible the number of square feet you expect to paint.

The label on a paint can will generally indicate the number of square feet of area the contents will cover. New, rough, or porous surfaces will require more paint. A gallon (3.8 L) of paint will cover about 400 square feet (37 sq m) of smooth surface in a finish coat, less area in a first coat. If you are uncertain of the amount needed, consult with the salesperson. It is more economical to buy paint by the gallon, unless only a small quantity is needed for woodwork.

Obtaining Equipment and Supplies

There is nothing more frustrating than to be all prepared for painting and find that you lack an essential item. Use the following checklist before beginning to paint:

— Paint and solvents or thinners Water-base paints may be thinned with water, and the brushes used with it may be cleaned with running water. Oil-base paints must be thinned with a paint thinner or turpentine, and the brushes used must be cleaned with these solvents.

— Brushes Buy good brushes, and take care of them. Bristles with split ends are more absorbent than those with pointed ends, and they hold the maximum amount of paint without dripping. You will need a 4-inch brush for large areas, a 2-inch brush for wood trim, and a 1-inch brush for very narrow places. Even though you paint with a roller, you will need to brush on paint in the corners and near any trim.

— Rollers Rollers may be used to paint any interior or exterior surface. Rollers with a short nap are recommended for wood trim; with a medium nap, for walls; and with a long nap, for outside brick, stucco, or cement block. The most popular roller has a ⅜- to ½-inch nap made of lamb's wool or a synthetic fiber resembling lamb's wool.

— Roller tray Buy a tray to accommodate the roller width. Line the tray with heavy wrapping paper or foil to simplify cleaning it later.

— Mixing buckets and paddles Cardboard mixing buckets are inexpensive and essential for mixing paint and cleaning brushes. Paddles are necessary for stirring paint.

— Putty and patching plaster Putty is used to fill holes in woodwork or those made in a wall by picture hooks. A patching compound is available in stick form for hairline cracks. If a crack is wider than a hairline, a groove must be chiseled out and new plaster set in with a putty knife.

— Putty knife This implement is used to scrape rough spots, to smooth over putty in holes, and to apply plaster in crevices.

— Sizing Sizing is needed to seal any new plaster or patched plaster before painting. It can be bought at a paint store.

— Sandpaper This item is needed to smooth rough spots in the plaster or to take the gloss off wood trim. Buy both fine and medium weights.

— Paint guards and masking tape These

STEPS IN PAINTING

Repair holes and large cracks before painting.

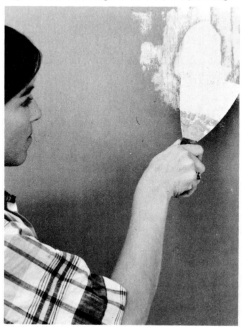

Use a brush to paint around wood trim.

Rollers are recommended for large wall areas.

Paint the trim last.

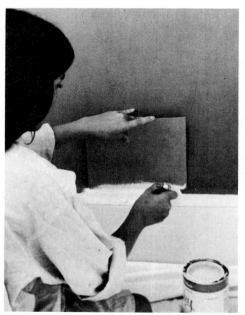

materials are used to protect the edges of wood trim as you paint, or to mark a clean line where one color meets another.

— Drop cloths Plastic drop cloths, which are fairly inexpensive, are needed to protect the floor and furniture. However, old sheets or bedspreads can be used instead.

— Old rags and newspapers Assemble plenty of old rags and newspapers. It will be easier to clean brushes and rollers if the excess paint is wiped, rolled, or brushed off first on paper or cloth.

— Ladders Two ladders and a long board to stretch between them may be needed to paint a ceiling or high wall. If you do not own ladders, it may be possible to rent them.

Preparing Surfaces for Painting

Before starting to paint, move all tables, chairs, lamps, pictures, and small objects from the room. Assemble large pieces of furniture in the middle of the room, and cover them entirely.

If the walls and ceilings to be painted are very dirty or greasy, the paint will not hold. The walls and ceilings in living, dining, and sleeping areas can be dusted quickly by going over the surface with a dust mop covered with a piece of soft cloth. The walls and ceiling in the kitchen should be sponged clean with a detergent, because they are usually greasy. Bathroom walls and ceilings should also be cleaned.

If there are any fine cracks in the plaster, they should be filled in with a special plaster stick. All loose plaster must be knocked away, and all deep cracks must be chiseled out and replastered. When the plaster is dry, these areas must be sized. If the walls are to have only one coat of paint, it is necessary first to paint the new plaster as nearly like the old surface as possible to eliminate the possibility of shading when the new coat is applied.

Sequence for Working

If an entire room is to be painted, the ceiling should be done first, the walls next, and the wood trim last. A different type of paint may be required for each type of surface.

When using a roller, load the cover uniformly with paint, and take the first stroke away from the body, whether working on the ceiling or a wall. Use only a moderate amount of pressure, and work fairly slowly.

It is advisable to use a brush around the edges of the ceiling, at the corners of walls, and around the wood trim. However, it is not advisable to paint all of these areas first, because of uneven drying. It is well to remember that wet paint over wet paint dries more evenly than wet paint over dry paint.

The following procedures will help to avoid streaking:

— Paint the ceiling across the width of the room, painting a strip 3 to 4 feet (about a meter) wide at one time and overlapping each strip before the paint dries.

— Paint the wall from the top to the bottom in the same manner as the ceiling. If you must stop, do so at a corner, a window, or a door.

— Paint wood trim with a brush, unless you are painting flush doors, in which case a roller works well. Paint the surface of a door first and the edges last.

— Protect areas not to be painted by using a paint guard or masking tape. (Avoid using masking tape on fresh paint.)

After painting, roll the excess paint off the roller onto newspapers to simplify cleaning. Remove the roller cover, and clean it in the proper solvent—water if the paint is water-soluble, and turpentine or paint thinner if the paint has an oil base. Clean brushes thoroughly before storing them. As the brush dries, comb out the bristles. To store, wrap the brush below the handle with brown paper.

APPLYING WALLPAPER

A number of considerations are important in buying wallpaper. The type of wallpaper should be suitable for the purpose. For example, wallpaper for a kitchen or family room should be very durable and easy to maintain. Certain types of wallpaper are easier to hang than others. A salesperson can advise you concerning the advantages and problems of various types, such as prepasted or regular. So-called *washable* paper will take only a moderate amount of sponging to remove paste marks left on the surface. Scrubbable wallpaper will withstand fairly hard cleaning. Some paper, especially plain paper, will show *every* spot and require a great deal of care in handling and cleaning.

In the room to be papered, any work on the ceiling should be done before the wallpaper is hung. If the ceiling is to be papered, that should be done before the walls. However, if the ceiling plaster is firm, painting it may be preferable. Because ceilings are difficult to paper, the job requires two people, unless it is done by an experienced paperhanger.

Estimating the Quantity of Wallpaper

Wallpaper usually comes in widths of 18, 20½, 24, and 28 inches (46, 52, 61, 71 cm) after trimming, though some wallpaper may be even wider. Regardless of the width of the paper, a single roll covers 30 square feet (.9 sq. m) of wall space, because narrow widths are longer than broader widths, and what is lost in width is gained in length, and vice versa. To estimate the wallpaper needed to cover the walls of a room, measure the perimeter of the room and multiply it by the height; then deduct 30 square feet (.9 sq. m) for every two doors or two windows or a door and a window. Wallpaper is generally bought by the double or triple roll, because the longer roll cuts to better advantage when the paper has a design.

Most wallpaper is pre-trimmed. However, if the paper does have a selvage, or narrow border along each edge, you will have to cut it off. Always keep leftover wallpaper; you may need to patch an area that gets damaged.

Obtaining Equipment and Supplies

Certain pieces of equipment are essential to the process of wallpapering. If you do not want to invest in all the items listed, you can make the substitutions that are indicated, or rent some items. The following equipment and supplies are basic:

—Patching plaster   This material is used to repair damaged plaster. It is available in small amounts, is easy to mix, and dries fast.

—Scraper and sandpaper   A scraper is needed to scrape rough plaster before sandpapering it, and the sandpaper is needed to smooth out the surface before applying wallpaper.

—Wall sizing   Newly plastered walls require a coat of size, or sizing, in order to make the paper stick.

—Wallpaper paste   Some wallpaper comes prepasted, making paste unnecessary. Otherwise, buy the type of paste recommended for the wallpaper you are using. Mix the paste with water to the consistency of mayonnaise. Make sure that the paste is free of lumps, because lumps will show under the paper.

—Bucket and paste brush   A bucket for paste should have an inside lip that serves to hold the brush out of the paste except when it is in use.

—Water tray   Prepasted wallpaper is soaked in water before being hung. Fill the water tray halfway and place it at the base of the wall. Roll up each wallpaper strip with the design side out and soak for the recommended time, usually about 30 seconds. Then unroll the strip out of the water and smooth it directly onto the wall.

—Table   A large worktable is needed for

TOOLS FOR WALLPAPERING

Stepladder

Plumb line

Old rags

Large table

Wide pasting brush

Paper-hanger's brush

Scissors

Pail for mixing paste

Knife

Yardstick

Old newspapers

measuring and cutting panel lengths and for applying paste.

— Yardstick or meterstick   This item is necessary for measuring panel lengths.

— Shears   Extra-long shears are needed for cutting off the selvage. You can make a sharper and more even edge by cutting along a straight-edge metal strip with a single-edge razor blade or a double-edge razor blade set in a holder.

— Plumb line and chalk   A length of firmly twisted string rubbed with colored chalk and with a weight tied to it at the bottom will serve as a plumb line for establishing a line perpendicular to the floor. Hold the ends taut and snap the cord. The chalk on the cord will mark a perpendicular line on the wall from the ceiling to the baseboard. This line is a guide for placing the edge of the wallpaper.

— Seam roller   This item is used to press seams flat when wallpaper is overlapped or pasted with edges adjoining. A furniture caster or small roller (often inserted in legs of heavy furniture) will suffice if it is clean and smooth.

— Wheel knife   This tool is a small rotary blade with a handle. It is used for trimming paper at baseboards, doors, and window frames. A razor blade inserted in a handle will do a satisfactory job.

— Brush   A long, slender, flexible brush is required for smoothing out the wallpaper on the wall.

— Sponge and bowl   A soft sponge wrung from clear water will be useful in wiping off smudges and paste.

— Stepladder   A sturdy stepladder is needed to stand on and to hold supplies while you are working.

Preparing Surfaces for Papering

The process of preparing walls for wallpapering is the same as preparing them for painting. See page 421 for suggestions about preparing walls for painting, and follow those directions accurately.

Sequence for Working

Hanging wallpaper involves a step-by-step procedure, which must be followed carefully for good results. This procedure is illustrated on these pages. Directions are given with each illustration.

The following suggestions may help you:

— Examine patterned paper to determine at what interval the pattern is repeated. Some patterns repeat straight across the roll, whereas others drop. Some papers may have patterns or repeats that require special consideration. Beginners should avoid using papers with drop matches or complicated patterns.

— If you are using a patterned paper, note where the top of the pattern occurs, and keep all panels parallel, starting at the top.

— When cutting strips, match them from the top and cut each strip long enough to extend over the baseboard slightly. Trim off the excess along the baseboard.

— Before you cut or hang any paper, study the room to see where to begin. It is usually best to begin in a corner behind the entrance door where the final joining will be the least noticed. However, if the wallpaper has a definite pattern, the pattern should be centered in the most prominent spot in the room—for example, over a fireplace or in back of the largest piece of furniture. In applying patterned wallpaper, it is a good idea to mark off the number of panels around the room and to check your wallpaper repeats before beginning to cut the wallpaper.

— If borders are used, they should be hung after all other papering is done.

STEPS IN WALLPAPERING

A. Use plumb line and mark;

B. Apply paste, or, if using pre-pasted wallpaper, dip in water;

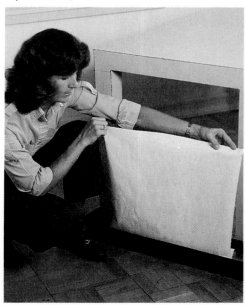

C. Fold wet sides together;

E. Smooth strip with brush;

D. Apply strip to wall;

F. Match next strip to first strip.

LAYING FLOOR TILES

Most resilient floor tiles, such as vinyl ones, can be cut with heavy shears to fit around pipes or to fill in around the edge of a room. Ceramic tiles can be cut with a special tile cutter. Power wet saws can be rented for cutting thick quarry tiles.

Obtaining Equipment and Supplies

Laying tiles, like painting and papering, requires the proper equipment and supplies for good results. It may be possible to rent some pieces of equipment and to improvise substitutes for others. The following items will be helpful:

—Chalk line   This commercial product is a firmly woven cord impregnated with chalk. It is used to establish a straight line on the floor before laying tile.

—Metal square   A square is needed to mark right angles and to use as a guide in laying the tile and checking the placement.

—Sharp knife and heavy shears or tile cutter   These tools are used to cut tiles in fitting them around pipes, wall extensions, and irregular areas around the edge of the floor.

—Adhesive or cement   Use the preparation recommended for the type of tile you are laying, and follow all the directions.

—Spreader   This item or a heavy trowel is needed to spread the thick cement for the tile.

—Roller or rubber mallet   Press resilient tiles in place by bearing down hard on them with a roller. With ceramic tiles, place a piece of plywood over the tiles and tap with a rubber mallet using moderate force.

—Grout and rubber-based grouting float   For ceramic tiles, use the float to work the grout into the joints between the tiles. Sponge grout off of tile surfaces before it dries.

Preparing the Surface

Tiles can be laid directly on smooth concrete or over a felt or paper base on a wood floor, provided the boards are perfectly smooth. On any other type of flooring, a base of plywood or masonite boards must be firmly nailed to the floor, snugly joined, and evenly fitted around the edges before tile can be laid. Ask the dealer from whom you are buying the tile for advice concerning your particular floor and its special requirements.

Sequence for Working

The procedure for laying resilient floor tiles is illustrated on pages 428 and 429. Directions for each step of the process are also given. Study the illustrations and directions carefully before you start to measure the floor and lay the tile. When you have finished, save any extra tiles for patching, because the color and pattern of the tile would be difficult to match later.

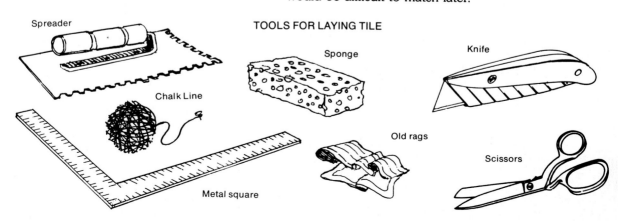

Spreader

TOOLS FOR LAYING TILE

Sponge

Knife

Chalk Line

Old rags

Scissors

Metal square

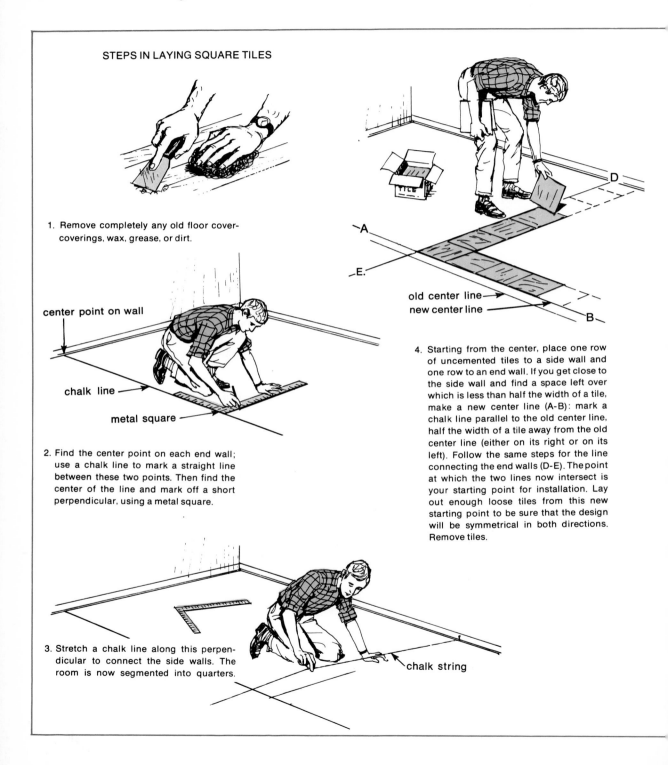

STEPS IN LAYING SQUARE TILES

1. Remove completely any old floor cover-coverings, wax, grease, or dirt.

center point on wall

chalk line

metal square

2. Find the center point on each end wall; use a chalk line to mark a straight line between these two points. Then find the center of the line and mark off a short perpendicular, using a metal square.

3. Stretch a chalk line along this perpendicular to connect the side walls. The room is now segmented into quarters.

chalk string

A
E.
D
B

old center line
new center line

4. Starting from the center, place one row of uncemented tiles to a side wall and one row to an end wall. If you get close to the side wall and find a space left over which is less than half the width of a tile, make a new center line (A-B): mark a chalk line parallel to the old center line, half the width of a tile away from the old center line (either on its right or on its left). Follow the same steps for the line connecting the end walls (D-E). The point at which the two lines now intersect is your starting point for installation. Lay out enough loose tiles from this new starting point to be sure that the design will be symmetrical in both directions. Remove tiles.

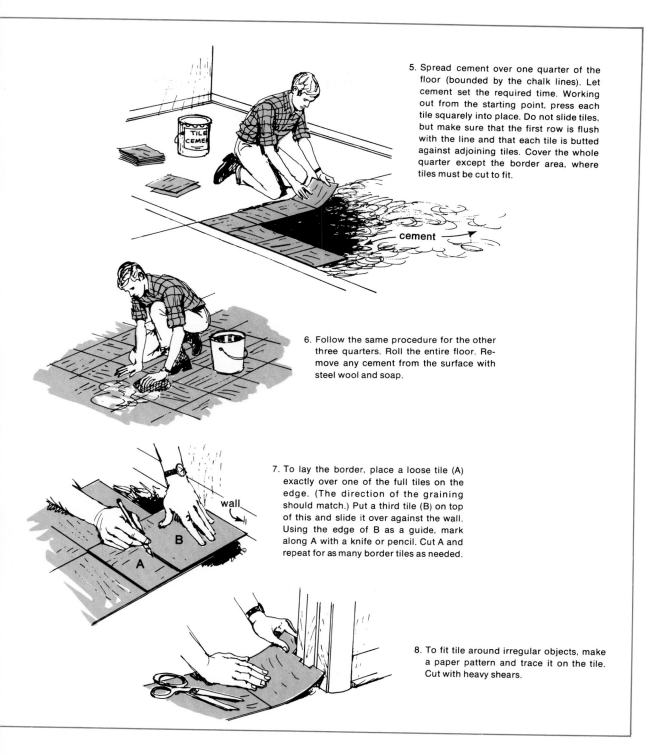

5. Spread cement over one quarter of the floor (bounded by the chalk lines). Let cement set the required time. Working out from the starting point, press each tile squarely into place. Do not slide tiles, but make sure that the first row is flush with the line and that each tile is butted against adjoining tiles. Cover the whole quarter except the border area, where tiles must be cut to fit.

cement

6. Follow the same procedure for the other three quarters. Roll the entire floor. Remove any cement from the surface with steel wool and soap.

7. To lay the border, place a loose tile (A) exactly over one of the full tiles on the edge. (The direction of the graining should match.) Put a third tile (B) on top of this and slide it over against the wall. Using the edge of B as a guide, mark along A with a knife or pencil. Cut A and repeat for as many border tiles as needed.

wall

8. To fit tile around irregular objects, make a paper pattern and trace it on the tile. Cut with heavy shears.

MAKING FABRIC CURTAINS AND SHADES

You can make curtains and shades for the windows in your home. Several styles are easy to sew, and special rings, clips, and pull tapes are available to make the job even easier. By sewing your own curtains and shades, you can select the fabrics, patterns, and colors that you want. In addition, you can save a great deal of money.

Preparations for Making Curtains and Shades

Making curtains or shades requires some planning. Before you select a style, study illustrations in magazines and in publications from manufacturers of drapery fixtures and trimmings. These publications are available for sale in fabric stores or draperies departments of larger stores.

The following guidelines will help you in planning window treatments:
—Determine the curtain length you prefer.
—Measure the windows and record the sizes before measuring and starting to cut the fabric.

—Select 48 inch (1.2 m) instead of 36 inch (.9 m) fabric whenever possible to avoid stitching extra seams.

Shirred Curtains

Cut fabric two to three times as wide as the window and about 4 inches (10 cm) longer to allow for hems. Press and stitch a narrow hem along each side of the fabric. Stitch a 2 inch (5 cm) hem at top and bottom of curtain. Stitch again about ½ inch (1.3 cm.) from edge of fabric at top and bottom to create a casing or tunnel for the curtain rods. Slip tension rods through the top and bottom casings. Place rods on the window frame and distribute the fullness evenly along each rod.

Pouf Curtains

Cut fabric three times as wide as the window and about two-thirds as long. Sew side hems and casings at the top and bottom, following directions for shirred curtains. Insert tension rods into the two casings and adjust fabric fullness. Position the top rod at the top of the window frame. To create the poufed effect, position the bottom rod just under the upper one.

Shirred curtains are gathered onto rods and mounted on the window.

For poufed curtains, the bottom rod is positioned just under the upper rod.

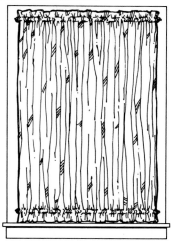

Shirred curtain

Pouf curtain

Café Curtains

Café curtains are hung from clips or rings that slide along a rod or are attached to a traverse café rod. A window can be partially covered by a single set of these short curtains, or an entire window can be covered by using two or three tiers. The top edge of café curtains can be finished in several ways.

Before measuring for café curtains, mount the curtain rods that you will be using. Measure the finished curtain length that you desire. To this measurement, add 6 inches (15 cm) for the top and bottom hems. The width of a café curtain should be two and a half to three times the width of the window.

The first step is to hem the sides of the curtain. Then finish the bottom edge with a 2½ inch (6.3 cm) hem. Turn the raw edge under 1/2 inch (12 mm) and press. Then fold the hem up and stitch.

The simplest way to finish the top edge is to sew a looped tape—a braid trim with fabric loops on it—to the finished hem at the top of the curtain. Then insert a café curtain rod through the loops.

You can make pleated café curtains by using special café curtain clips. Simply hem the top of the curtain. Then fold pleats in at the desired intervals and press the fold. Insert the pleat between two prongs of the three-pronged clip. The two outer prongs fasten to the front side of the curtain; the middle prong fastens to the back.

Pleater tape can also be used to pleat the top of café curtains. Sew the tape to the unfinished curtain top, turn to the inside, and stitch the bottom edge of the tape in place. Insert special pleater hooks into the slots in the tape and hang the curtain on the rod.

Café curtains can also be made with pleats along the top edge.

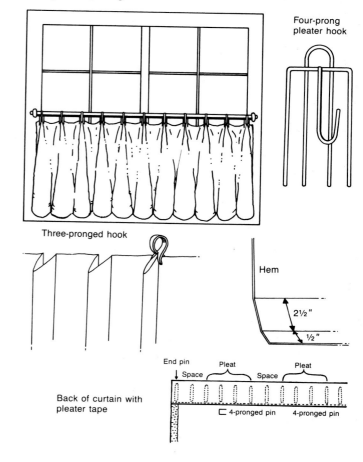

Four-prong pleater hook

Three-pronged hook

Back of curtain with pleater tape

Hem 2½" ½"

Some café curtains are made with special three-pronged hooks.

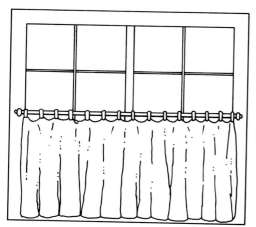

Austrian shades

Austrian shades can be easily made with special shirring tape.

When sewing the strips of tape to the back of the fabric, be sure that the rings on the tapes are horizontally level.

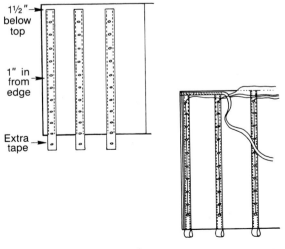

1½" below top

1" in from edge

Extra tape

To complete an Austrian shade, insert cords through the rings and gather together at one side.

Austrian Shades

Austrian shades are drawn up in gathers which form scallops. Before cutting the fabric, determine the length and width of the finished shade. The length to cut should be two to three times the finished length plus an inch for the bottom hem. To the finished width measurement, add 3 inches (7.6 cm) for the side hems, plus 2 to 4 inches (5–10 cm) for each shirred section.

To sew Austrian shades, stitch a 1½ inch (3.8 cm) hem at each side. Then sew a strip of ready-made shirring tape over each side hem, placing the tape 1 inch (2.5 cm) in from the finished edge. Begin 1½ inches (3.8 cm) below the top edge of the fabric and continue sewing the tape to the fabric until 3/8 inches (9 mm) from the bottom edge. Leave a few inches of tape at the bottom for stitching into loops for the rod.

Decide how many scallops you want; this will determine where the rest of the shirring tape should go. The scallops can be from 10 to 15 inches apart (25–38 cm). Stitch the shirring tape to the wrong side of the fabric. Make sure that each strip of tape is the same length and that the rings on the tape are horizontally level. Turn up the excess tape at the bottom and stitch it to make loops. Finish the bottom edge of the shade and insert the rod into the loops.

Next, finish the top edge of the shade. Place small pleats at either side of the shirring tape strips until the shade is the exact width of the window. Stitch a ½-inch (1.3 cm) hem at the top. Sew snap tape or nylon fastening tape directly over the top hem. The other side of the snap or nylon tape is attached above the window.

For each strip of shirring tape, tie a cord to the rod at the bottom and thread it up through the rings and through screw eyes on the window hardware. Gather the cords at one side of the shade. Lower the shade to its full length and knot the cords together at the top. Cut off all cords except the one used to raise the shade.

Roman Shades

Roman shades are very similar to Austrian shades but are drawn up in folds. Although both types are constructed in a similar manner, Roman shades require less than half the amount of fabric.

Cut the fabric at least 3 inches (7.6 cm) longer than the window measurement to allow for the bottom hem. The fabric width should equal the width of the window plus 3 inches (7.6 cm) for the side hems. Two types of pull tape are available for raising the shade. One type has rings sewed to it; the other is tape with punched holes.

Sew Roman shades by stitching the bottom and side hems. Cut each strip of tape 1½ inches (3.8 cm) longer than the finished shade length. Sew a strip of tape to each side edge. Sew additional strips of tape at evenly spaced intervals of 10 to 14 inches (25–35 cm), being sure that the rings or holes are parallel so the shade will pull up evenly. At the bottom, turn up the excess tape to form loops for the rod. Finish the top edge the same as that of the Austrian shade.

Thread the cord or pull tape through the rings or holes just as for the Austrian shade, and tie them together at one side.

Balloon Shades

Balloon shades have extra width and usually require two or more widths of fabric to be stitched together. Box pleats are stitched into the back of the shade to control the fullness, or the shade is gathered onto a curtain rod. Roman shade tape is stitched to the fabric to raise and lower the shade. Refer to a home decorating book for specific directions to make balloon shades.

Roman Shades

Roman shades are constructed in a similar manner to Austrian shades.

Balloon Shades

Balloon shades have extra width which can be controlled by box pleats or gathers.

REMODELING YOUR HOME

With today's high housing costs, more and more homeowners are choosing to remodel their present home instead of moving to another home that better suits their needs. Remodeling involves structural changes. It often means changing or adding to the electrical, plumbing, or heating systems. As a result, remodeling a home is usually an expensive project. For many of these jobs, professional contractors are hired to do some or all of the work. Popular projects include updating a kitchen or bathroom, converting an attic or basement, or adding on one or more rooms to the existing home.

Many people are deciding to do their own remodeling projects. In 1985, over 47 billion dollars was spent on remodeling or renovating residential buildings. According to building industry surveys, 73.5 percent of all American households undertook one or more do-it-yourself projects in 1985. This compared with only 39 percent in 1965. As the number of remodelers has increased, so has the number of publications and special products designed especially for the do-it-yourself market.

By doing most or all of the work themselves, homeowners are able to save a considerable amount of money. However, it is important to evaluate your own skill, interest, energy, and available time before undertaking a remodeling project. Do-it-yourself books are good sources of information. Building supply stores sell special tools and materials, some in kit form, that enable a remodeler to be more successful. Many of these stores have salespeople who can give helpful advice on various aspects of a project. Specific equipment or tools can also be rented for special jobs. Courses on how to complete specific remodeling projects, such as installing kitchen cabinets, are sometimes offered through adult education courses.

Hiring a Contractor

Before hiring a professional contractor for a remodeling job, ask for several references from other jobs. Then contact these references and ask for their evaluation of the contractor's performance. A few contractors are unskilled, unscrupulous, or unethical. A reputable contractor will be happy to provide you with references.

To avoid any misunderstanding and unexpected additional costs it is important that a contract be drawn up and signed by both the contractor and the homeowner. The contract should include a detailed estimate of costs, a listing of what materials will be supplied, and a description of what work will be done. Nothing should be left to an oral agreement that can be changed or misunderstood after the project has begun. For example, when remodeling a kitchen the agreement should list the brands, models, and colors of appliances that will be installed. Different models and colors vary in price. If a new room is being built or an attic is being finished, the agreement should specify whether painting and final cleanup is included in the price. Details such as who will cart away the trash can lead to major disagreements if not clearly stated in the contract.

The traditional way to arrange for remodeling is to hire a general contractor who oversees the whole job. The contractor hires the necessary subcontractors, such as the electricians, plumbers, and tile installers.

Some homeowners decide to act as their own contractor and hire the subcontractors themselves. Sometimes this can save money. However, in many cases the savings never materialize. When acting as your own contractor, you are responsible for scheduling deliveries and for coordinating the work of all the subcontractors. For example, you must arrange that the plumber finishes the installation of the pipes before the tile installer can lay the tiles. Or you must be sure the electrician completes the wiring before the plasterer can finish the walls. If the proper schedule cannot be arranged, delays and higher costs will result. Some subcontractors will charge a homeowner a higher price than a general contractor with whom they have done business in the past and plan to do more business in the future. Also, a general contractor knows of other subcontractors who can be called in if any unexpected problems arise. However, if you have the time and patience, you can successfully act as your own contractor.

When working with a general contractor or subcontractors, it is essential that any changes or additions to the project be stated in writing. For example, when remodeling a kitchen, the homeowner may decide to change the refrigerator to a model that has a built-in ice maker. This means that the plumber will have to run a separate water line to the refrigerator location, resulting in additional costs. If the new tile for the kitchen floor is changed from vinyl to quarry, the cost of both the materials and the installation will be increased substantially. To avoid misunderstanding or unexpected additional costs, ask the contractor for a written statement of exactly how much each change is likely to cost.

Many homeowners are deciding to do their own remodeling projects. If they have the necessary time, interest, and skill, they can save a considerable amount of money.

Remodeling a home can be a most rewarding experience, or it can result in extreme frustration, poor results, and unexpected costs. To be sure that the project will be successful, you must plan carefully, obtain accurate costs, and evaluate the amount of time and skill necessary to complete the project. Whether you decide to do it yourself or hire a contractor, remodeling your home may be the best alternative for meeting the housing needs of your family.

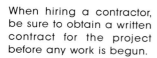

When hiring a contractor, be sure to obtain a written contract for the project before any work is begun.

CARPENTER

Carpenters construct, install, and repair structures and fixtures of wood, plywood, and wallboard. They study blueprints, sketches, and building plans for information about the types of materials required as well as their dimensions. They also must be sure that all materials and methods conform to local building codes.

Carpenters select the specific type of lumber or other materials to be used for construction. Then they prepare the layout of rooms using rulers and frame squares. Cutting and assembly lines are marked on the wood with pencil or chalk. Using saws, chisels, and planes, they must shape the wood to the specified measurements. Then they assembly the sections and fasten them together with nails, dowel pins, or glue. Carpenters use plumb lines and carpenter's levels to verify the vertical and horizontal trueness of a structure.

Depending on the project, carpenters may erect the framework, lay subflooring, build stairs, and install partitions and cabinet work. They may lay hardwood, parquet, and other wood-block floors, as well as install wood paneling or sound absorbant panels on ceilings and walls. Carpenters can fit and install prefabricated window frames, door frames, doors, weather stripping, trim, and hardware, such as handles and locks.

If you are interested in becoming a carpenter, you need good manual and finger dexterity. You should like working with hand tools and power tools and be able to work according to detailed specifications. You need the ability to observe the differences in form, color, and texture.

To become a carpenter, you can take vocational education courses, enter an apprenticeship program, or receive on-the-job training. You can then work for another carpenter as an assistant and eventually be self-employed. Carpenters are hired by general contractors or individual homeowners on a job-by-job basis.

REVIEWING CHAPTER 22

SUMMARY

Home improvement projects can update and enhance the appearance and livability of your home. By knowing how to do these projects, you can save money and gain personal satisfaction from your results.

It is easier to paint, apply wallpaper, and lay floor tiles if you are familiar with the procedures. Before beginning a project, you should estimate the quantity of materials needed, obtain the essential equipment and supplies, and prepare the surfaces. Then do the project in the proper step-by-step sequence to obtain good results.

Several styles of fabric curtains and shades are easy to make if you have basic sewing skills. Special loops, hooks, tapes, and cords are available to make these projects easier.

When remodeling your home, you can do the work yourself or hire a general contractor or subcontractors. Always get a written contract before work begins to avoid any misunderstandings or added costs.

FACTS TO KNOW

1. Explain how to estimate the quantity of paint or wallpaper needed for a room.
2. How should the surfaces be prepared before starting to paint or apply wallpaper?
3. What sequence of tasks should be followed when painting an entire room?
4. Describe the different procedures to use with prepasted wallpaper and with wallpaper that must be pasted.
5. Where should you begin wallpapering a room?
6. What sequence should be followed when laying resilient floor tiles?
7. What amount of fabric and additional materials, if any, would you need to make café curtains?
8. Explain why it is important to obtain a written agreement from a contractor before a remodeling project is begun.

IDEAS TO THINK ABOUT

1. What different reasons might people have for undertaking home improvement projects?
2. Explain the differences in the types of projects you might undertake as a renter and as a homeowner.
3. What type of home improvement project appeals most to you? What experience, if any, have you had in doing this? What kinds of projects might you consider doing for a future home of your own?

ACTIVITIES TO DO

1. Interview someone who has completed a home improvement project. Identify the project, the materials used, and the steps involved. Evaluate the final results in terms of time and energy involved, cost of materials, and benefits.
2. Prepare an estimate of the toal cost for redecorating a room, including wall and ceiling treatments, floor tiles or carpeting, and window treatment.

YOU CAN DO IT!

Enjoy the Outdoors

Bring a feeling of the outdoors into your home, or extend your living space outside. These do-it-yourself projects focus on enjoying the outdoors. Add a skylight or greenhouse window for added light and sunshine. For apartment dwellers, create a mini-garden on a terrace or balcony. In a house, build a deck, patio, or fence to create a special area for entertaining or just relaxing. Children always enjoy having a special play area that is designed just for them.

Install a skylight to let the sun shine in to brighten a room.

Convert a window to a greenhouse and grow plants and herbs all year long.

Turn an apartment terrace into a mini-garden area.

Build a deck and extend your living space to the backyard.

Build a fence to create a private corner in your yard.

Chapter 23

Future Housing Trends

What will homes be like in the year 2000? 2050? 2100? Perhaps some people will be living on floating islands in lakes and oceans, or below ground in deserts, or even on special platforms that float in space. Futurists are making predictions on how we will be living in years to come. Just as with most predictions, some will probably come true and some will not.

One thing is certain: with the rapidly increasing world population, there will be a growing need for additional housing in all parts of the world. What designs will best meet the needs of future individuals and families? With scarcity of land, where should new housing be built? With rapidly increasing costs, how can affordable housing be provided for all people? How can technology be used to make the dream of decent housing for everyone come true?

Shelter is one of the basic needs of people. Today's homes also help meet many other needs and desires, such as comfort, safety, relaxation, privacy, socialization, and self-expression. How will future housing trends change in relation to shifts in population, lifestyles, availability of resources, and economic conditions? Only time will tell.

PREVIEWING YOUR LEARNING

After you have read this chapter, you will be able to:
- Identify factors that influence where and how people live.

- Describe changes in the family that affect housing needs.

- Give examples of current and future trends in types of housing, housing design, construction methods, and new materials.

- Discuss the influence of high technology on the housing industry and homes of the future.

TERMS TO KNOW

automated—to operate by mechanical or electronic devices

cellular—containing cavities; having a porous texture

computerized—to carry out, control, or produce by means of a computer

elevation—an architectural drawing of the side view or vertical view of a building

high technology—computerized and automated methods used to produce objects and accomplish tasks

robot—an automatic device or machine that performs functions ordinarily done by human beings

spa—a place with facilities for exercising and bathing

time-sharing—purchasing a vacation home only for a specific number of weeks per year

HOME COMPUTERS

**F
E
A
T
U
R
E**

How are computers useful in the home? A computer is primarily a machine that stores and organizes information. It can be used to monitor household budgets, balance bank accounts, maintain tallies of tax data needed for IRS returns, keep a running inventory of valuables for insurance documentation, as well as educate and entertain children. And that's just the start. Personal computers can be adapted to give the homeowner immediate access to whole worlds of information. The addition of a modem (a device that connects the home system to the outside world over telephone lines) brings the problem-solving capabilities of national data services right into the home.

A computer system is made up of a number of components. It is not necessary to purchase all parts at once. The basic piece of equipment is the keyboard containing the central processing unit or CPU—the "brain" that carries out instructions and interprets data. The CPU is hooked up to a video display terminal. Some CPUs can be used with your own television. A disk drive or cassette recorder is used to store and retrieve information. It plays preprogrammed programs or software that you design yourself. A printer records data on paper.

Before purchasing a home computer, decide how you want to use it. Use determines what memory capacity your computer should have. Visit several computer dealers until you find one willing to take the time to explain the different models to you and help you design a system that fits your needs.

WHAT WILL HOUSING BE LIKE IN THE FUTURE?

We cannot predict what housing will look like one hundred years from now any more than those who watched the Wright brothers' first flight could have predicted the space age rockets of today. Changes in technology are occurring so rapidly that people of the future may live on a different planet or in homes built of materials not yet invented. Just as only a few people have been to the moon and many others have still not traveled on an airplane, history indicates that even if some people live on Mars, many others will still be on earth living in homes very much like the ones we have today.

Some Europeans are living in houses built over two hundred years ago. Often the same family has lived in the same house for generations. In general, basic house design and construction have been the same for centuries, except for the addition of conveniences such as heat, electricity, and plumbing. One reason for this is that new housing is just added to our current housing supply, it does not replace it. Therefore, new housing designs become a very small part of our total housing supply.

Today, over 60 percent of our housing structures are freestanding, single-family houses. Given a choice, most families would probably select this type of housing if it were available and affordable. Also, people tend to like the styles that they grew up with or have become accustomed to. New ideas take time to be accepted, if they are accepted at all. Radical housing designs have been offered in the past but have been met with public resistance. For example, dome houses made of connected igloo-type units, designed to provide inexpensive housing, were rejected. Such extreme styles do not fit into most existing neighborhoods and may be accepted only in remote areas.

In the future, certain factors will continue to influence how and where people will live. Some of these influences are economic costs, changes in the family, and job opportunities.

Economic Costs

The high cost and scarcity of available land are influencing housing design. Houses are being built on smaller and smaller lots. Attached houses and multi-family buildings are being built in suburban communities and smaller towns, not just in urban areas. In the future, land will become even more expensive.

Because of housing shortages and the high cost of new housing, many families are deciding not to move to another home when their housing needs change. Instead, they are remodeling their present homes by updating kitchens and bathrooms, converting attics and basements, and adding on rooms. This trend is expected to continue.

Because of the high cost of available land, more housing designs will be clustered or attached. As a result, more housing units can be built on one acre of land than if each unit was a one-family free-standing house.

Housing budgets are also influenced by the tax structure within a community or state. Adjacent communities may have very different real estate tax rates. When planning where to live, people must add the taxes they must pay to the mortgage cost. Some states have no income tax which enables people to spend more on their housing budgets.

Mortgage rates have a huge impact on the long-term costs of buying a home. When mortgage rates are high, fewer people can afford to purchase homes. When mortgage rates drop, money becomes available and more people are able to enter the housing market.

The cost of a house or apartment will also depends on its size, the size of the property, the materials used, the quality of the construction, its condition, and the age and condition of the basic systems such as the heating, electrical, and plumbing systems. The style of the home may also affect its cost. If you can make any needed repairs or renovations yourself, you can save money by purchasing a home that

The location of a home affects its cost. This rural ranch house may cost only one-half the price of an identical ranch house in a city suburb.

This couple is in their 30s and is looking to buy an apartment or house now that they have a child. Since they were married, they have saved regularly for a down payment on their own home.

This elderly couple is concerned about where they will live in the coming years when they are no longer able to maintain their own house by themselves.

needs improvements. Many families are purchasing older houses, apartments, and other living spaces, such as lofts, and restoring them. Many of these homes can be purchased very reasonably, have large, high-ceilinged rooms with extra space, and are conveniently located to transportation and work.

Changes in the Family

New houses are built with the characteristics of their future residents in mind. Our society has experienced major changes in the makeup of families. These changes will be reflected in the new housing that will be built.

In general, today's families are smaller. The average household contains only 2.75 persons. People are postponing marriage and postponing having children. Traditionally, houses are bought after the birth of the first child so first-time homeowners tend to be older now. At all age levels, the number of single-person households has rapidly increased. Many single people, with different housing needs than families with children, are choosing to buy houses or condominiums.

Both spouses of many of today's young couples work. Therefore, they are often willing to allot a higher percentage of their income for housing than was usual in the past. They also have less time to devote to the upkeep of their homes. People are more financially aware of the costs and benefits of home ownership as a form of investment. When a couple is ready to buy a house or an apartment, they generally have saved enough for the down payment and are willing to accept a larger mortgage. Families are more mobile than in the past and are often willing to move to a different part of the country for job and career opportunities. This results in different housing demands in different areas.

Due to ever-increasing life expectancy, there will be an increasing number of elderly people—singles and couples—for whom housing will be necessary. While retirement villages and community housing for the aged are two possibilities, many elderly people prefer to stay in their own homes. In some families, elderly parents move in with their adult children and space must be provided. More and more families have three generations living together as older children continue to live at home and grandparents move in too.

Today, an increasing number of families are headed by single parents. For these families, the financial costs and responsibilities involved in the upkeep of a home have become critical factors. Often there is limited income and little available time that can be spent on meeting the housing needs of the family.

Job Opportunities

The location of your employment is usually a determining factor in where you choose to live. While some people are willing to commute for long hours to their job, most people prefer to live relatively close to their workplace. As urban housing has become more scarce and more expensive, many families have been forced to live further and further from their work location. The availability, cost, and condition of public transportation also influence people's choices as to whether they are willing to commute to work.

In many areas, job opportunities are growing in suburban and outlying areas. This has resulted in changing housing needs as employees who live in the city want to move to suburban communities.

Within our country, job opportunities are constantly shifting and changing. During the past few years, there has been a steady population increase in the Sunbelt states as job opportunities developed. This brought about a construction boom of new housing in many southern areas. However, some major industries, such as the oil industry, have experienced periods of great growth followed by recessions and job layoffs. As a result, the housing demands have also fluctuated depending on the job opportunities in a particular area.

There is a boom in housing construction in many Sunbelt areas due to increased job opportunities.

This garden apartment complex seeks to attract young adults. It offers a swimming pool, two tennis courts, and an activities center where programs and parties are held.

NEW DEVELOPMENTS IN HOUSING

Builders are responding to the changing housing needs of families and individuals in many different ways. Increasing numbers of housing units are being built that are not freestanding, single-family homes. A wider variety of housing designs are being offered to help meet the vast range of space and price requirements of different people. New and faster construction methods are being developed that can provide new housing in less time and at lower cost. New materials and equipment are being developed that will increase energy efficiency, require little maintenance, and operate the home more effectively. Some of these new developments are being widely used; others are only in the experimental stage.

Types of Housing

With ever-increasing land and construction costs, cluster developments and multi-family housing units are usually more affordable than traditional single-family houses built on individual lots. These types of housing require less land and have lower construction costs per unit. In addition, they offer more security for their residents than freestanding houses that are located at a distance from their neighbors' homes.

Town houses and garden apartments appeal to singles and couples of all ages. They have the added advantage that all maintenance and upkeep services are provided by the management. Some developments or complexes are specially designed to appeal to specific age groups, such as young adults or retirees. They may include special features such as swimming pools, tennis courts, community centers, or support rails for the physically disabled. Some of these complexes discourage or even forbid families with young children from living there.

Within many cities and suburban areas, the growth of condominium and cooperative apartments continues to increase. These provide the financial and emotional advantages of home ownership, plus the convenience of apartment living. This style of living is appealing to many young couples who have dual incomes as well as older couples whose children are no longer living at home. Often these apartments are located within easy reach of job opportunities.

With increased leisure time for many individuals and families, builders are offering many different types of vacation homes. Some people buy these second homes to use for part of the year; others buy them strictly for investment purposes. The owners can hire rental agents to handle all arrangements for renting the vacation house or apartment whenever the owners do not plan to use it.

Time-sharing vacation homes have become popular in many resort areas. The cost for each property is divided into 52 segments—one for each week in the year. You then purchase a specific number of weeks; this determines your cost. For example, if you select two weeks you will pay 2/52 of the total cost of the home, and you will be able to use the home for those specific two weeks each year for the length of your ownership. Usually, the costs are adjusted so that people who choose weeks during the height of the resort season pay more per week than someone who purchases one or more weeks during the off-season. These properties can be purchased with a mortgage.

Time-share apartments and houses are completely furnished and have cleaning services to prepare the unit for the next owner's arrival. However, there are also several disadvantages to time-share ownership. You are limited to going to the same place at the same time each year. If you decide to go somewhere else, you do not get any reimbursement, although some time-share properties offer an exchange service with other resort areas. Also, the value of the time-share property depends not only upon the maintenance and upkeep of the grounds but of the individual units as well. Since they may each have 52 different owners using them per year, you are dependent upon many people's neatness and sense of responsibility.

Time-share apartments are sold on a weekly basis. Each year you can use your apartment for the specific week or weeks that you purchased.

Some housing designs feature combined living, dining, and kitchen areas. These open layouts are multifunctional centers for family living.

Housing Designs

The traditional-style house is still the most popular with home buyers. Most new houses are being built with traditional exteriors, such as Cape Cod, Southern Colonial, Spanish Mission, or expanded ranch. Adaptations in design are made to include new features such as added windows, porches, or decks, but the basic exterior retains a traditional look. Contemporary designs are the second most popular with home buyers, especially in newer communities. Modern or high tech housing appeals to the smallest group of homeowners. Although modern designs win many architectural awards, they continue to have limited appeal.

More design changes are taking place inside the home rather than outside. Floor plans are becoming more open, with space flowing together to create multifunction rooms. At the heart of the new design is the main room: a space that combines kitchen, dining, and living areas into a center for family living.

Kitchens and bathroom designs have been through many changes. Sleek, European-style kitchen cabinets in light colors are very popular today. Countertops need no longer be cluttered since storage areas for all small equipment and supplies are built in. Microwave ovens—in addition to conventional ovens—are being considered a basic appliance. A wide range of new floor and wall coverings and countertop materials that require very little care are being introduced.

A highly desirable type of bathroom today is a spa—a large room with a whirlpool bath, sauna, exercise equipment, and other fitness items. A separate dressing area may also be included. These new bathrooms are designed to be a luxurious retreat where a person can work out or relax.

Greenhouses and solariums are becoming popular additions to both new and remodeled homes. A new term is being used to describe these glassed-in areas of homes—*sunspaces*. Bigger windows, glass patio doors, and skylights help to admit more sunlight and open up homes to the outdoors. Backyards are becoming additional areas for living space with the construction of patios, decks, verandas, hot tubs, and whirlpools. Fireplaces continue to be popular, and many new homes have more than one.

Some new floor plans include separate living wings that can be used by elderly parents or adult children who still live at home. Bedrooms can be located at opposite ends of a home to provide extra privacy for different family members or guests.

Thus, new housing des᠍᠍.᠍᠍ns are reflecting changing family lifestyles in many different ways. Gone are boxy, single-purpose rooms. Instead, the use of space is being redesigned to better meet the needs and activities of today's homeowners.

An indoor sunspace with glass walls and southern exposure is an ideal location in which to relax or enjoy activities.

New Construction Methods

High technology is being used in the housing industry in order to produce homes faster and more efficiently and at less cost. Computers are being used to draw or customize house plans. Computer-controlled assembly lines are producing many different housing components. Someday, it may be possible to design, produce, and assemble entire housing units by computerized systems.

CADD house plans Computer-aided-design-and-drafting (CADD) systems are being used in many architectural firms. Designs on computers can be created quickly and accurately. Special computer programs that can create such designs are now available for use with personal computers. These enable an architect working at home or in a small office to draw designs freehand or to choose from an array of shapes and patterns stored in the program.

With a computer, an architect can increase or decrease the various rooms within a floor plan in seconds. Special design features, such as an extra closet, can be easily added or deleted. A floor plan can be flipped instantly to see if the reverse layout is preferred. Different exterior designs can be drawn in only a few minutes and can be evaluated immediately. For example, with computer drafting, an architect can create four different elevations, or side-view drawings, of the same house. Each elevation can have a different type of exterior siding and different window arrangements.

Computer-modified plans Today, you can buy basic house plans from a computer-assisted planning service. Then you can note any changes you would like on the plans, such as relocating windows and doors, changing window sizes and styles, or enlarging the home. The marked up plans go to a computer center and in two or three weeks your computer-revised plans are returned to you. The plans include elevations, materials and cutting lists, and printouts detailing the construction methods. Computer-modified plans for remodeling or planning kitchens are available through some stores. The salesperson enters data about your kitchen into a computer and printouts are provided of the floor plan, elevations, a list of needed cabinets, and the prices.

Assembly line houses Within a few years, over one-fourth of all new homes will be built in factories and assembled on-site. The required components would be factory fabricated in the two weeks before construction, while the foundation is being poured. Within 40 days, the new homeowners can move in.

The assembly lines of the future will be highly automated with the work performed by computerized equipment or robots. The quality will be carefully controlled. One assembly line will produce frames for walls, floors, and roofs. Another will produce wall panels using automatic nailers and will automatically install the plywood and insulation. Robots will weld components together, making two hundred welds in about eight minutes. Or they will move components from one section to another. A large warehouse will hold completed housing components in several thousand individual cubicles, and computers can be used to selectively pull together the inventory for any home design. The entire facility can be operated by a single worker at a computer terminal.

Automated factories are already producing housing units in Japan and Sweden. Some factories specialize in modular fabrication of individual housing components, such as walls and ceilings. Other factories produce housing modules that are then shipped to the site and erected, by crane, in four to five hours by a five-man crew. A completed house requires 12 to 17 modules.

Do-it-yourself house kits are also being created in factories. Logs literally come in one end of the factory and packaged kits go out the other. A house plan can be punched into a computer which then calculates exactly how much wood is needed and can direct the manufacturing process through production. The shell of a kit house can be erected in only two days.

New Materials and Their Uses
Traditional construction materials will continue to be used in the future, though sometimes in new ways. One award-winning design features a wood house with a

Architects use computers for designing and drafting.

skin of bolt-on plywood panels. Cellular concrete—a mixture of sand, cement, and foam—can be precast into panels and used to make the frame of a house.

Concrete has also been used in an experimental round house where it is poured without any seams or joints. Once the molds are in place, it takes only about four hours to pump in the concrete. When it sets, the molds are removed.

Plastics will continue to be used in many different forms in all areas of housing construction. Even dirt is gaining attention as a possible building material. Bricks are being molded out of earth using rammed-earth technology.

New construction materials are being designed to incorporate some form of insulation for energy efficiency. Sheathing is being made with layers of polyurethane foam or polystyrene for insulation. Doors are made with foam interiors. There is even an insulated lightweight concrete that includes foam or wood chips which cut down on heat loss. Foam-core wall and roof panels are made with advanced energy-saving technology. Quad-pane windows are proving more efficient for sunrooms than double-pane windows because the three insulating air spaces help retard direct transfer of heat through the windows to the outside.

Automated assembly lines can produce housing components or entire modular units.

INSIDE A HOME OF THE FUTURE

In the future, homes will probably have fewer rooms, but each room will be large and designed for several activities. Furniture will be more multi-purpose and will easily convert from one use to another. Such items as chairs and tables will be stackable so that they are readily available if needed but will free up space if stacked. Furniture will be designed to fit the human body rather than for appearance's sake alone. It will be possible to have plastic-framed furniture molded directly to your own body shape.

Computers will be used to monitor and control all the systems within a home. They will dim or brighten the lights and regulate the air-conditioning, heating, and air-purifying systems. They will be able to handle all forms of communication and provide increased security and convenience. The housing industry forecasts that such systems will be in many homes by 1995.

Some of these computer systems will respond to speech and voice recognition, others to touch. Many will be able to be controlled by telephone contact. Some systems will diagnose problems and suggest what is needed to fix them. One system will even be able to communicate in speech over the phone.

Household appliances will be able to communicate with the home's central computer. When a clothes dryer completes its cycle, it will no longer ring a bell or buzzer. Instead, it will communicate with the computer, and you will be informed of its completion via video monitors installed throughout the house. Appliances will recognize voices and obey commands. They will even be controlled long distance by a telephone call. Appliances may also be able to communicate with a central electrical system that monitors the energy needs for each appliance. When plugged in, each appliance will receive just enough power to make it work. Energy will be conserved, and the electrical system will be shock-proof and fireproof. Obviously, such complex systems mean that all manufacturers will have to work together to produce compatible appliances.

The home of tomorrow may be called a "smart house." Speak, and it will listen. Command, and it will control a variety of devices throughout the home. In addition, it will pass along information to you through a speaker system at the appropriate time. The use of computers, microprocessors, sensors, and robots to monitor and care for a home is one of the most exciting future prospects in housing technology.

The home-of-the-future will be monitored and controlled by a central computer system.

CAREER PROFILE

HOME ECONOMIST

Home economists work in one or more areas related to personal and family living: housing and home furnishings, food and nutrition, textiles and clothing, family relationships, child development, and consumer issues. Home economists may work in education, the extension service, or in business.

Home economics teachers prepare course outlines and lesson plans, demonstrate procedures, assign lessons, and correct projects and homework. They may teach at junior high or middle schools, high schools, vocational schools, or colleges and universities. High school home economics teachers may also serve as advisors to student groups, such as Future Homemakers of America (FHA) or Home Economics Related Occupations (HERO). College teachers and professors are also expected to conduct research and write articles for scholarly publications. Some adult education teachers are home economists. They teach courses in particular skills, such as cooking, sewing draperies, or refinishing furniture, that are usually offered in the evenings.

The Cooperative Extension Service is a division of the U.S. Department of Agriculture and has offices in every state and almost every county. Extension home economists are county extension agents with home economics degrees. They write leaflets and newspaper articles, conduct workshops, and work with 4-H and other youth groups. Some have regular radio or television programs. Many states have a housing specialist who is affiliated with the state's land grant university. The specialists train the extension home economists and develop a wide variety of programs on housing and home furnishings.

Home economists in business are employed by a wide variety of companies, including manufacturers of food, appliances, and personal products; textile and pattern companies; advertising and public relations agencies; magazine and book publishers; and financial institutions. Some specialize in research, product development, consumer education, writing, or advertising. Home economists can also be self-employed and write articles or brochures, coordinate projects, and demonstrate products for various clients.

If you are interested in becoming a home economist, you should like working with people. The characteristics necessary for a career in education, extension, or business are very similar. You must be able to communicate effectively, both orally and in writing. You need to know your subject thoroughly and have the desire and ability to share that knowledge with others.

To enter this field, you must obtain a college degree with a major in home economics. In addition, teachers must also take education courses and obtain their teaching certificate. Some states require teachers to have a fifth year of college or a master's degree.

REVIEWING CHAPTER 23

SUMMARY

Although no one can predict exactly what housing will be like in the future, certain trends and factors will influence new housing developments. Available land will become more scarce and expensive. Economics factors, such as housing costs and mortgage rates will continue to influence where and how people live. The many changes taking place in the family will also have a strong impact on housing needs. Current trends show an increase in smaller families, single-person households, dual-income families, single-parent families, and multi-generational families. Longer life expectancy will mean more housing will be needed for the elderly. Job opportunities will also influence the availability of housing.

As a result, more housing units are being built that are not single-family homes. Designs are changing more rapidly inside the home than outside. New construction methods include computerized drafting and automated assembly lines. In the home of tomorrow, a computer will monitor and control all household systems.

FACTS TO KNOW

1. What effect does the availability of land have on housing?
2. List four reasons why housing costs for similar housing may vary from one region to another.
3. Describe three trends in today's family structure that affect housing needs.
4. How do job opportunities influence housing choices?
5. What is *time-sharing*?
6. Describe how housing designs are changing. Are more changes occurring in the exterior design or the interior design?
7. How are computers being used to create house plans?
8. In what ways might the automated assembly line change construction methods in the housing industry?

IDEAS TO THINK ABOUT

1. Why are contemporary or modern housing designs less popular with home buyers than traditional designs?
2. What impact may high technology have on job opportunities in the housing field?
3. What special features would you want in a computer-controlled home? What disadvantages might there be if everything is operated by a computer?

ACTIVITIES TO DO

1. Design a "home of the future." Draw both the floor plan and the exterior elevation.
2. Research articles on the use of high technology in the fields of housing, home furnishings, or appliances. How are computerized and automated systems being used presently? What experimental designs or methods have been developed? What are some of the predictions for the future? Share your findings with the class.

Chapter 24

Careers in Housing and Home Furnishings

The fields of housing and home furnishings offer many opportunities for careers. Some of these careers are professional and technical, some are supervisory and managerial, and many of them are service-oriented. With so many opportunities available, how does a .person choose a career in these fields?

It is important to learn as much as you can about the jobs that interest you the most. There are many ways that you can do this:

- Talk with a vocational teacher in your school or a representative from a vocational or technical school about careers that you are thinking of choosing.
- Visit a local business where there are jobs that interest you.
- Interview a person who is employed in an occupation for which you want information.
- Visit your school library and read books, brochures, and pamphlets on occupations.
- Ask friends and family members about jobs they know about and can describe to you.
- Watch a filmstrip about a job that interests you.
- Take an after-school or summer job, either paid or unpaid, to gain experience.

PREVIEWING YOUR LEARNING

After you have read this chapter, you will be able to:

* Analyze your interests and abilities, and other personal resources.

* Locate information about different careers.

* Identify career opportunities that relate to the fields of housing and home furnishings.

* Describe the training or experience that is necessary in order to obtain a job in a particular field.

TERMS TO KNOW

apprenticeship—learning a trade by practical experience under the supervision of skilled workers

aptitude—natural ability

internship—gaining supervised practical experience in a professional field

merchandising—comprehensive sales promotion that includes market research, product development, marketing, advertising, and selling

professional—relating to a vocation that requires specialized knowledge and often long and intensive academic preparation

promotion—an organized or specific effort made to further the sale of merchandise through advertising and publicity

proprietor—owner

superintendent—one who is in charge or has responsibility

trade—an occupation that requires manual or mechanical skill

vocation—the work in which a person is regularly employed; occupation

LAURA ASHLEY: SUCCESS FROM SMALL BEGINNINGS

F E A T U R E

Small-scaled prints, ruffles, lace trim, and back-to-nature colors—these are the elements that create the countrified look of Laura Ashley designs. Believing that there is always a place for tradition in contemporary living, she designed fabric, wallpaper, home furnishings, and clothing that express English country charm.

Laura Ashley was born in Wales in 1925. After finishing school, she served in the Women's Royal Naval Service during World War II. Following the war, she lived in London and worked as a secretary. With encouragement from friends and neighbors, for whom she often made various kitchen accessories by hand, she and her husband founded the Laura Ashley Company in 1953. Production began right on their own kitchen table, using silk screens to print placemats, tea towels, and scarves.

Later, Ashley returned to her native Wales, where the business grew by leaps and bounds. Finding new inspiration in her native countryside, she designed clothing to add to her line of household textiles. With her husband's expertise in business matters and her own wonderful gift for design, success came naturally. In 1969, Laura Ashley opened her first retail shop in London and in 1974, the first Laura Ashley shop was opened in the United States. There are now 70 shops in the United States, over 220 worldwide, and the family-owned business employs over 4,000 people. Although Laura Ashley died in 1985, her prints continue to influence interior design and home furnishings around the world.

ANALYZING PERSONAL RESOURCES

Whatever career you choose, you should try to match your interests, abilities, and other personal resources to the job requirements. First of all, you should understand yourself—your special abilities, interests, preferences, skills, health, and ambitions—so that you can find the job that will provide the greatest satisfaction or offer the greatest challenge.

What are your interests? Have you enjoyed any special hobbies or part-time work? Do the things you enjoy most relate to being with people or working alone, working indoors or outdoors, traveling or not, and doing routine or creative work? Do you enjoy being competitive, taking risks, accepting challenges?

What special skills have you developed? Do you work well with people, ideas, or objects? Do you like work that requires patience and perseverance? Are you good at organizing work? Do you have initiative? Are you creative with your mind and hands?

Is your health or physical endurance equal to your work objectives? Some jobs require strenuous outdoor work in all kinds of weather. Some jobs mean being on your feet all day or stooping, bending, crawling. Some jobs mean working under tension for long periods.

What are your lifetime goals? It may be wise to identify your long-range goals in terms of career, avocations, and personal life. These goals may suggest a particular direction. With that knowledge, you can set up short-term goals for securing training and experience that will lead to your ultimate goal while also fulfilling other goals. If you are ambitious and want to advance in your career, you must be prepared to work very hard and devote additional time to gaining training, education, and experi-

ence. For example, a person starting as a carpenter, plumber, or electrician or in any other skilled trade may eventually become a supervisor or even own a construction company. A draftsman or surveyor may be able to take evening classes to become an engineer or architect. A clerk or stock worker in a store may become a buyer or manager. How intensively you want to pursue your career is your decision.

CHOOSING A CAREER

If you are interested in a career related to any aspect of housing or home furnishings, you have a wide choice of jobs. About 80 percent of these jobs do not require a college degree. Some jobs are available

Vocational education courses in high school offer an opportunity for learning more about different careers.

PERSONAL APTITUDES AND PREFERENCES

1. Do you prefer to work

_____ alone?   _____ with ideas?
_____ with a partner?   _____ with numbers?
_____ with a small group?   _____ with machines?
_____ with a team?   _____ with tools?
_____ with a large group?   _____ with materials?
_____ with your hands?   _____ with designs?

2. Do you like to

_____ organize?   _____ advance in career levels?
_____ supervise?   _____ paint large areas?
_____ carry out plans?   _____ paint art works?
_____ manage?   _____ draw?
_____ assume responsibility?   _____ work with measurements?
_____ be free of responsibility?   _____ study over long periods?
_____ remain at one career level?   _____ experiment with anything?

3. Would you be happy with

_____ a desk job?   _____ a job in a factory?
_____ moving about in a small space?   _____ a job in a small shop?
_____ moving about in a large space?   _____ a job in a testing laboratory?
_____ working on your feet all day?   _____ working in the same place?
_____ a job in a store?   _____ working in different places?

4. Would you like a job that is

_____ routine?   _____ competitive?
_____ varied?   _____ uncompetitive?
_____ creative?   _____ demanding?
_____ challenging?   _____ undemanding?

5. Would you like to be

_____ self-employed?   _____ employed by a large company?
_____ employed by a small company?   _____ an employer of others?

6. Will your health affect your career choices? If so, how?

7. Will family obligations affect your choices? If so, how?

through on-the-job training and apprenticeship programs. Under most of these arrangements, you earn while you learn. Distributive education programs in high school lead to jobs in merchandising and other fields. Through the U.S. Department of Health, Education, and Welfare, experience-based education or internships in numerous career fields are available.

Another entry method is through specialized training at a vocational, technical, business, or art school. This training leads to jobs in drafting, surveying, real estate, construction work, designing, and mid-management opportunities in housing and home maintenance. If you have health, ambition, and time, you can continue your education at evening school or take correspondence courses to increase your chances for promotion. Continuing education and experience are helpful in securing higher-level jobs in housing construction, maintenance, and management. A college education is necessary for careers in architecture, engineering, teaching, counseling, and many upper-level managerial jobs. Again, the courses required as preparation may be taken in part-time study, evening classes, and work-study programs as well as in full-time study.

Finding Career Information

Once you know what vocations or careers you are most interested in, you will want information about them. Start by making an appointment with your guidance or career counselor to learn all you can about opportunities in your field. The career section in the local library will have information about on-the-job training and special training programs, as well as the courses available at nearby technical and vocational schools and community colleges. Your library should also have books related to careers. The *Occupational Handbook,* published by the U.S. Department of Labor, and the *Encyclopedia of Careers*

Career information is available from your school, local library, newspapers, and other resources.

and Vocational Guidance, published by the J. G. Ferguson Company, are particularly helpful. Be sure to ask for the current editions.

Find out where the nearest state employment office is located and what jobs are handled by the office. The trade unions in various fields of construction have information about training programs and job opportunities. In addition, there may be a trade association of building contractors and suppliers that can advise you. The yellow pages of the telephone directory and newspaper Help Wanted ads are also sources of information about opportunities in many areas of housing.

Obtaining Training

Courses in high school that relate to careers in housing are interior design, family living, art, consumer education, psychology, merchandising, business accounting, drafting, and wood- and metal-working. Many people learn construction skills on the job, but it is also possible to work into a job through an apprenticeship program. Apprenticeship training is available to men and women from age 17 through 27 and to veterans over 27. The training runs from two to five years, depending upon the complexity of the job. Beginning salaries are about 40 to 50 percent of salaries for qualified workers. Apprenticeship training is available through joint labor-management programs registered with the U.S. Labor Department's Bureau of Apprenticeship and Training and through private employers in specialized areas such as textile construction, silk screen printing, and furniture making and cabinetmaking. The military services have in-service training in drafting, surveying, and skilled trades.

One- and two-year courses at vocational, technical, art, and business schools and two-year community colleges prepare students for entry at middle levels in many occupations related to housing and home furnishings. Courses in two-year community colleges may be credited toward a degree.

Gaining Experience

Any summer or part-time experience you can obtain will be valuable in applying for a job after training. Among the possibilities are office work; work in the construction industry; work at a hotel, motel, or resort; selling or keeping stock in a department, fabric, hardware, or furniture store; and work at a lumberyard, furniture factory, mill, nursery, or lawn-care establishment. You may find newspaper ads for summer or part-time work in housing construction, maintenance, or repairs.

Some young people organize crews to do housecleaning, care for lawns, paint, or make simple repairs. Volunteer service in hospitals, nursing homes, child-care centers, and community projects provide valuable experience in getting along with people, sensing their needs, and becoming familiar with the institution and its opportunities. Experience, together with a knowledge of opportunities in the areas of housing and home furnishings, will help you with career decisions.

CAREER OPPORTUNITIES

At some point in exploring careers, you may want to consider a wide range of possibilities. Always, there may be interesting fields that have escaped your attention. At this point, an in-depth review of opportunities in the fields related to housing would be valuable. The most important job areas related to housing, together with their requirements, are described in the section that follows.

Construction

The demands for all kinds of construction, including the construction of houses and apartment buildings, is expected to expand for at least the next five years. This means that the outlook is good for jobs in architecture, engineering, and management. The prospects are also good for surveyors, draftsmen, and people skilled in the construction trades. These trades include bricklayers, carpenters, masons, dry-wallers, electricians, floor-cover installers, insulation workers, lathers, equipment operators, painters, paperhangers, plasterers, plumbers, roofers, and tile setters.

Planning The careers in the construction industry that require a higher education for entry are those of the planners—architects and engineers, aided by surveyors and draftsmen. Architects may be self-employed, they may contract their services, or

Large construction projects involve a wide variety of occupations.

In planning large buildings architects often make scale models to represent the design.

Land-use planning is another aspect of housing and construction. Environmental impact studies are often required for large-scale development.

they may be employed by an architectural firm, a land-development contractor, or a real estate company. An architect's job ranges from working with a client in building or remodeling a single-family home to planning a high-rise apartment building or drawing up plans for a large open-space development. Some architects specialize in residential planning; others specialize in planning schools, hospitals, and other institutions, or in urban design and development. Another area of specialization is landscape architecture, ranging from landscaping highways, golf courses, and shopping malls to designing for open-space or planned-unit developments.

In addition to providing blueprints with floor plans, side elevations, and detailed drawings, the architect may be required to present color renditions and models, or miniature three-dimensional representations, of the project. A person who specializes in model making is often issued a contract to prepare a model.

Architectural training includes design skills, graphics (blueprints, diagrams, and charts), architectural and engineering principles, urban planning, the history of architecture, the use of building materials, and business theory. Personal qualifications are keen intelligence, creative and scientific aptitudes, interest in detail, business ability, and an interest in people. Deadlines often require working under tension. A five-year college course leading to a bachelor's degree is required at entry level, or the position of junior architect. Before starting to practice, an architect must pass an examination and obtain a license. The next levels are senior architect and designer. Many architects hope to be partners in a firm.

Engineers often consult with or work with architects on large projects. The engineering field is highly specialized. Civil engineers are responsible for site planning, land design, drainage and sewage systems, and large-scale construction projects such as building roads and bridges. Structural engineers are concerned with how well the land and skeleton framework will support a building, as well as the stresses and strains of structures. Mechanical engineers specialize in plumbing, heating, cooling, and ventilating systems. Electrical engineers are specialists in wiring systems.

A college degree is required to become a junior estimator or assistant engineer. The next ranks beyond junior estimator are those of estimator, senior engineer, business solicitor, and eventually, partner in a firm. Advancement beyond assistant engineer is to engineer, project engineer, general superintendent, and eventually, vice-president or president of a firm. Promotion in any field usually depends upon the person's experience and quality of work, as well as opportunities and personal qualities.

Surveyors work for construction companies; land developers; engineering and architectural firms; and local, state, and

A surveyor makes very precise calculations of the location of highways, buildings, and boundaries. Before a mortgage for a single-family house is granted, the exact locations of the property and its buildings must be confirmed by a surveyor.

federal governments on public works projects such as highways. Surveyors determine boundaries of real estate property such as farms, house lots, or tracts of land in a development. They also determine routes for highways, power lines, and water and sewer systems. Surveyors work both outdoors and indoors. Outdoors, a surveyor works with a crew of people who adjust instruments and measure distances between points and offset angles. Indoor work, following completion of outdoor measurements, consists of making drawings and writing specifications related to boundaries, land contour, and precise location. An interest in mathematics, science, and drafting is essential for anyone intending to study surveying. A surveyor needs to be rugged enough to stand exposure to all kinds of weather and to carry heavy instruments. Good eyesight, ability to make accurate judgments, and a good memory are personal assets. A surveyor may train on the job or as an apprentice; in military service; at a technical or vocational school; or at a two- or four-year college. A surveyor with a college degree may perhaps become involved in business management or ownership.

Draftsmen develop architectural or engineering drawings under the direction of an architect or engineer. To be a successful draftsman, a person must have good eyesight, be able to visualize space relationships, work with objects, and enjoy spending long hours at a drafting table making neat and accurate drawings. A background in mathematics, science, mechanical drawing, and shop courses is helpful. After on-the-job, apprenticeship, or technical training, a draftsman may later become a tracer, junior draftsman, senior draftsman, and design draftsman. By taking courses toward an engineering or architectural degree, a draftsman may branch out as a technical reporter, sales engineer, production foreman, or installation supervisor.

The skilled trades On-the-job and apprenticeship training provide entry to most skilled jobs in the construction industry. Workers usually enter at journeyman level upon completing the training period. Experienced journeymen may qualify for supervisory jobs. Often, there is a choice between working for a large construction or commercial company and establishing your own small business.

The following trades are among the most important in the construction industry:

— Bricklaying requires a number of special skills. Bricklayers may also work as gypsum-block setters, cinder block and concrete masons, hollow tile partition erectors, and terra-cotta masons. Skills are usually acquired through on-the-job or apprenticeship training. Basic skills include the proper use of tools, equipment, and materials, mixing and spreading mortar, and understanding blueprints or work layouts. As they gain experience, workers do the more difficult jobs of building arches, columns, chimneys, fireplaces, and floors; and setting and pointing bricks, cement blocks, and glass bricks. A bricklayer should have good health and be able to withstand all kinds of weather conditions. Good eyesight, a feeling for line and form, and manual dexterity are important personal qualifications.

The entrance to a job as journeyman is through on-the-job and apprenticeship training. The next step is foreman or forewoman. With ambition and administrative ability, the next rise may be to superintendent on a construction site. If a bricklayer pursues training in business or construction skills, it is possible to become an estimator, who obtains quotations for masonry work and submits bids to contractors.

— For becoming a cement mason, a high school diploma is not a requirement, but it may be important toward advancement. A cement mason must have three years of training. The program consists of learning to use and care for tools and materials, doing surface finishing, and using safety precautions. Classroom instruction includes mathematics, science, blueprint reading, building regulations, and cost estimates. High school courses in general mathematics, geometry, drafting, and shop courses provide a good background. Summer employment with a construction crew is valuable.

A cement mason enters the field as a journeyman and may advance to foreman, estimator for contractors, and perhaps job superintendent. The future demand for workers may be affected by the use of more automated equipment and prefabricated materials.

— Marble or tile setting is closely related to bricklaying and masonry work. People trained to set marble and tile are also usually trained to pour terrazzo floors, which are popular in Florida and southern California. Tile setters work indoors, but marble setters may work both indoors and outdoors. The trade requires an artistic flair, manual dexterity, and patience in making precision fittings. Although a three-year apprenticeship program is available, many people enter the trade through on-the-job training.

— Floor-covering installers may be qualified to install both carpet and resilient floor covering; some installers specialize in one type or the other. Every floor-covering installer must learn how to prepare floors for covering. This preparation may require resurfacing the flooring base with plywood, hardboard, or mastic cement. Installers must understand the use and care of tools and equipment and the use of adhesives for different applications. Installers must also know how to read blueprints and how to measure, cut, and fit floor coverings accurately. Courses in mathematics and shop, in addition to summer experience as a helper, are valuable.

After a training period of three or four years on the job or through an apprenticeship program, a person is qualified as a floor-covering installer. Advancement proceeds from journeyman to foreman, but few contractors have enough jobs to justify hiring a foreman. A floor-covering installer who can deal effectively with people and wishes to continue with an education sometimes becomes a salesperson or finds employment with a manufacturer of floor coverings. A few are able to establish a small business.

— To become a carpenter, it is helpful to have courses in drafting and woodworking at the high school level. Summer work with a builder is also good experience. On-the-job and apprenticeship training are also available. Trainees learn about the use and care of tools, properties of materials, building codes, blueprint reading, shop arithmetic, and sketching.

New employment opportunities for women have encouraged them to enter new career fields.

Many people enter carpentry through on-the-job training, but a four-year apprenticeship course provides more thorough training for entry as a journeyman. An experienced carpenter may become a foreman in charge of a small crew and perhaps a general construction foreman or estimator of carpentry work. Business courses can be a help toward promotion. Some carpenters become proprietors of their own business.

—Lathers work in construction, installing strips of metal or large pieces of gypsum to support backings for walls or supports for acoustical ceilings and wall tile. Because lathers spend a great deal of time on ladders and scaffolds, the work can be hazardous. A lather uses a large variety of tools. Courses in metalwork, woodworking, mechanical drawing, and mathematics provide good background.

A four- to five-year training program leads to entry as a journeyman lather. A lather may specialize in metal, rockboard, or wood lathing. A person with ability, good judgment, and business ability may move up to foreman, job estimator, or job superintendent.

—Insulation workers are employed in construction. They install insulation under roofs and floors and between walls to prevent the loss of heated or cooled air. They must know how to use hand and power tools, be able to reach out-of-the-way areas, and have manual dexterity. Because of problems with dust and fiber inhalation, this work involves certain risks to health.

Applicants for training enter an "improvership" program, which is comparable to an apprenticeship program. Advancement is from journeyman to foreman, and perhaps job superintendent. Some installers eventually set up an independent business.

—Electricians install components and equipment in residential, commercial, and industrial buildings and do maintenance and repairs. A four-year apprenticeship training period is required as preparation for becoming an electrician. Classroom training includes instruction in drafting and electrical layout; blueprint reading; mathematics; electrical theory, including electronics; and safety practices. As the field of electronics changes, the electrician must keep up with new developments. On-the-job training includes making all kinds of installations and repairs. Experience gained in repairing and assembling radios and model electric trains, as well as in repairing electrical appliances, is helpful. High school courses related to the electrician's trade are mathematics, physics, drafting, woodworking, and metalcraft.

A person may apply for apprenticeship training or become an apprentice to a local electrical firm. The steps for advancement are journeyman, foreman, estimator or job superintendent, and eventually, contractor. A master's license is required for an electrical contractor in most large urban areas. Some electricians are employed full-time to do maintenance work in large buildings. A number of electricians become independent proprietors.

—Plumbers and pipefitters install heating and air-conditioning units, water heaters, washers, dryers, and plumbing fixtures. Pipefitters install pipes for all liquids and gases, radiators, boilers, furnaces, and radiant-heating systems. The procedures are similar in both trades. Because most work is done indoors, employment does not depend on the weather. Although a high school education is not required for training, it is an asset. Courses in woodworking, mathematics, chemistry, and physics offer good background. In order to qualify for an apprenticeship program, an applicant must pass an examination administered by the state employment agency. The training period is five years. Summer experience as

Apprenticeships are available in some building and related trades. This apprentice is being given on-the-job training by a journeyman electrician.

It is also important to know how to prepare surfaces for painting. This includes mending cracks in plaster and holes in woodwork and using a blowtorch. Courses in art, mathematics, chemistry, and woodworking are helpful in the trade. Home experience and summer work as a helper in painting and paperhanging offer valuable experience.

Entry and advancement are similar to those for other skilled trades. Skilled workers may be employed by construction companies. However, painters and paperhangers have the advantage of working independently, with little money invested. Stores that sell paint and wallpaper frequently are asked by customers to recommend painters and paperhangers.

Manufacturing

Many categories of manufacturing industries relate to housing and home furnishing. These include exterior and interior building materials; woodwork and cabinetry; plumbing and lighting fixtures; heating/cooling and other equipment; awnings,

a plumber's helper will give valuable experience. The work of a plumber or pipefitter is strenuous and there are accident hazards, but employment and wages are good. The ability to work with people, together with knowledge of business practices, is an asset in this work.

In order to enter the trade, an apprentice must pass a special examination related to knowledge and skills. Before a plumber can become a plumbing and/or pipefitting contractor, it is necessary to pass an examination and obtain a license. After some experience, plumbers and pipefitters may advance to supervisory positions or work independently.

— Although painting and paperhanging are two different skills, many people in the building trades do both types of work. A painter must have a knowledge of all types of paints, varnishes, lacquers, and thinners.

Manufacturing provides a wide variety of jobs and career opportunities in all parts of the nation.

blinds, shades, and fabrics; carpets and resilient floor coverings; furniture and household furnishings; manufactured homes; and many more. In the field of ceramics alone there are many opportunities—in brick and cement materials; whitewares (including tile, cookware, dinnerware, and porcelain); glass (for mirrors, tableware, and cookware); and structural ceramics (roofing tiles, terra-cotta tiles, and patio tiles). The field of plastics includes products ranging from plastic drinking cups to home furnishings and equipment.

On-the-job training, apprenticeships, and programs at technical and vocational schools and two-year colleges lead to careers in manufacturing industries. Courses in chemistry, physics, and art provide good background. Although many jobs are routine, there are also opportunities for designing and for managerial jobs. A degree in home economics, business administration, advertising and promotion, merchandising, engineering, or architecture leads to professional entry-level jobs. A few colleges in Virginia and North Carolina, which are centers of wood furniture manufacture, offer degrees in furniture making.

Computer Technology

The growth of computer technology has expanded opportunities for housing-related computer careers. Many jobs that were once done by hand are now accomplished faster and more easily by computers. Computers are being used in research and development, manufacturing, and sales.

Designs for fabrics, furniture, and architecture can be developed by computer graphics. Details of the design can be changed in seconds without having to redraw the entire design. Computerized equipment can analyze the color of an item and determine the exact formula necessary to reproduce that color in paints, yarns, or fabrics. Computers are used to give instructions on how to set up the giant looms used for weaving fabric or tufting carpeting.

This programmer is working on a special computer program that will oversee the production of an assembly line

In manufacturing, computers can operate different types of machinery used for making almost any type of product, from appliances and cookware to building materials and modular homes. Computer-operated robots can move manufactured items along assembly lines from one spot to another or aid in the packing and shipping of the items.

Computers are also used in many business operations. They can compute costs, track inventory, analyze sales figures, and maintain records of suppliers and customers. In retail stores, cash registers can be linked to a computer system so that each item that is sold is automatically deducted from the inventory list. Computers are also used in homes to maintain records, compute budgets, store information, regulate temperature, and monitor security systems.

People with knowledge of computers are in great demand in many industries. Computer programmers are the ones who develop the programs or software that provide the information for the computer system. Technicians and operators are needed to run the computers for manufacturers, commercial businesses, and retail stores. Some special training is needed for a career in computers. You can take computer courses at a vocational or technical school. Most large computer companies have their own training program. A college degree in computer science, mathematics, or business is beneficial for the more technical areas of the computer field.

Real Estate

Opportunities in real estate exist in small towns, cities, and suburban areas. In a small community, one person may operate from a small office and perhaps sell insurance at the same time. In large cities, a dozen or more people may be employed by a real estate firm. Sometimes, real estate agents may enter into a franchise with a national chain of realtors for the privilege of using a nationally known name. However, real estate agents usually work for a real estate brokerage firm under contract. Some agents operate from model units in new developments. Most of these real estate agents are employed on a commission basis. Other agents may be salaried employees of large firms.

Every state requires that real estate brokers and agents have a license. This is obtained after they take prescribed courses in the principles of real estate, financing, appraisal, and property management. These courses may be offered by a local real estate board or a college, during the day or in the evening. After obtaining a license, brokers who are members of the National Association of Realtors receive the title "realtor," and agent members receive the title "realtor associate." In some states, agents must work for a broker for several years before they may obtain a broker's license.

A real estate salesperson's job is to obtain properties to sell and to find buyers. For this purpose, the agent develops lists of

The number of computer-related jobs has increased as the use of such equipment for recording, analyzing, and feeding back information has grown.

people who have property to sell and of people who are interested buyers. An agent discusses pricing, commission, and other terms with a seller and obtains a written agreement giving the agent the right to sell the property over a certain period of time. Often, if the property is not sold within a given length of time, it may be multi-listed so that any real estate company or agent in the area may sell the property. Practices for exclusive or multiple listing may differ from one state to another. A real estate agent should know the community and its characteristics; the zoning regulations; the value of other homes; the tax structure and water and sewage fees; the procedure for waste disposal; and the approximate cost of heating and cooling the home or apartment.

In addition to buying and selling property, some realtors specialize in rentals and management. They may manage a small apartment building with five or six units or a large high-rise building. The manager's job consists of collecting rents; paying for operating expenses, replacements, and redecorating; and employing and supervising maintenance help. The management fee is usually based upon a percentage of the gross income (that is, the income before expenses are taken out). A great deal of experience is needed to qualify as a real estate manager.

Although there are no educational requirements for becoming a real estate agent, a broad educational background is an asset. Some business schools and two- and four-year colleges offer courses in real estate. High school business courses and experience in selling are valuable. Honesty, patience, courtesy, tact, an interest in people, and an outgoing personality are all assets.

Upon passing an examination and qualifying as an agent, a person may apply for a position with a realty firm. To continue an affiliation with a firm, an agent must attain a certain sales record over a stated period of time. The field is very competitive.

Housing Maintenance

Jobs in housing maintenance may range from custodian of a single apartment building to maintenance superintendent of a large housing project. The work includes cleaning entrances, hallways, laundry rooms, and other areas in common use. It also includes outside work such as sweeping sidewalks, mowing lawns, and removing snow. Being able to use and care for cleaning equipment, make and keep schedules, and get along with people are important. In large housing projects, boiler room operators and general mechanics, as well as custodians, are employed. These people may work under a general building superintendent or through an agency. In some cities, unions and government agencies provide training programs in the use of cleaning equipment, scheduling, handling complaints, and making general repairs, and courses in basic arithmetic and reading.

Jobs are available through state employment offices and newspaper ads. A custodian may become a boiler room operator or mechanic assistant and eventually maintenance superintendent, supervising a staff of employees.

Housing Management

A housing manager must know how to run a private or government housing program efficiently and economically. This field includes low- and middle-income housing, cooperatives, condominiums, and retirement homes. The manager is the middle person between the tenants and the housing owners or the government. It is important to know how to get along with people, to understand housing policies, and to be able to handle complaints, worker strikes, and possible vandalism.

Housing management involves working with people more directly than real estate management does. Housing managers are concerned with the entire living environment or even an entire neighborhood. They try to involve the people who live in the project in combating vandalism, keeping the buildings and grounds attractive, and keeping play areas safe. Managers and staff members may be responsible for tenant selection, community relations, social services, security services, administration, and maintenance. Aides or trainees often collect rents, handle complaints, help to relocate tenants, and work with tenants to determine policies and set up social programs. One of the most important requirements is knowing how to work with tenants and to involve them in the activities of the housing community.

A high school diploma, experience in social services, and experience in working with people are entrance-level requirements to become an aide. An aide may become an assistant manager or eventually, a resident manager, supervising general manager, area district manager, or director of management. Jobs in accounting, public relations, budgets, and research also exist at the administration level. Each of these jobs may require specific courses, training, and experience as preparation.

Home Maintenance and Repairs

Many self-employed people in small communities, suburban areas, and cities provide basic services for homes and apartments. These repair and maintenance jobs include small appliance repair, TV and air-conditioning service, plumbing and electric repairs, lawn care, tile roof cleaning, general housecleaning, window cleaning, carpentry, rug and upholstery cleaning, upholstering and furniture repair, and drapery and slipcover making. A person may work alone or as a member of a group. Some people become managers of groups that provide a number of services.

If a person expects to become self-employed, it is advisable to obtain experience working for a large department or specialty store or—in the case of construction skills —working for a general contractor. It is also necessary to have some savings to live on until a business becomes established, with regular customers. Satisfied customers will continue to do business with the individual or business service and recommend it to friends.

To be successful, a person must have a knowledge of business and the ability to get along with people. A newspaper ad or cards to pass out to acquaintances will attract customers for a self-employed person.

Merchandising

Merchandising involves overall planning in advertising, promoting, buying, and selling products. Opportunities exist at the manufacturing or wholesale level with trade associations, and at the retail level with local stores. The largest number of opportunities exist in retailing. Positions related to home furnishings are available in chain stores and department and specialty stores in doing displays, promotion, and advertising. There are also opportunities in wholesale and catalog showrooms.

Although some jobs are highly specialized, it is usually possible to move from one area of buying or management to another. Supervisory and administrative jobs with large stores and retail chain stores are highly competitive. These jobs often require a degree in business management, marketing, or home economics. However, they are often open to graduates of two-year colleges who have experience, good work, and continued training. Summer and part-time experience, in addition to courses in business, marketing, interior design, art, equipment, and journalism, is

helpful. Students with enthusiasm, patience, tact, and an interest in people are likely to succeed in selling.

Distributive education courses in high school lead to entry into the merchandising field. After a training period and experience as a salesperson and stock assistant, a person may be promoted to assistant buyer or head of stock. These may in turn lead to the jobs of promotion assistant, assistant marketing manager, associate buyer, and senior buyer.

Designing

Interior designing offers the most opportunities in design-related fields. However, a broad range of opportunities also exists in design related to home furnishings. This includes the design of textiles, wallpaper, furniture, lamps, household linens, tableware, accessories, and floral arrangements.

An interior designer may work independently or be employed by a furniture, department, or chain store, a paint and wallpaper store, or a manufacturer in one of the categories of home furnishings.

An independent designer works with a client. Payment to the designer may be handled in a number of ways, including a set fee, an hourly fee for consultation or consultation and supervision of a job, or a percentage basis, or buying at wholesale prices and selling at retail prices, with an additional fee for professional services. The interior designer brings knowledge and experience to the wants, needs, present furnishings, and budget of clients.

Interior designers have access to the catalogs from manufacturers of furniture, floor and wall coverings, lamps and lighting, and accessories that clients otherwise would not see. Large decorating establishments have their own showrooms. Their designers prefer to handle large jobs, from making preliminary plans and estimates to completing the project.

An interior designer is not required to have a license, but membership in the American Society of Interior Designers (ASID) is essential. Interior designers need to be artistic, businesslike, responsible, communicative, and sensitive to others

An interior designer works with customers to select furniture, accessories, and fabrics that will match their needs and their tastes.

in order to work well with people. They need a background in art history (including architecture), color and design, furniture and carpet construction, journalism, marketing, and business principles. Some people enter the field of interior design through on-the-job training and taking daytime or evening courses.

A variety of jobs are available as home-furnishings counselors in paint, wallpaper, rug, drapery, and home-furnishings stores. More advanced jobs include those of interior designer with a department or furniture store, a manufacturer, a construction developer, or an interior design firm. Specialized fields include kitchen design with kitchen-cabinet manufacturers or floor-covering manufacturers, and assisting with the interior design or furnishing of school dormitories, apartment buildings, and retirement homes. Three-year specialized programs and college-degree programs provide the best background for professional-level careers. Entry levels in interior design include interior design assistant, editorial assistant on a magazine, design assistant with a manufacturer, and assistant buyer in retailing.

Other Professional Careers

Teaching opportunities in housing and home furnishings are available in high schools as part of the home economics program; in colleges, universities, and art schools; and in adult education programs. Home furnishings magazines, manufacturing firms, and trade associations also employ people to do research and writing in the area of housing and home furnishings. Utilities companies employ counselors in lighting and in the use of equipment.

As a large and basic industry, housing and its many related fields provide a great number and variety of jobs. These jobs cover an extensive range, from unskilled and skilled to managerial and professional. The information provided here about jobs and careers in housing-related fields is only a beginning. You should explore further, in terms of your own interests, preferences, and abilities.

The home furnishings editor is responsible for all the articles on housing, furniture, and household equipment in each issue of the magazine.

REVIEWING CHAPTER 24

SUMMARY

Choosing a career involves important decisions about your present and future. You should first analyze your interests and abilities and other personal resources to discover what career areas might suit you best. You should explore different career possibilities and obtain detailed information about those that interest you. Many people, including guidance counselors and specialists in various fields, can provide information.

Career opportunities within the housing field include a variety of jobs in construction, manufacturing, computer technology, real estate, housing maintenance and management, home maintenance and repairs, merchandising, designing, and other professional areas. Training for many of these careers can be obtained by taking courses at a high school, vocational or technical school, or a community or four-year college. Working part-time or during the summer will help you gain experience and discover whether or not this is a career field for you.

FACTS TO KNOW

1. Why is it important to identify your interests and abilities as part of your career planning?

2. Describe three ways that you can obtain the necessary training for an entry-level job.

3. Identify four sources of career information and describe the kind of help provided by each one.

4. List courses in high school that relate to careers in housing.

5. List as many jobs as you can in the field of construction.

6. What qualifications and abilities are needed to enter the field of real estate?

7. What training is necessary to enter the field of computer technology? housing management? merchandising? designing?

8. Identify specific jobs in the construction field and the home maintenance and repairs field in which you can be self-employed.

IDEAS TO THINK ABOUT

1. Describe three interests of yours that might influence your career choice.

2. Using the questionnaire on ''Personal Aptitudes and Preferences'' on page 460, analyze your own abilities and priorities concerning career choices. What conclusions about your choice of vocation or career can be drawn from your answers?

3. In your community, what summer or part-time job opportunities exist for teenagers that also offer good job experience?

ACTIVITIES TO DO

1. Survey the want ads in one or more newspapers for job opportunities in the housing field.

2. Prepare a career plan for yourself. Identify your career objective. What experience, training, and education will be necessary to achieve that objective?

GLOSSARY

abstract—having little or no resemblance to an actual object or scene

acoustical—having to do with sound

adhesive—a substance used to stick or glue things together

analogous—similar; two or more colors that are next to each other on the color wheel

appliance—a piece of equipment designed for a particular use and operated by gas or electric current

apprenticeship—learning a trade by practical experience under the supervision of skilled workers

aptitude—natural ability

archeologist—a specialist who studies the remains of past human life and activities

architecture—the art of designing and building structures; a style of building

armoire—a tall cupboard or wardrobe

attic—a room or a space immediately below the roof of a building

auger—a drilling tool for boring holes

automated—to operate by mechanical or electronic devices

balance—equilibrium of all elements

basement—the part of a building that is wholly or partly below ground level

blinds—horizontal or vertical slats that can be tilted open or closed

broadloom—carpeting that was woven on a wide loom

buffet—a piece of dining room furniture on which food may be served, with shelves or drawers for storage

bungalow—a style of house having one or one-and-a-half stories, overhanging roof, and a covered porch

café curtain—fabric curtain, attached by rings to a rod, that covers only part of a window

caulking—material used to fill seams, cracks, and joints so they will not leak

cellular—containing cavities; having a porous texture

chandelier—a branched lighting fixture suspended from the ceiling

china—fine porcelain dinnerware

circuit—the path through which an electric current flows

circuit breaker—a switch that automatically interrupts an electric circuit when an abnormal situation occurs

civilization—a cultural development that has a high level of technology and order

clapboard—a thin board usually thicker along one edge, overlapped to cover outer walls

classical—having to do with ancient Greece or Rome; traditional

cluster zoning—houses grouped together in clusters with undeveloped land between clusters

comforter—a bed covering filled with a batting or fiberfill that supplies warmth

commission—a fee paid to an agent

community—a group of people with common interests living in a particular area

compactor—an appliance that compresses or squeezes things together

complementary—completing or making up what is lacking; colors that are opposite each other on the color wheel

computerized—to carry out, control, or produce by means of a computer

condominium—an apartment house in which each apartment is purchased and owned separately

conductor—a substance that transmits electricity, heat, or sound

contemporary—of or having to do with the present time

contingency—a possibility that is likely but not certain to happen

contractor—one that makes a business arrangement to erect or remodel buildings

convection oven—an oven with fans that circulate heated air at a high speed

cooperative—an apartment house in which shares of stock are issued to the owner of each unit by the corporation which is made up of all the owners

cornice—a horizontal molding over a window that conceals the drapery rod

cove—a trough for concealed lighting at the upper part of a wall

crewel embroidery—needlework done with yarn and embroidery stitches

crystal—clear, colorless glass of superior quality

culture—the collection of ideas, skills, values, and customs of a group or society

decibel—a unit for measuring sound

deed—a legal statement of ownership of property

defrost—to free from ice

detergent—a synthetic, water-soluble cleaning agent

diagonal—something positioned at an angle

diffused—spread out over a large area

disability—a temporary or permanent mental or physical condition that is limiting in some way

disposer—an appliance that gets rid of food by grinding it to a very fine consistency

dormer—a window that projects from a sloping roof

down payment—initial payment made by a buyer at the time of purchase with the balance to be paid later

draw draperies—pinch-pleated fabric panels that can be open or closed by pulling cords at the side of the window.

duct—a pipe for carrying air or liquid

duplex—a house or apartment built for two families

easement—a right held by a person for the limited use of land owned by another person

eclectic—selecting what seems best from various styles

economics—production, distribution, and consumption of goods and services

elevation—an architectural drawing of the side-view or vertical view of a building

emphasis—a center of interest; a focal point; an area or object of importance

enamel—paint that dries with a smooth, glossy appearance

entrepreneur—a person who organizes and manages his or her own business

environment—the physical, social, and cultural conditions that influence the life of an individual or community

epoxy—a strong adhesive compound

equity—the amount a property is worth beyond what is owed on it

escrow—money held in safekeeping by a third party

etching—a print made by transferring a drawing or design from a metal plate

exposure—the position of a home in relation to the sun and wind

flashing—sheet metal used to waterproof the angle between a chimney and a roof

flatware—knives, forks, and spoons

float—a tool used for smoothing a surface

fluorescent light—light produced in a sealed glass tube which contains mercury vapor and has a coating of fluorescent material on the inside which glows brightly

footcandle—a unit of measure for illumination; the amount of light that a candle throws onto a surface that is one foot away

foreclosure—a legal proceeding resulting in owners losing their home because mortgage payments have not been made regularly

foyer—an entrance hallway

fuse—an electrical safety device that includes a strip of fusible metal that melts and interrupts the circuit when the current exceeds a certain level

gable—the triangular piece of wall between the sloping sides of a roof

gambrel—a roof with a lower steeper slope and upper flatter one on each of its two sides

goal—an objective or end for which you are aiming

grout—a material used for filling spaces between tiles

harmony—a pleasing arrangement of all parts

highboy—a tall chest of drawers

high technology—computerized and automated methods used to produce objects and accomplish tasks

hue—the name of a color

hutch—a chest topped with open shelves

illusion—an appearance or feeling that misleads by giving a false impression

improvised—made out of something conveniently on hand

incandescent light—light produced inside a glass bulb by a filament that is heated by electricity until it glows

inflation—a sharp increase in prices

inlay—to set pieces of wood or stone into a surface to make a design level with the surface

insulation—the material used in structures to prevent the passage of heat or sound

intensity—brightness or dullness of a color

internship—gaining supervised practical experience in a professional field

joint—a place where two parts are joined

kilowatt—1000 watts

lambrequin—a shaped frame for a window
laminated—composed of layers bonded together
landscape—the scenery around a particular area
latex paint—water-soluble paint
lease—the right to use real estate or other property for a certain length of time, usually by paying rent for it
life cycle—the stages of life that the average person or family goes through
lifestyle—way of living
lithograph—a print made by transferring an inked image from a flat surface
Lucite®—a type of clear plastic
luminous—throws out or gives off a steady light

maintenance—the upkeep of property or equipment
mansard—a roof with two slopes on all four sides, the lower slope being very steep
mat—a border around a picture between the picture and the frame, sometimes serving as its frame
medium—technical method of artistic expression
merchandising—a comprehensive sales promotion that includes market research, product development, marketing, advertising, and selling
microwave oven—an appliance that cooks food with tiny waves of energy that make food molecules vibrate, producing heat to cook the food
modular—a standardized unit that fits with others to become a finished product
monochromatic—having only one color
monotony—sameness; a lack of variety
mortgage—a long-term loan used to finance the purchase of a home
muslin—plain, woven cotton fabric that is coarser than percale

needlepoint—needlework done with yarn that completely covers the supporting canvas

opaque—does not allow light to pass through
option—a choice or alternative
outlets—points in an electrical system where electrical cords may be plugged in

parquet—a geometrically patterned design in wood floors
pediment—a triangular shape at the top of a cabinet used as a decoration

percale—a fine, closely woven cotton fabric
pile—yarn on the surface of a fabric or carpeting
place setting—a table service for one person
plaque—a flat ornamental piece used for decoration
plumb line—a weighted cord used to determine a vertical line
polyurethane—a very hard, durable finish that can be applied to surfaces
porcelain—a hard, nonporous, translucent material made from fine white clay and feldspar fired at high temperatures
prefabricated—items built in standardized sections at a factory and assembled during construction
prehistoric—existing in the period before written history
primary colors—the basic colors from which all other colors can be made; red, yellow, and blue
primitive—very simple
priority—something that ranks highest in order of importance
processor—equipment that causes a series of changes or actions
professional—relating to a vocation that requires specialized knowledge and often long and intensive academic preparation
promotion—an organized or specific effort made to further the sale of merchandise through advertising and publicity
proportion—size relationship of one part to another part or to the whole
proprietor—owner
provincial—relating to a country style of furniture that is more simple, plain, and informal
pumice—a lightweight rock used in powder form for smoothing and polishing
putty—a substance, with the consistency of dough, used to fasten glass in sashes

range—a cooking stove with burners or heating elements and an oven
resource—a source of wealth, supply, information, or skill
rhythm—a sense of motion that flows from one area to another
robot—an automatic device or machine that performs functions ordinarily done by human beings

sash—the frame that surrounds the pane of glass in a window or door
scale—relative size
sconce—a fixture consisting of one or more candlesticks which can be hung on a wall

secondary colors—equal amounts of two primary colors; orange, green, and purple

secretary—a desk topped with a cabinet with shelves and doors

sectional—furniture that can be divided into sections

security deposit—an amount paid by a tenant to a landlord to pay for any future damages caused by the tenant

selvage—an edge of fabric or paper that is meant to be cut off and discarded

shadow box—a shallow case used for displaying objects

sheers—curtains made of sheer or semi-opaque fabric that hang close to the window

shim—a thin often tapered piece of wood or metal used to fill in space between things

shingles—small thin pieces of building material laid in overlapping rows to cover a roof or the sides of a building

silk screen print—a print made by forcing dye through unsealed areas of a screen

sill—the horizontal piece at the base of a window

silver plate—a coating of silver on metal

sizing—a material used for filling the pores in surfaces such as plaster, paper, or textiles

society—a community, nation, or broad group of people having common traditions, interests, activities, and institutions

sofa bed—a sofa that opens up to form a bed

soffit—the underside of an overhang

solar heating—heating provided by energy from the sun

solvent—a liquid substance that can dissolve another substance

spa—a place with facilities for exercising and bathing

space—amount of distance or area that can be measured

spectrum—band of colors reflected by light through a prism

stainless steel—an alloy of steel, chromium, and nickel that will not rust or corrode

standard of living—the measure of how well a home and lifestyle meets basic needs

stretcher—a rod or bar that extends between two legs of a chair or table

structural—related to the construction of an item

stucco—a plaster that forms a hard covering and is used for walls

studio couch—a backless couch with removable back cushions that can serve as a single bed

sublet—a lease by a tenant to another person but with the original tenant still held responsible for the original lease

subsidy—a grant or contribution of money

superintendent—one who is in charge or has responsibility

swag—something hanging in a curve between two points

synthetic fibers—fibers produced from chemicals

technology—the methods used to produce objects that are needed by a society

template—a pattern used to form an accurate shape

tenant—a person paying rent for the use of a dwelling

tenement—a dwelling occupied by several families

terra cotta—a brownish orange clay used for vases, roofing, and building decorations

terrazzo—particles of marble set in cement used for floors

tertiary colors—any color produced by mixing a primary and secondary color

texture—the surface characteristics or feel of something

thermal—designed to prevent the loss of body heat

thermostat—an automatic device for regulating temperature

time-sharing—purchasing a vacation home only for a specific number of weeks per year

title—a legal claim proving ownership of property

tract development—a housing development of homes all with the same design

trade—an occupation that requires manual or mechanical skill

traditional—a style that is established and has been used for a long period of time

traffic pattern—the path people follow most often as they move around a room or from one room to another

translucent—permits light to pass through

trap—a bend in a drain or sewer in which the water forms a seal to prevent the passage of sewer gas

traverse rod—a metal rod with a pulley mechanism for opening and closing curtains or draperies

trestle—a braced frame that serves as a support

urban renewal—renovation of urban housing

utilities—the services of water, gas, and electricity

utility area—space for cleaning equipment and supplies

valance—a short drapery heading hung across the top of a window

value—lightness or darkness of a color

values—a person's ideals, beliefs, and attitudes

veneer—a thin layer of material used as an attractive finish for a surface

ventilation—the means of admitting fresh air

veranda—a large porch along one or more sides of a house

vinyl—any of various plastics used for coverings

vocation—the work in which a person is regularly employed; occupation

voltage—electrical potential expressed in volts

warranty—written guarantee of a product's performance and the maker's responsibility to repair or replace any defective parts

wattage—unit of power expressed in watts

weather stripping—strips of material used to cover the joints of a door or window and the threshold or sill so as to keep out rain, snow, and cold air

work triangle—the triangle formed by a kitchen's refrigerator, sink, and range

INDEX

Acknowledgements

Aetna Life & Casualty / Al Ferreira   469
Amana Refrigeration   183, 373, 379
American Plywood Association   1, 41, 129,
    137, 141, 143, 145, 213, 266, 299, 303, 322,
    331, 338, 440, 450, 453
American Society of Interior Design / Helen
    Schubert Public Relations   62, 63, 70,
    149, 204, 231, 282, 292, 308, 315, 324, 332,
    387, 457, 473
Brent Anderson   2

J. Barnall from Shostal   9, 10
Benchmark Preferred Wallcoverings   235
Binswanger Mirrors   179, 330
Hedrich Blessing   37, 43, 44, 45, 154, 155,
    163, 208, 220, 223, 232, 237, 239, 244, 300
Boston Public Library, Print Collection   6
British Travel Association   15
Brodegoard and Company, Inc.   354
Broyhill Furniture Industries   277
Burlington Industries   233

California Redwood Association   439
Cannon Mills Company   340, 345
Carolina Mirror Company   63, 330
Carrier Corporation   182
Pete Christie   cover
Freda Closs from Shostal   11
Continental Homes of New England   87
Hazel Craig   6, 16, 165
Croscill Home Furnishings   257
Dr. and Mrs. A.F. Cunningham   214
Charles Phelps Cushing   26

Dansk Designs   354
Wayne Davis   vi
John Deere and Company   101
Delta Faucet Company   179, 418
Department of Housing and Urban
    Development   42, 47, 52, 53, 54, 55,
    86, 123
Valentia Dermer   16
Robert Dustin   14

Editorial Photocolor Archives   17
Ethan Allen, Inc.   265, 267, 327, 331

Family Circle magazine   230
Scott Fishel   46, 48, 82, 84, 86, 91, 98, 335,
    444, 447
The Flately Company   111

Fleetwood Enterprises   452
Flexsteel Industries, Inc.   205, 275

Robert Gangloff   22, 57, 110, 132, 139, 153,
    157, 205, 256, 258, 260, 261, 284, 328,
    390, 393, 404, 430, 431, 432, 433
General Electric Lighting Institute   252, 310,
    314, 315, 319, 368, 371
Georgia-Pacific Corporation   73, 188
Greek National Tourist Office   12

Hamilton Beach Div., Scoville Manufacturing
    Company   380
Helios   420
Herrmidifier Company, Inc.   183
The Hoover Company   396, 397
Martin Hurliman   15

Illinois Laborers' and Contractors' Training
    Program   463
Independence (Missouri) Examiner   34

Johnson Camping, Inc.   5

Keller Advertising / Keller Windows   438
Kirsch / Cooper Industries   250, 254

Levolor Lorentzen   131
Laura Ashley, Inc.   458

The Maytag Company   376
McDonnell Douglas Automation
    Company   451
Robert McElwee   64, 71, 166, 183, 190, 226,
    236, 283, 295, 358, 388, 395, 400, 402, 445

National Gallery of Art   224
National Oak Flooring Institute   229
National Trust for Historic Preservation   33

Architectural Extension, Oklahoma State
    University   169
Emmett Osgood   174

Pella Windows & Doors, Inc.   198, 251, 438
Norman Peterson   456
Ply-Gems Manufacturing Company   236
PP&G Industries   56